Beyond the PhD

Prof Kenneth K Mwenda
PhD, LLD, DSc(Econ)

Beyond the PhD

International and State Recognition in Global Thought Leadership

VOLUME 1

Mereo Books

2nd Floor, 6-8 Dyer Street, Cirencester, Gloucestershire, GL7 2PF
An imprint of Memoirs Books. www.mereobooks.com
and www.memoirsbooks.co.uk

Beyond the PhD
ISBN: 978-1-9191788-5-1

First published in Great Britain in 2025
by Mereo Books, an imprint of Memoirs Books.

Copyright ©2025

Prof Kenneth K Mwenda has asserted his right under the Copyright Designs
and Patents Act 1988 to be identified as the author of this work.

A CIP catalogue record for this book is available from the British Library.
This book is sold subject to the condition that it shall not by way of trade or otherwise be lent,
resold, hired out or otherwise circulated without the publisher's prior consent in any form
of binding or cover, other than that in which it is published and without a similar condition,
including this condition being imposed on the subsequent purchaser.

The address for Memoirs Books can be found at www.mereobooks.com

Mereo Books Ltd. Reg. No. 12157152

Typeset in 11/17pt Garamond by Wiltshire Associates.
Printed and bound in Great Britain

TABLE OF CONTENTS

Chapter 1	Introduction	1
Chapter 2	At the frontiers of thought leadership	60
Chapter 3	Global thought-leadership inspires others	120
Chapter 4	Family roots	174
Chapter 5	My early childhood	235
Chapter 6	Moving to the Copperbelt	263
Chapter 7	The good ol' days of the African university	330
Chapter 8	UNZA Graduation and Bar admission	370

PREFACE

In a monotheistic religion such as Christianity, there are often two types of prayers. One is for thanking the Deity and the other is for asking the Deity for His providence. So, if you are a Christian and believe in God, then we can safely say that there is a time for thanking God and a time for asking God for His providence. Now, which one of the two types of prayers do you often throw at God, and why? As believers, we all need to examine ourselves and our attitude towards God. Are we selfish and egocentric in our prayers? Do we also pray for others or is it just about ourselves and our wants? Don't you think God notices these things? God is not a hospital or bank for you to turn to only when you are besieged with problems. Normalize thanking God, even when all is going well for you. Because if you cannot thank God, you are less likely to thank your fellow human beings who have been there for you. And so, in this autobiography, I proceed with a deep sense of eternal gratitude to God Jehovah Almighty, my Heavenly Father, for everything that He has done and made possible for me even when the road ahead did not always look quite promising, but He came through and paved a way. It is for this reason that I share my story.

That you have lived an impactful life globally is the very reason you cannot conceal or hide the story of your life. A star will not shine if it is hidden underneath the bed, for it was not meant to be there but up in the skies for mankind to see or admire. Your extraordinary life is meant to inspire and motivate others. Distinguished people and notable dignitaries, including Chief Justices, central bank governors, eminent Professors, Vice-Chancellors and Chancellors of top universities, leading businessmen and women, diplomats and parliamentarians as well as many other government and corporate executives, both in your home country and abroad, cannot just gather at the highest level to honor you at elaborate luncheons and dinners dedicated exclusively to recognize your global thought-leadership and impressive scholarly work, unless there is something worth paying attention to about your name. So, I do not take these rare momentous experiences lightly. They are all blessings from the Heavenly Father, God Jehovah Almighty.

Indeed, it is not every day, for example, that the world's best university, the University of Oxford, gets to confer on you the highest honor that any Oxford college can confer on an eminently qualified and distinguished individual. And it is not every day that you would find some of the most distinguished professors at Oxford as well as several distinguished Oxford alumni, Oxford administrators and friends of Oxford gathered at a special gala dinner held exclusively in your honor to celebrate your indelible and edifying global thought-leadership. To me, all these are blessings from God. And I am truly humbled. I am arguably only the second black African since the year 1314 when my alma mater college in Oxford, Exeter College, was established to receive this highest honor at Oxford's Exeter College. So I consider myself blessed.

It is also not an ordinary occurrence that various universities where one teaches host luncheons in your honor whenever you visit them to celebrate your scholarly contributions. I do not take all this lightly. Neither is it an ordinary accomplishment for two sitting governments and Heads of State to honor you for your outstanding scholarly work and distinguished global thought-leadership, in addition to a revered foreign Head of State asking for you to provide his country with professional technical advice. Indeed, I have advised several other States and governments across many regions of the world on various legal, institutional and policy reforms. Closely related to this, I have often been sought after, as a global thought-leader, and invited to appear in numerous print and broadcast media programs, including the *New York Times* (USA), *Voice of America* (VOA, USA), *CCTV* (USA), *The Times* (UK), the British Broadcasting Corporation (BBC, UK), and Sky TV (UK). And so, my public intellectualism has continued to transcend national boundaries, extending into the frontiers of knowledge at the global and international levels.

Further, not every scholar's name makes it into the official government or State gazette in their home country or elsewhere in recognition of their outstanding scholarly achievements and eminent global thought-leadership. So, again, I do not take anything for granted. Honors have come both from home and abroad. And some of my former students continue to serve or have served at the highest levels of government in various countries around the world. Among them are a Chief Justice, Supreme Court Judges, Constitutional Court judges, Court of Appeal judges, High Court judges, Attorneys-General, several cabinet ministers, an ambassador and many more. My other former students are now Professors, Deans and Vice-Chancellors at leading universities in their home countries, while some occupy top positions in international organizations. Indeed, it has been an extraordinary life well lived. And I am ever grateful to my Heavenly Father, God Jehovah Almighty, as well as to all those through whom He has made it possible. I hope this, my story, will help to inspire others.

I am mindful, however, that some folks with something inspiring to talk or write about choose to hide their life story, insisting that they are private people or that they would like to remain private. Various reasons could help to explain the inclination of such people towards the alleged 'privacy', which in many cases is simply 'secrecy'. Folks who are too superstitious tend to be quite secretive. They believe in hiding everything about their private or professional lives. Others, especially those that have a checkered past, want to lie low to avoid any detection. But some sections of the public often mistake such maneuvers for humility. There is a difference between humility and concealment. By parity of reasoning, there is a difference between confidence and arrogance. People who are overly sensitive, for example, can easily mistake someone's confidence for arrogance simply because that person's confidence rubs them up the wrong way. Yet it is their own insecurities that are at play.

Also, in life, there are folks who, with nothing of substance to write home about except for hot air, are too loud and try too hard to be noticed. Yet the facts on the ground do not match their talk. If you are going to tell your life story, the truth should match the talk. People who know something about your background will even implore you to say something. Indeed, many people have approached me, asking me when I will write my autobiography. The writing of this book took longer than expected due to some competing academic and professional engagements, but I have finally delivered my life story. I am, however, mindful that some people could have expected me to talk about, say, any presidential ambitions I hold. Others would want me to revisit my first experience with snow when I first arrived in Europe close to four decades ago. It is always one thing or another, insisting on asking why you did not talk about this or that, or why you decided to include ABC, and not XYZ. Almost everyone has something that they expect you to say or write about. Others already know the kinds of things they expect you to say and how you should say them. Then there are those who will try to judge you based on your garb, as if your designer clothes can adversely affect your intellectual faculties. But remember that your autobiography is your life story, not theirs. Some people might want you to include them in your life story, but you can't please everybody. You just have to tell your life story as you, not for others.

As a global thought-leader and public intellectual, your life story is already a public book. You simply have to bring the book to your audience. Many people want to read it. The story does not belong to you alone. The impact of your life story has benefited many people near and far, so your story must be shared. That your story has touched the lives of many people around the world is a compelling reason why it must be shared, especially that it will continue to inspire many more. Through God, you owe that responsibility to humanity. As a leader, you are a role model that many people look up to. So, you have the moral responsibility, through your life story, to provide authentic leadership, even to people who have not met you but follow you and your works closely. Otherwise, it would be a grave injustice to deny people a glimpse into your extraordinary life. Many people have been inspired by your works and life story. And many others will continue to be inspired. Together, they are a part of your story. Therefore, you must tell your story, and nobody can tell it better than you yourself.

Neglecting to tell the story of an impactful life, I contend, is unfortunate if one has indeed lived such a life. It is like asking someone to deliver a distinguished lecture on your behalf when you are available to speak. The audience expects to hear from you, not from your delegate or surrogate. What comes from the horse's mouth is often treated more seriously than any hearsay from a third-party. But if you choose to retreat from this responsibility of telling your life story, your truth might get distorted one day by naysayers, haters and superficial cynics. So, if today you have a chance to tell your story, then do it right. Tell your story yourself, since you know it best.

It is a truism that some leaders are an enigma. Many people out there want to know what drives or motivates you to reach the heights that you have reached professionally and academically. People want to know how and where you grew up. They also want to learn something about the schools you attended so that they too can be inspired. Some young people have dreams modeled around your life story. They want to understand your career choices or decisions and how you approached them, as well as how they have impacted your professional and academic life. People are eager to hear from you. So, tell your story not only because your life has impacted the lives of many others in a positive and progress way, but also because, as a leader, you owe society that moral responsibility. You must tell your story not only because posterity will one day look back to see what your generation accomplished and left behind for them, but also because those in the present times deserve a chance to learn from chapters in your life. Indeed, you must tell your story not because you just want to be heard, but rather because you inspire many people around the world and your name is a household name both in the Global North and Global South, especially among those who follow leading African intellectuals.

Further, remember that your family members, friends, professional colleagues, mentees, students, former students, followers and other members of the public want to hear from you about your life story. You cannot allow them to sit and wait on gossip about it. Such a thing would not only be doing yourself a disservice but also dishonoring your legacy. Although oral tradition is still an acceptable method of transmitting knowledge to posterity, documenting one's life story is a more reliable method of avoiding any distortions or the misrepresentation of facts by others.

In this autobiography, I have endeavored to document facts as accurately and objectively as I can. Understandably, not everyone will agree with me on everything. But what I have stated is nothing but my truth as it stands. I am also awake to the political realities inherent in certain dogmas that are often veiled as objective critiques but are simply a charade of misconceived anecdotal conjectures. For some parochial cynics, the value of some of my ideas might not sit well with them. For others who have not yet been initiated globally, the ideas might not register immediately until they get initiated.

The perspectives that I have shared in this autobiography cannot be reduced to a monolithic cultural perspective, for they are global and universal in scope and scale, as opposed to parochial and insular perspectives. So the reader is invited to take off the local lens of, say, a monolithic Zambian or African cultural perspective, to look at issues from a more global and heterogenous perspective. It is that transition which many people struggle with. Ever wondered why some celebrities in Hollywood will ask members of the public for privacy if, say, some news was to break out about a scandal or some development affecting the concerned celebrity's personal or professional life? Other celebrities will show up at a social event just for a few minutes and then leave, claiming that they are off to another engagement even if there is no such other engagement. It is all about managing expectations. Something that is too common can easily lose value and become cheap, especially because we know that familiarity often breeds contempt. Rarity is a virtue. Some folks can visit you in hospital, that is, if, as a celebrity, you are ill, just to take a glimpse at how bad you are looking so that they can broadcast to the whole world. Others can pretend to commiserate with you when things are not going too well for you, say, in your marriage, work, or business, but all they want is gossip. You can pre-empt such people by asking them to buy and read a copy of your autobiography if they have any burning questions to ask you.

It is my sincere hope that this autobiography will also serve as a useful contemporary and historical guide to the generations of the Mwenda family to come so that they may know who their ancestors were and where they came from. As one Pan-African activist, journalist and entrepreneur, Marcus Garvey, once wrote: "A people without knowledge of their past history, origin, and culture is like a tree without roots." In a work of this kind, I am mindful that I owe my gratitude to many people. Indeed, it is not without difficulty that I record my indebtedness to all the people that I owe my gratitude. If I omit or forget to mention anyone, please forgive me.

Let me start by thanking the Good Lord, God Jehovah Almighty, and my dearest parents, Mr. Joseph T Mwenda and Mrs. Esther M Mwenda. To God, our Heavenly Father, His mercy endures forever. The fear of the Lord is the beginning of wisdom. To my dearest parents, though you have crossed over, your fatherly and motherly love endures forever. Your words of wisdom will forever remain indelible in my heart, edifying my thoughts and aspirations. I thank you for everything.

My thanks also go to my lovely wife, Dr Judith Mvula-Mwenda, and my adorable son, Joseph. They have been my rock. I cannot thank them enough. I am grateful for their patience, understanding and support, as I worked tirelessly long hours in the night and on weekends to bring this book to fruition. Further, I would like to thank my many friends, colleagues, mentors and mentees across the world, whose names are too numerous to mention, for their inspiring camaraderie and warm support.

Finally, I would like to express my gratitude to my siblings and other extended family members not only for their familial support and encouragement, but also for sharing some helpful information on the various genealogical aspects of the Mwenda family tree. Other sources on possible origins of the people from the region where I hail from in Luapula Province of Zambia included academic colleagues and reliable contacts in and from the neighboring countries of the Democratic Republic of Congo, Tanzania, Kenya, Uganda, Rwanda and Burundi. I remain ever grateful to all of them.

The interpretations and conclusions expressed in this book are entirely those of the author.

They do not represent the views of any institution, organization or other individual. All the facts presented in this book are as at the date of publication of the book.

Kenneth K Mwenda, PhD, LLD, DSc (Econ)
Washington DC
March 28, 2025

CHAPTER 1

Introduction

I was a youth when I left Africa, almost forty years ago. Africa taught me some good family values. In Africa, it was mainly about sharing even if you did not have much. You learned the values of philanthropy at an early age such that when such values started to manifest themselves in your adulthood and began to impact positively on the lives of others, it was primarily because Africa, and your faith in God, gave you a strong foundation of being humane towards fellow human beings, especially the less fortunate. However, sometimes the emphasis on sharing in Africa created a moral hazard of laziness among those who often expected free handouts from family members and friends.

I moved from Africa to live, study and work in Europe for almost a decade. The cultures of the two worlds were quite different. England taught me conservative values of not being wasteful and to be independent and responsible. However, in England, a bit like in Africa, what others thought about my character was as important as how I carried myself. I found that in much of British culture, as in many African, Asian, Latino and Pacific cultures, there was something of an emphasis on conformity, although cultures that stress conformity, though often successful at maintaining social order, can inhibit self-discovery of one's hidden talents because people are often preoccupied with conformity and avoid experiments that could lead to innovation.

From Europe, I moved to live, study and work in a third continent, North America, where I have spent the last three decades. In the US, I learned the value of being exceptional without being apologetic. You can just be yourself and it is okay. In the US, I also learned to be happy for myself and to strive for the best. In addition, I learned how to create and claim value, without waiting for others to create it for you. But then, I often missed the traditional African values of extended family networks. Life, as an old adage often attributed to one Phillip Calvin McGraw teaches us, is a marathon, not a sprint. Indeed, as the English playwright John Heywood often averred, Rome was not built in a day.

As you read this autobiography, may you be the light that lights and illuminates the path of others so that you may bring forth hope where there is despair. To achieve this, we must, among other things, learn to listen in order to understand, not in order to respond. There are people out there who can pretend to be listening to what you are saying yet are just waiting to respond or attack you verbally as soon as you are finished talking. Such people will by design or default miss or gloss over your reasoning and could even overlook the substantive points that you made, as they focus on trivialities that suit their narrative. They often can't even distinguish between substance and form or between deductive and inductive reasoning. Others will google up something without a demonstrable semblance of erudite grit. Armed with whatever they may find on the internet, they will spiritedly try to take you on and disagree with almost everything you have said or written. A little knowledge, as they say, is more dangerous than none at all, for it often gives the unenlightened person a false sense of confidence, even if he or she hardly knows anything worth writing home about. Superficiality typified in anecdotal conjectures should not be confused with enlightenment or being learned. Even a charlatan can appear impressive to the uninitiated.

It is important to understand that many enlightened folks spent years in school for a good reason. Before a learned person opens his or her mouth, he or she is expected to think through what will come out of it. And the thoughtfulness of those utterances often comes from several years of encountering the baptismal fire of critical erudition in school. And so, to try to speak a learned person's intellectual language if you have not climbed the mountain of knowledge that he or she has climbed would be an exercise in futility. It would be like pursuing a red herring. Your tongue and mind must first taste the baptismal fire of erudition before you can speak his or her language. Otherwise, you can end up exposing your ignorance. Indeed, if one cared to read, say, about the theory of dynamic systems or the complexity theory and the principles associated with these theories such as uncertainty, totality, interdependence and spontaneous emergence, they will appreciate the value of critical thinking. The same can be said if one took time to study and understand a critical learning tool such as Bloom's taxonomy of learning. By contrast, the traditional or classical thinking approach characterized by determinism, analytical reductionism, materialism and linearity, like the Cartesian approach of reducing an organism under observation into smaller elements, is less helpful. Classical thinking is akin to rote learning. With rote learning, you get to cram and memorize some basic facts and information repeatedly in order retain them. Rote learning could involve the memorization of such basic facts and information as multiplication tables, scientific equations, names of countries, names of cities, alphabetical letters, historical dates, and language translations. So let us take a more reasoned look at this issue.

A rudimentary version of rote learning that lacks intellectual sophistication is 'microwave thinking'. This type of thinking can occur where a person is deluded enough to think that they can just open their mouth without spending some time in school. Microwave thinking is commonly found where someone who just attended some short seminar or course, or one who googled up stuff or picked some anecdotes and conjectures here and there (e.g. from a newspaper, television, social media or radio source), wants to posture as if he or she is very learned and knowledgeable about some complex issue. Such people often think that they can just wing it or cut corners without spending some time in school. Among them are charlatans, superficial cynics, naysayers, wannabes and social media trolls. They want to rush to talk even before their ideas are fully conceptualized. They are in a hurry to be heard and are impatient for fame and attention. Yet they forget that it takes time to come up with brilliant ideas, as opposed to spewing anecdotes and conjectures all over the place in a subjective, incoherent and unsystematic manner. Education is important. Not even experience can beat it. Knowledge is power. Those who hate education lack knowledge. And those who lack knowledge lack power. While few people are born with the gift of natural wisdom, not everyone has such a gift. Many people need to get an education before they can even open their mouth to say something sensible. Education helps you to improve your thinking.

Unlike some stories that one gets to read or hear about, my story is not a story of political connections, embellishments, self-exaltation, narcissistic sentiments, placing oneself on a pedestal or vanity. Far from it. Neither is my story one of sympathy or regret. Also, it is not a story of nepotism, tribalism, cronyism, superstition, bootlicking, schmoozing or favoritism. Rather, it is a story of honesty, vision, clairvoyance, prophetic truth, hope, faith and charity. It is also a story of dignity and hard work as well as perseverance, discipline, vision, compassion, empathy, authenticity, and effective leadership. My story is underscored by the value and importance of earning respect on merit at every stage of your life without lifting your hand for attention or to be noticed. It is a story that tells you that you don't always need a godfather, sponsor or godmother to make it in life. God is enough, and He will speak for you. In fact, in many cases, what people call, 'networking' is simply a euphemism for corrupt and unethical behaviors. As a people, we have gotten accustomed to the business of trying to legitimize certain unacceptable behaviors in the workplace by giving them polite euphemisms such as 'networking' or 'social capital' to make them appear and sound legit. In many instances, networking is just an offshoot of mediocrity where someone with average or mediocre credentials is trying so hard to make up for what is missing or lacking in his or her résumé. Experience has shown that the weaker one's résumé or CV is, the more aggressive such people become at networking. Their insecurities are easily noticeable from their exaggerated efforts of networking. Such people often lack something that they are trying to cover up for through excessive schmoozing and bootlicking.

The path that I have traversed, without doubt, is harder than asking, say, a powerbroker to place a phone call that will set you up in life. The path is even harder if you are a highly educated African black man in a world where not everyone is treated the same. Indeed, the path that I have travelled is harder than a bootlicker securing some business deal or job offer or promotion on the golf course, in dark secret societies or behind closed doors. My story is different. It is transparent and clean. My story is about coming up on merit. It is about substance, not who you know or who put in a 'good word' for you to get in. My story is about choosing meritocracy over mediocrity. It is a path of honesty, not dishonesty. Such a path requires no lobbying and will stand you in good stead wherever you go. You must always remember that life is not always a straight road. Those who try to fake it eventually get caught or derailed. Those who try to use connections only last as far as those connections last. After that, they can't stand on their own two feet. But if you earn your respect on merit, even if someone tries to mess you up, they cannot take away the respect that you have earned. You can't buy respect. You must earn it. And it is not an overnight thing. The record must speak for itself before you can earn that well-deserved respect.

Generally, it is not uncommon for some people to have preconceived views about someone based on that person's race, tribe, ethnicity, gender, religion, age, physical appearance, traits, educational background or other closely related factors. But the truth is that if you don't know me, for example, and I don't know you, never assume anything about me. To illustrate, you cannot assume that you are more righteous than I am, or that you are more important or sophisticated than me. An enlightened person does not think or behave like that. You might think that because you are a son of a chief the world should be on its knees before you. But I could be a son of a king. You just never know. Royalty is not something you claim. Rather, you are born into royalty. And it is not something you make noise about if you are truly of royal blood. If you are royalty, it will show. You will often stand out.

In Chapter 4, I explain my royal family roots. Here, suffice it to say that assumption is the mother of all mistakes. If you are meeting someone for the first time and have no knowledge, or limited knowledge, about that person, learn to be open-minded. You cannot assume anything, because you do not know who or what you are dealing with. Personally, I have nothing to prove to or against anyone, so I have no time or room for inflated or bloated egos, because I am not one who looks elsewhere for validation or acceptance. I am content with who I am. Therefore, what I share in this autobiography is about my life and just my life.

Knowing who you are is important in defining your values and identity. That I am an African does not mean that my values are all African. Neither are they all Western. I am a mosaic of many cultures. And I have a decolonized mind. So I have chosen purposefully to share the photo appearing above where I am wearing African traditional Kente cloth as the first photo in this autobiography. That photo speaks to my African roots. And I am not shy about my roots. If anything, I am a proud African who can easily and comfortably venture into the foray of other cultures too.

By contrast, there are folks out there who are constantly and egoistically seeking validation of one kind or another and trying so hard to compete against the world or prove a point to others instead of just living and enjoying their life. In my case, I simply let gratitude to God define my attitude. You are less likely to find real happiness in life if you are all about impressing other people or trying to meet their expectations. If you look carefully at some of these folks, you will notice, for example, that they drink certain expensive beverages just to fit in. They want to be like the who's who in town. Others play golf and smoke cigars just to fit in as well. The insatiable quest for acceptance is real. There are also folks who want to dine at famous restaurants and hotels, or to know famous people, just to fit in. They too are constantly looking for validation through one obscure channel or another. If you are financially broke, for example, you are not their friend. If you are no longer in that high office that you once occupied, you are no longer their buddy. They will even delete your phone number from their phone, because you are of no use to them anymore until you make it again. But, if you are up there, the whole world will know that you are their 'closest' buddy or best friend. Others will even claim you as their relative. Folks are constantly seeking validation of one kind or another. They will even smoke what famous people are smoking just to fit in or get close to those famous people. It's a stressful life. Folks are constantly in financial debt while keeping up appearances, buying luxury cars, taking expensive vacations, living in mansions and flaunting expensive lifestyles just to fit in. Folks can no longer be happy without trying so hard to fit in. Your lifestyle must match your station in life and your affordability. Do not stress yourself too much just to fit in if you do not belong.

Whenever I meet someone, whether through reading about them or in person, I try to approach the encounter with an open mind. I do not let outside noise distract me. Unconscious bias must be avoided. even though many people struggle with it. For example, an elderly white woman in an elevator holding dearly to her purse might be fearing that the other person in the elevator, a black man, will attack her and steal from her. But not all black men are thieves, and some white men commit crimes. By parity of reasoning, you cannot assume that the black lady playing with a white child at the park is the child's babysitter. She could actually be the child's stepmother, adopted mother or foster parent. Learn to be open-minded. Neither can you assume that all white people are rich or that black men are uneducated and unfaithful to their wives. Your isolated personal experiences cannot be the basis of making such wild and sweeping generalizations. So do not generalize or stereotype, because you are most certainly going to find some white folks out there who are poor and uneducated. And there are white men too who cheat on their wives.

On one of my visits to Africa, I recall an incident of an African driver in one of the government ministries who was tasked to pick up a team of visiting businessmen and women arriving at the local airport from America. When he saw the businessmen and women at the airport, he immediately assumed that the black man in their company, since the rest were all whites, was the least important team member. The African driver just assumed that a black person cannot be more important or senior than a white person, without realizing that the black man was the team leader. In fact, the African driver did bypass the black guy while showing his tainted teeth to the white folks and offering to lift their bags until they all reminded him that the black guy that he had just bypassed was the team leader. Unconscious bias is real.

Armed with these illustrations, let us now debunk five common myths about highly educated people before this author's life story is shared. This discussion is important because it will help to set in context everything that you will read and see in this book.

First, some people assume that highly educated people must be shabby-looking and that they lack humor, with no sense of fashion or finesse when it comes to aesthetics. This is a wrong perception, as

I will demonstrate in this book. Here, suffice it to say that rich guys can't have all the fun. Let the smart kids also have some fun. Because all work without play makes Jack a dull boy.

Secondly, others believe that most highly educated people live their lives like paupers, engrossed in their books and divorced from the material trappings of this world. Again, this is not true. There has to be a fine balance between work and life. I will demonstrate this point in the book.

Thirdly, there are also those who believe that highly educated people cannot afford the finer things in life that are associated mainly with the affluent. This prejudicial view is misleading and assumes that highly educated people can't afford a luxurious lifestyle and should just be spectators while those with so-called 'money' enjoy opulence. I will illustrate in the book that not all highly educated people who spend many years in school end up as spectators of rich folks enjoying a good life. Indeed, rich boys can't have all the fun. In the two pictures below, I have shared images of my favorite Burberry and Hugo Boss shoulder bags that I carry when I am lecturing at various universities.

Fourthly, there is a section of society that believes that highly educated people, especially academicians, have no place in industry and that their home is the university. That view is misleading. There are a number of distinguished academics who have held senior leadership roles in the corporate world and in international organizations, for example. Many continue to juggle between industry and academia. They bring to both worlds what is lacking in either. And that is a path I have followed after leaving full-time academia in the United Kingdom. Indeed, focusing exclusively on

one career path or track much of your working life can lead to counterproductive exclusive homogeneity and tunnel vision where you become oblivious of what is obtaining outside the tunnel that you are trapped in. It is good to have a balanced and symbiotic approach to what obtains both inside and outside the tunnel. In the picture below, I stepped outside the academic tunnel and wore my other hat as a seasoned international development practitioner and leader, as a I led a World Bank delegation of about thirty team members at the United Nations in New York, US.

In the picture below, taken at the International Monetary Fund (IMF) in Washington DC, US, I can be seen again stepping outside the academic tunnel, as I led a large World Bank delegation to the IMF.

In the picture below, I can be seen leading my thirty-member World Bank delegation at the US Securities and Exchange Commission (SEC) in Washington DC, US.

In the picture below, switching gears into academic life while on leave from the World Bank, I can be seen with my international law students (JD class) when I served as the 2024 Archibald McDougall Visiting Professor of International Law at West Virginia University College of Law in Morgantown, West Virginia, USA.

And, of course, the professor has to carry with him some decent shoulder bags and attendant accessories when he is in the academy.

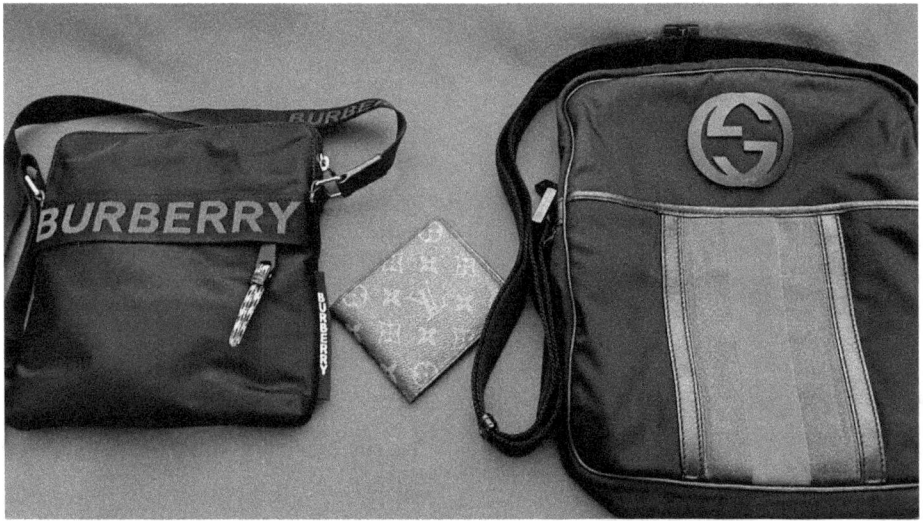

Additionally, that one is associated with the academy does not mean he or she should fall short of expectations of the corporate world. Even as a scholar, it is wise, though not mandatory, to have options of business cardholders to suit each occasion.

Fifthly, there is a misconception and fear that academicians can be too theoretical and lack practical experience. Such fears and concerns are unwarranted, for there is nothing so practical as a good theory. In the social sciences, theories are born out of empirically observed facts and do not exist on their own in the abstract. Put simply, education does matter. Even if you do not make much money using education, at least your faculties will have developed, making you a more enlightened human being who can make some meaningful contribution to socio-economic development. Education liberates you from the shackles of ignorance. In the pictures below, I can be seen delivering speeches and officiating at events at the World Bank in Washington DC, US.

We should, however, be mindful that highly educated folks are also human. Like any one of us, they too have needs and wants and thus should not be discriminated against when it comes to what some leftist radicals call 'bourgeois tendencies.' Most of us, including those same radicals, want the best in life, so why should academicians or highly educated people be treated differently?

It's always healthy to enjoy some good humor, smile and not take life too seriously.

And if I have to do a hoodie, it matters what type of hoodie I am wearing.

Against this background, there is nothing wrong with a professor showing up for lectures in a Lamborghini, Ferrari, Maserati, Aston Martin, Range Rover, Jaguar, Mercedes-Maybach, Bentley or Rolls Royce, if he or she can afford one. Indeed, it is not a sin or crime for the highly educated to drive a luxury car that is often associated with people that are considered financially wealthy. The problem is not the professor, but people who tend to judge the educated through the lens of our own prejudiced and subjective mindsets. We are the problem, because we carry with us a whole load of baggage of value judgements and stereotypes.

We often want to place people in various boxes based on their background. Surely, why should someone's decent and fine taste of clothing or dressing appear offensive to anyone? Or why should someone's prestigious and admirable quality education be a bother to anyone? Have the learned committed any crime by going to school to get a good education or dressing up elegantly? Many times, people just project their own insecurities and frustrations onto innocent parties. Yes, it is true that some people settle for less whilst others are content with just being average, but not everyone is like that. Those who choose to live a low or average life when they can actually do better should not expect others to follow their path. Each one of us is free to choose his or her own destiny.

There are people out there who want to be inspired by great success stories of exceptional people, not some low-life story veiled with fictitious humility or modesty. Indeed, there are people out there who want to be inspired by stories of high-flying careers, high levels of education, modern trends in fashion and dressing, worldly travels, fine wines, quality food and so forth, and we should not hate on those who have lived such a life just because of our own lives are average or low. Rather, we should look for inspiration from various walks of life, and not hating on those who have done better than us.

Some people have a tendency of trying to justify or glorify poverty as humility. Poverty is poverty. It is not humility. If you choose to live like a pauper when you can actually to better, do not expect others to follow your path.

In life, mediocrity should not be an option. You only have one life to live. In that life, you can choose to be either amazing or amazed. There is hardly any grey area in between, especially for minorities who cannot claim the equivalent of white privilege. Put simply, whatever talent God has given you, use it wisely and strive to go beyond the norm. If, for example, you hold a PhD and are a schol-

ar, strive to go beyond the PhD. Look for what lies beyond. Whatever you touch, strive to go beyond. That is how real champions are made. They always go an extra mile while others are resting. Similarly, do not let a mere job title define the limits of your capabilities, especially if you know that you are worth more than the job title or position assigned to you by an employer. Go an extra mile beyond the job title. For we have seen cabinet ministers come and go. We have even seen chief executive officers come and go. Ambassadors have come and gone. Even presidents have come and gone. The question is, what is there beyond your job title that you can claim if you no longer have that job title or are stripped of the same?

Your whole life as a professional should not be limited to a job title or position. People get hired and fired from high-profile and low-profile jobs. Others retire or become frustrated and quit. Nothing appointed or elected is sacrosanct in this life. People do get disappointed at some point. So, if your whole professional life is anchored to a job title, and consequently you have become very bigheaded, what will become of you should you retire or get stripped of your job title? The questions to ask oneself are how impactful your job title or position has been and whether or not it provides you with some sustainable hope for tomorrow. Many people with big job titles lose themselves in a delusional maze of grandiose postures, as they shield themselves in a cocoon of power from the commoners. It all looks good until the bubble bursts. Thus, one is well-advised to ensure that one's professional life is bigger than one's job title and position. Otherwise, you will easily get frustrated in situations where, for example, you cannot get a big job title or position, especially if you know full well that you are worth more than the job title or position that has been assigned to you by your employer.

There are instances, for example, due to adverse organizational politics, a toxic corporate culture or simply operating in a less congenial habitat, where some suitably qualified individuals do not get a chance to actualize their full potential in the workplace, especially if such individuals do not have a godfather, godmother, advocate or sponsor. Indeed, certain corporate maneuvers and shenanigans often require more than just networking or having a mentor or coach. That is where the role of an advocate or sponsor comes in, that is, someone who can speak for you when you are not around or someone who can lobby for you to open doors on your behalf.

One of my mentees called me to complain how he was being bypassed for promotions at work and was thinking of quitting his job because he could not take it that someone who was far less qualified than him had just been promoted to be his supervisor. I let him vent out all his frustrations, and then, through some active listening, started paraphrasing slowly all that he had been saying to ensure that he understood that I had heard him well and fully. With the advantage of old age wisdom, I then proceeded to share some life lessons with the young man, saying: "Son, in life, merit is a minority. It has never been a majority. Merit, in contrast to the dominant mediocrity in this world, is only a small fraction. Only when we go to Heaven shall we find absolute meritocracy. Otherwise, mediocrity continues to dominate much of this world. Pray to God that you find the wisdom to know right from wrong and to distinguish good from bad. And pray to accept what you cannot change while remaining positive and hopeful that one day God will open the right doors for you where you will be respected and appreciated."

My mentee went quiet for a while before he responded: "But should I just sit and watch while this nonsense goes on?"

I smiled calmly and said to him: "Son, it is not every fight that you must fight or win. Choose your battles wisely. Some people are where they are because they have benefited from organizational politics of patronage in the workplace. Promotions or appointments to senior positions are not always performance based. It is easy for cronies to get rewarded for bootlicking or schmoozing. Others even join secret societies or clubs where their bosses are found just to advance their careers. Is that what you want?"

He went quiet. I then pressed on, "Son, some folks are rewarded for sexual favors. Yes, it can and does happen sometimes even though it is unethical. Some folks are brave. They can sleep their way up the corridors of power. Others might go for milder forms of seduction such as constantly giggling and flirting with their bosses. There are also those who wear provocative clothes at work just to catch the attention of bosses. The world out there is a jungle. Also, do not forget certain obstacles you have to deal with in the corporate world which include white privilege, racism, tribalism, gender discrimination, homophobia, and religious intolerance. All these barriers can affect your career development, and, if not handled properly, can even derail your career. When promoting their staff to leadership roles, bosses don't always choose the most qualified person or the best performer. Rather, they often choose someone that they are comfortable with. That's the real world out there, son. For example, a Latino boss might warm up quickly to a fellow Latino. An Asian boss might warm up quickly to a fellow Asian. A white boss might warm up quickly to a fellow white person. It happens a lot, though, of course, not everyone is like that. By contrast, for a number of you black folks, when you are given some leadership role, you often like to surround yourselves with white folks so that you feel important that you have white people reporting to you. Other black folks don't just trust their fellow black folks. You are often not comfortable in your own skin. That's just the reality. You like to seek validation from outside. Otherwise, son, many career opportunities for which you are suitably qualified will just bypass you if all you want is meritocracy where everybody sings kumbaya."

Taking a bird's eye view, how then does one retain some sanity in a world filled with such contradictions? Some people choose fearfully to stay put in the same place while nagging and complaining the whole day. Others opt to quit and look for better opportunities elsewhere. But there is also a third route that you can take to remain motivated and engaged in whatever you are doing. Let us take a more reasoned look.

Instead of just staying put and complaining every day, or quitting and moving somewhere else, the third viable option would be to embrace an ambidextrous strategic approach to professionalism. What do we mean by this? You can remain executing and implementing for today while envisioning for tomorrow. To achieve this, your professional life must be bigger than your job title or position. For example, ask yourself: what are your career prospects after you leave your current job? Do you have any skills that are saleable outside your current organization? And at what level do you think you can land? Or will you just be looking lost once you retire, as you quietly fizzle out into oblivion? To deal with such uncertainties, you may want to consider a dual or parallel career track that runs concurrently as long as (a) neither of your two careers is a distraction to the other, (b) there are no conflict of interests between the two careers, and (c) the staff policies at your main workplace do not proscribe outside work professional engagements.

In a similar way, if you are an academic, you might want to ensure that your academic life is bigger than just holding a PhD. Go beyond the PhD. For example, publish scientific works, break academic records and overcome stereotypes. It is always wise to generate options for yourself and find those alternatives that make you unique and stand out. Your uniqueness is what will differentiate you from others and create value for you. That said, in carrying out a generic strategy of differentiation, one must ensure that it is done at a cost leadership where the benefits outweigh the costs. Also, it is important to focus while pursuing an ambidextrous approach or a dual career track, meaning to say, do not diversify too much or you will be all over the place. Further, be mindful that, no matter how spirited the justifications of some people on why they hold a job, jobs are there mainly to pay your bills and they should not be taken as a measure of your capabilities. For you could be more capable than your job, and all you need to thrive is to be given a chance. Thus, it is your unique attributes that differentiate you from others and speak to your true worth. Once you appreciate this reasoning, you will be amenable to the idea of finding a safe space and a more congenial habitat where you can flourish under a secondary or parallel career and make a greater impact with what you bring to the table. Your unique attributes and skills-set are what will set you apart from the others. And these will drive the impact that you make. Indeed, the strategic deployment and application of your core competences is what will be helpful in differentiating and separating wheat from the chaff.

Put simply, how different are you from the others? And what is it that you possess or are bringing to the table that others do not possess or cannot bring to the table? Indeed, there are many people out there, including some prominent public figures, wealthy folks, celebrities and other socialites, whose former teachers, for example, have nothing good to say about them. A number of these fellas were just rascals or a menace when growing up. So, for me, I am humbled by the kind words posted on a social media page in January 2025 by one of my former high school teachers, Mr Charles Suwali, regarding my substantial intellectual contributions and inspiring published scholarship.

In the picture below, I can be seen at sunset in the Fellows' Garden at my alma mater, the University of Oxford's Exeter College, with the famous Radcliffe Camera in the background, shortly before I was honored at a special Oxford gala dinner held in my honor on Sunday, June 16, 2024. Such honor is rarely granted at Oxford and is reserved only for the most highly qualified and eminently distinguished persons whose contribution to the international community is worthy of special mention and recognition.

In November 2023, following the publication of my thirtieth scholarly book, my alma mater, the University of Oxford's Exeter College, posted the following statement about my scholarly journey on its college website: 'Until 2019, he was the only known legal scholar in the English-speaking world to hold Higher Doctorates in two different disciplines.'

> 03rd November 2023
>
> # Honorary Fellow Kenneth Mwenda publishes The Recognition of Global Higher Education Qualifications in International Law
>
> Honorary Fellow Professor Kenneth Mwenda (1992, BCL) has just released a new contribution to the study of international law and higher education. Professor Mwenda is the Manager and Executive Head of the World Bank Voice Secondment Program (VSP) in Washington DC and Extraordinary Professor of Law at the University of Western Cape (UWC) in Cape Town. Until 2019, he was the only known legal scholar in the English-speaking world to hold Higher Doctorates in two different disciplines. In 2019, the President of the Republic of Zambia Edgar C. Lungu awarded Professor Mwenda the Presidential Insignia of Meritorious Achievement, Zambia's highest civilian honour.

Source: Exeter College, University of Oxford, "Honorary Fellow Kenneth Mwenda publishes The Recognition of Global Higher Education Qualifications in International Law," (November 3, 2023), available Online at: https://www.exeter.ox.ac.uk/honorary-fellow-kenneth-mwenda-publishes-the-recognition-of-global-higher-education-qualifications-in-international-law/, accessed on March 1, 2025.

I was born in Africa, though I have lived much of my life elsewhere. The Africa I left is not the same anymore. Over the years, my tastes have changed even though my roots remain African. So, there are certain things that I might say or do innocently that could appear alien or strange to the African context. Yet I mean well and do not intend to cause any trouble. It is just that I have been away from Africa for far too long. So much has changed since I left Africa. Over the course of my life, I have lived, studied and worked in three different continents, namely, Africa, Europe and North America. While living in England, I spent some time in Oxfordshire before moving up north to Yorkshire. After a year in Yorkshire, I moved to Warwickshire, where I spent a number of years. While based in the United Kingdom, I also travelled widely to other European countries such as Netherlands, Hungary and Romania as well as to some African countries that include Zimbabwe and South Africa. At the time, South Africa was just about to transition from a white minority apartheid government to a black democratic majority government, and Zimbabwe had just won independence a few years before I got there.

I left the UK for the US in the late 1990s. I have been in the US ever since, working at the World Bank. In the US, I started off living in the affluent parts of downtown Washington DC close to Foggy Bottom area. I lived in DC for about five years before relocating to Virginia. My family I had spent a few years in Virginia before we finally decided to buy our family home in Maryland. While in the US with the World Bank, I have also had the opportunity of working extensively on European and Central Asian economies and frequently travelling to those regions.

In addition, I have travelled extensively within and outside the US and have had the privilege and opportunity of working in several countries leading work on law, policy, regulatory and institutional reforms as well as capacity-building. These countries include Albania, Antigua, Armenia, Barbados, Bulgaria, Canada, Commonwealth of Dominica, Croatia, Estonia, Ghana, Guyana, Hungary, Iceland, Jordan, Kenya, Kyrgyz Republic, Latvia, Lithuania, Libya, Moldova, Poland, Romania, Russia, Serbia, Slovenia, St Vincent's and the Grenadines, Tajikistan, Turkmenistan, Uzbekistan, and Uganda. Sometimes travel can become overwhelming. You are either in the air or in high profile meetings with senior government officials. There are times where within a day I have had breakfast in America, lunch in England and dinner in Germany, Switzerland or Austria. The burden of regular international trips is, however, lifted slightly by the perks of First Class and Business Class air travel. Apart from the countries listed above, I have also worked in and on countries such as Slovakia, Kosovo,

Philippines, Nepal, Sri Lanka, Bangladesh, Maldives, Mongolia, Lao PDR, China, Solomon islands, Papua New Guinea, Vanuatu, Kiribati, Tuvalu, Tonga, Samoa, Afghanistan, Azerbaijan, Bhutan, Ukraine, Croatia, Ireland, Cambodia, India, Pakistan, Iran, Iraq, Kuwait, Kazakhstan, Oman, Syria, Lebanon, Saudi Arabia, Vietnam, Thailand, Myanmar, Marshal islands, Micronesia, Jamaica, Haiti, Belize, St Kitts and Nevis, Grenada, Brazil, St Lucia, Dominican Republic, Paraguay, Columbia, Suriname, Mauritania, Cameroon, Senegal, Cote d'Ivoire, Comoros, Angola, Algeria, Botswana, Rwanda, Tanzania, Benin, Ethiopia, Gambia, Somalia, Sudan, South Sudan, Chad, Sierra Leone, Liberia, Egypt, Burundi, Burkina Faso, Gabon, Equatorial Guinea, Guinea, Guinea Bissau, Togo, Central African Republic, Namibia, Nigeria, Mozambique, Eswatini, Lesotho, Malawi, Zimbabwe, Zambia, West Bank and Gaza, and Yemen. In addition, I have visited and worked on other countries that include Germany, Georgia, Montenegro, Switzerland, Belgium, Italy, France, Austria, Turkey, Dubai, Qatar, Bahamas, Trinidad and Tobago, Nigeria, Cote d'Ivoire, Senegal, Botswana, Rwanda, Ethiopia, Democratic Republic of Congo, and Cabo Verde. Within the US, I have been to almost all major states and cities.

So I am not sure where that leaves me. Put simply, I consider myself a global citizen, even though am a dual national of the US and Zambia, as my views of the world and humanity are informed by an eclectic taste of various global and international cultural experiences. Indeed, my intercultural global and international experiences have given me the unique exposure which transcends the parochial limits of tribe or the insular norms of race, creed, and ethnicity. As a global thought-leader, I am also open to secular and non-secular views. My life is shaped by a mosaic of different intercultural values and norms. You cannot, for example, say of me that 'As an African, he cannot say this or that about Africa.' Yes, I am an African, but my value systems are not exclusively or entirely confined to the African experience. I have lived more than half of my life outside Africa. I left Africa in my early twenties. I am now in my mid-to-late fifties. So, it would be unfair to hold me to, or judge me strictly by, African standards simply because I come from Africa. Neither can you judge me exclusively by American or British standards. Along the way, as noted above, my tastes have changed. I am not only a product of Africa. I am a product of many other cultures around the world. Wherever I have studied, lived and worked, I have picked up various cultural norms. So, I am a product of the various environments where I have not only lived but have also studied and worked.

Let me use a metaphor here to contextualize what I am saying. Both my parents are originally from Luapula Province of Zambia. Our traditional Luapula folklore has it that some years back it was considered too risky to go swimming in some lakes or rivers of Luapula because some malicious villagers near those waters who practiced witchcraft would turn mysteriously into alligators or crocodiles and hunt down whoever they had a beef with. It is alleged that, out of pure malice, jealousy and envy, the culprits would lie low in the waters after turning into a gator or croc, as they waited patiently to pounce and drown their innocent victims once the victim stepped in the water. This vice went on for years until, according to Luapula folklore, some traditional chiefs warned all the villagers about engaging in such retrogressive superstitious practices. Otherwise, according to folklore, there would have been no other solution to the problem and even the police or courts of law would not have solved it.

Generally, a croc or gator is known as 'ing'wena' in almost all the Luapula dialects as well as in Bemba. But a croc or gator formed out of the superstitious enterprise of the locals is not called 'ing'wena'. Rather, it is called 'ichi bokolo'. Now you might be wondering what I am trying to say here. If you have only been exposed to our native and indigenous African culture in Luapula, you might be tempted to think that even in places such as Florida and California in the US, or Australia, the common shark attacks in the summer are a result of superstitious enterprise of 'ichi bokolo'. You might even start wondering why the US Government or the Australian Government doesn't consult some of our traditional African chiefs in Luapula how to manage those shark attacks emanating from the 'ifi bokolo' version of sharks.

By contrast, if you are someone who has been exposed to different cultures globally or internationally, you are likely to understand issues differently. You are likely to think of global warming and the changing ecological factors in the environment as some of the factors that are causing sharks to come more closer to the coastline. You are also likely not going to insist that the shark attacks 'fya ku Bantu' (English translation: 'the shark attacks are a result of the superstitious enterprise' of some bad people). But a person whose perspectives are limited, say, to our indigenous folklore of 'ichi bokolo' will say that the shark attacks in America and Australia are being carried out superstitiously by some bad people who turn into sharks to attack their victims. It would even be worse if such a superstitious person were to see alligators loitering around the neighborhoods of Florida. The person might be tempted to think that there is no way a normal alligator can be found in the neighborhood, and that it should be a product of the superstitious enterprise of some old man or woman nearby. Put simply, exposure changes your thinking. Travelling is knowledge of and by itself. You begin to see things differently. And so, I see things differently from the many lenses that continually shape my global experiences, given the many places that I have lived in and visited. And I should be understood from that perspective.

To place the discussion in further context, let us take another example from Zambia. If, say, someone tells you that some really bad folks in some villages of Eastern Province of Zambia have a habit of turning mysteriously into a lion or hyena at night in order to attack their nemeses or someone who refused to help them out during the day, including someone that they are simply envious of, you would, if you are an individual whose experiences are limited parochially to Eastern Province folklore and culture, end up believing everything you hear. By contrast, one who is exposed to other cultures might be tempted to think that perhaps the animal attacks are simply because the villages are situated near a game reserve where some wild animals in those reserves escape from at night to hunt for food in the nearby places. Indeed, different societies have different emphasis. So it will all depend on the societal emphases that you have been exposed to. Those emphases will shape some of your thinking.

Growing up in Africa, I remember that when I was a young boy, some of my friends believed mischievously that they could derail a train by simply placing a sewing needle on the railway tracks. They tried several times, but no train got derailed. So, you begin to ask yourself: how valid are some of these myths? It is always good to be open-minded, though not to be recklessly dismissive or to throw caution to the wind. Let us take a more reasoned look.

When I completed my four years of university education in Zambia, I stayed on in the country for a few more years to complete graduate education for my Bar admission before commencing my university teaching career at the University of Zambia (UNZA). I took the Bar exams in 1991 and passed at first attempt as the best overall graduating student. At a tender age of twenty-three (23) years, I left Africa for Europe, that is, shortly after Zambia's founding father, His Excellency (H.E.) President Kenneth Kaunda, lost presidential elections to H.E. President Frederick Chiluba. The 1991 Zambian Presidential and General Elections saw an end to the One-Party State System in Zambia, ushering in a new era of multiparty politics. From 1964, when Zambia gained political independence from Great Britain, to 1973, Zambia enjoyed a multiparty political system. The three main political parties were the United National Independence Party (UNIP), the African National

Congress (ANC), and the United Progressive Party (UPP). Of the three parties, only UNIP, the party that became the ruling party after independence, had a nationwide appeal, while the other two were mainly regionally based. ANC had support mainly from Southern and Western Provinces while UPP had support mainly from the northern provinces and other Bemba-speaking areas of the Copperbelt. The One-Party State system was introduced under Zambia's 1973 Constitution mainly to unite the country against tribal and sectarian politics. The introduction of the One-Party State system in Zambia effectively banned ANC and UPP, leaving only UNIP as the sole constitutionally mandated political party in the country.

Today, when I look at contemporary sub-Sahara Africa, much of what I see is that the greatest generation of African nationalists and Pan-Africanists was the generation that fought for Africa's independence. They were enlightened and socially conscious folks. By contrast, what we are left with in Africa, as in many other parts of the world, are simply businessmen and women. Many don't even have any semblance of an ideology on which their ideas of leadership and governance are anchored. Some are just plain conmen. The reintroduction of multiparty politics in many parts of Africa, including Zambia, has had its own shortcomings.

Though viewed as an important tenet of Western democracy, a notable shortcoming of the reintroduction or introduction of multi-party politics in Africa is the resurgence of sectionalism and tribal politics which the One-Party State had somewhat managed to quash. I contend here that many African nations could have benefitted from simply reforming and democratizing the One-Party State system instead of rushing to reintroduce multiparty politics. If only fixed-term limits for each president were strictly adhered to under the One-Party State system, in order to allow for other aspirants to succeed the presidency, the One-Party State system would not have been perceived as a dictatorial system. However, the problem with the One-Party State, as it was, is that it did not entertain or tolerate any opposing views that were contrary to the position of the ruling party, thereby stifling any semblance of internal democracy.

To appreciate the reasoning behind the proposal above of reforming the One-Party State system, we have to be mindful that different societies have different emphasis in their ideological or cultural outlook. The socio-economic conditions which support multiparty politics in the Western world, for example, might not be the same as those obtaining in Africa. To illustrate, tribalism is a big thing in Africa, whereas the Western world does not have to deal with such things. By contrast, their problem is racism.

Often where sectionalism and tribal politics are rife, as is the case in much of contemporary Africa, it is hard to distinguish those who have gone to school from the unenlightened. Even some Africans living in the diaspora, including many with a good university education, have not been spared from the scourge of tribal politics. Often tribal politics are fueled by primitive and opportunistic behaviors. Africans and tribalism are a whole doctoral thesis on their own. Tribalism is like a plague. In many cases, education has failed to detribalize the African intellectual. Prior to the introduction of multi-party politics in many parts of Africa, the One-Party State was viewed by many commentators as an undemocratic system of governance. It was also seen as an oppressive authoritarian rule by one man and his political party, especially given that no other political party was allowed to operate constitutionally in Zambia.

Laudable as this view may seem, the One-Party State system could have been reformed internally, as I have argued above, to allow for democratic centralism that provided an avenue for change of leadership within the ruling party itself by introducing and adhering to fixed presidential term limits. Instead, the One-Party State system, as seen in many parts of Africa, created a political cult around one absolute leader. The system cultivated a culture of absolute loyalty and patronage to the head of state. Any form of dissent was seen as unpatriotic. A dissident, as dissenting persons were called, would often be met with State-orchestrated brutality. Many people thus thought that the reintroduction of multiparty politics was panacea to the ills of the One-Party State.

Zambia was one of the first African countries to move away from the One-Party State system. In Zambia, multi-party politics were reintroduced in 1991, marking an end to it. However, with the reintroduction of multiparty politics in Zambia, as in many other African countries, came the resurgence of sectionalism and tribal politics. For example, in an interview that aired in Zambia as the country was preparing for the 2021 Presidential and General Elections, President Kenneth Kaunda, the founding father of the Nation of Zambia, expressed some concerns about the divisive tendencies of sectionalism exhibited by some political leaders, but many people ignored his warning, much to their detriment. Understandably, in a protest vote, many people will take anything but the status quo. Often there is not much thoughtful consideration of the available options, just a protest for urgent change to vote out the sitting government. When people are hungry, they become angry and don't have time to negotiate or think deeply into issues.

Today, many folks look back and recall the wise words of President Kaunda. Yet in 2021, anyone who raised concern about the rising tide of tribal politics was seen as endorsing or supporting the (Patriotic Front) government that was in power at the time. This was so because the main opposition to the PF Government had grown out of a largely ethnic-centered movement and morphed eventually into a national protest. This trajectory was also reflected in the ethnic-centered voting pattern of the main opposition (see the red coloring in the map below) which for the first time was aided by a national protest vote from other parts of the country against the PF Government. The data on the results of the 2021 presidential elections in Zambia, as demonstrated in the table below, is self-explanatory. Numbers don't lie.

Overall Election Results by Party Winning Margins

Overall: 2021 Presidential Election Results by Constituencies

Source: L. Phiri, "Learning from Data: Mapping Regional Voting Patterns in the 2021 Zambia Presidential Elections," General, Technical, Zambia, (August 23, 2021) (based on data collected from the Electoral Commission of Zambia) available Online: https://lightonphiri.org/blog/learning-from-data-mapping-regional-voting-patterns-in-the-2021-zambia-presidential-elections, accessed on July 3, 2024.

There was a strong element of denial and defensiveness in the then main opposition camp whenever anyone raised concerns over the issues of tribal politics and primordial separatist tendencies. Whoever raised such concerns was accused instead of being a tribalist. It was a way to contain the elephant in the room. Others in the opposition camp saw it as an opportunity for affirmative action to redress the supposedly limited opportunities that had been accorded to people from their region. But all these defensive counterarguments were unfounded. Zambia has always been a largely inclusive nation.

Over the last three to four decades, tribal politics have been gaining traction in Zambia and are getting overtly worse after each presidency, notwithstanding some intermittent periods of remission. To illustrate, on December 11, 2023, the *Diggers* newspaper, a leading Zambian media publication, carried a headline pointing to some growing sentiments against what appears to be an emerging culture of sectionalism and tribal politics among some reactionary forces within the governance class of Zambia.

Within only seven days, there were more media reports in Zambia on the emerging culture of tribal politics. To illustrate, on Tuesday, December 19, 2023, following the headline article in the *Diggers* newspaper highlighted

above, two other media publications, *The Mast* newspaper and the *Daily Nation*, carried closely related headline articles, as shown below.

On March 20, 2024, *The Mast* newspaper, as seen in the picture below, carried a headline alleging tribalism and sectionalism in the hiring and firing of employees of Zambia's State-run electricity supply company, ZESCO.

To try to contest these media articles taken from three different independent media sources, all of which point to primordial separatist tendencies, would be pursuing a red herring. We have to be honest with ourselves. Denials and counter-accusations in the face of overwhelmingly visible and disturbing trends of sectionalism and tribal politics are nothing but a manifestation of cognitive dissonance. And cognitive dissonance is not only unhelpful, it is counterproductive. Besides, if a large faction of the public perceives a regime to be too tribal or defending sectarianism, that can make those who were in the preceding regime and who are accused of having engaged in corrupt practices look like angels. People will shift their attention to you instead. They will even forget about those whom you are accusing of having stolen from the State coffers. On Thursday, February 27, 2025, the *Mast Newspaper* of Zambia carried a front-page article whose headline, as seen in the picture below, points to the same worrying issue of sectarianism.

It is a truism that ever since the UNIP Government lost elections in 1991, the successive Zambian governments that have come to power in Zambia have struggled with the issue of corruption among some of their political elites. The fight against corruption can easily lose momentum if we allow tribal politics to fester. On Thursday, November 21, 2024, another screaming headline appeared in the media on tribal politics in Zambia, as depicted on the front page of *The Mast* newspaper.

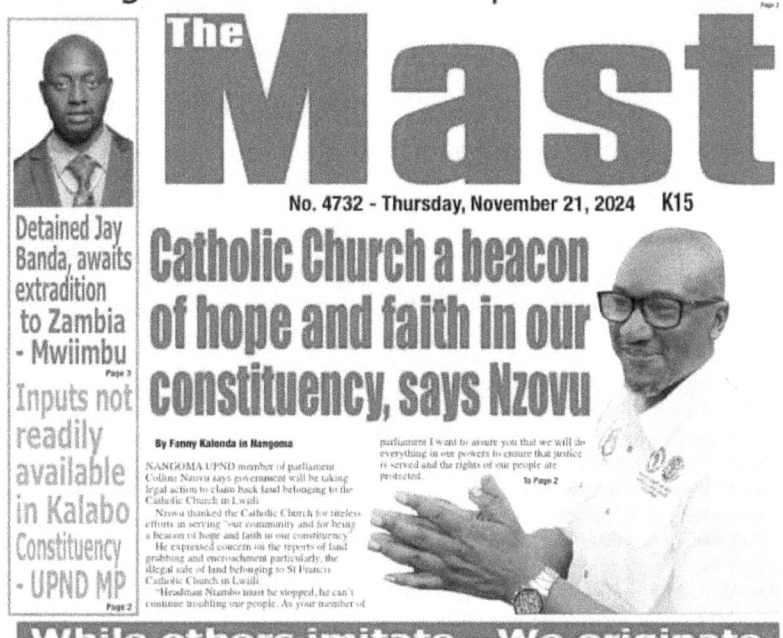

We are comforted by the words of Thomas Paine who once said 'He who dares not offend cannot be honest.' We must all dare to be honest. As a scholar, I do not write to appease or pacify the audience. Neither do I write to cause trouble. Rather, I simply pursue the truth wherever it leads me. So if, for example, I write down my view on something that hits you hard, you will think that it is personal and I am targeting you, yet it is your own guilty conscience that betrays you. The truth is never kind to anyone who is guilty. If I tell you that as a football coach, I would like to fill a position in my team, but I am faced with a dilemma of choosing between a player who is quite talented but is said to have some issues with alcohol and one who some people fear will only be passing the ball to his tribemates or folks from his ethnic regional base, notwithstanding some occasional passes to other folks who are married to his tribemates, you will think I am talking politics. Indeed, that is how dishonest people think. Their own guilty conscience betrays them. Yet I am talking about football, not politics. If all you want to hear is what you suspect, then you will definitely hear your own misconceptions, because your mind is already made up a priori. But if you have an open mind, you will be open to the possibility of other interpretations.

Indeed, why not assume that I am talking about the corporate world where such things do happen as well? On the higher echelons of the corporate ladder, it is not uncommon, say, for a white man who is racist to consider more favorably a black man who is married to a white woman, on the premise that the black man is taking care of his white sister, than to accommodate a black man who is married to a black woman. The black man with a white woman is likely to be seen as looking after their white sister. So you will find some black men spiritedly exploiting this avenue of inter-racial marriage in order to secure a 'passport' to climb up the corporate ladder. But because some people are not honest, they are likely to enter into cognitive dissonance at the sound of such truths. History, however, has a way of vindicating the truth. You will know the truth by looking at the people that someone passes the ball to as soon as you put him in a position of power.

When I taught at the University of Warwick in the United Kingdom in the 1990s, the President of the Republic of Zambia at the time was His Excellency President Frederick Titus Jacob Chiluba. President Chiluba, who was pursuing his Master of Philosophy (MPhil) degree program in political science at the University of Warwick, was, like me, from Luapula Province in Zambia. He was from Kwa Musangu village, while I am from Pa Mwenda. But at no time did I go looking for President Chiluba and try to ingratiate myself with him or his political party simply because we are from the same region or province. Tribe, village or region did not matter to me. In fact, I never even met President Chiluba or made an effort to him. To me, he was just one of our students at Warwick. That's it. As the former president of Mozambique, President Samora Machel, once said, "For the nation to live, the tribe must die."

Ironically, a number of my Zambian friends who hail from the same province or region as His Excellency President Hakainde Hichilema, including some folks who I thought were well educated and above petty tribal politics, came out at election time in support of their tribesman primarily on parochial grounds that he was 'one of their own'. Prior to that, when the Patriotic Front (PF) Government was in power, most of these folks were in hiding, pretending to be intellectuals and apolitical. While people have a right to support any party or candidate of their choice, it is wise not to base such support on primarily tribal, regional, or ethnic considerations. For how else can we call it? For me, if I have to align myself to any cause, or adopt any political affiliation, it has to be based on purely logical and sound ideological bases, not mere sentimental attachment to my tribe, race, region or ethnic group. Indeed, it cannot be a mere coincidence that most of my friends and colleagues referenced above supported their 'own'. Without doubt, many had been pretending to be apolitical intellectuals until it was time to vote in their own.

As soon as the results of the 2021 presidential elections were announced, it was clear that some people had not been honest. They started posting on social media some never-before-seen photos they had taken with President Hichilema shortly before and after he was elected as president. All along, they were mute while quietly supporting him and pretending to be apolitical. That's why we say people are not honest. Even those who have smoked weed before will never admit it, especially if their children ask them, 'Daddy, did you ever try to smoke weed when growing up?' And they are not the only ones. Young people will never admit to their parents that they are sexually active until trouble catches up with them. People are not honest.

Anyhow, unlike most of the fellas who were busy flashing photos taken with the newly elected president, I had never had any photos taken with President Chiluba or travelled long distances just to meet him at his home or wherever he was addressing a gathering simply because we are from the same region. Neither did I make any financial contributions to his political party. I was not even a member of it. For me, I always think of the nation first, not the tribe, race, region, ethnic grouping or religion. Those that I have interacted with, including many that I have helped, assisted and mentored from different tribes, races, religions and ethnic groups, can attest to this fact. I tend to look at the bigger picture, not taking a small myopic insular or parochial view of life. That is who I am. I am a scholar. And I live by my erudite thought-process, not primordial separatist tendencies.

Unfortunately, for some people, you can offer them shelter when it's raining, get them career or educational opportunities, give them rides in your car to save them from walking or commuting long distances, and even introduce them to your professional networks, but as soon as they think that one of their 'own' is now in power they will disrespect you and tell you to your face that there was no good Samaritan who helped them when they needed help, irrespective of the fact that the so-called 'their own' actually neglected and abandoned them while you sacrificed to salvage them when they were in distress. Indeed, such ungratefulness and inherent prejudice are easily discernible. You can vote for someone today, thinking that he or she will have your back or interests at heart if he or she wins the election, but you will be shocked at how quickly you will be forgotten once the person gets into office.

Although some sentiments in the Zambian media, masked as a clarion call for affirmative action, have tried to counter the views that condemn tribal politics and primordial separatist tendencies, many such countering sentiments are simply veiled attempts to promote and protect sectarianism. Two wrongs don't make a right. Groups of people who gather simply because they share a common ethnic background, notwithstanding, say, a handful of outsiders among them, often tend to work against norms of diversity, inclusion and equity. Tribal politics thrive on tribalism and are usually a function of the middle class and disgruntled intellectuals who use tribalism to access economic resources and opportunities at various levels of the State. Indeed, it is about accessing resources and opportunities. Where peasants and the proletariat are found to be engaging in tribal politics, they are often drawn into it and co-opted by opportunistic elements of the middle class and some disgruntled intellectuals.

On their own, peasants and villagers are generally good people and rarely practice tribalism. They are often driven by their sense of 'Ubuntu'. By contrast, it is the schematic shenanigans and machinations of the middle class and petit bourgeois elements, as well as some frustrated intellectuals, that draw peasants and the proletariat into sectionalism and sectarian tribal politics. Quite often, we think of extremism as the holding of extreme and fanatical religious or political views, but it can also manifest itself in the form of tribalism. In the Global North, especially in North America and

Western Europe, extremism is often underscored by racial bigotry. In some parts of Eastern Europe, it has mainly been about racial and ethnic bigotry. Such prejudices have led to violence and the displacement of people. In some parts of Asia, extremism has often been about religion, race, caste and ethnic divisions. In Latin and South America, it has mainly been about ethnicity and racial bigotry. In the Middle East, extremism has often been about religious and racial bigotry. In the Pacific region, including Australia and New Zealand, it has mainly been about race and ethnicity. In Africa, it has mainly been about tribal bigotry within states, with closely related bigotry across sub-regions based on the religion practiced in those sub-regions and the colonial language spoken by people from a particular sub-region. In some cases, this form of extremism has led to misguided notions of self-determination. Unfortunately, a number of failed attempts of secession under the guise of self-determination have often ended up as criminal offences of treason. But let us take a more reasoned look at how a tribal mind works amongst some Africans.

You could be with a fellow Zambian colleague in the middle of New York in the US, and the moment the two of you meet another countryman or woman whose name is from the same region or tribe as your colleague, that colleague of yours will suddenly brighten up excitedly as he or she switches immediately into his or her native Zambian language to greet and converse with the third party that you have just met, leaving you out of the conversation. I mean, in the middle of New York, how do you begin to ask a stranger if he or she is from the same village in Zambia as yours? Nobody cares about your African village in the streets of New York. Why not ask someone, say, about their profession or the college or university that they attended, as a way to build some possible professional or alumni networks. How can you ask someone you have just met in New York if they come from the same village as yours? Of what relevance is your village notion in America? Some people struggle with leaving the village out of their head even if they have lived abroad for years.

For the middle class and the petit bourgeoisie as well as the disgruntled intellectuals, many envy the glamour associated with bourgeois tendencies, so they try to morph quickly into a cabal of the governing class so that they can form links to, and benefit from, international capitalists or the ruling class. But to do so, the middle class and the petit bourgeois opportunists, as well as the disgruntled intellectuals, try to win political legitimacy by framing their parochial sentiments of sectionalism as a legitimate cause against the so-called socio-economic disenfranchisement of their ethnic group. Yet, we know that you cannot use or adopt tribal sentiments to correct the ills of what you perceive as tribalism against your people. Indeed, you cannot defeat tribalism by using or adopting another form of tribalism. Rather, why not become a nationalist? A jealous and envious person will condemn a thief not because he wants to stop the theft but because he wants to be the one stealing. Parochialism leads to nothing but sectionalism and sectarian tribal politics, and such political dispensation often lacks global and international appeal. Tribal politics are just too insular and parochial to become global or international in scope and scale. Wherever you find tribal politics, group-think is the dominant ideology and identity of the culpable parochialists or those who subscribe to such politics. These individuals are like football fans. They will not want to hear anything else but the support of their team.

On December 19, 2023, the Zambian House of Chiefs, a constitutional body of traditional chiefs established pursuant to Article 169 of the Constitution of the Republic of Zambia 1991 (as amended through to 2016), is alleged to have issued the following statement on the resurgence of sectionalism and sectarian tribal politics in Zambia:[1]

Then, on January 31, 2023, an opposition party leader in Zambia, Dr Fred M'membe, wrote an article on what he considered to be some of the reasons fueling the emerging debate on tribal politics in Zambia. The said article, published on the website of the Socialist Party of Zambia and titled, "What's fueling tribal politics debates?" was accessed online by this author on December 20, 2023. In that article, Dr M'membe, a media mogul and leader of the Socialist Party, states:

> **HOUSE OF CHIEFS CONDEMNS DIVISIVE REGIONAL GROUPINGS THREATENING NATIONAL UNITY**
>
> *19th December 2023*
>
> The House of Chiefs, strongly condemns the emergence of regional groupings such as Chuunda Chaita, Kola Foundation, Luapula United, and Umozi ku Mawa. These entities, purportedly fostering unity, are instead contributing to the division of our beloved nation.
>
> We should all remember the sacrifices made by our founding fathers who championed the principles of co-existence under the banner of "One Zambia, One Nation." The House of Chiefs firmly advocates for national unity and rejects any efforts that threaten the unity of our diverse country.
>
> I am urging every peace-loving Zambian not to allow politicians to exploit these divisions for personal gain. We should not forget that the peace-loving Zambia, standing as a beacon of peace in our region and Africa, is at stake. Politicians may have the means to leave the country, but it is the ordinary citizens who will bear the effect of instability and unrest.
>
> The House of Chiefs calls upon all Zambians to uphold the ideals of unity, diversity, and peace that have defined our nation for decades. Let us stand together against divisive forces and work towards preserving the harmony that is essential for the prosperity of our great nation.
>
> As traditional leaders we stand firmly in support of any efforts that promote peace and coexistence. Let us not permit our nation to descend into the chaos that has afflicted other countries. We have only one Zambia, and it is our collective responsibility to safeguard its peacefulness and unity.
>
> HRH Chief Chisunka (Dr)
> Chairperson – House of Chiefs
> Chairperson – Luapula Province Council of Chiefs

---

1   See, for example, W. Zylum, "House of Chiefs Condemns Regional Groupings: A Call for Societal Unity," (December 21, 2023), available Online: <<https://bnnbreaking.com/world/zambia/house-of-chiefs-condemns-regional-groupings-a-call-for-societal-unity/>>, accessed on December 31, 2023.

"It seems Mr Hakainde Hichilema and the UPND are perched on the defensive over accusations of tribalism. Why? Probably it is because of the promises they made to have a tribal and regionally balanced and representative government. Critiques are asking if what they are seeing is equal to what they were promised."[2]

Dr M'membe goes on to submit the following list of key office holders in prominent government positions under President Hakainde Hichilema:[3]

- President (Tonga)
- Vice-President (Bemba married to a Lozi)
- Speaker (Lozi)
- Chief Justice (Lenje)
- Acting President of the Constitutional Court (Lozi)
- Attorney General (Lenje)
- Solicitor General (Tonga)
- Chairman of the Judicial Service Commission (Lozi)
- Chairman of the Judicial Complaints Commission (Tonga)
- Commissioner of Lands (Tonga)
- Chief Legal Advisor to the President (Lozi)
- Minister of Justice (Tonga).

Referring to expectations of a large section of the electorate, Dr M'membe avers further that,

"They are saying the key state institutions and the country's justice system are basically in the hands of Tongas and Lozis (with very little or no meaningful participation from the rest). They are saying the same about the key government ministries (Ministries that are not easily done away with by any government):

- Home Affairs (Tonga)
- Local Government (Tonga)
- Education (Tonga)
- Tourism (Tonga)

---

2   F. M'membe, "What's fuelling tribal politics debates?" *Socialist Party of Zambia*, (January 31, 2023), available Online at: <<https://socialistpartyzambia.com/2023/01/31/whats-fuelling-tribal-politics-debates/>>, accessed on December 20, 2023.

3   See *Ibid*.

- Justice (Tonga)
- Foreign Affairs (Lenje)
- Health (Soli)
- Defence (Luvale)
- Infrastructure (Lozi)
- Finance (Lozi)
- Lands (Lunda)
- Governor of Bank of Zambia (Tonga).

The rest are, in the main, pushed to ministries that can easily be done away and receive very limited budgetary allocations."[4]

Dr M'membe furnishes additional evidence to support his submission, contending that:[5]

"They say the picture is the same for key defence and security agencies:

- Zambia Army Commander (Lozi)
- Zambia Air Force Commander (Kaonde)
- ZNS Commandant (Luvale)
- Inspector General of Police (Kaonde)
- Director General of Intelligence (Lozi)
- Commissioner General of Correctional Services (Tonga)
- Chief Immigration officer (Lozi)

In substantiating his claims, Dr M'membe postulates:

"They are saying in all these key command defence and security positions there's no one from the East or the North as the political leadership to keep the tribal and regional balance the political leadership had promised. They are also pointing to the Electoral Commission of Zambia:

- chairperson (Lozi)
- vice-person (Mambwe)
- the other three commissioners are Tonga, Lozi and Lunda

---

4   See *Ibid*.
5   See *Ibid*.

There's no one from the East or the North proper. These concerns are raised about lower positions in these and other state, government and quasi-governmental institutions and agencies. These are the concerns they are raising and the response is to label them tribalists and divisive elements and prosecute or persecute them on charges of tribal hatred. With these concerns and the debates they are generating, our multiparty political dispensation is back on the spot. The concern is no longer the lack of political pluralism or diversity, but the hijacking of the political processes by tribal politics. The challenge to our multiparty political dispensation is not the prevalence of ethnic diversity, but the use of identity politics to promote narrow tribal interests. It is tribalism."[6]

Public perception in politics is important. How a regime is perceived by large factions of the public can either give it legitimacy or deny it of the same, so legality alone is not enough. You can ignore the issue of public perception if you want, though at your own peril. If people are complaining that you are being too tribal in your job appointments and promotions, including in the nomination or endorsement of candidates from your country for international jobs, you can choose to ignore those complaints as you try to justify your seemingly biased decisions as 'affirmative action'. If a large section of the public can point to individuals that you are spiritedly sponsoring for top positions in international organizations as coming mainly from your region, you can choose to ignore such complaints if you want. But at what cost? If people are saying that even the so-called 'talent' that you are poaching from some international organizations is predominantly from your region, you can choose to ignore those complaints. But you will, no doubt, meet the voters' wrath at the next elections. It would, however, be different if the complaints were only coming from one or two persons, but not a wide population. A quick investigation shows that even within the ranks of those promoting regional or tribal politics, some felt left out in the distribution or sharing of power after the elections. It is easy to gang up and grab the carcass from a lion, but hard to share the carcass equally afterwards. Without doubt, you can be united against a common enemy, but as soon as you overcome the enemy and are left to your own devices, greed comes in.

Historically, even some past presidents of Zambia, although not all of them of course, are alleged to have formed cabals of tribal loyalists around them when they were in power. For example, during President Levy Mwanawasa's presidential term, the rise to prominence of some political appointees from among the Bantu Botatwe ethnic grouping was not uncommon. The story of the infamous

---

6   See *Ibid*.

'family tree' was all over the media, pointing to political appointments of relatives and in-laws. The same could be said of many notable Bemba appointments during President Michael Sata's presidential term. The man resuscitated the careers of some of his old Bemba friends and, like his predecessor, President Mwanawasa, had some of his relatives and in-laws appointed to the foreign service. The emergence of tribal appointments continued with President Rupiah Banda, who surrounded himself at State House with a number of advisors from among his own Easterners, including an Attorney-General. Quoting the then President of the Republic of Zambia, Mr Michael Sata, in the *Lusaka Times*, an online article dated July 21, 2012, that was first published in the *Zambia Daily Mail*, then republished on the *Lusaka Times*' website, and titled, "President Sata accuse former President Rupiah Banda of tribalism", postulates as follows:

"PRESIDENT Sata has said that he is hugely disappointed that his predecessor Rupiah Banda is allegedly using a tribal card to determine who should be Zambia's next President. However, we are comforted because Zambians know Mr Banda when it comes to tribalism. His record at NAMBOARD, Ministry of Foreign Affairs and as Lusaka district governor speaks for itself. It is this record that makes him feel at home when dealing with certain well-known tribally-based political establishments in the country,' the President says."[7]

The problem with tribal politics is that almost all the beneficiaries involved never admit to practicing such politics. In an online article published by the *San Diego Union Tribune* on June 29, 2012, and titled, "Zambian President Sata under Scrutiny," Lewis Mwanangombe writes:

"President Michael Sata made his uncle his finance minister, appointed other relatives to other high government posts… He appointed his uncle, Alexander Chikwanda, as minister of finance. The local government minister is his niece, and cousins have been appointed ambassador to Japan and acting chief justice. Giving family members government jobs is something of a political tradition in Zambia. Under Mwanawasa, some dubbed the government 'the family tree.'"[8]

After President Kenneth Kaunda, one notable president who appeared not to have made it a

---

[7] Lusaka Times, "President Sata accuse former President Rupiah Banda of tribalism," *Lusaka Times*, (July 21, 2012), available Online at: <<https://www.lusakatimes.com/2012/07/21/president-sata-accuse-president-rupiah-banda-tribalism/>>, accessed on March 2, 2024.

[8] Lewis Mwanangombe, "Zambian President Sata under Scrutiny," *San Diego Union Tribune*, (June 29, 2012), available Online at: <<https://www.sandiegouniontribune.com/sdut-zambian-president-sata-under-scrutiny-2012jun29-story.html#:~:text=Zambia's%20populist%20president%20portrays%20himself,the%20year%20since%20taking%20office.>> accessed on February 2, 2024.

habit of appealing to his ethnic base in how he governed, was arguably President Edgar C. Lungu. If it were not for his middle name and surname, you would not even know that President Lungu was from the East. President Lungu, like President Kaunda, was more of a cosmopolitan leader and often spoke in English or Bemba, but not Nsenga, Tumbuka, Ngoni or Chewa, as one would expect. How many political leaders can operate comfortably in politics without using their native language? It matters less that President Lungu grew up on the Copperbelt. He was still not Bemba, though he did not show any disdain towards Bembas or any other ethnic or tribal group. That versatility is rare. Like President Mwanawasa and President Kaunda, President Lungu was also not known for telling lies or making false promises to the electorate. But what worked against President Lungu in the 2021 presidential elections was arguably the apparent indiscipline of some of his political cadres and the mismanagement of resources by some key government officials while he was in power. I would not say that the leading opposition party, the United Party for National Development (UPND)), was that popular. Rather, what helped UPND to win the elections was simply that the electoral result was a protest vote against the thuggery and untamed corruption that was associated with the then ruling party, PF, which shot itself in the foot by not listening to the cries of the people. Even so, UPND did not succeed purely on the basis of exclusive support from its regional and tribal strongholds but was aided by the support of a large faction of other voters from various parts of the country who were just tired of the indiscipline in the PF Government. By its own misdeeds, PF had become unpopular and thus lost the elections on a protest vote. Interestingly, after UPND won the elections and formed a government, they spent much of the first term blaming the PF Government and accusing it of having mismanaged the Zambian economy instead of delivering on its electoral promises. A man who divorces his wife to marry another woman does not spend most of his time blaming her for having mismanaged his finances each time his new wife asks him for money to buy groceries or food for the house. Rather, he must focus on the promises he made to the new wife.

In 1991, after the rebirth of multiparty politics in Zambia, the Chiluba Movement for Multiparty Democracy (MMD) Government embarked on an ambitious privatization program. I was just about to leave Zambia then for my graduate studies as a Rhodes Scholar at Oxford. Throughout the Chiluba MMD Government and the subsequent Zambian governments of H.E. President Levy Mwanawasa (MMD), H.E. President Rupiah Banda (MMD), H.E. President Michael Sata (Patriotic Front (PF)), H.E. President Edgar Lungu (PF) and H.E. President Hakainde Hichilema

(United Party for National Development (UPND)), I have been away from Zambia, though I am well-informed of developments on the ground. As a scholar, I am alive to the realities of the political dispensations in the country, though the only Zambian government I have lived under for a long time was H.E President Kenneth Kaunda's United National Independence Party (UNIP) Government. Dr Kaunda's UNIP Government was in power during Zambia's first republic, lasting twenty-seven (27) years from 1964 when Zambia got political independence from Britain to 1991. I remember that first Zambian republic as arguably the best in the political-economic history of the country. What came after the first republic is best left to the younger generation to tell, that is, if, or when, they decide to write their autobiographies.

When I left Africa for Europe more than thirty years ago, I left on a fully funded and highly competitive graduate studies scholarship tenable at the University of Oxford. I did not have to do odd jobs in England to survive. If anything, I was very comfortable. I arrived in England in 1992 as Zambia's 1992 Rhodes Scholar-Elect after beating fierce competition at home which included a colleague who later became a State Counsel in Zambia as well as another colleague with a Masters degree from the prestigious University of Cambridge. I will explain my story later, regarding the Rhodes Scholarship interviews. Here, suffice it to say that I was the only Rhodes Scholar selected for Zambia that year. I left Zambia for Oxford in August 1992. After completing my graduated studies at Oxford in 1994, equipped with a top British education, I remained in England to continue my academic career at a leading British university. Following a successful university teaching career in England, which started in 1995, I left England in 1998 and moved to North America for a career with the World Bank. While in the US, in addition to working for the World Bank, I not only completed advanced leadership and management studies at such top US universities as Harvard University, Yale University, Stanford University, Massachusetts Institute of Technology (MIT), University of Pennsylvania, Cornell University and Georgetown University, but also taught at a leading US law school, American University Washington College of Law (WCL). At the time of writing this book, I have lived in the US for more than twenty-five years now. Before that, I spent almost a decade in England. All in all, I have been away from Africa for more than half of my life, though I do visit the continent annually for some academic engagements. I was only 23 years old when I left Africa. It is now more than 30 years ago.

While living and working in England and the US, I have been blessed with the opportunity to travel to many other parts of the globe. I can safely say that I have seen the world. Accordingly, the views and experiences that I share in this book are informed not only by my youthful experiences in Africa, but also by my global and intercultural views of the world.

I would best describe my views as a mosaic and eclectic taste of different cultural experiences, informed by various global and international perspectives. To illustrate, my exposure to different cultures is not only limited to North America, Europe and Africa. I have also travelled to and worked in the Middle East, for example. Further, I have travelled to and worked in the Caribbean islands and South America. And I have travelled to and worked in Central Asia and Eastern Europe. In addition, I have worked on many countries in South Asia as well as East Asia and the Pacific. There is no major region of the world that I have not covered. Even within Africa, I have travelled to and worked in West Africa, North Africa, East Africa, and Southern Africa. So, in sharing my story, I will be wearing different hats at different times or occasions, as my wardrobe of experiences is not limited to one hat.

Against this background, I submit that, if one does not tell his or her story, the story may never be told. Nobody owes you the obligation to tell your story on your behalf. And even if your story is told, it may end up being distorted or misrepresented. Sometimes, only half the truth of your story gets to be told. At other times, the truth can be watered down deliberately and intentionally just to dim your light. If that were to happen, you only have yourself to blame for not having told your story yourself. Only you know your story best, for you are the best witness of yourself. All the same, avoid embellishments and stick to the truth. Nobody can dispute facts, even if they don't like those facts. And facts are different from value judgements or theories. You can question value judgements and challenge theories, but facts are facts whether you like them or not. For example, X works hard and owns a posh car, but his neighbor, Y, a lazy chap who has never owned a car in his entire life, is bitter and envious of X. Y keeps accusing X of bragging just because he can't afford X's luxury car. Instead of being inspired by X to work hard so that he too can excel, Y chooses to hate X, as if that will change or improve his miserable life. Unfortunately, hating will not change a thing. The fact remains that X drives a posh car while Y keeps walking on foot daily, pounding the tarmac relentlessly with the soles of his cracked shoes, as he complains in the heat of the sun about how unfair life is. Y can only drench his misery in the company of his fellow miserable cynics, as they gather to discuss how X got his posh car. Some cynics might say that X stole money, benefited from proceeds of corruption, or is into illicit drug trafficking. Others could accuse him of engaging in supernatural activities or belonging to a dark secret society. When people are hallucinating, they can imagine anything.

Then, there are also those cynics who might claim that X is not the first one, or the only one, to own such a car. Such cynics will even claim that another man down the same street where X lives owns and drives a better car. But the fact remains that X owns a posh car while the cynics don't, whether they like it or not. Instead of focusing on improving their own lives, the cynics such as Y and his fellow miserable friends, will be busy trying to bring down X.

So, if you want to own and drive a posh car like X, you can choose either to sit down with X and learn from him or to sit down with the superficial cynics and learn from their misery. The choice is yours. Thus, instead of complaining that your friend is full of it simply because he is flying First Class or Business Class whilst you are all squeezed up in a tight seat in Economy Class, try to understand the steps that he took to find himself in that First Class or Business Class. You can't just be mad at him because you don't have what he has. Rather, learn from him or the steps he took to fly First Class or Business Class. The choice is yours.

Against this backdrop, in this modern age of technology, we can no longer rely solely on oral tradition to tell our stories. Neither can we rely on oral tradition alone to store and transmit our historical facts. Oral tradition worked well in a time and place where the culture of writing had not evolved much. But today, we have no excuse. We must document our history, especially those facts that can, and will, inspire posterity.

My personal philosophy in life is that, firstly, in anything you do, you should aim to be among the best. There is no point in playing second fiddle. Secondly, ideas, not money, are what separates men from boys and women from girls. Boys and girls can play around with money, not ideas. That is why boys with money are often called 'the big boys.' Great ideas are for great men and great women. At the outset, it is important to point out that a basic tenet of consumer theory in economic thinking is that individuals are utility maximisers, meaning that they make economic decisions that can assure them the highest level of gains or consumer satisfaction. Put simply, we all want gains, not losses, don't we? I doubt you would just want to internalize the costs of a decision without taking any benefit. So, all factors being equal, we can assume that individuals are likely to act rationally in maximizing the utilization of the opportunities before them so as to achieve an optimally efficient outcome. Some become big boys or big girls, while others become great men or great women. Remember, your race is not against anyone or others, but against your own goals. While it is strategically sound to audit the internal and external environments before coming up with your personal development strategy, you must not forget to set your own goals and targets. If it means beating your own record whilst others are complacently watching, do so. For you are competing against your own goals and ideals, not against those of others. And so, if my goal or target were to become financially wealthy, I would have aimed at becoming one of Africa or the world's richest men. There is no point in thinking small or playing second fiddle. Money, however, has never been my primary motivator. Even a criminal or fool can have money. Don't ask me how. Suffice it to say that some seemingly rich people cannot even explain their wealth. Never pay attention to anything that a man cannot explain. I can explain my education and won't get upset if you asked me how I got it, yet some people don't want to talk about how they acquired their wealth. They even get upset if you try to ask them how they accumulated their riches. It tells you something. If I can explain my education, why can't you explain your riches? What are you hiding?

Money is just a medium of exchange. There is nothing for people to get excited over or to fear. Money is there to help us to trade in goods and services, that's it. But others see money as a status symbol. For me, erudition has always been my primary and edifying motivator. Money can run out, but your *magnum opus* of ideas will never run out. Besides, your name is not written anywhere on that money, but the expression of your ideas, if you have any noteworthy ideas, is protected by copyright law. Your name is written all over those ideas, as can be seen when you come up with an invention or write a book. That state of permanency embedded in matters of erudition is an indelible feature of products of the mind. The police can follow someone over his money, especially if he looks suspicious, but they will rarely follow a learned person over his ideas. If anything, the police can sit down and listen to an erudite man explaining something. The learned don't have to hide or panic each time they see a cop. But a man with questionable money, especially money that he cannot explain, often has to keep looking over his shoulder. Often, sleep eludes such a man, for he knows that even robbers go where they expect to find money, not where there are books. Indeed, nobody robs a library. They rob a bank, or what looks like a bank.

The writing of an autobiography is often a journey filled with different emotions, as expressed through the various life experiences of the author. It is a journey embarked on sometimes with nostalgic sentimental value, and, at other times, with a sense of loneliness or some sad memories. Indeed, some memories bring nostalgia while others invoke mixed feelings of pain and joy. From inspirational moments to those of a comical nature or tragedy, an autobiography can sometimes cast light on incidents that invite the clairvoyant introspective mind of the reader. An autobiography can also be a tragicomedy, bringing forth tears to the eyes of the reader. They could be tears of both joy and sadness. For, in life, there will always be highs and lows. We may not know the whens, hows and whys, but we do know that life isn't always perfect. And so, it is not the whens, hows and whys but the character of the man or woman in the story that helps to enrich the lives of others.

In this book, I start with the now or the present, akin to the famous backward design model in curriculum development, and then work backwards to how it all started. The idea here is to prioritize the learning outcomes for my audience, as opposed to prioritizing topics to be covered in the book. Indeed, what lessons can we draw from what will be shared in this book, for example, as opposed to worrying about what has been left out or what should not have been disclosed or included. Are there things that can help to inform, for example, our own experiences? What parallels can we draw from what we are about to read?

In this book, I not only begin by looking at the now before working backwards to talk about how it all started, but also make some cross-references to the past and present so as to provide a better-informed narrative. This approach gives the reader a fuller and more meaningful context. For, our lives are not lived in a linear manner. We sometimes pivot by stepping forwards or backwards before we advance. At times, we sidestep before we make a move. The same is true for the reader. He or she might be rushing to board a flight at the airport and therefore has no time to read the whole book but simply wants to skim through quickly. That reader must be able to find something meaningful in any part of the book that he or she turns to. Likewise, where the reader is not in a hurry and is comfortably enjoying the book, he or she must be able to find something that he or she can relate to easily. Whichever part of the book the reader turns to, he or she must be able to find something meaningful.

I have presented this story of my life with the eclectic taste of a mosaic sculptured from African beads that are scattered all over the world. As noted earlier, I left Africa when I was only twenty-two years old, and have since studied in, lived in, worked in, and traveled to many other parts of the world. Every station has been a learning experience. As noted earlier, I have been away from Africa for more than half of my life. At the time of writing this autobiography, it is more than three decades since I left my motherland, Africa, though I make time to visit Africa now and again. So, some things that I might say could appear or sound strange, or even offensive, not because I want to cause any problems, but because I am no longer the person I was before I left Africa.

Having spent more time outside Africa, I have picked additional norms and values from various other cultures where I have spent much of my life. My life and perspectives are a mosaic of complementing, or sometimes conflicting, cultures. So once in a while, I might say, understandably, things that will not sit or resonate well with some people from a certain cultural background. It is simply because I do not view the world through one lens only, but multiple lenses. Therefore, I hope that the reader will bear with me and show some understanding. For if we do not appreciate the value of variable learning, we might not capture the value of the author's life experiences.

For the most part, variable learning, as opposed to rote learning, invites us to draw and learn from a variety of experiences, and not simply by following a singular, linear or monolithic type of experience. Some experiences that I will share might understandably cause some readers some discomfort, but it is not my intention, as noted above, to cause any trouble. I would like to stress that different contexts have different emphasis. That is why it is important for the reader to approach issues in this book with an open mind. That way, both the value created by the author in writing this book and the value to be captured by the reader in reading it can be optimized and realized in a harmonious and fulfilling way without losing the broader vision through which the story is told.

The starting point of our discussion is that nobody is perfect. Yet a lot of people struggle with this basic fact of life. If, for example, you do not understand something, you are better off asking for someone to explain it to you. Only a fool will laugh at you. You do not have to pretend that all is okay when clearly you are struggling to comprehend issues. Some people find it difficult to ask for help when they are stranded or in need of help, maintaining that, if someone helps them, that person will end up telling the whole world. Well, so what if the whole world gets to know? Is it not a fact that you got some help? Be honest and stop pretending. Is it not a fact and the prophetic truth that you went to ask someone for help, and that he or she helped you? Be honest. It would be different if that person only carried out or executed a civic duty or responsibility that he or she is already mandated or required to carry out and did not go over and above his or her usual call of duty, but where someone has gone the extra mile over and above his or her normal call of duty in order to help you, do not be a fool by trying to downplay that person's help. Have some manners.

Manners do matter. I know that because of foolish pride, some people have difficulty being honest and admitting the truth. Instead, they will try to justify their foolish ego and pride with disingenuous arguments just to try to conceal their ungratefulness. Such levels of dishonesty are often hidden behind selectively quoted Bible verses just try to legitimize one's pitiful pride and lamentable dishonesty. Here, the one with a problem is not the person who helped you. Rather, you, who were helped, are the problem. Because why would you want to hide the fact that you were helped? Why do you have difficulties with being transparent? And why should receiving or giving help be a secret? There are no data privacy issues here. So do not quote Bible verses disingenuously to cover up for your foolish pride and insecurities. Just be honest. The person that helped you can even help you more if he or she hears that you have been acknowledging to others the help that he or she rendered to you. Be smart. If through your own foolishness, pride and inflated ego, you would rather downplay the help that you received by staying mute. The other person is left with no option but to spill the beans and tell the world about the assistance that he or she rendered to you. Once we grasp this simple formula of life, we all can become better human beings.

There are going to be times when people will judge you unfairly or even doubt you. Sometimes they will disrespect you or deny you the respect you deserve or have earned. Take courage, my friends. Even some promotions or appointments at work or elsewhere might bypass you, not because you are not good enough but simply because you are not 'one of them' or you don't belong. Also, your CV alone can intimidate some bosses as well as other people around you. Many people's unfounded hate cannot be substantiated. It is simply a reflection of their own insecurities.

There will be times when people who are less qualified than you get promoted or appointed over you. Sometimes, you will be asked to do most of the work while someone else gets the credit. There are times when you will not even be acknowledged for all the effort you put in. Someone else will take all the credit. What to do? It is the nature of the beast. You can also find yourself reporting to someone who should have been reporting to you. How do you deal with that? That too is the nature of the beast. It's an ugly beast.

It is not always the brightest or smartest who get to the top. Rather, a lot of average and mediocre folks as well as some plainly incompetent quacks are able to swing it through patronage and cronyism. Such people can be very mean if they are serving as your boss or supervising your work, constantly finding fault in whatever you touch or do just to break your spirit and make you feel their weight. However much you try to put in, it is not good enough for them.

But do not be fooled. It is not that these people can't see your worth or value. Rather, it is their own deep-seated insecurities. They can see your worth and value but are deliberately trying to frustrate you. They will even be quick to commend and applaud one of their cronies who could be your junior or who is nowhere close to your capabilities, just to spite you. It is the nature of the beast. It is very ugly. Sometimes, a role or responsibility that should have been assigned to you will be given to someone else, perhaps someone junior. At other times, you won't be invited to a meeting whilst everyone else is in attendance. The problem is not you. The renowned Princeton scholar Professor Albert Einstein, a 1921 Nobel Laureate in Physics, was allegedly rejected by some German university when, as a young scientist, he applied to read for his PhD at a German university. He put it more eloquently in one of his famous quotes:

"Great spirits have always encountered violent opposition from mediocre minds. The mediocre mind is incapable of understanding the man who refuses to bow blindly to conventional prejudices and chooses instead to express his opinions courageously and honestly."

To be accepted in this world, you are expected to belong or to conform. Conformists appear to excel simply because they live a fake life of pretense and are not a threat to the system or establishment. Otherwise, if you are independent-minded, you might be sidelined or left out. Further, you cannot realize your true worth if you keep listening to the ill-informed and misguided opinions of mediocre and insecure people. At some point, you have to find a way to be who you are without getting too comprised with mediocrity. On October 6, 2023, in an article titled, "Researcher Demoted

By University Of Pennsylvania Wins Nobel Prize For mRNA Discoveries—And Some Academics Urge Penn To Apologize," *Forbes* reported: "Katalin Karikó won this year's Nobel Prize in Medicine alongside Drew Weissman for their research that led to the development of mRNA Covid-19 vaccines, but a post from the University of Pennsylvania—where Karikó was demoted from tenure track in 1995—claiming her as a Penn researcher angered the medical community."[9]

People will reject you today, like the story of Joseph and his envious siblings in the Bible (Genesis (37–50), and then acclaim you tomorrow after they see or hear that you have now made it. Don't we all have people like that in our midst? For, as the old English adage says, 'success has many fathers, but failure is an orphan'. The same people that rejected you will be the first to clap when you make it, yet all along they have been trying to dim your light. Reporting on Nobel Laureate Katalin Karikó's experience at Penn, *Forbes* notes that 'her colleagues have also recognized the difficulties she faced: Cardiologist Elliott Barnathan said Karikó was treated as a "second-class citizen" at Penn.' In short, Katalin was deemed by some quarters of authority at Penn as not belonging. The *Forbes* article continues:

"Karikó was hired by the University of Pennsylvania in 1989 as an adjunct professor and researcher, where she met and began collaborating with Weissman, a professor of medicine at Penn, in 1997. Though initially on track to become a tenured professor, the university reportedly offered Karikó a choice to either leave or be demoted with a pay cut in 1995—which she said was 'particularly horrible' because she had just been diagnosed with cancer and her husband was stuck in Hungary because of a visa issue—because her mRNA research was deemed too risky and did not attract enough grant funding."[10]

There will be moments in your life when you might even begin to doubt yourself, that is, if you are not careful enough, just because of the opinions of the naysayers. As *Forbes* reports, 'Karikó has spoken in numerous interviews about her difficult experience at Penn, stating in 2020 her demotion made her feel that she was "not good enough, not smart enough".'[11] Sometimes you will even be

---

9   See C. Murray, "Researcher Demoted By University Of Pennsylvania Wins Nobel Prize For mRNA Discoveries—And Some Academics Urge Penn To Apologize," *Forbes*, (October 3, 2023), available Online at: <<https://www.forbes.com/sites/conor-murray/2023/10/03/researcher-demoted-by-university-of-pennsylvania-wins-nobel-prize-for-mrna-discoveries-and-some-academics-urge-penn-to-apologize/?sh=60d212ef68b1>>, accessed on February 6, 2024.

10 See *Ibid*.

11 See *Ibid*.

forced to play second fiddle just to survive, yet many of those mistreating you actually know your true worth. Thus, "Karikó took the demotion and continued her work, but later left her senior research investigator position at Penn (where she retains an adjunct professorship) in 2013 to serve as vice president at BioNTech—co-manufacturer of the Pfizer-BioNTech Covid-19 vaccine—because Penn refused to reinstate her to a tenure track position, reportedly considering her research 'not of faculty quality'."[12]

But when you make it, the same people who questioned the quality of your work will want to be associated with you. Forbes reports: "Penn, however, wasted no time congratulating Karikó and Weissman for their Nobel Prize win… calling them 'Penn's historic mRNA vaccine research team' and attaching a university news release (which does not acknowledge Karikó's tense history with Penn)—but a community note applied to the post calls the wording 'misleading' because she left the university as a researcher a decade ago."[13]

Life can be unfair sometimes. But take courage, my friends. Someone bigger out there is watching and seeing everything, and you will be rewarded with something much bigger than what those who denied or rejected you can ever dream of. God has a way of humbling arrogant and mean people. The *Forbes* article concludes:

"Members of the medical and academic communities criticized Penn in response to the university's post. Eric Feigl-Ding, chief of Covid Task Force at the New England Complex Systems Institute and former Harvard Medical School researcher, urged Penn to apologize to Karikó but praised her for persisting in her research despite being demoted. Nicole Paulk, founder of Siren Biotechnology, criticized Penn Medicine for its post congratulating Karikó, stating: 'You shunned her and put roadblocks in the way of her and her research when she was at Penn. You should feel immense shame, not pride, today. You played no role in this.'"[14]

Some people think that success is simply racing to the top of the corporate ladder or landing a big job title. If that is what you want, then just try to 'belong', 'conform' and get yourself a 'sponsor' to advocate for you. Otherwise, the case of Nobel Laureate Katalin Karikó shows that she was not even a tenured professor at the University of Pennsylvania, yet she won arguably what is considered

---

12   See *Ibid*.
13   See *Ibid*.
14   See *Ibid*.

the most prestigious award in the field of medical science. Katalin Karikó had allegedly been sidelined as an adjunct faculty member only. But look at the power that she now wields with that Nobel Prize. If you do not understand the concept of power, you will think that it is more prestigious to have an important title such as an endowed professorial chair until you get to learn more about awards such as the coveted and esteemed award the Nobel Prize. In life, it is often wise to ask what else someone has achieved other than his or her big job title, that is, since a job title per se is not an achievement. Even a criminal or a corrupt person can have a big job title. We have seen, for example, how some mediocre or poorly educated folks rise to the helm or higher echelons of the corporate ladder. Those are not achievements. They are merely appointments, because an appointment can easily be muted by removal of the officeholder from office. But a well-deserved achievement cannot be muted easily. Such achievements are a form of real power and are hard to mute. The horn will continue to play no matter how much you try to drown a person. The person will keep floating back to the surface because of the real power that he or she possesses. Put simply, you cannot mute real power by simply removing someone from office or withdrawing some perks from him or her.

Another place where you find a form of authority or power that is easy to mute is among some folks occupying senior government positions. Once there is an unexpected change of government, they often panic, scampering in all directions and looking lost. For, they know that their power or authority is temporal and only contingent on their holding public office. In life, generally, you do not need to be smart or have done something extraordinary to get promoted or appointed to a big job title. You simply need to know the right people or be in the right place at the right time. I kid you not. Using ichi-Copperbelt language, which I will explain in Chapter 4, one would surmise as follows:

> You can be a cabinet minister or president of a country. You can even be a director or vice-president of a big company. We are not disputing. But your friend went to Oxford iwe! Kasako if you went nangu ku Harvard! Oxford na Harvard fya ibela. Na fi pusana from ilyashi lya tu fulo. Ta tu tina aba tu fulo. Tu tina aba amano!
>
> Ifya ma vote fye na ma appointment can't be compared ku fya ma somo. Na fi pusana iwe! Umu nobe ali jober. Iwe ba ku sontele fye. So, tu le pelena ko umu chinshi bane.

If you have ever had the opportunity of swimming next to dolphins at an aquarium, you will realize that there are three forms of power that you are likely to encounter in any organization. Dolphins are smart mammals. They often exude referent and expert power as well as informational power. They are in control of their environment and relate well to their audience. It is not by default or chance that they are able to do so, but by design. The research conducted by social psychologists French and Raven (1959), on understanding the basis of power, lists inter alia legitimate power, reward power, and coercive power as different forms of power, but quite often, none of these outlasts expert power, referent power and informational power. Your expert skills, together with your personal warmth and the valuable information you possess, will often outlive any high-powered job title you may hold today or any of your temporal relationships with power brokers. Even incentive structures of reward as a form of power tend to be temporal. It's just a matter of time. You can be a cabinet minister today, but tomorrow, if you are fired or kicked out, you are a nobody, especially if you do not have any other form of power. As a matter of fact, not everyone who gets these seemingly lofty positions is deserving of them. Anyone not barred by the constitution, for example, including a street vendor, can be appointed as a cabinet minister, depending on the whims of the appointing authority.

If your brand is limited to your job title, it ends the very moment you step outside the door of your workplace, because nobody knows you out there. Only your workmates know you. A CV that is built around a job title is not worth admiring. The moment the job title is removed, the CV will run out of fuel and the noise that was coming from it becomes mute almost instantaneously. To avoid such issues, it is wise to build yourself an authentic brand of longevity that outlives your job title, one that is global in both scale and scope. Workplace job titles or connections remain at the office, for they are like obscure local brands that are not known elsewhere. They have little clout, if any, once you step into some unknown territory or domain. You can be a CEO or cabinet minister today, but once you are fired the next day nobody will remember you because your brand is just about office connections and your job title. By contrast, other people have global and international brands that go beyond mere national, hometown, workplace, neighborhood, golf club, tribal, racial, ethnic, religious, village or local pub confines. Anything other than a global or international brand tends to have little or no significant presence and impact globally. I remember someone introducing me to their local idol in Lusaka, Zambia, saying:

"Nde mona mwa li bomfwa po, Ba Kantwa. Eyaba!" (English translation: "I am sure you have heard of Mr XYZ. This is the man.")

How on earth do you expect me to know your local brand or idol when I am not even based locally and am coming from outside the local jurisdiction where trends are mainly about international and global brands? It is the same thing as a Lusaka socialite trying to impress you by saying, 'Oh, I know XYZ…we hang out in the same circles.' Which circles? I don't live in Lusaka. You can try to impress someone who is not exposed, travelled or a fellow local, but not someone who operates at the international and global levels. Put simply, 'ilyashi lya pa njinga ta ba li leta pa ba mu ndeke' ('Topics discussed by folks who habitually travel local distances on a bicycle are often different from topics discussed by those who fly around the world.') So you can schmooze your way up the corporate ladder and become a director, vice-president or even a CEO, but the moment you retire or just step outside the building of your workplace, who knows you out there? Probably nobody has ever heard of you or read anything about you. If your powerbase is limited to your workplace, where else could you go if you were to retire today? Unless and until you cultivate a distinguished professional career and a reputation that goes beyond your job title and workplace, you will be running back desperately to your former employer to be taken care of, as a retired and tired former employee, through some part-time consultancies. It happens a lot. Some people look lost when they retire, not knowing where to go and what to do next with their life. Even the people that used to suck up to you when you were a big boss begin to shun and avoid you because you are no longer of any use to them. Such is life. You can try to run into academia, as many retired folks try to do, but if you have been away from academia for such a long time and have not been publishing any serious scholarly work, academia can be quite unfriendly and unwelcoming. Others try to go into farming, yet they don't even know how to plant a seed. There are also the ambitious ones who try to go into politics, but if you are not used to stomaching insults and mud-slinging you will need to see a doctor every now and again to check your blood pressure.

Real power, I submit, is not contingent upon, say, cronyism, patronage, schmoozing or lobbying for a promotion or an appointment to a lofty position. Rather, it is the intrinsic value that lies in you regarding the skill set, capabilities and reputation that you have developed over the years and which no external force can take away from you. For example, Edson Arantes do Nascimento, better known by his nickname Pelé, was Pelé even after he retired from playing football. He continued to appear at many FIFA global events, not because he was still playing for the Brazilian national football team, but because of his immutable reputation and expert skill in the game of football. Not every former football player gets that kind of attention worldwide once they retire. Muhammad Ali had the same kind of aura as Pelé to a point where people would momentarily stop paying attention to any boxers about to start a boxing match if they saw Ali walk into the boxing arena. Even the boxers themselves would start to cheer. With or without a boxing championship belt, Muhammad Ali was 'Ali'. He remained, irrefutably, the greatest boxer of all time. Ali left an indelible mark that did not require a title or belt for validation. And so was Pelé in football. Now that is what I call real power.

I have found myself at certain high-level forums where seemingly powerful and politically connected people have been invited, based on their glamorous job titles, to make presentations. I will also be there to give my presentation, but not on the basis of my job title. Rather, I will be there in my private capacity on the basis of my immutable and indelible expert power which goes way beyond the walls of my workplace. If I were to step outside the building of my workplace, I should not be a stranger, say, to the academic community in my field. Expert power, like referent power and informational power, unlike legitimate power that is associated mainly with a job title, transcends insular and parochial institutional structures. Even more interesting is the fact that you do not retire or resign from your expert power, referent power or informational power. To me, that is what I call authentic power.

CHAPTER 2

At the frontiers of thought leadership

Chapter 1 provided the underlying objectives and the political context to this autobiography. It gave the political context of my native homeland, Zambia, at the time of writing my autobiography. I was born in Zambia. I spent twenty-three years of my life there before I relocated to Great Britain for further studies. After my graduate studies in England, I settled there. I lived and worked in England for almost a decade before moving to the United States of America, where I currently live and work. I have been living in the US for three decades now. The Africa that I knew back then is not the same anymore.

While it is not my intention to make generalizations here, there have been cultural shifts in Africa over the years. For example, the culture of political resistance against imperialism in the African university around the 1970s and 1980s, evidenced through radicalism and leftist ideological orientation of many students and academics, has been watered down significantly. The African university has lost its social consciousness. Many of our African intellectuals are compromised by economic hardship at a personal level. We now have a culture of personal survival among our intellectuals.

Building on my submission above, there are two misconceptions generally about religion as it applies to scholars and intellectuals that I would like to debunk at the outset. The first is that a highly educated person cannot or should not be associated with such belief systems as Christianity or other religions that are not rooted in empiricism. Religion, for example, is criticized by many scholars who are so fascinated with empiricism as lacking objectivity. For them, anything that is not backed by empirical evidence is not scientific or objective. But I have reservations about such cynicism. For, science cannot know, and has never known, everything. That is why we have discoveries every other day. Perhaps, one day, science will discover God. We cannot rule out that possibility. We must remain open-minded.

The second misconception about scholars and intellectuals is that highly learned people must look overly obsessed with books and appear uninterested in material things or all manner of bourgeois tendencies. I touched on these stereotypes briefly in Chapter 1, and thus I beg to disagree. That you are poorly dressed, with unkempt hair, does not mean you are a genius. Neither is the wearing of the same old sweater daily by a professor, as he delivers his lectures, a mark of intellectual sophistication. Professors and scholars can, if they want, look presentable. They are only human like anyone else. In this autobiography, I have tried to demonstrate this 'cool' side of a scholar using pictorial images. While academia has its own culture which often extends to the dress code of many academics, you can still look presentable as a scholar in that dress code. My reasoning here is that if we do not make academia and intellectualism appealing to the young folks, they will shun the world of ideas. Put simply, academia and intellectualism must be appealing to young people. Education and learning should not look boring. If anything, it should be fun and must accommodate style and fashion. If fashion and style are part of the popular culture of the day, why not embrace it to make learning even more interesting and popular for the learner? Professors and scholars in these communities cannot be blind to such reality. Indeed, this is my philosophical view as a scholar.

As a participant-observer in communities of highly educated people, I have noticed that it is not uncommon for intellectuals to avoid acknowledging or even mentioning God in public spaces. For me, I am not ashamed to acknowledge God in my life. The Bible instructs us in Matthew 10:33 that Jesus Christ, whose Hebrew name is *Yehoshua*, reminds us: "But whosoever shall deny Me before men, him will I also deny before My Father who is in Heaven."

As Proverbs 1:7 in the Bible promulgates, 'But fools despise wisdom and instruction.' Generally speaking, in civilized parts of the world we are past the age of Christians being persecuted over their faith, notwithstanding some vicissitudes of such dark ages rearing their ugly head in some less civilised parts of the world. Unlike some secret societies whose belief systems are shrouded in mystery and whose members only meet in dark secret corners and cannot come out publicly, there is hardly anything to hide about being a Christian. In fact, Christians don't have to hide or deny that they are members of the Christian faith. Almost everything about Christianity is in the open. That said, it is not uncommon to find some notoriously mischievous individuals, including some unscrupulous fellas, in Christian church circles masquerading as religious leaders. Such individuals often confer on themselves sleazy grandiose 'religious' titles to deceive the masses. A number of them, through the use of trickery, cajolery, some heretics and what could be termed ostensibly black magic, with almost no deep theological and philosophical articulation of issues, like to profit from their gullible followers who are desperately looking for 'miracles'. Other such imposters and charlatans are just plain unsophisticated motivational speakers with no recognized formal training in theological matters. Their deceitful acts of trickery are often characterized by a certain type of mysticism steeped in theatrical and pretentiously charismatic stunts and are arguably not of the true Christian faith. *Yehoshua* Himself said (Matthew 24:5): "For many will come in my name, claiming, 'I am the Messiah,' and will deceive many."

In all His preaching, *Yehoshua* never asked for money from any of His followers or from the people that would gather to receive blessings and healings from Him. Neither did *Yehoshua* sell Holy Water or anointing oil like some of the so-called 'men of God' do today. These people are laboring hard to commercialize Christianity to the extent that some of them even ask their blind followers to donate money to buy them a luxury jet, claiming fraudulently that that is the desire of God. There are simply too many conmen in the church today. People are hoodwinked into submitting to magical and unchristian practices that don't even make sense. Religion without common sense and logic is nothing but dogma. The things that you believe in should always be subjected to common sense. You have the right to question and probe pertinent aspects of your own faith or institutional beliefs. That is not the same thing as questioning God. Religion and God are not the same. Religion is manmade. Therefore, you can question aspects of your religion. In Christianity, it is part of Christian faith to ask questions so that you can learn more. Let no man mislead you by saying that all that you need is the Holy Spirit in order to discern issues. Why did Jesus Christ spend time teaching His apostles before God sent them the Holy Spirit? God did not say, 'all you need is the Holy Spirit'. By parity of reasoning, there is no such thing in Christianity as 'touch not the anointed', as is often propagated by some indoctrinated religious people in defense of their religious leaders. Jesus Christ was often asked questions. He never got upset or annoyed with anyone who asked Him questions. Neither did His apostles get upset and run to His defense. Asking questions is part of your faith.

As a Christian, I believe truthfully that if my faith in God were in vain, I would not have come this far. Neither would I have ascended to the pinnacles of erudition that I have reached, nor accomplished the coveted and much cherished intellectual milestones that I have attained. Science without religion is incomplete because science does not have answers to everything. By parity of reasoning, religion without science is dogma. So, there is a symbiotic relationship between science and religion. For, where dogmatism creeps in people cannot even ask questions. And that is how cults are born. Cults often emerge from dogmatism. Enlightened faith, however, embraces science, appreciating the view that science and religion are not contradictory but complementary. Many highly educated people are not ready to ask themselves, for example, why science does not have all the answers to life, that is, if at all science is the all-definitively supreme solution to our life problems. But aren't there things around us that are incapable of explanation? Many intellectuals would rather focus on discounting religion, as if it is mere anecdotal conjectures steeped in superstition and fear. And they often try to distance themselves from what is sometimes known as the 'opium of the people'. Karl Marx, for example, is alleged to have said: "Religion is the 'opium of the people.'"

But isn't it being dogmatic if we are not prepared to even entertain the thought or possibility of the existence of a deity out there, choosing instead to remain fixated on the primacy of materialism? Shouldn't we be more open-minded to the possibility of a body of knowledge parallel with, beyond, or outside science? The underlying premise of Marx's dictum is that religion only serves to console and pacify the poor or uneducated. Some highly educated people look at religion as just some form of superstition. Others equate it to an irrational myth. The obsession with materialism in scientific inquiry leaves little room, if any, for any form of idealism, notwithstanding the influence, for example, of Hegelian idealism on Karl Marx's conception of dialectical materialism. And so, for various reasons, many highly educated people choose wilfully not to acknowledge God publicly. Some only associate religion with those who commit atrocities against humanity in the name of religion.

While it is a truism that, in some cases, religion has been used for centuries to advance wrongful acts of selfish individuals against humanity, the sins of your cousin or brother are not your sins. Those who commit atrocities in the name of religion have themselves to answer before God for their sins. We do know for a fact that many have promoted, practiced and encouraged slavery using religion to justify their sins by jettisoning the idea of a heaven where there will be no suffering. The victimized were often encouraged to look up to heaven while continuing to suffer on this earth.

Some slaveowners would even quote Bible verses to justify their actions. And some churches and clerics participated in slavery and even owned slaves. We are awake to that fact.

For a long time, the church accommodated and encouraged such ills as slavery, racism, apartheid and colonialism. Thus, many critics of faith today find no comfort in religion whatsoever. Others even wonder why Christianity, for example, has very few followers in the land where it originated from in the Middle East, yet has a huge following in lands afar. We are therefore invited by critics of 'Western religions' to reconsider subscribing to our indigenous African ideas of a deity, as practiced by our ancestors. Yet, I submit, the deity that our African ancestors prayed to is the same God as that of the Christians. Just as different people turn to different television channels to watch the same news, it is the same news. If, for example, you look at any map of a city, you will notice that there are many roads leading into downtown. You can take any one of them, depending on where you are. The destination is the same – downtown! I am a Catholic Christian, for example, not because I am mesmerized by or a blind follower or fanatic of the Vatican, or because my parents were also Catholics, but rather because the Catholic Church embraces intellectualism in matters of faith and allows me to ask tough questions that I would not ordinarily ask elsewhere. The selfie appearing below was taken in church after Ash Wednesday Mass at St. Stephen Martyr Catholic Church in Washington DC on March 5, 2025, as I and many other church congregants waited for the heavy rain outside the church to subside. When I was going to church, it had been drizzling but I remained determined not to find excuses to miss church. I braved the rain and walked to church from work at lunchtime, not just because it was Ash Wednesday, but because God does not give us excuses whenever we turn to Him to ask for help. So, why should I give Him excuses? Whether I have had my lunch or not, I must go and pray. I can always eat later.

Those who love have no time for excuses. They simply

love unconditionally. We must not only love God when it suits us or when it is convenient for us. The other selfie here was taken against the backdrop of the blessed statue of my patron saint, St Jude Thaddeus, on the Ash Wednesday at St. Stephen Martyr Catholic Church in Washington DC.

As in many other Christian denominations or religions, there are also some Catholics who are unreasonable in their approach to the Word of God. Indeed, some religious fanatics, irrespective of their religion, can be quite unreasonable in their approach to the Word of God. Many such fanatics, including some clerics, have a tendency to advance questionable and misguided theological interpretations based on such weird things as stereotypes and other subjective value-laden traditions, and projecting these as the Gospel truth. Such misguided views only bring confusion among the faithful. Although I am a Christian, I submit that Christianity, as a religion, does not have the monopoly of Heaven. And Christians are not the only people that know God. They certainly don't own Heaven. Heaven belongs to God for all His children. Although I am a Catholic, the Catholics, like any other Christian denomination, do not have the monopoly of Heaven and they do not own Heaven. As noted above, we are all just hustlers trying to get there. In short, even the Pentecostals, the Jehovah Witnesses, the Seventh Day Adventists, the Evangelicals, and any other protestant Christian denomination have no monopoly over Heaven and do not own Heaven. Neither does any race or group of people have priority seats in Heaven. Nobody on this earth has a monopoly of Heaven. Heaven is open to everyone unless and until you drop the ball through your own wicked and pitiful sins.

A good analogy here is when students are sitting for exams in school. Each student is assured of getting a distinction or First Class grade until and unless he or she decides to start throwing away marks in the exam room.

So, to me, faith should not be about a self-conceited sense of self-righteousness, not even among the clerics. This means that any cleric, including a Catholic priest, Anglican priest, Pentecostal or evangelical pastor, a Bishop of any kind, or a self-proclaimed prophet, is only human and should be humble enough not to behave like a deity. Nobody is perfect. Even those fellas who like to loiter around the church premises and holding leadership positions in church-related associations should not think of themselves as having a right of safe passage to Heaven by virtue of holding such earthly positions. That mentality of acting ostensibly pious or holier than thou is simply not faith, but hypocrisy. For, nobody is perfect. Some clerics, for example, can be quite promiscuous and have girlfriends in their church congregations. We cannot run away from this truth.

If we claim to be Christians, we must not compromise the prophetic truth. Many clerics may look holy and saintly in those church robes and attire, but they are not what they appear or purport to be. As Christians, we are, however, not discouraged by the shortcomings of fellow men and women, because it is to God we submit, not fellow mortals. Our prayers are to God, not to fellow human beings. There is no human being, be it cleric or not, who is a deity. And so, no cleric, pastor, or papa is perfect. We all have to be humble enough to accept this fact.

For example, I myself am not perfect. I am a work-in-progress. So, I doubt that many folks in the Catholic Church would scoff at me for asking a priest or a bishop some tough moral questions about social life. How else can I learn if I do not ask such questions? We must be prepared to deal with uncomfortable truths.

Unfortunately, many people would rather pretend that being a Christian means that life is blissfully kumbaya. And this could explain why many church folks like to share spiritedly Bible verses that only suit their narrative, as opposed to verses that also rebuke their deeds. Indeed, the problem with quoting Bible verses is that many people only quote those verses which console them, not those which rebuke them. For example, pay attention to the status updates on the social media pages of some church folks. Many just post Bible verses of how God loves us, as if we are in doubt, but will never post any Bible verses that reprimand them, say, for illicit sex and sexual immorality. They act as if the sins of adultery and fornication do not exist. Others will even refrain from eating pork or, if they are ill, decline to have blood transfusions from the medics. Yet when it comes to illicit sex, the same people will hypocritically indulge, as if illicit sex is a lesser sin than eating pork or having a blood transfusion.

I am confident that in the Catholic Church, notwithstanding some cases where you find yourself before some misinformed or unreasonable Catholic priest or church community leader, I can ask some tough questions without facing the risk of retribution, excommunication, punishment or being threatened with all manner of intimidatory shenanigans just for asking such questions. We all have to ask our religious institutions and leaders some tough questions, not because we want to cause trouble, but in order for us to discover the truth for ourselves. And religious leaders must be prepared and ready to answer tough questions. Against this background, I trust that I can speak freely and ask tough questions in the Catholic Church which I cannot ask elsewhere without facing the risk of offending some people. In some churches or religious circles, you can end up being stoned, kicked out, or reprimanded by being told 'touch not the anointed', or you can be subjected to other forms of punishment for raising uncomfortable issues. But the truth is that religious leaders are not deities. Like you and me, they are just as human as any of us and are not perfect at all. So why should we be afraid to ask them tough questions? If they hold public office, like parliamentarians or civil servants, they must not only be seen to be accountable but be held accountable. For they are not immune to scrutiny and criticism.

From an epistemological point of view, the word 'catholic' means 'all-embracing'. Thus, the universality in the pursuit of knowledge is at the heart of Catholicism. Catholics even run decent and highly regarded schools and universities as well as many reputable hospitals everywhere around the world. And their clerics, that is, the people to whom I might want to pose some tough questions, are highly learned and competent folks who have spent many years in university and seminaries. It is thus unlikely. that they could feel intimidated by any intellectual challenge. If anything, they could help me to reach a good understanding of matters of faith, as opposed to seeking speculative guidance from an intellectually questionable source. As a scholar, I find intellect and intellectualism more assuring even in matters of faith. And intellect is something that the Catholic Church has not shied away from. But that is not to say that the Catholics are perfect or that they know everything. No, that is not the point. Nobody is perfect. Personally, I find that the enlightened teachings of the Catholic Church do not constrain or confine my power of reason, but rather empower me with the autonomy to make well-reasoned choices. And this, I submit, is as it ought to be. Religion devoid of reason and logic is nothing but dogma. So, where religion is not clear or does not make sense, we will not stick to it religiously for the sake of being seen to be holy. Rather, we will introduce reason and logic, and leave the rest to God. For, we cannot reason for God. The Bible, in *Isaiah 55:8-9*, makes it clear when it says that the Lord God Jehovah Almighty tells us that:

"'For my thoughts are not your thoughts, neither are your ways my ways,' declares the LORD. 'As the heavens are higher than the earth, so are my ways higher than your ways, and my thoughts than your thoughts.'"

Where human intellect is weak or lacking, even a modest understanding of the ways of the Lord, God Jehovah, might turn out to be a red herring. There is indeed a reason why God gave us a mind of our own. Those who argue that all you need is the Holy Spirit when it comes to matters of faith, and not education, often get it wrong. Ignorance is certainly not a substitute for enlightened reasoning. For even Jesus Christ taught his disciples before He sent them the Holy Spirit. He never left them ignorant by just comforting them that all they needed was the Holy Spirit. Rather, He taught them first, and kept repeating to them "The things that I have taught you", (see, for example, *Matthew 28:20*), before He sent them the Holy Spirit.

While nobody is perfect, for many intellectuals, talking about matters of faith in public spaces is as if that will detract or take away from the scholarly or professional recognition that they have earned and enjoyed over the years. We often behave as if only the uneducated and poor should find solace in matters of faith. And we sometimes even feel embarrassed to introduce God anywhere in our intellectual discourse, as if all matters of faith and science are contradictory and mutually exclusive. After all, we tell ourselves, we are scholars. We convince ourselves that we are scientists and believe only in science and empiricism, not things that cannot be proven scientifically. We tell ourselves that we are driven by objectivity, not speculative things. Yet in the darkest moments of our lives, when we are left alone, we are not only scared about what tomorrow holds but the thought of God also often pokes our minds.

There is so much out there that science is yet to discover. Science does not and will not know everything. So how then can we discount things that we do not even know yet? If there is some good sense in something, it is wise, I submit, to at least give it a chance. You do not want, as a scientist or scholar, to be seen to be ignorant if or when science makes that discovery. While we acknowledge and respect the fact that society is heterogeneous, not homogeneous, and that in any democracy people are free to choose whatever they want to believe or not believe, our love for humanity is what invites us to share this polite word 'hope'. After all, sharing is a precept of any polite society.

Otherwise, each one of us is free to choose whatever suits our situation. Some are atheist and believe that there is no God. Others are into agnosticism, postulating that human reasoning is incapable of knowing God or providing a rationale justification that God exists. Then there are those who subscribe to irreligion, rejecting all forms of religion or any belief in the supernatural. We also have people who believe that there is a God while others say that they believe in some 'superior being' but not God. We cannot force religion or faith on anyone. It's okay whichever way you choose to go. It's a personal choice. We can only share but not force. At the end of the day, nobody is perfect. We are all sinners, only asking God to look not on our sins but our faith.

Human wisdom sometimes implores us to use metaphors and comparative perspectives. Wouldn't it be safer to believe that there is God, just in case in the afterlife we find that God actually exists, than not to believe and be caught off-guard and unprepared after discovering that He does exist? Put simply, if, say, hypothetically, God does not exist, but I have believed all my life that He does exist, what will I lose? I will lose nothing. But if I had lived a recklessly crazy life and then discover in the afterlife that God does actually exist, and that I had offended Him gravely without even repenting, where will I run to and what remedy do I have? And to whom can I appeal for help? You are better off insuring your car even if you may never get involved in a car accident than driving around in an uninsured car and then suddenly finding yourself in an accident. As one elderly Ghanaian colleague and eminent scholar, Oxford-educated Professor Ferdinand Akuffo, who taught at the University of Zambia for many years, once told me: "My good friend from Oxford, you know… I go to church just in case there is a God out there. You never know."

But again, matters of faith are a personal choice. In my native Bemba language, we say "Akoni ke kala umuti ka temenwe." ("A bird chooses the branch of a tree it wants to perch on. You cannot choose that branch for it to sit on.")

The English have a similar saying: "You can lead a horse to water, but you can't make him drink."

By parity of reasoning, those who believe in God must also appreciate that faith alone is not enough. As long as we are on this earth, we are only human, not Heavenly beings. So our understanding of God is limited, but it can be aided by some educational tools. The starting point here is appreciating that faith without education can lead to dogmatism. Education and faith go hand in hand. You cannot bring ignorance into matters of faith and expect to understand God.

While the Holy Spirit works in each one of us, God has given us all a mind to reason with. And that mind must be nurtured and developed through education, especially scientific knowledge, not just parochial religiosity. That you are a person of faith does not mean you must discard secular ideas. Science is as important as faith. Science can help you to think and reason logically without projecting your own ignorance as faith. Put simply, religion and science go hand in hand and are not mutually exclusive. Sometimes, where one ends, the other begins. In the Bible, *Proverbs 1:7* tells us that, 'The fear of the Lord is the beginning of knowledge, but fools despise wisdom and instruction.' That Bible verse says that the fear of the Lord is the beginning of knowledge but does not say that the fear of the Lord is the end of knowledge. So, there is room for science in religion.

In *Proverbs 9:10*, we are told that, 'The fear of the Lord is the beginning of wisdom, and knowledge of the Holy One is understanding.' It is important here to highlight that you might not have such an understanding if you do not embrace learning. For, as I have explained above, even the Twelve Disciples in the Bible had to go through some rigorous education under the guidance of the Teacher, Jesus Christ, himself. I pointed out above that Jesus Christ repeatedly reminded the disciples (see, for example, *Matthew 28:20*), 'The things that I have taught you', before He sent them the Holy Spirit on Pentecost Day. Jesus Christ taught them first before He sent them the Holy Spirit. What does this tell us? Education cannot be avoided.

In *Proverbs 3:1-12*, we are told, 'My child, never forget the things I have taught you. Store my commands in your heart. If you do this, you will live many years, and your life will be satisfying. Never let loyalty and kindness leave you! Tie them around your neck as a reminder. Write them deep within your heart. Then you will find favor with both God and people, and you will earn a good reputation. Trust in the LORD with all your heart; do not depend on your own understanding.

Seek his will in all you do, and he will show you which path to take. Don't be impressed with your own wisdom.' Yet some folks are impressed with their own wisdom and contest what they do not understand just because they choose not to see beyond and outside science.

Against this background, I want to acknowledge the presence of God in my life. And I make no apologies. I may not be perfect, but this is the path that I have chosen. It's my choice and I am happy with it. In a world influenced widely by a popular culture of secularism, I hope that others will respect my choice as much as they would want their choices of secularism respected.

There have been moments in my life when, like many of you, I have doubted myself. And even where I know that I am humanly prepared and ready for a challenge or battle, I still have had to kneel down and pray quietly before God for strength and His divine intervention. 'For we wrestle not against flesh and blood, but against principalities, against powers, against the rulers of the darkness of this world, against spiritual wickedness in high places.' (*Ephesians 6:12*) This is something that is not easy to explain to someone who chooses consciously or unconsciously not to see or accept the divine work of God in their life, believing selfishly that they themselves are the only heroes in their lives and have made everything happen. For me and my household, we shall continue to 'Give thanks in all circumstances; for this is the will of God in Christ Jesus...' (*1 Thessalonians 5:18*) so as to 'Enter His gates with thanksgiving and His courts with praise; give thanks to Him and praise His name.' (*Psalm 100:4*).

On Thursday, June 1, 2023, almost thirty years after I had graduated from the University of Oxford in England, I received electronic mail from the Rector of my alma mater, Oxford's Exeter College, informing me that I had been elected by the Governing Council of that college to the prestigious status of Honorary Fellow of Exeter College, the University of Oxford. The news came as a pleasant surprise. But I know that, 'Nothing is impossible for God' (*Luke 1:37*). I was not even aware that I was being considered for any esteemed honor or that my name had been put forward for consideration. But *Psalm 23:5* is instructive, as to what God promises: "Thou preparest a table before me in the presence of mine enemies: thou anointest my head with oil; my cup runneth over."

I read the Rector's email over and over, and looked carefully at the email address to ensure that it was real. It was, indeed, as genuine and authentic as one would wish for. I called my wife to break the news. She looked at me intently, smiled calmly and said:

"You deserve the best and nothing less, Honie. You work so hard! We thank God for this."

I was silent for a while, as I tried to take in the magnitude of the honor. These are things you do not lobby for or ask anyone to put in a good word for you. It is not like some job offer or promotion at work that depends mainly on the decision of some boss. Some people get appointed or promoted to top corporate and government positions based on friendships, cronyism or other dubious criteria. In cultures of cronyism, patronage and similar uninspiring norms, anyone with a minimal level of education can make the cut. But to be elected by a body of eminent scholars who are not related to you and are not in any way influenced by any favors or bias is no mean achievement. You are chosen on merit. You truly must earn the respect of your peers in the academic community of eminent scholars to get such honor. And so it came to pass.

I looked back at my long scholarly journey, remembering, among many great memories, my student days at Oxford as well as my parents' visit to Oxford when I invited them over to spend the summer of 1996 with me in the UK. I did not want my wife and son to see my emotions, so I bottled it all up inside as I sat down to reply to the Rector, Professor Sir Richard Hughes Trainor, a fellow Rhodes Scholar and a highly distinguished academician and academic administrator, accepting the prestigious and highly coveted honor with much humility. In the picture below, I can be seen six months later with Professor Sir Rick Trainor at the World Bank in Washington DC when I met him for the first time. It was an honor for me to host him to lunch at the World Bank, as we explored various themes of common interest pertaining to international development and the University of Oxford, generally and Exeter College at Oxford, in particular.

Shortly after I was elected as Honorary Fellow of Exeter College at the University of Oxford in May 2023, one of Zambia's leading newspapers, the *Daily Nation*, carried the following front-page headline on June 29, 2023:

Below is the full text of the media article that appeared in the *Daily Nation* newspaper of Zambia.

Oxford confers highest honour on Zambia's celebrated scholar, Professor Kenneth K Mwenda, PhD, LLD, DSc(Econ)

By

Dr Austin M Mwange

(Published in the Daily Nation (Zambia) on June 29, 2023)

Oxford's Exeter College, one of the oldest and most prestigious colleges within the University of Oxford, has elected Zambia's celebrated scholar, Professor Kenneth K Mwenda, for the highest honor that any Oxford college can confer on an eminently qualified person. Founded in 1314, Oxford's Exeter College is one of the 44 constituent colleges of the world's leading university, the University of Oxford. At 54, Professor Mwenda is the first and only Zambian scholar to be elected as an Honorary Fellow at Oxford. As an Honorary Fellow, he also becomes a member of the Senior Common Room (SCR) at Oxford's Exeter College. But what does it mean, or entail, to be elected as an Honorary Fellow?

Awarded to eminently qualified and distinguished persons who have achieved the highest distinction in academia or public life, *Honorary Fellowships* at Oxford are prestigious and rare honors to recognize and celebrate the extraordinary achievements of exceptional individuals. This category of Oxford fellowships does not constitute an employment contract and should not be confused with tutorial or research fellowships. As the American Society for Legal History in the US avers, regarding its *Honorary Fellowships*, 'Honorary Fellows are the scholars we admire, whom we aspire to emulate, and on whose shoulders we stand.'

In a recent letter from Oxford's Exeter College to Professor Mwenda, informing him that the Governing Council of Oxford's Exeter College has elected him as an Honorary Fellow of the College, the following statement was conveyed:

"This is a category of Fellowship reserved for individuals, usually with a significant connection to the College, who are both distinguished in their field and who have also contributed to society more generally. It is the highest honour that the College can bestow, and we hope that (in some small way) it serves to demonstrate the very high regard within which you are held by our community."

Currently, Professor Mwenda serves as Extraordinary Professor of Law at the University of Western Cape in Cape Town, South Africa, and has previously taught at the University of Warwick (UK), the University of Cape Town (South Africa), the University of Pretoria (South Africa), American University Washington College of Law (USA), Miskolc University (Hungary) and the University of Zambia. He also continues to serve as Extraordinary Professor of Law at the University of Lusaka in Zambia. In 1995, at a tender age of 26 years only, Professor Mwenda became the first Zambian legal scholar to be appointed to a full-time Law Lectureship at one of the top ten (10) British universities, the University of Warwick. In 2015, he gave the 2015 Distinguished Lecture at the University of Nairobi School of Law in Nairobi, Kenya. Over the last three decades, Professor

Mwenda has taught at leading universities in three different continents, namely, North America, Europe and Africa.

A Rhodes Scholar and Oxford graduate, Professor Mwenda concurrently serves as the Manager and Executive Head of the World Bank Voice Secondment Program at the World Bank in Washington DC, USA. He has also served previously as Senior Counsel in both the Legal Vice-Presidency and Integrity Vice-Presidency of the World Bank. In addition, at the World Bank, he has worked on almost all geographical regions of the world, covering many sectors. Professor Mwenda is a Fellow of the British Royal Society of Arts and a Fellow of the Zambia Academy of Sciences. Admitted as a Fellow of the International Compliance Association in the UK and a Fellow of the British Institute of Commerce, he holds a British PhD in Law from the University of Warwick as well as a Higher Doctorate in Law (LLD) from Rhodes University in South Africa and a second Higher Doctorate, the degree of Doctor of Economic Sciences (DSc(Econ)), from the University of Hull in the UK. Further, Professor Mwenda is a US-certified Anti-Money Laundering Specialist as well as a US-certified Mediator and Negotiator.

At Oxford, Professor Mwenda attended Exeter College from 1992 to 1994 and read for the famed two-year graduate law degree, the Bachelor of Civil Law (BCL I & II, now structured sequentially as a one-year BCL, followed by a one-year MPhil in Law). He has also studied business and leadership at other leading universities such as Harvard, Yale, Stanford, INSEAD, Wharton, MIT, London Business School, Cornell, Kellogg, Georgetown and Hull. Professor Mwenda joins the elite ranks of other eminent and distinguished scholars as well as learned and notable statemen and statewomen who have been elected as Honorary Fellows of various colleges at Oxford. These Honorary Fellows include some famous Nobel Prize Laureates such as (i) Professor John Goodenough (Honorary Fellow of St Catherine's College at Oxford, who, in 2019, was awarded the Nobel Prize in Chemistry for the development of the lithium-ion battery), (ii) Professor Elizabeth H. Blackburn (Honorary Fellow of Jesus College at Oxford, who, in 2009, was awarded the Nobel Prize in Physiology or Medicine for her research and contributions to the understanding of telomeres and the enzyme telomerase), (iii) Professor J. M. Coetzee (Honorary Fellow of the Oxford Animal Centre for Ethics, who, in 2023, received the Nobel Prize in Literature); (iv) Professor Sydney Brenner (Honorary

Fellow of Exeter College at Oxford, who, in 2002, received the Nobel Prize in Physiology or Medicine); (v) Professor Thomas S. Eliot (Honorary Fellow of Merton College at Oxford, who, in 1948 was awarded the Nobel Prize in Literature); (vi) Professor Rudolph A. Marcus (Honorary Fellow of University College at Oxford, who, in 1992, was awarded the Nobel Prize in Chemistry); (vii) Chinese writer, Mo Yan, (Honorary Fellow of Regent's Park College at Oxford, who, in 2012, was awarded the Nobel Prize in Literature); (viii) Professor Stanley Whittingham (Honorary Fellow of New College at Oxford, who, in 2019, also received the Nobel Prize in Chemistry; (ix) Professor Michael Kosterlitz (Honorary Fellow of Brasenose College at Oxford, who, in 2016, was awarded the Nobel Prize for his work on the exotic state of matter), and, (x) Ms Malala Yousafzai, the world's youngest Nobel Peace Prize winner, who was elected as an Honorary Fellow of Oxford University's Linacre College in 2023.

Other Honorary Fellows at various Oxford colleges include such intellectual luminaries as the following Higher Doctorate degree holders: (a) Lord Andrew Stephen Burrows, DCL (Oxon) (Honorary Fellow, Brasenose College); (b) Sir John Ashworth, PhD (Leicester) DSc(Oxon) (Honorary Fellow, Exeter College); (c) Sir Jack Beatson, LLD (Cambridge), DCL (Oxon); (d) Sir Anthony John Patrick, DPhil (Oxon), DLitt (Oxon) (Honorary Fellow, Balliol College); (e) Sir Anthony James Leggett, DPhil (Oxon) DSc (Oxon) (Honorary Fellow, Balliol College); (f) William Graham Richards, DPhil (Oxon) DSc (Oxon); and, (g) Andrew Douglas Garrad, PhD (Exeter), DEng (Bristol) (Honorary Fellow, New College).

Closely related to this, Her Majesty, Queen Sofia of Spain, was elected as an Honorary Fellow of Oxford's Exeter College in 1989. In 2002, the President of the Republic of Ghana at the time, President John Kufuor, who, like Professor Mwenda, is also an alumnus of Oxford's Exeter College, was elected as Honorary Fellow of Exeter College. President Kufuor attended Oxford's Exeter College from 1961 to 1964, studying philosophy, politics and economics (PPE), and graduated in 1964. In an online article dated Wednesday, May 8, 2002, and titled, 'President Kufuor honoured by Exeter College', the GhanaWeb reported that:

"The Governing body of Exeter College of Oxford University has bestowed on President J.A. Kufuor an Honorary Fellowship of the College. A release signed by Mr J.O. Obetsebi-Lamptey, Minister for Information and Presidential Affairs, said the message about the honour was sent to the President through Ghana High Commission in London. A letter signed Madam Marilyn Buttler, the President of the College, explained that the Honorary Fellowship had been a category reserved for *old members who have reached a special eminence."*

More recently, in 2018, former US First Lady and (former) US Secretary of State, Ms Hilary Clinton, was elected as an Honorary Fellow of Oxford's Mansfield College while her husband, a Rhodes Scholar and former US President, President Bill Clinton, was elected in 1993 as an Honorary Fellow of Oxford's University College. Then, in 2022, Simon Woolley, Lord Woolley of Woodford, and Principal of Homerton College, Cambridge, was elected as an Honorary Fellow of Oxford's Magdalen College. As noted on Magdalen College's website: 'Simon Woolley was knighted in the Queen's Birthday Honours in June 2019 and was created a life peer in December of the same year. He sits as a crossbencher in the House of Lords.'

In reputable international organizations and multilateral institutions, some of the eminent persons who have been elected as Honorary Fellows at Oxford include Ms Katherine Susan Allen, Director of Amnesty International UK since 2000 (elected as Honorary Fellow of Oxford's Brasenose College in 2006), Sir Nicolas Bratza, former President of the European Court of Human Rights (elected as Honorary Fellow of Oxford's Brasenose College in 2011), and Mr William Lacy Swing, Director-General of the International Organization for Migration (IOM) (elected as Honorary Fellow of Oxford's Harris Manchester College in 2013). IOM is part of the United Nations System.

On his election as Honorary Fellow of Oxford's Exeter College, Professor Mwenda had the following to say:

"This coveted and esteemed award from my alma mater, Oxford's Exeter College, came as a pleasant surprise. I had no idea that I was being considered. It is a humbling experience, and is, without doubt, an indelible and edifying mark of the highest levels of scholarly recognition. As a scholar, I can think of no greater honor than one from Oxford, especially given the unparalleled academic standing of the university internationally."

With a great sense of humility, Professor Mwenda avers that his election to the prestigious *Honorary Fellowship* at Oxford has put Zambia on the world map. Looking back at the road leading to this Oxford honor, he notes further:

"This is the highest honor that a college at Oxford can confer on its alumni. As you might know, I graduated from Oxford almost thirty (30) years ago. Since then, I have maintained a sustained trajectory of notable thought-leadership. As a result, I have received many scholarly awards and honors that include the President's Insignia of Meritorious Achievement (PIMA), two earned Higher Doctorates from two leading universities in the UK and South Africa (an unparalleled feat across the entire African continent), a competitive fellowship from Yale University Law School (that is, the best Law School in the US), the recognition as Honorary Tourism Ambassador for Zambia, and several senior academic appointments at various leading universities as Extraordinary Professor of Law and Visiting Professor of Law. In addition, I have published close to thirty (30) scholarly books and more than a hundred (100) articles in leading peer-reviewed academic journals as well as supervised and examined several PhD theses across many universities around the globe. Furthermore, I have mentored many young professionals as well as contributed meaningfully to philanthropy, educational causes and improving the lives of many young vulnerable people. Today, most of the students that I have taught and mentored are global leaders in many parts of the world, including Zambia. So, I can safely say that my contribution to society at home and abroad has not gone unnoticed."

In his concluding remarks, Professor Mwenda posits that election as an Honorary Fellow of an Oxford college is not only prestigious but also a testament of how the international community views you as a leading pundit, thought-leader or public leader. He concludes by saying:

"I am eternally grateful to God, our Heavenly Father Almighty, for this rare and very prestigious honor from Oxford, as well as to all those who made it possible, especially the distinguished members of the Governing Council that elected me. I look forward to giving my best as Honorary Fellow of Exeter College at the University of Oxford."

After reading the above article in the Zambia *Daily Nation* newspaper, my nephew, Bernard M Fungamwango, sent me the following excerpt from the website of the University of Oxford:

Oxford University is the world's top university for a record eighth year

PUBLISHED 27 SEP 2023

SHARE THIS

UNIVERSITY

The University of Oxford has once again topped the Times Higher Education World University Rankings as the best university in the world for a record eighth consecutive year. The rankings – announced in Sydney, Australia today – rate 1,904 universities from 108 countries around the world.

Source: University of Oxford, "Oxford University is the world's top university for a record eighth year," *News and Events*, (September 27, 2023), available Online at: <<https://www.ox.ac.uk/news/2023-09-27-oxford-university-world-s-top-university-record-eighth-year>>, accessed on October 1, 2023.

Bernard then added as follows:

"Uncle, you are the real G.O.A.T (Greatest Of All Time)! You deserve a national monument in your honor. Let me get this right. You not only attended the best university in the world, that is, the University of Oxford, but also went there, arguably, on the most prestigious scholarship in the world, the Rhodes Scholarship. Yes, I know that there are other Rhodes Scholars, but you have not only taught at some of the top universities in the world… you have also received two earned Higher Doctorates since obtaining your PhD, in addition to having published close to thirty scholarly books and over a hundred journal articles. Not even a hundred PhDs can add up to one Higher Doctorate! Now you have also been honored at the highest level by the best university in the world,

that is, not Harvard, Yale, Cambridge, MIT, Princeton, or Stanford, but Oxford itself! Even within the University of Oxford, you are getting the highest honor that any Oxford college can confer. Uncle, you are one of a kind. I doubt you have any equals in your field in Zambia or Africa. All I can say is, wow! Two Higher Doctorates, plus a PhD is not a joke. And now this award from Oxford…Umwaume pa baume ni Mwenda! Eh, Dangote, atemwa, Jeff Bezos nangu Bill Gates wa ma sambililo (English translation: 'You are a man worthy of note, Uncle. If books were money, you would be the Aliko Dangote, or rather the Jeff Bezos or Bill Gates of academia')!"

In the picture below, I can be seen with my good nephew, Bernard Mofya Fungamwango, when he was seeing me off at Kenneth Kaunda International Airport, as I was concluding my 2024 visit to Zambia.

On Wednesday, May 15, 2024, a colleague from Zambia, Wadde Stephen Bwalya, who is a close friend of my young brother, Joseph, upon hearing that I had been elected as an Honorary Fellow at Oxford, sent me the following edifying and inspiring message, spiced with a sense of wit and humor:

"Bushe chumfwika shani uku wina Ballon d'Or ya ku Oxford?" (English translation: "How does it feel to win a Ballon d'Or from Oxford?")

As my young brother, Joseph, would put it, 'If academia were to be translated into soccer, this Oxford award would be like joining the ranks of Ronaldinho, Messi and other soccer legends who have won the Ballon d'Or. It does not get any better than this.' Around the same time, the following headline appeared in *Lusaka Times*, a leading online media publication.

A childhood friend of mine who has followed my scholarly work over the years wrote the following:

> "Ahhh, mdala, kanshi te Ba Lungu fye beka aba mwene ubu kali bobe. Pantu na Ba RB nabo ba li ku subile bu Honorary Tourism Ambassador for Zambia. Elo, apa nomba, na Ba Oxford nabo ba lunda po. Impalume pa mpalume. Put simply, mdala, all we can say is that mpaka pa last na Ba Oxford ba suka ba landa ati, 'Uyu Mwenda ena mwaume sana. Wa ku leka fye!' Ta fi chila apa, mdala. Na upesha metre." (English translation: "Not only did two Zambian Presidents, H.E. Dr Edgar C Lungu and H.E Mr Rupiah Banda, respectively, acknowledge your immense

and outstanding scholarly contributions to the world, but Oxford too has now done the same. Your scholarly work speaks for itself, my brother!")

It is difficult to explain Oxford to someone who has never experienced it if they have a closed mindset. As a graduate law student, for example, you might arrive at Oxford thinking that you know all the law that there is to know out there until you get into the BCL lectures, seminars and tutorials. The experience is life changing. Oxford is not Harvard, Yale, the Sorbonne, or Cambridge. Oxford is Oxford. You have to experience it to understand and appreciate it. Those wooden doors at the porters' lodge as you enter each Oxford college are not only heavy, but also provide you with some insight into the weight of knowledge that you are about to encounter at Oxford. Therefore, for the coveted and distinguished rank of Honorary Fellow at Oxford to be conferred on you, the pinnacle and the highest honor that any Oxford college can confer on a distinguished and eminent scholar or statesperson, is no mean achievement. I have provided below some pictures that I took of my alma mater, Exeter College, at the University of Oxford, on one of my many visits to Oxford.

Then, following below are some pictures taken with my family when we visited Oxford in 2014. I took my dear wife, Dr Judith M Mwenda, and my beloved son, Jojo, to England for a family visit of, *inter alia*, the University of Oxford, the University of Manchester (*i.e.* my wife's alma mater) and the University of Hull in Yorkshire, where I was receiving a Higher Doctorate. I was sharing with them some of my fond memories of England.

RHODES
HOUSE
OXFORD PRESERVATION TRUST
AWARD
2017

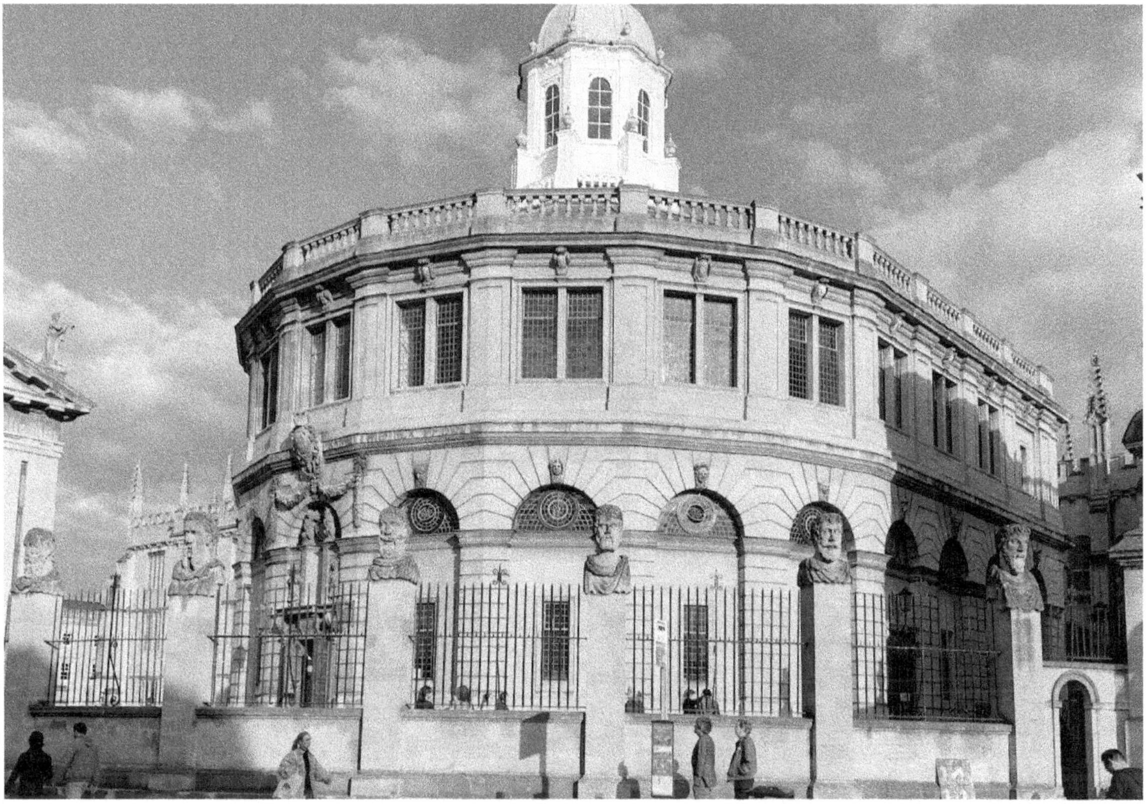

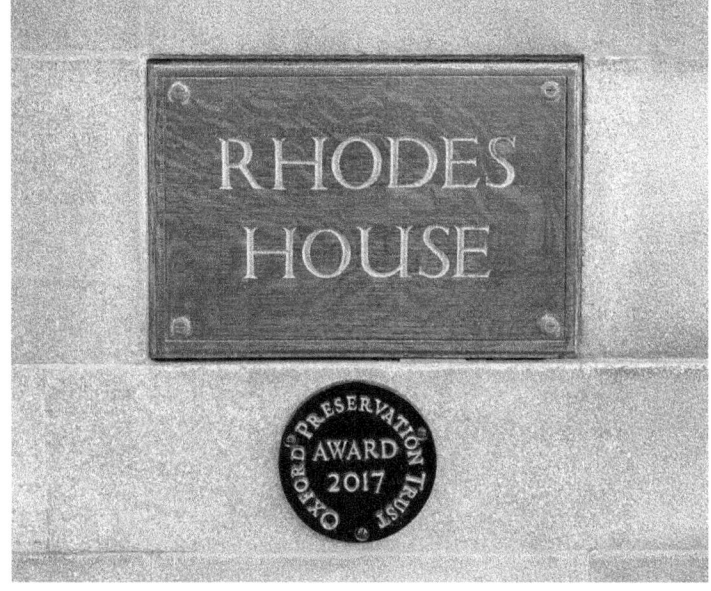

UNIVERSITY OF
OXFORD
St Cross Building
Bodleian Law Library
English Faculty Library
Faculty of English
Faculty of Law
← Reception

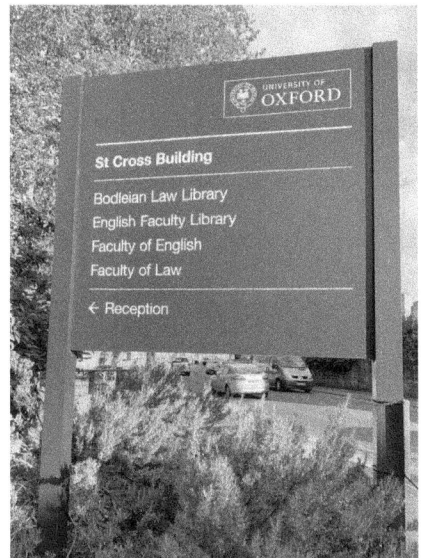

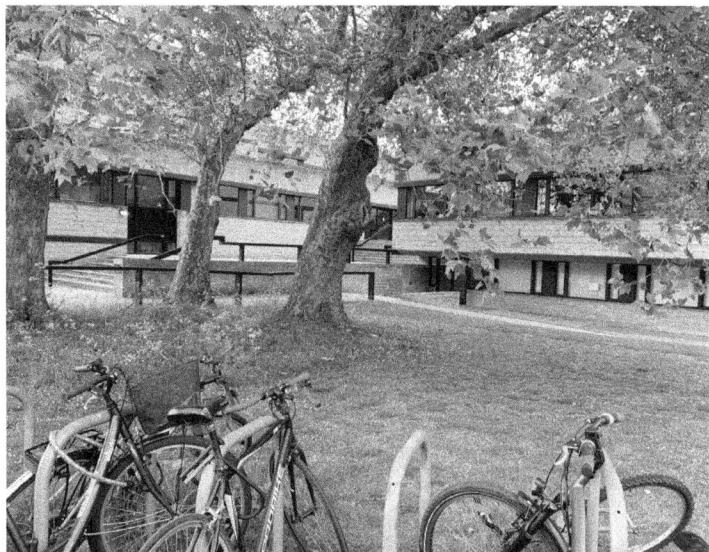

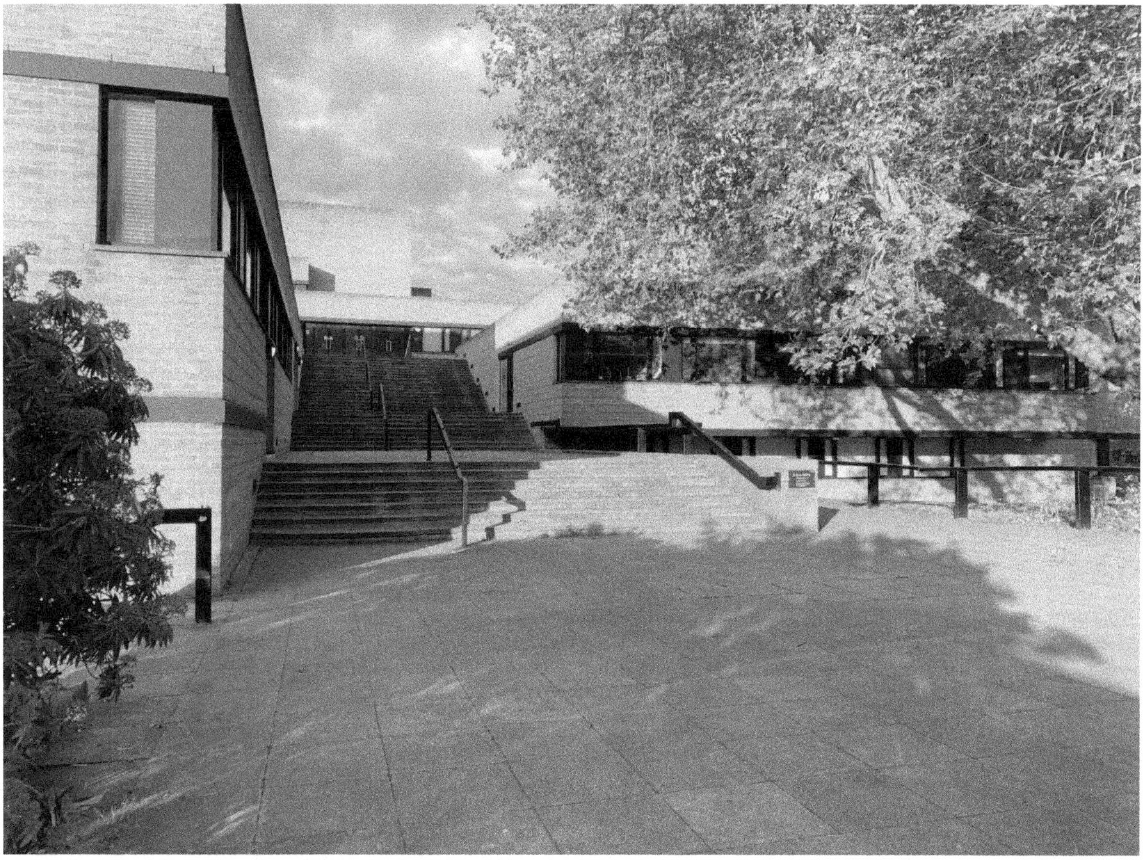

Someone will tell you that you don't need all those degrees and papers, and that all you need is just good work experience. Such superficial cynicism is born out of nothing but insecurities and envy. As one who has travelled both lanes at the highest international levels, that is, higher education and professional practice, I can tell you most candidly that you need to have a strong footing in both. Many a time, if, say, you are hired, even though you have work experience or a big job title, you will still have to undergo a probationary period before you can be confirmed in your new job. Why? Because your employer cannot just rely on stories of your work experience or your former job title. The same is true for degrees or academic papers. You have to undergo probation even if you have high-level degrees. So, it is best to have both degrees and work experience so that your probationary period is not fraught with question marks about your suitability.

Some people say that experience is the best teacher, but education remains an indelible equalizer. The problem with experience, however, is that it is not easy to measure or quantify it. Yet many insist that it is the best teacher. But how can we tell if the experience being claimed is going to lead to the expected outcomes once the person is hired? Some people have experience in doing things wrongly. You can't just look at the number of years that a person has been working and assume that they have valuable experience. Even where a person has worked in a closely related or similar job before, you cannot assume that he or she was able to thrive because they are good at what they do. It could be that the person was protected by a godfather or helped by other networks. And reference checks or interviews can only help you up to a certain point. Some people are good at faking it or pretending.

The point here is that claims of experience alone, without any meaningful formal education or qualifications, are as good as speculation! For there is significant distance between darkness and light. To be certified as a surgeon in a certain country, for example, a doctor needs to have performed a certain number of surgical operations. Knowing how difficult it would be in his European country for a junior doctor to carry out such a high number of complex surgical operations, a newly graduated physician volunteered to go to Africa where, in less than a year, he had performed twice the number of the required operations. He then returned to his home country in Europe and produced a report confirming that he had met and exceeded the requisite 'experience' to be certified as a surgeon. What to do now?

Also, at a certain workplace, to frustrate a young Ivy League-educated engineer, some old folks working under him (most of the old folks had no university education, only many years of 'work experience') decided to teach their boss a lesson. Working behind his back, they mischievously removed a small but vital component from the production equipment at the plant. The idea was to get the equipment or machine to malfunction and see if the boss would figure it out. They knew it would be hard for the boss to detect was wrong with the machine.

The crafty old folks then sat and waited for their boss to show up. When he arrived, he was told that the machine was not working. After the young engineer struggled for hours, without much success, to figure out what was wrong with the machine, one of the old men stepped forward and offered to help. The others lured their boss to a nearby coffee machine for a short break, as their friend started to 'fixing' the machine. Within a minute, the machine was working. The boss was shocked, as the old folks smiled and cheered in unison: "Experience is the best teacher!"

On July 5, 2023, the Zambia *Daily Nation* media article referred to earlier in regard to my Oxford honour was republished on the faculty website of the University of Western Cape (UWC) Faculty of Law in South Africa, the university where I have been serving as Extraordinary Professor of Law. Further, excerpts of the Zambia *Daily Nation* media article kept flooding my email and social media inboxes. Many well-wishers and individuals whose lives I have impacted as well as those who have been inspired by my works over the years kept sending in congratulatory messages. I am one person, however, who remains level-headed and does not let success to get to his head. Even with all these accolades, I know that there is still more work to be done. Following below are additional excerpts of the front-page headlines in the Zambian newspapers on the Oxford award.

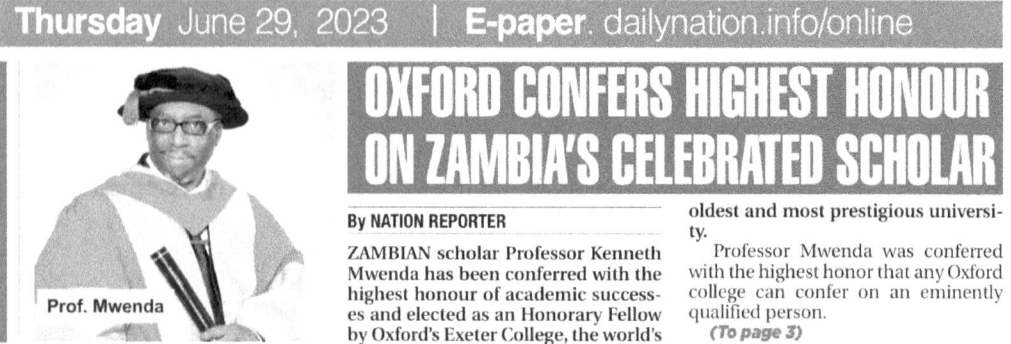

Oxford confers highest honour on Zambia's celebrated scholar

From page 1

At 54, Professor Mwenda is the first and only Zambian scholar to be elected as an Honorary Fellow at Oxford and as an Honorary Fellow.

He becomes a member of the Senior Common Room (SCR) at Oxford's Exeter College.

And Professor Mwenda said this coveted and esteemed award from his alma mater, Oxford's Exeter College, came as a pleasant surprise.

He said he had no idea that he was being considered and it was a humbling experience, and was, without doubt, an indelible and edifying mark of the highest levels of scholarly recognition.

"As a scholar, I can think of no greater honour than one from Oxford, especially given the unparalleled academic standing of the university internationally," he said.

Prof. Mwenda said that his election to the prestigious Honorary Fellowship at Oxford had put Zambia on the world map. Looking back at the road leading to this Oxford honour.

Along the way, we have inspired and continue to inspire many. For example, on June 29, 2024, I received the edifying message below from the class of postgraduate law students that I taught earlier that year at the University of Western Cape in Cape Town, South Africa. They were all pursuing the Master of Law (LLM) degree program in International Trade and Investment Law.

Dear Dr Mwenda

I hope this letter finds you in good spirits. On behalf of the LLM Trade '24 Group, I would like to thank you for taking time out of your busy schedule to teach the newest additions to the UWC LLM Trade legacy all about International Finance and Financial Regulation

Your engaging teaching style and humorous character made every lecture interesting. From the very first class, it was evident that your approach to teaching was one-of-a-kind. You have a rare talent for breaking down complex concepts into understandable and relatable lessons, which not only made the material accessible but also sparked a bit of introspection in each of us.

The lively and stimulating environment you created does not go unappreciated. You managed to turn a challenging subject into an enjoyable and interactive experience. The connections you built encouraged active participation and definitely kept us all on our toes.

Moreover, your anecdotes and pearls of wisdom were invaluable. Each story and piece of advice you shared provided real-world context to the theoretical knowledge we were gaining. These moments were not only educational but also deeply inspiring, often leaving us with much to ponder long after the class had ended. Your ability to weave these insights seamlessly into your lectures added a layer of depth to our understanding and appreciation of finance.

Thank you for your dedication, enthusiasm, and the positive atmosphere you cultivated. Your influence has undoubtedly shaped our academic journey and left a lasting impact on us all. We are truly grateful to have had the opportunity to learn from you and to benefit from your expertise and wisdom.

We wish you all the best, and we hope to make you proud.

Warmest regards,
LLM Trade Class '24

Similarly, I have often received messages from people from various walks of life on how they have been inspired by my scholarly work and professional life. For example, on June 7, 2024, a dynamic young Zambian scholar, who is completing her Masters degree at a leading US university, posted the following article on her Linkedin page:

Loretta Ching'andu • 1st
Communications Specialist | Social Change Advocate | SDG Enthusiast | CEO S...
3d • Edited • 🌐

OF HUMBLE GIANTS AND GREAT MEN !!

Just had the privilege of meeting the incredible and distinguished Professor of Law, Kenneth K. Mwenda.

Like many people, I have long admired Profs rare accolades and contributions to the fields of law, economics, politics and academia.

Prof. Mwenda is a renowned scholar, professional, and thought leader with a remarkable track record of achievements. He serves as the Program Manager and Executive Head of the The World Bank Voice Secondment Program(VSP), a major capacity-building initiative for the World Banks Board of Executive Directors in Washington DC.

Until 2019, he was the only known legal scholar in the English-speaking world to hold Higher Doctorates in two different disciplines. Infact in 2019, former President of the Republic of Zambia Edgar C Lungu awarded Professor Mwenda the Presidential Insignia of Meritorious Achievement, Zambia's highest civilian honour.

Three years ago I casually commented on a Facebook post about him wherein I said in my next life I would love to be like him..... alas today I got the very rare honor of sitting under the distinguished council of a man of high professional and academic standing. I was so struck by his humility and willingness to listen to and encourage young people like me.

Despite his very impressive accomplishments, he remains approachable and kind, and you can feel the passion he has for empowering the next generation of leaders. In his words and firm voice he said to me "Loretta I am proud of you and how far you have come, don't lose focus and remain humble, education will always open doors for you." 👏👏👏 I don't take these words lightly especially that many great men and women continue to invest in my growth and success.

I'm grateful for the opportunity to learn from him and look forward to applying the nudgets of wisdom he shared especially as I prepare for a critical stage of my life.

You can read more about this great man here
https://lnkd.in/dqmR-ejs

Prof. Mwenda thank you for all the encouragement and for embodying excellence, humility, and a passion to uplift others! You have jumpstarted my spirit

Also, recently, Hon. Dr Masiye W Banda, who, not too long ago, served as the Permanent Secretary in the Ministry of Home Affairs of the Republic of Zambia and earned his Doctor of Business Administration (DBA) degree from ZCAS University, sent me a WhatsApp message expressing his gratitude for the inspiration that he continues to draw from my scholarly work. Dr Banda has also served previously as a director in the office of the Auditor-General of Zambia. In his WhatsApp message of December 1, 2024, Dr Banda wrote the following:

"Mudala uzatipayisa...you are a model to many young and middle-aged professionals. Got my DBA and am enrolling for PhD at UNZA."

Translated into English, the Nyanja words 'Mudala uzatipaisa' mean 'Big man, you will get us killed, as we get fired up by your inspiration to excel to greater heights.' It was very humbling to receive such edifying and unsolicited thoughtful words. I called Dr Banda to thank him and congratulate him over the phone. He was pleasantly surprised to receive my call. After we spoke, I sent him the following message:

"Congratulations, Ba Doc. This is awesome! I just had to call in person to offer you my sincere congratulations. Please keep up the good work."

And Dr Banda responded:

"Your humility does not match your status. You are too humble for your status. Thank you so much, Prof. We keep looking up to you."

Another high-ranking government official, Hon Mr Mwamba Peni II, who once served as a presidential advisor at State House in Zambia, and later as Permanent Secretary at Cabinet Office in the Government of the Republic of Zambia, posted the following message on his social media page on October 24, 2024, to mark Zambia's 60th Independence Day anniversary.

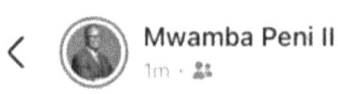

Zambia@60. Prof Kenneth Kaoma Mwenda, PhD, a Rhodes scholar, has written 30 scholarly books and close to 100 scholarly articles in top-rated peer-reviewed journals. He has also taught at leading universities in three continents, namely, Europe, North America and Africa. Until 2019, Prof Mwenda, was the only known legal scholar in the entire world with two earned Higher Doctorates, in addition to a PhD, and all three doctorates earned from leading prestigious universities.

On Tuesday, April 2, 2024, one of my mentees, Mr Charles Shachinda, , now completing a second Masters degree program at Oxford, posted the following update on his WhatsApp status.

Similarly, on Wednesday, March 20, 2024, I met up with a young and dynamic economist from the Ministry Finance in Zambia who was on an academic visit to the Bretton Woods institutions from Williams College in Williamstown, Massachusetts, US. We were meeting for the first time. He stopped over for a courtesy call at my office at the World Bank during lunch hour. His name is Mr Boyd Lumbwe. I have shared a picture below of Mr Lumbwe and me taken in my office at the World Bank.

We exchanged some pleasantly enlightening thoughts on contemporary global issues, especially as they relate to Africa. I have shared below the post that Mr Lumbwe published on his LinkedIn page the evening after our meeting.

Boyd Lumbwe · 1st
Budget Analyst at Ministry of Finance and National Planning-Zambia
6h · Edited · 🌐

My first meeting with Professor Kenneth K. Mwenda was an encounter suffused with veracity.

In the midst of Washington DC's bustling energy, amid the cherry blossoms' delicate sway, I walked to the World Bank Group Headquarters this morning. There, Professor Mwenda, a beacon of intellect, wisdom and humility, welcomed me warmly, and waited patiently for me as I completed the entry formalities to the World Bank building.

Within the confines of his office, we engaged in discourse that transcended mere conversation. His intellect, like a wellspring of enlightenment, flowed flawlessly, suffusing our dialogue with depth and insight. He imparted not just knowledge, but a profound sense of encouragement, igniting within me a renewed sense of purpose.

In my reflections, I realized that inspiration need not be sought in distant lands, it resides within the hearts and minds of individuals like Professor Mwenda. His journey, a testament to the power of intellect and perseverance, serves as a guiding light for all who dare to dream. We often times shun our very own, and draw inspiration only from people from afar, whom we seldom know. This trend ought to stop.

Professor Mwenda, a thought leader, and true embodiment of "Brain Gain," has enriched not just Zambia, but the global community with his immense contributions. As he continues to inspire and uplift, I wish to register my heartfelt gratitude and best wishes for his continued success.

I was humbled by Mr Lumbwe's thoughtfulness and kind words. I sent him a 'thank you' note via WhatsApp soon after reading his LinkedIn article the following day on Thursday, March 21, 2024. He replied immediately with an additional edifying note:

"Thanks Prof. So much wisdom and truth in your words. My coming to your office was the key highlight of my visit to Washington DC. One thing that has really stood out from the time that I have known you as a netizen is how you take time to respond to people's comments and have dialogue. You make time for everybody. That is a trait that most influential and well accomplished people like you don't possess. You have a deeper sense of humility. Even when I was coming to visit you, I had nothing to offer you. Yet you welcomed me like I had something to offer you. Clearly, that's why some people are blessed and go far in life. May you live long and may you achieve all that your mind can conceive."

A few months earlier, that is, on Friday, January 19, 2024, to be specific, another outstanding alumnus of the University of Zambia (UNZA), Mr Twaambo Hamoomba, who had gone back to UNZA to study law as his second degree, sent me the following edifying note via LinkedIn:

TODAY

Twaambo Hamoomba · 2:12 am
Good morning Prof. I just got my results for my law degree and I'm finally done 😁
You are the person I look up to and you have been the driving force behind me getting this degree.

The following day, Saturday, January 20, 2024, less than 24 hours after I received the message highlighted above from Mr Twaambo Hamoomba, one of my mentees, Ms Margaret Mwape, then a postgraduate scholar at the University of Sussex in the United Kingdom, posted the following update on her WhatsApp status:

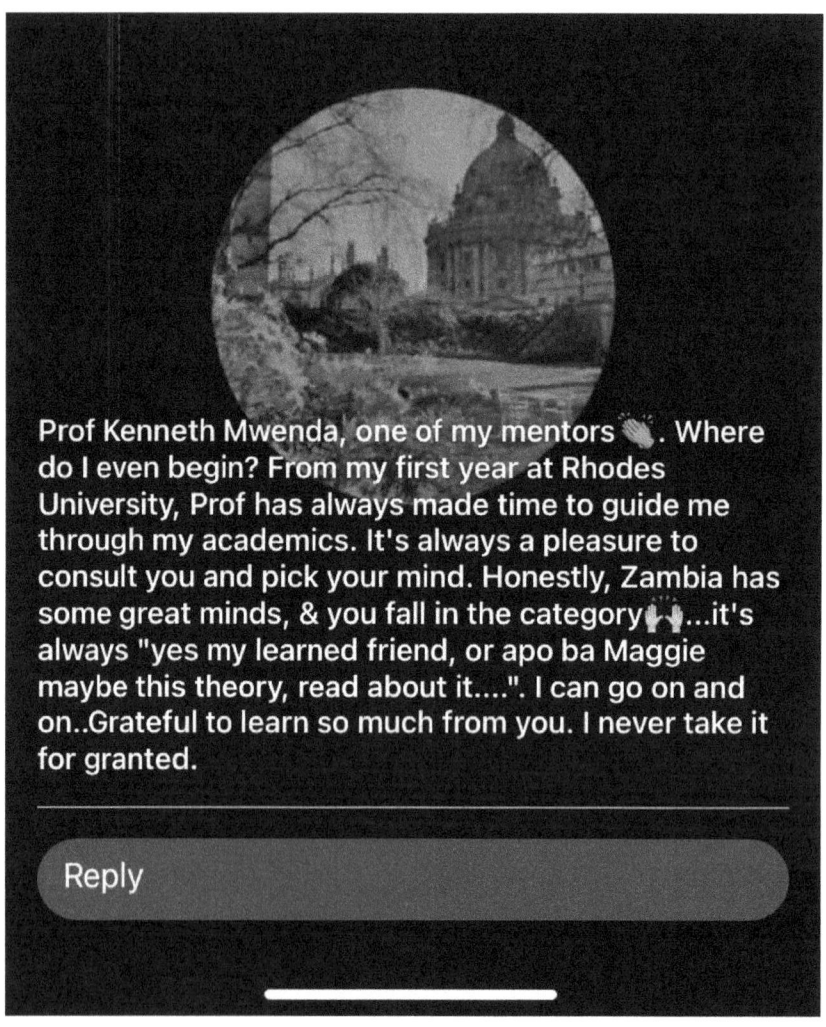

On Monday, April 22, 2024, Ms Margaret Mwape shared another inspiring WhatsApp status update, averring as follows:

"When I went to Rhodes, my lecturer told me about a Zambian who was the first to be conferred a Higher Doctorate in Law at Rhodes University… I was intrigued, and so I had to find this person. That's how I connected with Prof K…I am glad I reached out, because that top tier mentorship, hmm ."

I receive several such inspiring messages from various young and upcoming leaders. For example, one Ms Vanessa Samba Samulyata, a successful commercial farmer in Zambia, commenting on a post I shared on social media, responded as follows:

"You do inspire me. You inspire me to do good, to be the best I can be, to value myself and set high standards for a mate. You inspire me to think big and aim high. I can achieve anything I work towards. This is evident in you, and so I have no reason to doubt my own capabilities."

Then, one Mr Troy Kabungo, a Zambian mining engineer, sent me the following message on LinkedIn:

"Good day Professor,

I was going through your profile and was inspired by your exceptional achievements. What is so incredibly inspiring is that you are from Zambia and are now representing our country at the biggest stage of it all. A remarkable professor of international law and business studies! I just want to take this time to appreciate you for your service. Thank you for standing up for the motherland. I am happy to learn so much about you."

On July 18, 2025, one of my mentees, Ms Valerie Mwinji Nambeye, a UK chartered accountant and lawyer, who served as a member of the Board of Zambia Revenue Authority (ZRA) before joining the World Bank and completing her second Masters degree in the US at George Washington University, wrote: "Prof. Kenneth K. Mwenda, I am ever grateful for your invaluable guidance, wisdom, and encouragement over the years. Your mentorship has been a profoundly influential part of my academic and professional journey. I can confidently say that you saw potential in me even when I struggled to see it myself. You challenged me to think more deeply, aim higher, and never settle for less than I am capable of. You pushed me to the point where I started questioning things that I took for granted, but it was only because you believed in me. Through your example, I have learned that true leadership is grounded in integrity, patience, and a genuine desire to uplift others.

Indeed, it's about selflessness. Your contribution to the growth of my professional and academic life remains indelible. The lessons you shared go well beyond skills or knowledge. They are principles that I will hold dear throughout my life. Thank you for believing in me, investing in me, and showing me what it means to be both excellent and kind. May the Almighty God continue to bless you!"

In early July 2025, I sent a congratulatory message to my good learned sister, Hon Dr Dora Siliya, who has held previously some key cabinet positions in the Government of the Republic of Zambia, on her appointment to a faculty position at the University of Lusaka. In the 1990s, when I was lecturing at the University of Warwick in England, Dr Siliya had just commenced her Masters degree studies at the University of Cambridge. I was honored to have served informally as her mentor when she was pursuing her Masters degree studies at Cambridge. The following is Dr Siliya's inspiring feedback which she shared on her Linkedin page, responding to my congratulatory message:

Dr Dora Siliya Author 1d ···
Leader, Researcher/Policy Analyst, Business/M...

Kenneth K. Mwenda I thankyou so much. You know that you were always an inspiration for me too and teaching now, even as a new bee, is really coming full circle after our conversation back in Cambridge ...more

Like 1 Reply

Dr Siliya served not only as Minister of Transport in the Government of the Republic of Zambia, but also at various points in time as Minister of Education, Minister of Energy and Water Development, Minister of Agriculture, Minister of Information and Broadcasting Services, and Deputy Minister of Commerce.

A few years ago, I received the photo appearing here to the right from a university student in Zambia who was preparing to sit for his law school exams. The two books in the photo are some of my works on securities regulation and the development of capital markets. Sometimes we don't realize how much our work touches and influences the lives of others until we get a pleasant surprise such as the one below. Indeed, ideas can transform lives. And ideas can change a society.

On Friday, November 24, 2023, a Nigerian PhD student, Puja C. Albert, who recently completed his PhD and who I taught on the Masters of Law degree program (LLM) in International Trade and Investment Law at the University of Western Cape (UWC) in South Africa, posted the edifying and uplifting update on his WhatsApp status shown here:

A decade ago, that is, on Tuesday, June 3, 2014, to be specific, the *Post* newspaper in Zambia published an article written by the current Ambassador of the Republic of Zambia to the United States of America, His Excellency Ambassador Dr Chibamba Kanyama, who was at the time serving as Advisor/Deputy Director at the International Monetary Fund (IMF) in Washington DC. In that article, Ambassador Kanyama, who is also a former Director-General and CEO of Zambia's leading and State-owned television network, the Zambia National Broadcasting Corporation (ZNBC), explained the progressive camaraderie that he and I have shared over the years. I have provided below a copy of that inspiring article by Ambassador Kanyama.

When a cat gets mirrored as a lion!

Talking Business
With Chibamba Kanyama

IN OCTOBER 2013, I received a phone call from Dr Tukiya Mabula, Bank of Zambia Deputy Governor, asking me to apply for a job in an international organisation.

She started, 'I do realise that the position you hold at ZNBC as Director General is very important to the nation. There is, however, another opportunity I believe would be of equal importance to Zambia if you got it.'

She unpacked the advertisement and in less than ten minutes, she had emailed a copy to me. By virtue of its position, the Bank of Zambia had direct access to the information and it was against this backdrop the bank management looked for Zambians that would take the chance.

The job was certainly beyond me after reading through the job requirements and qualifications. The reality is that when you are confronted with an opportunity that sits beyond your imagination, you would rather let it pass than waste your time. My mind was clouded with a defeatist attitude as it got flooded with challenges of the past and my personality. There was no way a person like me with the *Mutwiwambwa* life-orientation would attempt to compete for a high-profile job in a very high-profile organisation that many have just known through academic textbooks.

However, upon reflecting on Dr Mabula's convictions, I decided to comply. If I had seen the advert on my own, I would never have had the courage to even read through it. That is the kind of assignment that suits Kenyans, Brazilians, Australians but not a Zambian, I thought!

I hired Namucana Musiwa, senior partner of Career Prospects to rewrite my Curriculum Vitae. The copy she submitted reminded me of a picture of a cat that saw itself as a lion in a mirror. I phoned her why she thought I fitted the description that was in the reworked CV. 'Do not think you are that simple, Chibamba,' she responded. 'You have achieved a lot and your CV is of international standard. Why do you under-value yourself when you have everything within you considering your record of achievements?'

Within two months, I had successfully gone through the first two rounds of interviews that were held via conference calls and skype. Seeing that I needed to travel to Washington DC for the next round of interviews, I decided to alert Dr Mabula again, someone I had been in touch with throughout the process. This time, I was before Dr Michael Gondwe, the Governor himself. I received the most reassuring encouragement and motivation of my life, to go to Washington DC with a mindset of a winner. He reminded me of my strengths and asked me to believe in them. It was through this consultation I was advised to formally inform my principals so that the government stood behind me.

The encounter with Dr Roland Msiska, Secretary to the Cabinet, was like listening to a digital video encyclopedia of knowledge. He believed just as much as ZNBC needed me, the job at an international organisation was equally beneficial for the nation. He oriented me around global economic politics, debates and issues. I left with a lot of confidence about operations and systems that govern international organisations. He was more than certain I was cut for the job.

Even on the day prior to my flight, I had another moment with him, receiving the 'half-time' pep-talk to enable me to have the right mentality for the challenge ahead. It was the same Dr Msiska who called me to his house stimulation about the need for me to take up the ZNBC job at the time I was dilly-dallying.

The day before the interview, I had dinner with Professor Kenneth Mwenda. When I failed my first Corporate Finance test at the University of Reading, it was Dr Mwenda I had consulted to help me comprehend how to rise against failure. By then, he had just left Warwick University, where he was lecturer. He shared some titbits about the UK academic system and that to get a distinction in a British University; you had to present facts only and in a succinct manner. I followed the instructions to the letter and saw myself being an MBA lecturer in the same subject I had failed.

On this particular evening in Washington DC, he gave me life-changing morsels about how to succeed in a job interview under an American setting: 'Americans generally believe in self-exaltation,' he advised. 'In Zambia, we do not glory in our achievements. If ever you did under our culture, society would think you are pompous, rude and proud. It is the opposite here. They want you to explain your achievements, your record of achievements and do not be afraid to tell them about how good you are. That is what makes an American society, and this philosophy resonates even among institutions that operate here!'

I had known by then that there were two of us called for the final interview. I did not want to know who the other person was for fear of psychological intimidation, 'What if he came from some high-profile country, far bigger and richer than Zambia?' I told myself.

I went through what I would define as 'three phases of interviews' the following day. I never exaggerated anything about myself. All I did was to merely acknowledge and highlight my credentials. To my surprise, the panel already knew so much about me, and that they saw me as a lion and not as a cat!

I have decided to share this story to motivate my fellow Zambians to rise to the business challenges and opportunities before us. We should not be dwarfed by many foreign investors who are erecting shopping malls at every junction, winning government tenders by the hour while we whine and cry in our offices and bedrooms. In the past fifty years, a lot of investment was made to reposition us, Zambians, as winners and achievers. It is now time we accepted ourselves as initiators and drivers of change. We cannot be underdogs and underachievers in a world of plenty. At times, it helps to see ourselves as what neighbours think of us, as Zambians and not how ugly spots of our history define us.

I regret to announce that my new assignment requires me to take a break from platforms that will require me to comment on economics, finance and business. It is against this backdrop I thank Post Newspapers for having accorded me this rare opportunity to run this well-followed column.

I particularly acknowledge my editor Chiwoyu Sinyangwe for his rare editorial skills. My readers should take this break as a resourcing experience so that I come back a different person. For individuals mentioned in this article (without their permission), accept my apologies. I needed to use my experience to motivate Zambia's young people who are on the road to prosperity. The Lord bless you all.

In the picture below, I can be seen standing next to my good learned brother, His Excellency, Ambassador Dr Chibamba Kanyama (in the middle), with Dr Akashambatwa Mbikusita-Lewanika, a distinguished senior citizen who has held a number of key cabinet and corporate executive leadership positions in Zambia. This picture was taken in Washington DC after the three of us had lunch together.

In 2021, I had written a musing on my Facebook page which was taken out of context by some sections of the public, given the prevailing political climate in Zambia at the time. The country was preparing for the 2021 Presidential and General Elections. Tempers were flaring up and things were getting really heated up. I must admit that I had a huge following on Facebook which went beyond Zambia. I was, arguably, the only leading Zambian scholar with such a huge Facebook following. A number of my musings and posts on Facebook would find their way on other social media platforms in Zambia and elsewhere. Others would be published on websites of leading media outlets both in and outside Zambia. Even some prominent radio stations in Zambia, such as Q-FM, would publish some of my musings as part of their news items.

As recently as 2024, some of my old Facebook posts are still being shared and appreciated by many factions of society. To illustrate, I have shared below one of my old Facebook posts which was re-published in February 2024 – tmany years after I had closed down my Facebook page – by three leading Zambian media platforms, namely, *Zambia Reports, Smart Eagles* and *Hot FM-Zambia*.

BEYOND THE PHD

Many people now look back and realize the value and sense of much of what I used to share on Facebook. We only aspire to inspire.

 **Zambia Reports** · Follow
Dec 20, 2020

Professor Kenneth Mwenda wrote...

"A picture or pictures can tell a great story. What you see in the first picture is the swimming pool that I left in my home town, Luanshya, Zambia, after completing high school in 1985. What you see in the second picture is the same swimming pool, as it stands today, after the privatization of the copper mines in Zambia."

 **HOT FM Zambia**
36m

THROW BACK THURSDAY.

In 2020, Professor Kenneth Mwenda wrote...

"A picture or pictures can tell a great story. What you see in the first picture is the swimming pool that I left in my home town, Luanshya, Zambia, after completing high school in 1985. What you see in the second picture is the same swimming pool, as it stands today, after the privatization of the copper mines in Zambia."

 **Smart Eagles**
51 m

THROW BACK THURSDAY.

In 2020, Professor Kenneth Mwenda wrote...

"A picture or pictures can tell a great story. What you see in the first picture is the swimming pool that I left in my home town, Luanshya, Zambia, after completing high school in 1985. What you see in the second picture is the same swimming pool, as it stands today, after the privatization of the copper mines in Zambia

So it was clear that my voice on the political dispensation in Zambia, as the 2021 Presidential Elections were approaching, would have attracted wide interest and attention had I spoken out openly or endorsed a presidential candidate. I never did. I chose to keep quiet. Many people expected me to say something or endorse their preferred presidential candidate. They just wouldn't take my neutrality and impartiality for an answer.

While I have never been into partisan politics, some people feared that whoever I was going to be perceived to have endorsed would benefit from the influence of my public personality and, thus, end up securing a number of votes from my social media followers. This caused some people a lot of sleepless nights. I have never in my life endorsed any presidential candidate.

A number of colleagues from the then leading opposition party, the United Party for National Development (UPND), approached me discreetly before the 2021 Presidential Elections, asking me to endorse and support their presidential candidate. I declined. Yes, I declined. I have always maintained impartiality and insisted that I am not into partisan politics. That I did not distance myself from or disown the other camp, that is, from some colleagues and friends in the then ruling party, the Patriotic Front (PF), made things worse. Some colleagues in the pro-UPND camp thought that I was supporting PF, especially that H.E. President Edgar C Lungu (PF leader), the then Head of State, had awarded me the prestigious and coveted President's Insignia of Meritorious Achievement (PIMA) a couple of years before that for my unparalleled academic accomplishments as a noteworthy global thought-leader as well as a distinguished scholar and eminent authority in the field of law. However, I was honored by President Lungu not because of politics, but purely on professional and scholarly merit. The intellectual gravitas of my scholarly work and contributions speaks for itself and remains indelible. Even the most superficial cynic knows it, yet he or she might choose to be willfully blind to this prophetic truth. I was honored by President Lungu not only as a doyen of knowledge in the field of law, a uniquely rare quality among many a Zambian legal mind, but also for my pioneering global thought-leadership that

John
@juan_avanzando

Replying to @isaacjanets @VictorK37728806 and @StudentsZed

Elo Prof. Mwenda doesn't beat around the bush😆😆,

remains indelibly evident in what I have produced and contributed to the world at large. In Bemba, we say: "Sonta epo wa bomba ("Show me your works before you start arguing)". Those who know me will know that:

I remember vividly the clairvoyant words of H.E. President Edgar C Lungu, as we walked together on the presidential red carpet at State House to take the photos below. The man looked at me respectfully, and said candidly, with a sense of wit and humor:

"Ema professor aba…abakweba ati we have seen his scholarly works, noti aba bambi who just come to Zambia to make noise yet we have not even seen anything they have written." ("This is what it means to be a real professor…we have seen this man's massive body of scholarly publications, unlike some people who claim to be professors and come to Zambia to make noise, yet we have not even seen anything they have written".)

H.E. President Lungu was himself a distinguished senior lawyer, had been a brilliant student during his student days at the University of Zambia (UNZA) Law School, so he knew what he was talking about. His sentiments were valid. Scholars are not all cut from the same cloth. To become a professor of note, you must have professed knowledge publicly through serious peer-reviewed scholarly publications. Scholarly publications matter more than anything else in academia.

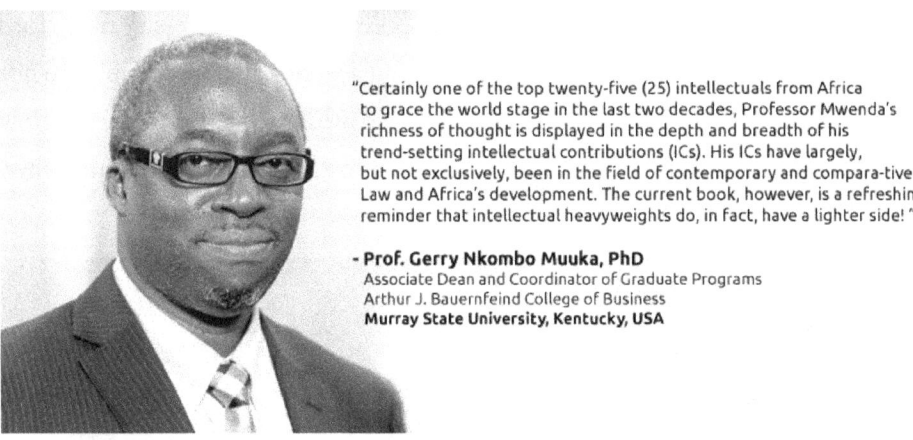

"Certainly one of the top twenty-five (25) intellectuals from Africa to grace the world stage in the last two decades, Professor Mwenda's richness of thought is displayed in the depth and breadth of his trend-setting intellectual contributions (ICs). His ICs have largely, but not exclusively, been in the field of contemporary and compara-tive Law and Africa's development. The current book, however, is a refreshing reminder that intellectual heavyweights do, in fact, have a lighter side!"

- **Prof. Gerry Nkombo Muuka, PhD**
Associate Dean and Coordinator of Graduate Programs
Arthur J. Bauernfeind College of Business
Murray State University, Kentucky, USA

I must add that before I was honored for my distinguished scholarly contributions by the PF Government, I had been honored previously by the Movement for Multiparty Democracy (MMD) Government under Zambia's President Rupiah Banda. I remain eternally grateful to both governments for these admirable and rare State honors. I was honored by both the MMD and PF Governments for my distinguished scholarly contributions. The MMD Government appointed me as Honorary Tourism Ambassador for the Republic of Zambia. So, how can some superficial cynics out there claim that I was honored by H.E. President Lungu because I was a PF cadre? I have never been into politics. If you cannot get me to endorse your preferred presidential candidate, or to hate your political opponent, then do not speculate with anecdotal conjectures. Is MMD the same thing as PF? Yes, I was also honored by the MMD Government, and more recently I have been honored by my alma mater, Exeter College at the University of Oxford in England. So, where is 'cadre-ism' in all this? As I used to say on Facebook, (some) people are not honest. They will try to twist facts to suit their political agenda. I have shared some pictures below from the occasion where I was honored by the MMD Government in Zambia for my distinguished scholarly contributions.

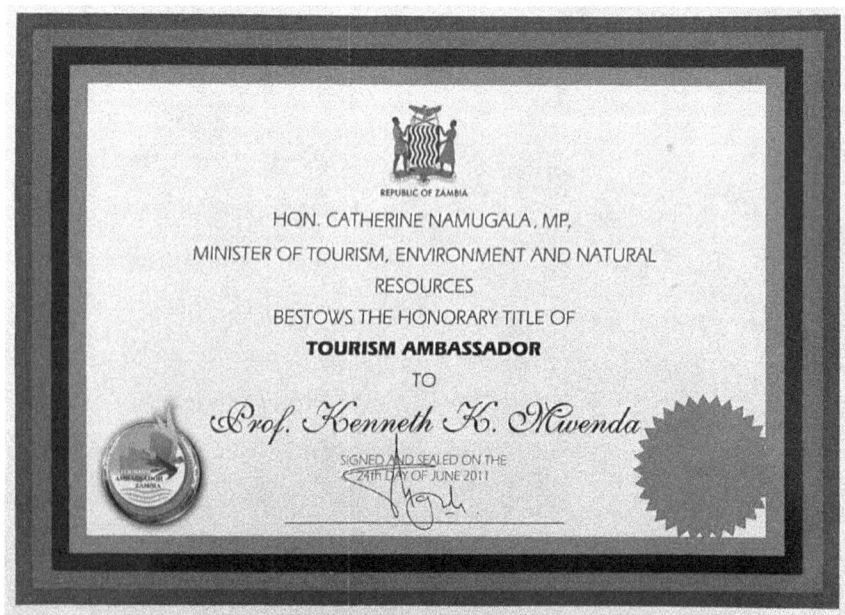

Until 2019, there was no other known legal scholar in the entire English-speaking world with Higher Doctorates in two different disciplines than Zambia's Kenneth Kaoma Mwenda. Put simply, and objectively speaking, my influence as a thought-leader could not be downplayed or ignored and that is why it would bother some people before the 2021 President Elections in Zambia. I had larger audiences beyond Facebook which extended to academia, countries beyond Zambia and various international television channels where I am often invited to speak. Even to this day, a common phrase that I coined while I was active on Facebook, namely, 'People are not honest', continues to do rounds on social media in Zambia and is widely referenced by many.

As the 2021 Presidential Elections in Zambia drew nearer, a lot of people were anxious to see me take a position between PF and UPND, but I always refuse to do things just to appease people. And that infuriated some people. They wanted me to support their presidential candidate. By contrast, I chose to remain impartial and apolitical. Here, an analogy can be drawn with developments leading to the 2024 US Presidential Elections. The *Guardian*, in an Online article titled, '"She could absolutely change my mind": readers on Taylor Swift's political influence', dated

Tuesday, February 6, 2024, quoted a PhD student and prospective voter as saying: "If Taylor Swift endorsed a presidential candidate, I would be angry. Americans do not need more noise in their already noisy election."[15]

In Zambia, as the date of the 2021 Presidential and General Elections drew closer, there was a lot of political intolerance of divergent views and things were seen mainly as either white or black, with no middle shades of gray or brown in-between. It was like a cult. But today many who espoused that high level of intolerance due to the psychology of mob mentality have woken up to the harsh reality of life. Others even regret. Many have either sobered up from the illusory expectations that drove much of their insensitivity towards divergent views or are trapped in a pitiful state of denial and cognitive dissonance. Indeed, you can choose, if you want, to disrespect and insult a friend who has treated you with nothing but respect over some politician who doesn't even know you, but the day that politician gets to win the election is the day you will realize how unwise you were. You will be lucky if you get anything for your blind political sycophancy.

When people make a noise, do not look at the position they have taken. You will be misled. Rather, look at their interest. It is the person's interest in a matter, not his or her position on the matter, that exposes him or her. Many folks making noise and agitating for change were looking for jobs and procurement deals from State institutions only to learn that, with a few exceptions, if you didn't belong then there was no seat for you at the table.

While hunger was looming under the PF Government, it got worse under the UPND Government. Many people today feel deceived. Folks were hungry and had been promised heaven on earth by some functionaries of the then main opposition party, UPND. Some people who had lost business deals, girlfriends and mistresses to functionaries of the then ruling party, PF, had become so bitter with the PF Government that they could not wait to vote them out of power. Others suffered from the lawlessness of some low-ranking PF functionaries known as 'cadres' who would at times grab land and other forms of property with impunity from helpless citizens. So, the bitterness against PF was at an all-high, leading to the protest vote that ousted the PF from power. But after PF lost power another wave of bitterness ensued against those that took over power from

---

15. J. Otte, "'She could absolutely change my mind': readers on Taylor Swift's political influence," *The Guardian*, (February 6, 2024), available Online at: <<https://www.theguardian.com/music/2024/feb/06/taylor-swift-political-voting-election-influence>>, accessed on February 6, 2024.

PF, the UPND Government. Indeed, hunger has gotten worse under UPND. Many people still don't have jobs despite the promises that some politicians in the UPND camp had made to the public prior to the 2021 presidential and general elections.

In 2021, prior to the aforesaid elections, when I wrote the controversial musing on social media referenced above, some supporters of the then ruling party, PF, used it for their own political mileage to attack my good friend and learned brother Ambassador Kanyama, insinuating that the musing was directed at him, and especially that he was associated with UPND. Some supporters of UPND responded, together with those that just wanted to fan the fire. It became a national saga on social media that even had one of the cabinet ministers issue a public statement to clarify matters.

Fortunately, Ambassador Kanyama is an intellectual. He could see through the entire charade of the PF and UPND cadres. He and I had been close friends even before the PF and UPND political parties and governments, respectively, were conceived. Yes, I have friends in PF and cannot deny knowing them. They are my friends. I am a man of principle. I don't deny or distance myself from people just because they are no longer in power. Some of them even attended my mother's funeral in Luanshya. So I am ever grateful for such friends. Equally, I have friends in UPND who I have known since my student days at the University of Zambia (UNZA) and before UPND was even formed. That is just how life is.

In today's world of international diplomacy, we only have friends and are not against anyone. However, some UPND sympathizers got upset with my musing, as they suspected that I was supporting PF because I was not siding with UPND to condemn PF. But did I have to condemn anyone or take sides? Absolutely not! And it is not about sitting on the fence. Being apolitical is not betrayal and it is not the same thing as sitting on the fence. I have a constitutional right to remain silent, especially if I cannot reason at the same level as the people around me making unnecessary noise. Indeed, I can propose to myself, and choose to agree, to remain silent. I don't need anyone's approval or permission for that, for I am under no obligation to talk to or hate the person you hate. The problem with social media is that even people who ordinarily would not have access to you or be privileged to interact with you, given that you are in a totally different social class and rank from theirs, feel that you are now at the same level just because you are all together on social media. As one quote attributed to Mike Tyson reads: "Social media made y'all way too comfortable with disrespecting people and not getting punched in the face for it."

Indeed, familiarity breeds contempt. And as Tyson is also reported to have said, "Everybody has a plan until they get punched in the face."

So, mu kwi pifya, as we say in Bemba ('put simply'), I cannot be recruited to hate the person or people that you hate. That is not my plan. And you cannot recruit me to be a hater. You can't even use my name for your own selfish political agenda by demanding that I endorse the person that you like, or that I criticize or condemn the person that you hate. I don't work like that. That said, I am awake to the fact some prominent Zambian academics originating from a certain regional base in Zambia only supported a presidential candidate from their home regional base. One would have expected such people to continue making noise in the media after the elections. But suddenly, they have all gone mute even though the economy has continued to underperform and has probably even gotten worse. Human rights violations are also rife.

In my case, it is a truism, for example, as established earlier, that His Excellency President Frederick Titus Jacob Chiluba, like my humble self, originated from Luapula Province in Zambia. Yet at no time did I start writing media articles spiritedly supporting his ascendancy to power in 1991 just because he was my fellow Luapulan. I am above such pettiness. You cannot hide behind intellectualism, yet the underlying thrust of your noise is that of tribal politics. Indeed, you don't behave like that as a scholar. For me, I did not even make spirited efforts to meet President Chiluba, especially that, while he has the Head of State of Zambia, he was also one of our graduate students at the University of Warwick in England where I was teaching at the time. Others, if they were in my shoes, would have hustled to meet President Chiluba and get themselves introduced for any possible political benefit. But that's not me. You'll find me as I am.

I do not suck up to people and I am not into tribalism or partisan politics. Rather, I am a scholar and intellectual. That is who I am. The rest follows from there. If you ask me to condemn or endorse someone, I will do neither. You should expect me to treat another person the same way you expect me to treat you. I don't take sides anyhow, unless there is an absolute necessity for me to do so. I am a critical thinker. Clairvoyantly, I would rather watch, observe and listen. I have always chosen to remain apolitical, impartial and neutral. But for some people, even just sharing a picture on social media where you appear, say, with the then sitting President of the Republic of Zambia, His Excellency President Dr Edgar Chagwa Lungu, it would offend them. The problem is that some people want to recruit you to hate the person or people they hate. It does not work like that. As noted above, I have friends in both PF and UPND parties. And so, whatever differences the two parties could have had between them it had nothing to do with my friendship with some members of both parties. That I do not side with you to condemn your nemesis does not mean I am against you. Get this right. And this is where some people don't get it. I don't have to agree with you to be my friend or compatriot. I have an independent mind of my own. Besides, there is no reason for me to hate a person who has not done me any wrong. It just does not make sense.

My good learned brother, His Excellency Ambassador Dr Chibamba Kanyama, called me from Zambia when the whole hullaballoo on Facebook broke out regarding one of my musings alluded to earlier. We spoke at some length. As noted earlier, when I was on Facebook, I used to write some daily inspirational musings, but some people would catch feelings, especially if they saw their own shadow in a musing, while others would get inspired and learn something from the musings. Most importantly, there will be people with no idea of how far you have come with someone or how close the two of you are.

I have shared Ambassador Kanyama's media article above, demonstrating where we have come from and how far we go. When I lost my mother in 2019, I flew to Zambia for the funeral. As soon as Ambassador Kanyama learned of my mother's passing, he reached out to me and graciously offered me one of his vehicles to help me get to the Copperbelt for the funeral. It was very kind of him. That is how far we go as friends. I replied to him, thanking him and mentioning that I was already on the Copperbelt. I had taken a connection flight from Lusaka to Ndola, and then picked up a car hire at the airport to connect to Luanshya.

My friendship with Ambassador Kanyama dates way back to the 1980s. We were together as undergraduate students at the University of Zambia (UNZA) in the 1980s before many young people on Facebook were born. Further, we have been friends since before social media existed. Our friendship also predates the establishment of both UPND and PF. And we remain friends to this day.

In the pictures below, taken on Friday, January 17, 2025, I can be seen with my good learned brother and friend Ambassador Kanyama at the Zambian Embassy in Washington DC when he invited me over to give the keynote address at the hoisting of the Zambian flag at the newly renovated premises of the Zambian Embassy.

And in the three pictures below, Ambassador Kanyama and I posed for some photos after the hoisting of the Zambian flag.

In some of Ambassador Kanyama's books, he has written extensively and generously about me, acknowledging and endorsing my global thought-leadership. He even invited me to give a keynote address at one of the youth development conferences he and his business team held in Lusaka, Zambia, just before the 2020 pandemic broke out. That is how close we are. And I am ever grateful to my good learned brother, Ambassador Kanyama. But many people have no clue how far Ambassador Kanyama and I go back, and that is the problem of believing everything you read on social media instead of spending your precious and valuable time in the library reading on more sensible things.

CHAPTER 3

Global thought-leadership inspires others

For a long time, I had been wanting to do some philanthropic work back home in Zambia. I always told myself that if my thought leadership could inspire someone out there, then I would have served my purpose on this earth. For that is one of the greatest talents that God has given me. And I cannot hide my talents under the bed. Rather, I must learn to share.

Not too long ago, I received the email reproduced here from a university student in Zambia. I woke up in the morning only to find this unsolicited and uplifting email in my inbox. Truly, thought leadership inspires others. For, if you cannot inspire or motivate others, then you are not an effective leader. Even in much of the literature in organizational psychology, there is a correlation between leadership and motivation.

Raised as a Catholic, I saw at a young age how the Catholic Church carried out their socially uplifting work of attending to the poor and vulnerable in my native country. The church helped the poor and marginalized through offering valuable educational, social and health

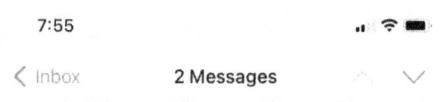

Thank you for the inspiration

Dear Prof. Mwenda,

My name is ▓▓▓▓▓▓▓▓▓. I have been following your achievements and truth be told you have really inspired me to go back to school.

I recently enrolled at The National Institute of Public Administration (NIPA) Ndola Campus under the Legal Division and I am studying LLB in year one. I am going all the way to LLD and I am doing it at The University of Western Cape.

I just wanted to say thank you for the inspiration and one day God willing I look forward to meeting you.

Kind regards,

services. The Catholic Church built schools and hospitals in some of the remotest parts of the country, where even the State and other religious groups had a limited presence. To me, that was a true attribute of the Christian faith, as opposed to simply shouting in purported 'tongues' and looking for 'miracles' daily, without any demonstrable works of love, caring for others and charity. Some folks will tell you defiantly that it is not by your works that you will be saved, but by your faith. Yet, faith without works, I contend, is disputable love. For, the fundamental precepts of the Christian faith are drawn from love, as espoused in the following two Old Testament Commandments, captured in Matthew 22:34–40, Mark 12:28–34, and Luke 10:25–28:

"But when the Pharisees heard that he had silenced the Sadducees, they gathered together.[35] And one of them, a lawyer, asked him a question to test him.[36] 'Teacher, which is the great commandment in the Law?'[37] And he said to him, 'You shall love the Lord your God with all your heart and with all your soul and with all your mind.[38] This is the great and first commandment.[39] And a second is like it: You shall love your neighbor as yourself.[40] On these two commandments depend all the Law and the Prophets.'"

So, if I have my faith in God but show no love to my neighbor, but simply shout in tongues and look for miracles, of what good is my faith? Your works, I submit again, especially where they are born out of genuine love for others and from your personal sacrifice, are a manifestation of true Godly love, for you cannot give or share the little that you have if you have no love for others. Rather, you will selfishly hold on to whatever little you have. And so, works born out of faith in God are not in vain. Your fear of the Lord God, Jehovah Almighty, is your conscience. It permits you to discern right from wrong and good from bad. You do not have to be perfect, or appear pious or sanctimonious, but you must learn to love others as you love yourself. For, there will never be a time when you can say that you now have enough to share with others. Otherwise, you can wait a lifetime.

So, around 2021, I reached out to Dagama School in Luanshya, Zambia, a school for children who are differently able-bodied that is run by some Franciscan Catholic nuns. I grew up in Luanshya, so I knew the school very well. As a young altar boy at the Immaculate Conception Catholic Church in Luanshya, I would see Catholic nuns walk the children from Dagama every Sunday for Mass at church. Those memories of the good work of the Catholic nuns never left me. Thus, after so many years, I reached out to those nuns to explore possible ways in which I could, in my humble way, give back to society. I could have chosen to offer my philanthropic efforts to my former high school, Luanshya Boys' Secondary School (LBSS), which has been actively fund-raising to refurbish the infrastructure at the school. But I chose quietly to work with the Catholic nuns at Dagama School.

The reason for this decision was simple. While some of my childhood friends from my LBSS days wondered why I was not visible in the fundraising activities of LBSS alumni association, I knew that LBSS, unlike Dagama School, had a strong alumni base with several alumni who had become very successful in life and could easily help LBSS with its fund-raising. By contrast, Dagama School had no one to turn to but the Catholic nuns. As one Catholic nun shared with me: "We hesitated initially when you reached out to us because it is not common for our own people to offer to assist us with the work that we do here. You are probably one of the few, if not the first. I discussed the matter with the other Sisters. But now that we know who you are and about your Christian family background here in Luanshya, it gave us a lot of trust and confidence."

So, since 2021, I have been working closely with Dagama School to assist children for whom help is critical and who society, for the most part, overlooks, neglects and abandons. For, in Matthew 25:34-40, we are told:

"Then the King will say to those on his right, 'Enter, you who are blessed by my Father! Take what's coming to you in this kingdom. It's been ready for you since the world's foundation. And here's why: I was hungry and you fed me, I was thirsty and you gave me a drink, I was homeless and you gave me a room, I was shivering and you gave me clothes, I was sick and you stopped to visit, I was in prison and you came to me.' Then those 'sheep' are going to say, 'Master, what are you talking about? When did we ever see you hungry and feed you, thirsty and give you a drink? And when did we ever see you sick or in prison and come to you?' Then the King will say, 'I'm telling the solemn truth: Whenever you did one of these things to someone overlooked or ignored, that was me—you did it to me.'"

I have shared below a few pictures taken in May 2023 when I visited Dagama School and met up with some of the Catholic nuns running the school. It was the first time we had met in person, though I had been working with the nuns remotely from my base in the US. I was welcomed by Sister Ruth Ndhlovu, through whom I got to meet the other Franciscan Sisters, including Sr Aretha Ngoma, at the said school. I felt at home. I was in awe of the great work that the Catholic nuns were doing to take care of the marginalized and the often forgotten. For me, every experience is a learning experience. I learned a lot from my visit and have continued my engagement with Dagama School. God speaks to us in many different ways.

At Dagama School, I did not need lengthy introductions. Some of the older nuns already knew my parents since both my parents were very active in the community work of the Catholic Church in Luanshya. So, the nuns could easily see me through the edifying Christian exemplary life of my parents, as a son who had returned to his community and people.

With the permission of the school, I have shared below some photos taken in late 2023 at a Christmas and graduation party that I supported for the children at Dagama School. It was so heartwarming to see the smiles on the faces of the young graduands when I received these photos as well as a few videos of the event.

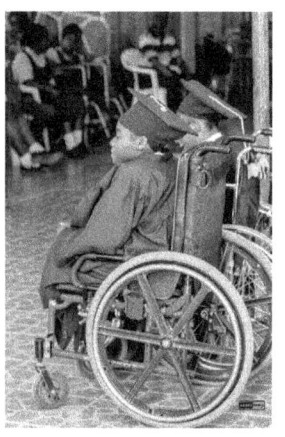

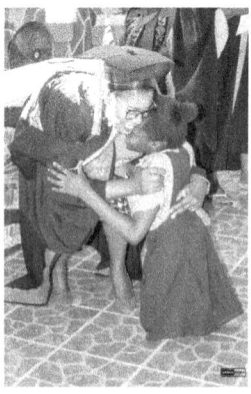

On December 31, 2024, I received the following message of thanks from one of the Franciscan Sisters at Dagama School:

"Dear Ba Professor, Doc Mwenda and family,

Let me take this opportunity to express my sincere gratitude for your unwavering love, care, concern, support, and generosity in having a heart to support our children… Each time we've received something from you, it has been a great relief. Words cannot express my deepest gratitude. The greatest gift to the family is our prayers for you and the generation to come. May the good Lord continue to bless you abundantly. That's all we can say. A very simple and humble family despite the high caliber you possess. You are Franciscans at Heart."

When I started my philanthropic initiative at Dagama School, one of my friends who I sought advice from encouraged me to have the media cover the work that I was doing, insisting that I should also invite, say, one of the Catholic Bishops or a prominent politician to officiate at one of the events. I reflected deeply and decided against the idea. If you are doing something from the heart, you do not need to publicize it. I have only written about this work here because I am writing my life story. Indeed, this is an autobiography. I am not a politician who tries to gain political mileage out of any works of philanthropy. I do not do things like politicians to gain political mileage. I know that it is very common in Africa for some politicians and First Ladies to set up non-governmental organizations (NGOs) and drum up a lot of publicity for them, but that is for them, not me. You only do that if, say, you would like to attract more donors to your NGO or you have a political agenda, say, as part of your electoral campaign strategy. As noted above, I am not a politician. Rather, I am simply a humble child of God.

On Saturday January 18, 2025, I received the following message from one of my mentees, Ms Chola Mwansa, who is based in Ndola, Zambia, and recently obtained her Masters degree:

"Today, when I went to church, the priest spoke about selflessness and gave you as an example. The work that you are doing in Luanshya… He was saying you are in America living a good life, but you choose to give to people who need it more. That is the way I would want to be remembered in life."

Ms Chola continued:

"I didn't get the priest's name. I don't often attend Mass at that parish, but it is St. Joseph's in Itawa, Ndola. I don't think you know them."

As a Christian, I feel that there can be no more edifying and uplifting words than those said in the House of God by a genuinely humble servant of God who you are yet to meet, though he appreciates your work. Indeed, I am ever grateful to that priest as well as to my mentee, Ms Chola, for conveying the message. You don't get to be mentioned easily in a homily at church during Mass. To me, that honor exceeds many citations of honor that one would get to receive in the mundane world out there. Because the Church is a house of God whose is the Alpha and the Omega. And on the kind words said by the priest in Itawa, Ndola, one of my good friends, Dr Chola Kafwabulula, whose doctoral thesis I supervised, had the following to say:

"Iyeee!!! But I too want to agree that what you are doing there, very few in your privileged position would even find time to think about those children, especially looking at your comfort and then for you to think of those kids…mhhh kwati tebengi mwe (very few people would do that). Above all, you are so mute about it. Even in your postings, ine palwandi, I have never seen or heard you talk about your charity works. Ba Prof, for all these things you do for us, God will continue to bless you. I know you have a great IQ, but, my brother, there is also the invisible Hand of God in your life."

Dr Kafwabulula continued:

"Kalebalika (God bless you). It is the reason why you have heard me say several times that, 'It's a blessing for some of us to know you at a personal level.' In life, for people like who we cannot repay in full, as my Mum used to say, 'We must always commit such good people in prayer to the Lord, our God.'"

Equally, the children at Dagama School are so grateful for my philanthropic work at their school. I remember one time when one of the Catholic nuns there called me on video in order for the students to sing me a Christian song and say their thanks. I shed tears quietly afterwards. I could feel the Spirit of God. I was really touched, though I could not let the children and the Catholic nuns see my tears during the video call. I pretended to be strong, as the children sang and delivered their gratitude speeches. I was overwhelmed and really touched.

My wife knew about my work to support the kids at Dagama School, though I am not sure that she understood fully the spiritual and emotional side of the work until she joined me on that videoconference call. I could tell when she saw the kids singing that her emotions were no different from mine. My wife continues to partner with me and support me on this journey. And I am eternally grateful to the Franciscan Sisters at the school for welcoming me to give back to my people. This has been one of the most enriching aspects of my life: to give back freely and without expecting anything in return from the young and poor, marginalized, neglected, abandoned and different able-bodied children, who are not even my relatives.

For me, it does not matter that someone is not from my tribe, race, ethnic group. We are all made in God's own image. We all deserve to love and to be loved. Everyone you see out there is a wonderfully made human being, made in God's own image, just like you and I. And in these children, God is always present.

The pictures shared below were taken when I returned to Dagama School the following year, 2024. I had travelled back to Zambia for my young brother's funeral who died on March 6, 2024, while he was working as a volunteer for the school. My young brother, Francis, gave his best for the good and honor of God to serve the often overlooked and neglected. Francis, like a true Franciscan, made us proud in a world where many people today only do things for money or political gain. His was selfless.

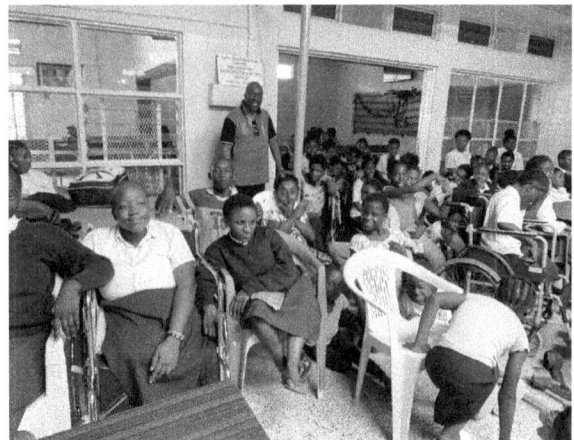
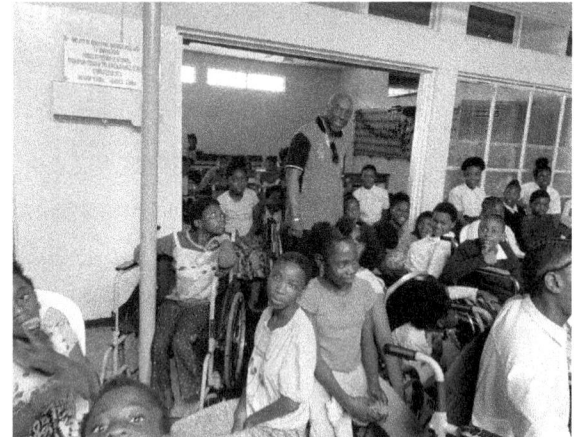

In life, if you are a true leader, you will inspire many people. Some will acknowledge the inspiration that they have drawn from you while others, out of foolish pride or envy, will not admit it openly even when you helped to open doors for them that they themselves could not open.

Also in life, do not expect everyone to like you. It explains why President Nelson Mandela is reported to have said, "If nobody hates you, you are doing something boring. I have never seen a successful person without haters." Even our Lord Jesus Christ faced several haters from among the Pharisees and magicians, including the ranks of many other evildoers, who could not perform the kind of miracles that He would perform. Envy and jealousy are not only evil but are also the root of much hate in this world.

So, Mandela was right. Some people will see your success as a threat. For not everyone was raised well. Others are going through issues of their own and will project their frustrations on you. There are many insecure folks out there, and your hard work and success only reminds them of where they should have been had they not messed up in their lives. Some others just want to be where you are or have what you have without appreciating how you got there. And if they cannot have it, they will be mad at you, as if you owe them something or anything. They will behave as if you caused or are responsible for their situation. *These are people who are fully able-bodied and have everything one needs to succeed in life, but choose instead to be lazy and irresponsible, as they put the blame on others.*

Everyone knows at least one or two family members, relatives, friends, workmates, colleagues, or acquaintances who fit this description. You can help them, but you will be lucky if they even say thank you. As a metaphor, many a patient will be quick to celebrate their recovery after receiving medical treatment but will be slow in thanking the doctor or nursing staff who attended to them. The 'thank you', if it ever comes, is usually relayed as an after-thought or a by-the-way kind of thing. Some patients just leave jubilantly without even saying thank you, not even to family or friends who were by the bedside throughout.

By parity of reasoning, an accused person can jump in jubilation once acquitted by a court of law without even thanking his or her lawyer. Again, a 'thank you', if it comes, is usually relayed as an afterthought or a by-the-way kind of thing. And so it is with many a student after passing their school exams. Few, if any, look back to thank their teachers, parents, guardians or mentors. Even the politician who was begging for your votes before the elections begins to act funny once he gets your votes.

People are quick to celebrate their victory but slow to celebrate, or even acknowledge, the help that they got to get to the victory. In Africa, for example, we have seen a Head of State appoint some unknown person to a cabinet ministerial position or as a vice-president. Later, the appointee starts scheming behind the scenes to take over the presidency from the man who 'made' him politically. Indeed, once these fellas get close to power, they become too comfortable and start to think that they can also rule. Familiarity breeds contempt. And if the Head of State drops the guy, the next thing you will hear is that that disappointed fella, instead of being grateful for having been given a chance to serve the people, has now joined the opposition or formed his own political party to wrestle power from the Head of State. Disloyal people are usually not honest. That is why someone got kicked out of Heaven by God. God does not like disloyal folks, especially those who engage in such sinful machinations as betrayal or malevolent, spiteful, vengeful and malicious shenanigans. One of my good mentees, Mr Denny Kamutadi, a thoughtful and clairvoyant young man based in Northwestern Province of Zambia, sent me the following edifying message via WhatsApp on Monday, January 29, 2024:

"How many of the people you've helped financially, academically, educationally and much more have made [WhatsApp status] posts showing their gratitude for what you've done for them? Secondly, how many of us have sat back to reflect on life and the people who've helped us and spared some time to post or say something to show how grateful we are for what they ever did for us in one way or the other?"

Denny was right. Put simply, do not expect everyone you help to be thankful. Some people were raised badly. They simply lack manners. Perhaps, there was no charity to learn from in the homes where they grew up. You can be trying to help them, yet deep inside their hearts they are busy harboring evil thoughts of competing against you and outdoing you. They will even badmouth you to other people without ever mentioning your good deeds that helped them and from which they benefitted. Their intentions are not always good. For, they want to be in your shoes, especially folks who are not so gifted or talented but are overzealously ambitious as well as those who started off badly but are in a hurry to prove a point. As soon as they get your help, just watch for their behavior and attitude. They start to behave as if you are now equals.

Most ungrateful people try to compete with you as soon as they get your help. I remember one incident where someone was trying to get into graduate school to pursue a Masters degree program somewhere in the US. The individual graduated with poor grades from the University of Zambia (UNZA) such that even a well-known and highly regarded professor who that individual was claiming to be related to refused to write the individual's reference letter for graduate studies. Indeed, the so-called relative or uncle declined to assist the person. That person came running to me and crying for help. I simply smiled and wrote the reference letter. And the person was admitted to graduate studies. The Bible, in Luke 17:11-19, however, helps us to understand that:

"On the way to Jerusalem Jesus was going through the region between Samaria and Galilee. As he entered a village, ten lepers approached him. Keeping their distance, they called out, saying, 'Jesus, Master, have mercy on us!' When he saw them, he said to them, 'Go and show yourselves to the priests.' And as they went, they were made clean. Then one of them, when he saw that he was healed, turned back, praising God with a loud voice. He prostrated himself at Jesus' feet and thanked him. And he was a Samaritan. Then Jesus asked, 'Were not ten made clean? But the other nine, where are they? Was none of them found to return and give praise to God except this foreigner?' Then he said to him, 'Get up and go on your way; your faith has made you well.'"

In a desperate moment, some people will come to you for help, pretending to be humble, but as soon as they get what they wanted they will either disappear or become disrespectful and insolent, belittling the help that you gave them. For a person who rarely helps others but simply lives off them or just waits to exploit them, it is easy to say ungrateful things once the person has been helped, claiming that those who render help should just help without expecting anything in return or any form of gratitude. Such self-serving statements are nothing but pitiful dishonesty. Just where are your manners? Do such people even have manners? Until someone screws them, we will not know their true character.

There are also those who will try to compete with you, as you help them out, or after you have helped them. They think you are now equals and are at the same level. This attitude even creeps in when they are talking to you, dismissing or treating lightly whatever help you could have rendered to them. Such people, instead of being humble and showing appreciation, can disingenuously tell you that it takes a village to raise a child and that we should just help others for the sake of helping, not because we expect something in return, or that when the righthand gives out something the left hand should not know. Put simply, they have a weird sense of entitlement. They behave as if the world owes them something. Yet, in reality, where have you seen an investor, if I may ask, put his time and money that is, the concept of 'time' and 'money' here as a metaphor of helping someone where there are absolutely no returns? Unless you are in Heaven, individuals on this earth are utility maximisers. And any rational being understands the implicit logic in utility maximization. Therefore, to try and push misguided arguments of pursuing altruism without any reciprocity in the form of some kind of appreciation is simply disingenuous.

In America, for example, you even get tax incentives from the government for giving to charity. Yes, you are donating for free, but the government has to show some appreciation in the form of tax incentives. As a 'belief in or practice of disinterested and selfless concern for the well-being of others', altruism does not negate or eliminate the need for the recipient of help to show appreciation to the altruistic person. To illustrate, we go to church to pray, not just because we are good people, and we don't expect any reward from God. Rather, we do it mainly because we expect something in return from God, that is, that God will keep His promise and allow us into Heaven when our time is up. Let us be honest with ourselves and stop pretending to be holier than thou. Similarly, we go to work every morning, not just because we love our work and don't expect anything in return from our employer. No, that would be a lie. We expect something in return from our employer, that is, a salary and other perks for the work that we do and the hours that we put in. It is as simple as that. Even economists talk of incentives to influence certain forms of human behavior. So let us not kid ourselves.

Where there are no incentives, don't expect much. Just ask a politician who lost an election, or a retired corporate executive or one who was forced out, if he or she ever hears from the people that used to bootlick him or her. People can be schmoozing and kissing your ass today, and even fighting on your behalf while you are fast asleep, just because you are in power or have power. But the day you lose that power, you will be lucky if your phone ever rings, or if anyone picks up or returns your calls. You will even start to think that there is something wrong with your phone. Ungrateful people move on quickly, distancing themselves from you as if you have a plague or are radioactive. You will only see them with their new boss, notwithstanding all the favors that you have done or did for them. Ungrateful people have a tendency of downplaying the help or gift they got from you, often quoting Scriptures or proverbs, out of convenience, to justify the selfishness of their ingratitude. You will know a person by his or her attitude towards gratitude. Some of them will even start praising someone else who hardly knows them and who does not even talk to them, just to get at you as they try to insinuate that he or she is a better person than you. If you are dealing with people who are driven or possessed by the dark spirit of entitlement and receiving only, as opposed to those who exhibit good values of reciprocal gestures of returning favors and being able to give something in return to others as well, the former tend to have a weird sense of entitlement. Such people will only remember the things that they believe you should have done for them, and not what you actually did for them. Their selective memory is anchored in an abyss of dishonesty. Out of frustration, such people can even betray you. Their selfishness is simply about taking and taking away from you, without ever giving you anything in return, not even a 'thank you'. Some people can be funny, with an obnoxious sense of entitlement. If we should not expect the people that we help to say thank you, and if we should just help for the sake helping, why then did Jesus Christ ask the healed leper who went back to thank Him, "Were not ten made clean? But the other nine, where are they?"

Why did Jesus Christ not just let it go or forget about it? Indeed, if Jesus Christ, as one who remains consubstantial with God, the Eternal Heavenly Father, through the Doctrine of the Holy Trinity, could express frustration and disappointment at the nine lepers who got healed but did not go back to Him to say thank you, what about us mere mortals? If one is a Christian, surely, you ought to know that even God expects us to show gratitude for the life that He has given us. We are all made in God's image and likeness (See: Genesis 1:26-27; Genesis 2:7; and James 3:9), meaning that, as humans, we borrow from God's likeness. You cannot therefore tell God 'After all, I have already said thank you for the life that you gave me, so what more do you want?' How you behave after you have been helped, as the Bible story of the ten lepers in Luke 17:11-19 shows, is what determines how grateful you are. Personally, I always take time to acknowledge those who have been there for me even if I may not agree with someone on everything. You lose nothing in showing gratitude and being honest.

In this book, I have listed a number of my mentors and former teachers, for example, including my primary and secondary school teachers, as well as many lecturers and professors who taught me at university, acknowledging the inspiration that I have drawn from them. I could have chosen to omit them all and just write about myself only, arguing that, after all, the book is about me, not them. But I am not a narcissist. I am who I am because of those people that God put in my life. I am not shy to say or admit it. Some people are too proud to even acknowledge their former teachers or lecturers, especially if one thinks that he or she has now made it. For me, I cannot pretend that my teachers, mentors, lecturers, and professors were not there for me. They are a part of my story. A number of them helped me in various ways, including writing so many reference letters on my behalf. I cannot therefore behave as if I just made it on my own. That would be extremely disingenuous. You don't behave like that unless you were not raised up well or are just uncultured and lack manners.

Your sense of gratitude and your attitude will often determine your altitude. Indeed, as noted above, you will know a person by his or her attitude towards gratitude. A man once told me how he put his girlfriend on a flight for the first time in her life when they went on a vacation together to Europe. She had never been on plane until that moment. She had never been anywhere outside Africa. When they got back to Africa, she started telling him how one of her friends who was dating an old white man had gone with him to some beautiful places in Miami and the Big Apple. Instead of being grateful and thankful for the opportunity of her maiden international travel that her man had given her, she felt that she deserved more. In her narrowmindedness, she was of the view that what her man had just done for her was not good enough. She even forgot where she was coming from and that none of her former boyfriends had ever put her on a plane, not even on a domestic flight. How do you expect your man to show you those other places if you can't show gratitude for what he has just done for you?

Similarly, a married African lady working as a professional nurse in England got her family over to the UK from Africa. She bought her husband and their two children, including a child he had fathered outside marriage, air tickets to join her in England. The man was not working in Africa. Life had become so harsh on him. When the man arrived in England, it was all nice and there was no drama, at least, for the first six months. His wife would take care of the family as the sole breadwinner since he was not in gainful employment. And she would never complain. She simply kept encouraging him to apply for jobs and go back to school.

What did he do? He started eyeing some white ladies in the neighborhood and fell in love with one of them. The man abandoned his African wife and children for an old widowed white lady in the neighborhood after being rescued from the excruciating poverty he was facing in Africa by that same woman he had chosen to abandon. How do you expect to go far in life like that?

If you speak with some elderly folks, say, on the Copperbelt Province of Zambia, they will tell stories of how some Zambian miners would go back to their home villages to find themselves a wife, only to be abandoned by that same wife after she had been introduced to modern life in the city. Women, too, will tell you that some of them have regretted taking out a loan to buy their man or husband a luxury car only to find him with other women in that same car or to assist him financially with a purported business venture which never gets to see the light of day. Other women have supported their uneducated men or husbands go to school only to discover that the man has started misbehaving with other women after getting his education and finding a steady job. It happens. It is like buying beers for someone who is busy praising another man as a well-known spender on drinks, yet that other man doesn't even know him or has no time for him. Some people can be so ungrateful.

Other folks, as alluded to earlier, try to compete with the person that is helping them or bad-mouth that person to other people. They behave like serpents. A serpent may bite the hand of the person trying to rescue it from a pit. People of this kind often pretend that they just made it on their own. They will never admit that you inspired them or helped them, yet it is obvious from their journey that they keep imitating much of what you have done, including the strategic choices that you have made in your professional career and academic journey. For example, if you join academia in a competitive and attractive setting, they also want to do the same. If they see you in an international organization, they also want to join an international organization. If they see you publishing or writing scholarly books, they also want to start writing and publishing scholarly work. You receive an esteemed award in recognition of your scholarly work, they also want to hustle around for a similar award. You just wonder whether such shenanigans are a mere coincidence or not, especially if you know each other or you know that the other person has been busy following you quietly, hoping that you do not notice their machinations. But such is life. We cannot change people. So, we just sit back and watch where someone does not want to give credit where it is due. Only time will tell.

On the bright side of life though, as we turn to progressives who have no issue in acknowledging the inspiration that they have drawn from others, one young brilliant Zambian professional shared with me on social media a picture of his birthday cake. The cake was ordered for him by his wife. She knew that her loving husband had been following my scholarly works very closely. Although I have not met the couple, we were connected virtually on social media. To put a smile on her man's face

on his birthday, the gracious wife asked the company that was making the birthday cake to custom-make it with a picture of the front-cover of one of my books, as the final 'icing on the cake'. And this is the picture that you see below. Such honor simply melts your heart with gratitude to the young and loving couple.

Below are two excerpts from a media article that appeared recently in one of the leading newspapers in Botswana. The gentleman in the picture below, Prof Goemeone Mogomotsi, one of the leading legal scholars in Botswana, was one of my graduate law students at the University of Western Cape in Cape Town, South Africa. He shares in the opening paragraph the inspiration that he has drawn from my scholarly journey. When this media article came out, a nephew of mine based in Botswana proudly sent me the excerpts.

Sometimes we do not realize how much our ideas and works inspire others to excel to greater heights professionally. A few years ago, a young African lawyer walked into my office in Washington DC and introduced herself. She then said: "So, finally, I have met you. Sir, you are one of the reasons why I came to work for the World Bank. When I was at Harvard Law School, we used a number of your scholarly works on securities regulation and capital markets in emerging economies."

Today, I look back at how it all started more than thirty years ago when I arrived at Oxford as a young Rhodes Scholar. One of my professors there had a whole bookshelf filled with books he had written. Indeed, here was a man whose ideas occupied a whole bookshelf. It was quite intimidating yet inspiring. Today, some of the books that I have written rest on a shelf of their own (see the picture below). My many other books as well as several dozens of my scholarly articles published in leading academic journals worldwide are not even on this shelf. Like the young Harvard educated African lawyer, I too was inspired by someone from Oxford.

A fuller representation of the scholarly works appearing above is captured in the picture below.

Indeed, ideas, not money, are what separates men from boys and ladies from girls. Boys and girls, as noted earlier, can play around with money, but won't be found anywhere close to great ideas. Such ideas are for noble men and women.

Many professors in full-time academia enjoy the privilege of having research assistants to assist them with scholarly writing, especially in regard to data collection and analysis as well as in preparing preliminary drafts of some of their scholarly work. Many other professors receive research grants from the universities where they teach as well as from outside sources to support their academic writing. I have not benefitted from either. Much of my scholarly writing has been carried out almost exclusively by myself, with no research assistants. Also, I have had to use my own financial resources where necessary to support my writing, as I am no longer in full-time academia where one can easily access research grants. So, for the most part, my scholarly work has not benefited from any kind of help such as research assistantships, research grants or subsidies provided by of some organization or institution. I have had to work extra hard all by myself, producing top-notch quality scholarly work of the highest international academic standard.

I left full-time academia in 1998 to join the World Bank. At the age of only 26 years, I was an Assistant Professor of Law at one of the top ten British universities, the University of Warwick. Previously, I had taught at the University of Zambia (UNZA) from 1991 to 1992 before I won a Rhodes Scholarship to proceed to the University of Oxford in England. I started teaching at UNZA when I was only 22 years old, and I joined the World Bank when I was 29 years old. I have since continued to hold several prestigious secondary appointments as a law professor in academia while working for the World Bank. In essence, I have been on my own in much of my writing, as an established scholar, and have not had the privilege of getting institutional support in the form of research grants or research assistants as full-time academics do. If anything, I have had to work twice as hard, or even more, while holding a full-time job outside academia, than a number of my colleagues who are in full-time academia and are paid to write and teach. Despite these limitations, I have excelled and received several prestigious scholarly awards in recognition of my outstanding scholarly work. This is by no means an easy feat. Like the parable of a prodigal son in the Bible, I found myself returning to where it all started from, that is, it started in academia in 1991, to collect some of the most coveted scholarly awards and honors. It is not easy as an outsider to excel at the frontiers of thought leadership where many an insider dare not go or can only dream of. And the story does not end there. As stated above, I also continue to hold coveted secondary academic appointments at various leading universities worldwide.

When I obtained my PhD more than two decades ago, I never felt I had achieved all there is to achieve in school. Put simply, I never felt as if I had arrived. Something kept telling me, 'You can do better.' It is that urge to keep improving myself that has taken me to greater heights in global thought leadership. The first half of my PhD thesis was written at the University of Oxford in 1993/94, as a graduate (now MPhil) thesis for the then two-year Oxford BCL degree, while the other half was written at the University of Warwick where I was at the time serving as a full-time Assistant Professor of Law. I read the doctoral regulations at the University of Warwick and noticed that the said regulations, like parallel regulations at many other universities, allowed for the development of a Masters degree thesis into a PhD thesis, provided that the candidate: (i) identifies clearly which part of the thesis has been submitted and examined previously for a Masters degree while the candidate continues to develop that very part and integrating it masterfully into the overall framework of the PhD thesis; and (ii) ensures that the overall PhD thesis makes a substantial contribution of doctoral standing. So I went for it. I realized that there was no point in writing my PhD thesis on a new topic altogether when the regulations allowed me to develop my Masters degree thesis into a PhD thesis. So, I picked it up from there and expanded my Oxford BCL thesis into my Warwick PhD thesis by adding some critical regional and global perspectives that went beyond the national perspective covered in the Oxford Masters degree thesis. As an Assistant Professor of Law at Warwick, I did not have to pay any tuition fees for my PhD studies, except for minor examination fees. Also, the doctoral regulations only allowed me, as a member of the academic staff, to have an advisor, not a supervisor. Typically, if you are already a faculty member and would like to pursue a PhD program, you are only given an advisor, since you are assumed to be peers with other faculty members. Only PhD students who are not faculty members at, say, Assistant Professor level and upwards get a PhD supervisor. And these students include Graduate Teaching Assistants (GTAs) and research assistants. Although an advisor, like a supervisor, is a faculty member, the difference is that the advisor is your faculty-peer and will thus not supervise the writing of your doctoral dissertation or thesis. By contrast, a supervisor will supervise the writing of PhD thesis.

As a full-time faculty member at the University of Warwick Faculty of Law, I worked mainly independently on my PhD thesis, receiving only minimal guidance from an advisor. The advisor would simply provide limited guidance, since he or she is your faculty-peer. For the most part, you were expected to be on your own since you are a faculty member and thus cannot be supervised by a fellow faculty member.

I started working on my PhD thesis around August 1996. By the end of 1997, the first draft was ready and had already been accepted for publication into a book. I continued to work on it, finalizing it in the summer of 1998 as a different version from the book. At the time, I was preparing to join the World Bank. Word this World Bank offer had gone around at Warwick. Initially, my plan was to proceed to Yale University Law School in New Haven, Connecticut, US, where I had been offered a fully-funded prestigious graduate fellowship, but I had to decline the prestigious and coveted Yale Law School offer after I got a second offer from the World Bank to join that leading international development institution on its highly prestigious Young Professionals Program (YPP).

It was not an easy decision to make, but the fact that I had already secured both the 'Oxford' and 'Rhodes Scholar' brands on my résumé or CV made things easier. I was not going to lose much by declining the Yale Law School offer. After all, I reasoned, I already had Oxford on my résumé. And besides, the World Bank was undoubtedly the ultimate premier brand in international development. So I reasoned that it would be best for me to go to the World Bank even though Yale Law School remains the best law school in the US, beating even Harvard Law School. Many would ask: who turns down Yale? Yes, I did. I turned down Yale for the World Bank. I proceeded to the World Bank in Washington DC in September of 1998, becoming the first Zambian to join the Bank as a Young Professional on the prestigious YPP.

When I arrived in Washington DC, I found only one Zambian black professional member of staff at the World Bank. The few other black Zambians that I found there were mainly administrative staff. The sole Zambian lady who was on the professional staff was fairly elderly. In a sense, my joining the World Bank helped to demystify the World Bank to many middle-aged Zambian professionals who could only admire the institution from afar. Soon, many Zambian Rhodes Scholars who came after me on the Rhodes Scholarship started following my footsteps by applying to join the World Bank through the YPP. I have often found myself as a pioneer, setting trends for others to follow.

When I got my PhD from the University of Warwick, I had just turned 32 years old. I knew even back then that this was just the beginning of the story. Many PhD graduates celebrate and jump excitedly upon earning their PhD. Some even indulge in a euphoric sense of intellectual invincibility while their friends battle with finishing their PhDs. Others rally with exhaustion to the finish line. For me, I celebrated calmly when my good friends, Dr Zakary Tamainot-Telto and Ms Susan Sitemba, graciously threw me a surprise PhD graduation party in Coventry, England. I knew even back then that my PhD was just the beginning of a long scholarly journey. Ambidexterity has always been a key strategy of my professional life exploits, attending to the present while envisioning the future.

I would like to think that it is a bit risky to ignore the future and focus only on the present, or to neglect the present while living only futuristically. You are best placed to balance the interests of the present with those of the future so that tomorrow you can continue to thrive in a new world. To achieve this calls for some social and emotional intelligence. While emotional intelligence can help us to understand and deal with our emotions, in addition to recognizing and influencing the emotions of others within our environment, social intelligence allows us to understand and deal with interpersonal relationships within the environment. Thus, an effective ambidextrous strategy invites us to continue auditing our internal and external environments while attending to the present and envisioning the future.

I arrived in England from the US on Wednesday, January 10, 2001, to receive my PhD from the University of Warwick. The graduation ceremony was scheduled for Friday, January 12, and was held on the campus of the university. A quick look at various notable university league tables in the UK will tell you that the University of Warwick is one of the few British universities, together with Universities of Oxford and Cambridge, that has been ranked consistently among the top ten universities in the UK. Warwick, like Oxford and Cambridge, is part of the Russell Group of Universities, that is, a group of 24 leading research-intensive universities in the UK. In the US, the transatlantic equivalent of the Russell Group of Universities is the Ivy League. So, I was excited to be back in England, a place that I had become so accustomed to as my second home before I moved to the US. My Warwick PhD graduation had been delayed by some human and administrative hurdles. As Voltaire once said: "Lord, protect me from my friends; I can take care of my enemies."

Since I was a faculty member at Warwick, I had to have two external examiners, with no internal examiner. I had proposed the name of one of the two external examiners to the university for appointment. The other was a former faculty member at Warwick who had since moved to another university in the UK. Little did I know that there would be some political undercurrents, or rather what I would call a 'festivity of academic egos', from some key stakeholders. Luckily, it all turned out to be a storm in a teacup. I managed to pass my PhD exam and graduate.

Ten years later, at the age of only 39, I was receiving my first Higher Doctorate. Allow me to highlight a few points here. First, it is extremely rare to receive a Higher Doctorate at such a young age. Secondly, I know of no other person who has been awarded an earned Higher Doctorate at that age or below. Thirdly, even among the most senior scholars in full-time academia, a higher doctorate is rare. Fourth, I was coming from outside full-time academia to claim an award that even those who are in full-time academia rarely make an attempt at. Put simply, it was like beating military snipers at a shooting range when you are no longer in full-time military service. If you understand this analogy, you can appreciate the magnitude of my scholarly enterprise and endeavor. Fifth, I know of no other person outside full-time academia who has been awarded an earned Higher Doctorate. The reason for this is simple. If you are not in full-time academia, you are likely to be distracted with other professional work and life engagements such that you hardly get the time to publish any serious scholarly work. Indeed, it is not easy to find time between a full-time job outside academia and writing scholarly work and excelling even where those in full-time academia rarely go. That has been my journey, stepping into academia and going where even the brave dare to go. I have provided below a taxonomy of doctorates in higher education in Commonwealth countries. Canada, however, though a Commonwealth country, does not have the concept of a Higher Doctorate. The highest doctorate in Canada, like in the US, is a PhD or its equivalent.

> A TAXONOMY OF DOCTORATES IN HIGHER EDUCATION, RANKED IN ORDER OF SENIORITY
> 1. The Holy Grail: the rarely awarded High Doctorate
> 2. PhD/DPhil: (a) PhD by thesis (monograph or 3 long essays); (b) PhD by coursework and a one to two years dissertation; (c) Phd by published work (usually a published monograph or 3 journal articles on related topic
> 3. Professional doctorates such as a DBA
> 4. Other professional doctorates: JD, MD, DDentistry

A few South African universities, such as the University of Cape Town (UCT), Rhodes University and the University of Witwatersrand (Wits), do have provision for a Senior or Higher Doctorate. By contrast, some continental European countries have what appears to be a watered down or lighter version of a Higher Doctorate that is taken immediately, or a year or two, after completing a PhD. In a number of these countries, that lighter version of the Higher Doctorate is known as 'Habilitation' or 'Docent'.

Sixth, it was the first time ever in the rich history of one of South Africa's oldest and most prestigious universities, Rhodes University, that a Higher Doctorate in Law was being conferred when I was received the esteemed Higher Doctorate degree of Doctor of Laws (LLD) from the said university. A Higher Doctorate, it must be emphasized, ranks significantly higher than a PhD and is only awarded in rare and exceptional cases of distinguished scholarly contributions carried out by a senior scholar who is recognized as an international authority in a field of research that forms the basis of that degree. The concept of an earned Higher Doctorate that is significantly higher than a PhD is one that is rare in the United States and Canada, but more established in the UK, Ireland and other Commonwealth countries. Higher Doctorates, it should be stressed, are very rarely awarded. They are reserved for those senior scholars that have made exceedingly significant contributions to a science or body of knowledge through exceptionally insightful and distinctive scholarly publications, earning them recognition as international authorities in the field of research that forms the basis of the degree.

When I submitted my application for the Higher Doctorate at Rhodes University, the first step was for the Faculty of Law to carry out an internal scrutiny of my published scholarly work to determine if that body work was fit enough to proceed to examination for a Higher Doctorate. The university made it clear that I should submit only those scholarly publications for which I was the sole author, not co-authored works or other works that appear, say, as a compendium of cases, statutes and materials or edited volumes of chapter contributions from different authors.

FIRST TIER
(i) Sole authored monograph published by leading academic press, and (ii) Sole authored peer-reviewed articles in top-rated academic journal

SECOND TIER
(i) Co-authored monographs published by leading academic press; and (ii) Co-authored journal articles in top-rated academic journals

THIRD TIER
(i) Edited books comprising chapters by various contributors; (ii) Compendiums or compilations of cases and statutes; (iii) The publication into a book of academic conference proceedings; (iv) Articles published in lowly regarded academic journals as well as basic introductory textbooks; and (v) Working paper series

PUBLICATIONS WHICH DON'T MATTER IN ACADEMIA
(i) Newspaper and magazine articles; (ii) Blogs; (iii) Consultancy reports; (iv) Proceedings of non-academic conferences; (v) Social media posts; and (vi) Television and other media appearances

The Onion Layer theory of academic publications

Many universities, knowingly or unknowingly, are influenced by taxonomies that are closely aligned with, or structured alongside, what is captured in the figure above, regarding the recognition of faculty scholarly publications. I call the taxonomy highlighted above the 'onion layer theory'. There could be some variations of emphasis in the taxonomy between different disciplines, but the underlying thrust is that of peer-reviewed scientific scholarship. The dry outer layer or shell of the 'onion' can be equated to a newspaper article or a blog that is not peer-reviewed. Such writings are often not taken seriously by scholars and receive less recognition. As you peel through the onion layers, you begin to get to the finer fresher layers, which get better and better as you peel on. You start to move from newspaper articles, social media posts and blogs to published or unpublished conference proceedings, as well as edited volumes of chapter contributions written by various authors and compendiums of statutes and judicial decisions. From there, the recognition begins to deepen and increase as you move to the heart of the onion, where you now find peer-reviewed monographs and textbooks published by leading academic publishers, as well as scholarly journal articles appearing in top-rated peer-reviewed journals. Some faculties or universities distinguish scholarly publications written by a single author from those that appear as co-authored works, especially where several authors crowd 'suspiciously' on one journal article. The reason for this distinction is that where you have several co-authors crowding on one journal article, it is not easy to determine the extent of the contribution made by each one. Indeed, co-authorship often invites the 'free-rider problem' of some individuals taking more scholarly credit than they deserve, because they did not put in much work or effort.

In short, the concept of the Higher Doctorate is for you to furnish appropriate scholarly evidence that you are an international authority and that the body of published scholarly work you have submitted for examination comprises your own scholarly ideas, as opposed to hiding behind other people's ideas in co-authored works, compendiums, edited book volumes, or cases and materials type of books. The preliminary assessment of my published scholarly work by the Faculty of Law at Rhodes University was thus successful, and a panel of three eminent senior professors was constituted to examine the said body of work. The three examiners were senior professors drawn from Germany, the UK and South Africa. I waited patiently, with anxiety, for months to hear back from the university on the outcome of the examination process. Then the news eventually came. All the three examiners had unanimously approved my work, with high praise and strong commendation. The decision was unanimous, with no referrals for corrections, further review or adjustments. I had been accepted for the award of Rhodes University's first ever Higher Doctorate degree of Doctor of Laws. I received the Higher Doctorate degree from Rhodes University on March 28, 2008. It was the first time ever that a Zambian residing in any part of the entire English-speaking world was being awarded such a prestigious degree. No other Zambian had ever reached this height in any academic discipline. I was writing history both at Rhodes University and in my home country, Zambia. A week later, my wife put out the following congratulatory message in the media back home in Zambia.

Higher Doctorate Awarded to Distinguished Legal Scholar
Professor Kenneth K. Mwenda, PhD, LLD
CONGRATULATIONS

At thirty-nine (39) years only, you have become Zambia's first and only Higher Doctorate Degree holder. Congratulations my dear husband, Professor Kenneth K. Mwenda, PhD, LLD! Yes, you have held many Visiting Full Professorships at various leading universities internationally. And you have been a Rhodes Scholar at the University of Oxford as well as a full-time academic at a top British University, the University of Warwick. Currently serving as Senior Legal Counsel in the Legal Vice-Presidency of the World Bank, Washington DC, you have indeed practiced law at the highest international level. And you have won many international academic awards from top universities such as Yale University Law School in the USA. And, now, you have truly distinguished yourself, earning that highly prized Higher Doctorate Degree – the Doctor of Laws Degree (LLD) from one of Africa's best three universities, the esteemed Rhodes University in South Africa. As author of seventeen (17) scholarly books and over seventy (70) academic journal articles, your unblemished scholarly record clearly speaks for itself.

After careful and critical examination by an international panel of distinguished and eminent senior professors drawn from the United Kingdom, Germany and South Africa, your published scholarly works, particularly those for which you are the sole author, were unanimously adjudged to be of exceptional scholarly brilliance and, thus, constituting authoritative academic work internationally. Arguably, Commonwealth Africa as a whole has no more than five (5) to six (6) individuals with the Higher Doctorate Degree of Doctor of Laws (LLD). And you are one of them. Higher doctorates, as many can attest to, are very rarely awarded and stand at the pinnacle of all academic achievement. These academic awards are NEVER the immediate step after a PhD. We therefore continue to give thanks to the Good Lord for His Kindness.

Your loving wife,

Dr. Judith M Mvula-Mwenda,
BSc, MD, MBA, MPH

Word started spreading around fast in Zambia about my unprecedented academic achievement. Many who had followed my academic career over the years were not surprised. They knew me very well. But the superficial cynics were left with no words. As I grow older, I have come to understand that some people will try to pretend to have been with you or on your side once you make it, yet they were among the naysayers. It is always good not to look at the position taken by an individual, but rather to focus on the interest that drove the individual to that position. This is a scientific approach that we use in negotiation. We don't look at a person's position on a particular matter, but at the interest that led to that position. For example, some people will tell you that they would like to stop by your house or office just to say hello since they are within the vicinity. But not everyone means well. As soon as they show up, you will discover that they have some financial problem or personal crisis going on in their life and that they came to ask for help, not to check on you or just to say hello. Others can pitch up just to show you that they are dressed elegantly that day, as if you are competing in a pageant. Then there are those who will show up just to show you the type of luxury car they are driving. The motive matters.

You will see it even in their demeanor, posturing restlessly and pacing around, especially if you do not comment or appear moved by their shenanigans. Not everyone means well. You can see that someone is trying so hard to make a statement. That is why it is not uncommon if, say, you have gone out for drinks for someone seated nearby or at the same table as you are to bring out his or her car keys and place them on the table right next to his or her smartphone so that you see from the car keys or key tag the type of car he or she is driving. And the smartphone is there too, not in the pocket or bag, for you to see the type of latest and expensive smartphone he or she uses. Such is life.

Others will invite you to their mansion, not because they are just being nice, but because they want you to see how well they are living, just in case you have not heard. And they will not hesitate to show you around the house while dishing out unsolicited details, with a lot of embellishments, regarding the Western country or countries from which they imported the building materials. Some will even add exaggerated details of how much it cost them, while stressing that the prices were nothing to them and that they have already paid off everything and don't owe anyone any money. People can be funny.

In life, I have come to realize that some people can be competing with you without you knowing it. That is why, for example, if the institutions and good offices that have honored you deservedly with all the distinguished awards you have earned over the years were to ask some of your so-called 'friends' to nominate you for any of those awards, your name would probably not even reach the draft shortlist of nominated candidates. We thank God Jehovah Almighty for keeping such 'friends' far from the table of honor that He Himself has prepared for us. 'He is not the only one', but they will not find any equal or parallel equivalent, except some inferior imitations. Others could try to say that it was just another PhD that he received, just to dim the thunder and water down the Higher Doctorate buzz. For a good number of our people, major intellectual milestones are often associated mainly with white people, not a fellow black person. It is a colonial mindset that continues to persist even to this day. I'd guess it is not a common thing for many of our people in the part of Africa where I come from to hear about one of their own breaking international or world records, especially when it comes to academic records. Many folks are accustomed to, I would imagine, clapping for people from other races or cheering foreigners. Maybe if it was one of the white students that I have taught in the various European, North American or South African universities where I have taught receiving such an esteemed award some of my fellow black people would have believed it easily simply because the person was white. We do not often believe in ourselves and in our own.

On Wednesday, September 20, 2023, *BBC News*, in an online article titled, "Half-million-year-old wooden structure unearthed in Zambia," reported:

"The discovery of ancient wooden logs in the banks of a river in Zambia has changed archaeologists' understanding of ancient human life. Researchers found evidence the wood had been used to build a structure almost half a million years ago. The findings, published in the journal *Nature*, suggest stone-age people built what may have been shelters. 'This find has changed how I think about our early ancestors,' archaeologist Prof Larry Barham said."

This archeological finding in Zambia, as reported by *BBC News*, was awash on many social media platforms, with a large section of the Zambian public clearly elated at that finding. In many parts of Africa, we are somewhat accustomed to waiting for outsiders to come and tell us about our own treasures. Then we begin to clap at their finding in awe. And that is how in 1855 the Scottish missionary, Dr David Livingstone, allegedly 'discovered' the Victoria Falls in Zambia before I could even 'discover' Loch Coruisk in the Isle of Skye in Scotland, Dr Livingstone's native homeland. He beat me to it. Surely, where were the Zambian researchers and archeologists while outsiders were making the 'ancient wooden logs' discovery in Zambia? One could argue that Zambia has no archeologists. But then, aren't there archeologists in the neighboring country of Zimbabwe? The Faculty of Arts and Humanities at the University of Zimbabwe does have a reputable degree program in archeology. Zimbabwean archeologists could have helped Zambians excavate those archeological sites instead of Zambians waiting for Europeans to make the discovery for them almost sixty years after gaining independence. I bet you understand now where I am coming from.

Let us take another example for more reasoned insights. In Zambia, it is not uncommon to see opposition political leaders running to embassies of Western States in Lusaka to report a sitting Zambian Government for mistreating them. You would think you were watching small kids in kindergarten competing to report each other to the teacher. Why don't our opposition political leaders run to report a sitting Zambian Government to embassies of fellow African States? Have you ever heard of a Zambian opposition political leader running to the Embassy of Angola, Embassy of Mozambique, Embassy of Algeria, Embassy of Burundi, High Commission of Malawi, Embassy of Democratic Republic of the Congo, High Commission of Botswana, Embassy of Egypt, Embassy of Libya, Embassy of Namibia, High Commission of Nigeria, High Commission of Tanzania, or High Commission of South Africa to report a sitting Zambian Government? Why are our opposition political leaders always running to the Europeans, Americans or Chinese? Why not even try embassies of other regions such as the Caribbean islands or South America? Why just focus on the attention of European, American or Chinese people? Is it because of money? Is it because the Europeans, Americans or Chinese are the ones with money, and you believe that it is best to cut the supply of donor funds to your own Zambian government by reporting the government to wealthy donor nations?

Put simply, you would rather have the supply of donor funds to your own country get cut in order to squeeze the ruling party out of power even if it means the general populace in the nation suffering. Or is it that you believe that nothing good can come out of Africa and you would rather look to people from outside Africa for a solution? Colonialism surely left a big dent on the psyche of many an African. When did you ever hear of an opposition party in the UK, Germany, France, the US or the Nordic countries run to an African embassy in London, Berlin, Paris, Washington DC, Copenhagen, Stockholm, or Oslo to report their own government? Your friends in the Global North believe in themselves, whilst some folks in the Global South doubt themselves and don't even believe in their own.

So, I was not surprised that the news about my receiving a Higher Doctorate shocked a number of people back home in Zambia, including some of my former academic colleagues at the University of Zambia (UNZA) where I started my academic career in 1991. The problem with some people is that if they taught you, say, at undergrad, or were your seniors, they often struggle to accept the fact that you have now surpassed them in terms of international scholarly repute and standing as well as in terms of intellectual gravitas as a global scholar. Much to their chagrin, they remain stuck parochially in the past, struggling to accept that the status quo has changed. They can't fathom the idea that one of their own boys has now excelled to such unparalleled scholarly heights. But the Bible, in *Psalm 110:1*, is instructive and provides as follows:

"A Psalm of David. The LORD says to my lord: 'Sit at my right hand until I make your enemies a footstool for your feet.'"

More recently, in an article titled, "A prophet is not without honour except in his own kingdom: Oxford University honours Prof Mwenda," published in *The Mast* on Monday, July 3, 2023, my good learned brother and fellow esteemed legal scholar, Dr Munyonzwe Hamalengwa, the Dean of the Law School at Zambian Open University, addressed the issue of many sections of the Zambian public being slow to 'honor their own prophets'. Dr Hamalengwa submitted as follows:

"On Wednesday June 28, 2023, there was a full-page article in the *Daily Nation* reporting about the top award Oxford University just recently awarded to…Professor Kenneth Kaoma Mwenda. Oxford University's Exeter College, Mwenda's Alma Mater made him a fellow of that college. Being made a fellow of a University college in an old and prestigious university like Oxford or Cambridge and so on is a big deal in England and everywhere else. It is equivalent but at a bigger scale than an alma mater like University of Zambia giving its alumnus, Kenneth Mwenda, an Honorary Doctorate in Law, which it has not done."

Dr Hamalengwa observed further: "The honour or dishonour of not honouring its own extends beyond the University of Zambia, to all Zambian universities without fail. Name any Zambian university that has honoured its alumnus with an Honorary Doctorate. It has taken foreign universities to honour prominent Zambian academics like Mwenda… Zambia is literarily living up to the famous biblical truth that a prophet is not without honour except in his homeland. Yet our universities, including the leading and oldest university, UNZA, have seen fit to honour some fit and unfit political leaders with Honorary Doctorates."

Dr Hamalengwa's submissions are on firm ground. His arguments are valid. For some reason, many Zambian universities, including the nation's leading university, UNZA, rarely confer honorary doctorates on any of their exceptionally outstanding alumni. Why? Your guess is as good as mine. Let us take the case of UNZA, for example. Arguably, the first two alumni of UNZA to be awarded honorary doctorates in any field were two sitting Heads of State, namely, President Edgar Chagwa Lungu, as sitting President of Zambia, and Zimbabwe's head of state, President Emmerson Dambudzo Mnangagwa. President Lungu graduated from UNZA Law School in 1981 while President Mnangagwa graduated from the same law school in 1976. Both individuals were conferred upon by UNZA the honorary doctoral degree of Doctor of Law *Honoris Causa* (LLD (Hon)) on June 21, 2019. Then, on August 15, 2024, an Honorary Doctorate of Business Administration degree (Hon. DBA) was conferred by UNZA on the seventh president of Zambia, President Hakainde Hichilema, who succeeded the sixth president, President Edgar Lungu. It remains unclear, however, why UNZA decided to award President Hakainde an honorary degree titled after a professional doctorate, in contrast to one titled after a Higher Doctorate. If anything, an honorary doctorate titled after a PhD would have been closer to one titled after a Higher Doctorate since a PhD is an academic doctorate while a DBA is a professional doctorate. Generally, in many universities worldwide, honorary doctorates are often titled after Higher Doctorates akin to the doctoral awards that UNZA bestowed on Presidents Edgar Lungu and Emmerson Mnangagwa.

All in all, few other individuals have been conferred upon an honorary doctorate by UNZA, and these few individuals have often not been UNZA alumni. The majority are, in fact, non-Zambians. Why? Again, your guess is as good as mine. Apart from Presidents Lungu and Hichilema, the additional names of Zambians who have also received honorary doctorates from UNZA include the following:

(a) 1974 – Zambia's first and founding President, President Kenneth D Kaunda;
(b) 1984 – Zambia's former Speaker of the National Assembly, Mr Robinson Nabulyato; and
(c) 1984 – UNZA's former Vice-Chancellor and Zambia's former Minister of Foreign Affairs, Prof Lameck Goma.

Other recipients of UNZA's honorary doctoral awards have been non-indigenous Zambians and non-alumni of UNZA, and these include Professor Elizabeth Colson, who taught at UNZA and received her honorary doctorate from UNZA in 1992, Professor Doug Anglin, who was the first Vice-Chancellor of UNZA from 1965 to 1969 and received his honorary doctorate from UNZA in 2011, and President Jacob Zuma, who, as sitting President of South Africa, received his honorary doctorate from UNZA in December 2009. To validate Dr Hamalengwa's submission above where he states: 'Name any Zambian university that has honoured its alumnus with an Honorary Doctorate. It has taken foreign universities to honour prominent Zambian academics like Mwenda', the University of Cape Town (UCT) in South Africa, in an online article titled, 'Honorary doctorate for Kelly Chibale in Switzerland', dated November 28, 2023, regarding the award of an honorary doctorate on one of its distinguished Zambian professors who is also a graduate of UNZA, explained as follows:

"Leading University of Cape Town (UCT) scholar and scientist Professor Kelly Chibale has been awarded an honorary doctorate from the Faculty of Science at the University of Basel, Switzerland – a world-leading research university – and one of the oldest in Europe...The University of Basel is the oldest university in Switzerland; its goal is to remain one of the best research universities worldwide and to make important contributions to research and social development through scientific knowledge and innovation."

I'd bet UNZA did not see any need to recognize Prof Chibale with an honorary doctorate, notwithstanding everything that he has achieved internationally as a leading authority in his area of specialization. Suffice it to say, the UCT media update reads further:

"*Exceptional and inspiring*'... Chibale is a South African National Research Foundation A-rated scholar and holds the Neville Isdell Chair in African-centric Drug Discovery and Development at UCT... At the Dies Academicus of the University of Basel, the faculties award honorary doctorates to outstanding personalities in science or society. I am delighted to inform you that the Faculty of Science has decided to award you with this year's honorary doctorate. It is to honour your exceptional and inspiring curriculum vitae, your outstanding academic achievements... Professor Kelly Chibale [is] one of the most influential scientists in the research and development of new drugs for malaria, tuberculosis and understudied tropical diseases."

On January 24, 2012, the *Cornell Chronicle*, a publication of Cornell University in the US, in an online article titled, 'Law School's Ndulo named distinguished Africanist', published the following:

"Muna B. Ndulo, professor of law at Cornell Law School and director of Cornell's Institute for

African Development, will receive the New York Africana Studies Association (NYASA)'s 2012 Distinguished Africanist Award for his scholarly achievements and contributions to Africana studies. Ndulo will receive the award at NYASA's 37th annual conference, Feb. 24-25, at Penn State University. Previous recipients of the award include Chinua Achebe, Joseph E. Harris, Mamood Mandani, Molefi Kete Asante and Ali A. Mazrui."

Again, can we argue that UNZA did not see any need to recognize Prof Muna Ndulo, a distinguished alumnus of UNZA, with an honorary doctorate, given everything that he has achieved internationally as a leading authority in his area of specialization? When are we going to learn to respect, and give formal recognition to, our own heroes? When I received my earned (*not* honorary) Higher Doctorate degree from Rhodes University, that is, on March 28, 2008, Zambia's leading university, UNZA, had by then not even awarded a single Higher Doctorate in any academic field. Yet, UNZA was established forty-three years prior to my receiving the Rhodes University Higher Doctorate. UNZA was set up, on November 12, 1965, by an Act of Parliament (No. 66 of 1965). Since its establishment in 1965, UNZA has not conferred a Higher Doctorate degree on any of its distinguished alumni in any academic field or discipline.

UNZA officially opened its doors to the public on July 12, 1966. However, it was not until late 2021 that UNZA awarded its first ever Higher Doctorate, conferred posthumously on the late Professor Michael J. Kelly, who was also a Jesuit priest of Irish origin. Professor Kelly, an accomplished scholar of international repute, died in January of that same year (2021) at the age of 92. Does it have to take a man to die before UNZA can recognize his outstanding scholarly contributions? Professor Kelly joined UNZA's School of Education in the Department of Administration and Policy Studies as a senior lecturer in 1974. He then rose through the academic ranks to become Full Professor. Professor Kelly, who, however, was not an alumnus of UNZA, joined as Deputy Vice-Chancellor of UNZA between 1979 and 1983. Other than that, no other person, living or dead, has ever been awarded an earned Higher Doctorate by UNZA.

So, when I made history in 2008 by becoming the first Zambian scholar to receive a Higher Doctorate in any academic discipline, that is, even before Zambia's premier university, UNZA, had awarded its first ever Higher Doctorate, the then Bank of Zambia Governor, Dr Caleb M Fundanga, and his dear wife, Mrs Rosario Fundanga, were gracious enough to sponsor and host a major celebratory event to recognize my exceptional and outstanding scholarly achievements. It was a fabulous and momentous occasion, with five-star hotel outside catering befitting the intellectual gravitas of the Higher Doctorate degree that I had received from Rhodes University. I learned something from this experience. This was the first time ever in the history of Zambia that a scholar was being celebrated at such a high level and in the presence of many other distinguished scholars and academicians. For that, I remain eternally grateful to the Fundangas.

Dr Fundanga and his dear wife have been like family to my family and me. Whenever they visited Washington DC, we would spend some family time together. Whenever we visit Zambia, our visit would be incomplete if we did not spend some quality family time with the Fundangas. That is how valuable and deep our family ties go. And I value that friendship highly. A devoted Catholic, Mrs Fundanga was like a mother to my family and me. There was never a vacation that my family and I made to Zambia that the Fundangas were not there for us, treating us to great hospitality, lovely meals and edifying camaraderie.

Dr Fundanga, a man for whom I have so much respect, not only taught me at UNZA in my first year of undergraduate studies but has also been a great mentor and supporter of my professional work and career. When I visited Abidjan, Cote d'Ivoire, from Washington DC in the early 2000s, Dr Fundanga was then serving as an Executive Director at the African Development Bank (AfDB). I had been invited to Abidjan by AfDB to interview for the position of Chief Counsel for Good Governance. I stayed at a hotel not too far from the AfDB headquarters. After the interviews, as I was preparing to fly back to Washington DC, Dr Fundanga invited me to stay on a few days at his residence. The Fundangas hosted me for the remaining days of my stay in Abidjan. I cannot thank them enough. They have been more than family to me. A man who opens the doors of his home to you deserves nothing but respect.

As family, we have shared so much with the Fundangas over the years. When I lost my mother in March 2019, Dr Fundanga drove all the way from Lusaka, the capital city of Zambia, to Luanshya town on the Copperbelt to attend her funeral. I was so touched. It was an extremely humbling gesture. When I received news of my mother's passing, I rushed quickly from my base in the US to Zambia, without informing many close friends. As you might know, when you are faced with such devastating news it is hard to think straight. All you want to do is get on that plane quickly, so I hurriedly posted a message on my social media page and took off for Zambia. Dr Fundanga saw the message and did not wait to hear from me directly. He got his driver ready, and they started off for the Copperbelt to join me in mourning my mother. In my native language, Bemba, we say: "Ukwangala kwa chila ulupwa" ("A good friend is better than your own relative"). Truthfully, not all blood is thicker than water. Indeed, water can at times be thicker than blood.

At the 2009 event hosted in my honor by the Fundangas in Lusaka, shortly after I received my first Higher Doctorate from Rhodes University in South Africa, the Guest of Honor was the then Chief Justice of the Supreme Court for the Republic of Zambia, Hon Mr Chief Justice Ernest Sakala. Also in attendance at that event was the Deputy Chief Justice, Hon Ms Justice Lombe Chibesakunda, as well as the Deputy Governor of Bank of Zambia, Dr Denny Kalyalya, the then Vice-Chancellor of UNZA, Professor Robert N Serpell, the Secretary of the Rhodes Scholarship Selection Committee for Zambia, Professor Oliver S. Saasa, and many other important dignitaries, including some Members of Parliament, former State Counsels, the President of the Law Association of Zambia (LAZ), Mr Stephen Lungu SC, and other members of senior management at the Bank of Zambia.

In the picture above, the longest serving Bank of Zambia Governor, Dr Caleb M. Fundanga, and his dearest wife, Mrs Rosario Fundanga, can be seen presenting me with a national award of meritorious achievement. May God continue to bless them.

In the picture below, the Guest of Honor, the then Chief Justice of the Supreme Court for the Republic of Zambia, Hon Mr Chief Justice Ernest Sakala, can be seen officiating when I was being recognized formally for attaining unprecedented scholarly heights. I am ever grateful to him as well.

In the picture below, I was asked to stand as the host, Governor Dr Caleb M. Fundanga, read out my biographical profile and the long list of my scholarly achievements. Seated in the background, and wearing a white Cubavera shirt, is the then Vice-Chancellor of UNZA, Professor Robert Serpell.

Additional pictures from the event follow below. In the group picture appearing immediately hereunder, my mother can be seen seated next to me and wearing a lovely hat. I was happy that she was alive and present to witness this moment. It is very rare that one's scholarly work brings together such distinguished men and women for a celebratory moment. It speaks to how well and highly regarded you stand among your peers. Personally, I have not witnessed or heard anything like this anywhere in Zambia.

This event brought together some notable CEOs and distinguished academics as well as political leaders. It was the first time ever that such an event had been held in Zambia. I had just flown into Zambia after my lecturing engagements at the University of Pretoria in South Africa where I was at the time serving as Extraordinary Professor of Law, concurrent with my position in Washington DC as Senior Counsel in the Legal Vice-Presidency of the World Bank. So from Washington DC, I flew to South Africa first and then proceeded to Zambia after giving lectures in South Africa. My wife and son had remained behind in the USA could thus not join us for the event in Zambia.

Six years after receiving my Higher Doctorate from Rhodes University in South Africa, having produced another substantial body of scholarly work, I submitted the new body of published scholarship for a second Higher Doctorate, the degree of Doctor of Science in Economics (DSc(Econ)), from the University of Hull in the UK. Some of my writing has been quite interdisciplinary, since I am an interdisciplinary scholar with an MBA degree from the said University of Hull.

At the University of Hull, the Business School received and put my application through an initial screening and review for fitness of purpose, as was the case for my first Higher Doctorate at Rhodes University. The idea is to determine if the application merits to proceed to full examination for a Higher Doctorate or not. The outcome of the preliminary assessment was successful, so two senior professors were appointed as examiners of my DSc(Econ) work at Hull. One of the two examiners was a senior professor from within the UK, while the other was a senior professor from a parallel jurisdiction outside the UK. I waited patiently for almost a year. Finally, the examiners' reports were in. I was recommended unanimously by both examiners for the award of the Higher Doctorate degree of DSc(Econ). I was only 44 years old and had managed to bag another Higher Doctorate. I would hasten to add that very few African scholars have ever had a Higher Doctorate confirmed upon them by a leading British university. Arguably, I could be the first African to have received a Higher Doctorate at my alma mater, the University of Hull. Without doubt, the requirements for one to be admitted to a Higher Doctorate are extremely stringent. A Higher Doctorate is never the immediate step after a PhD. It is a very demanding senior doctorate. Many professors simply retire without ever attempting a Higher Doctorate. I was thus quite humbled and honored to receive an inspiring email of commendation from the Vice-Chancellor of the University of Zambia (UNZA), Prof Stephen Simukanga, and the Deputy Vice-Chancellor, Prof Enala Mwase, when UNZA received news of my second Higher Doctorate. A lead article on the website of UNZA, as seen below, was published by UNZA immediately, capturing the said commendation from senior management.

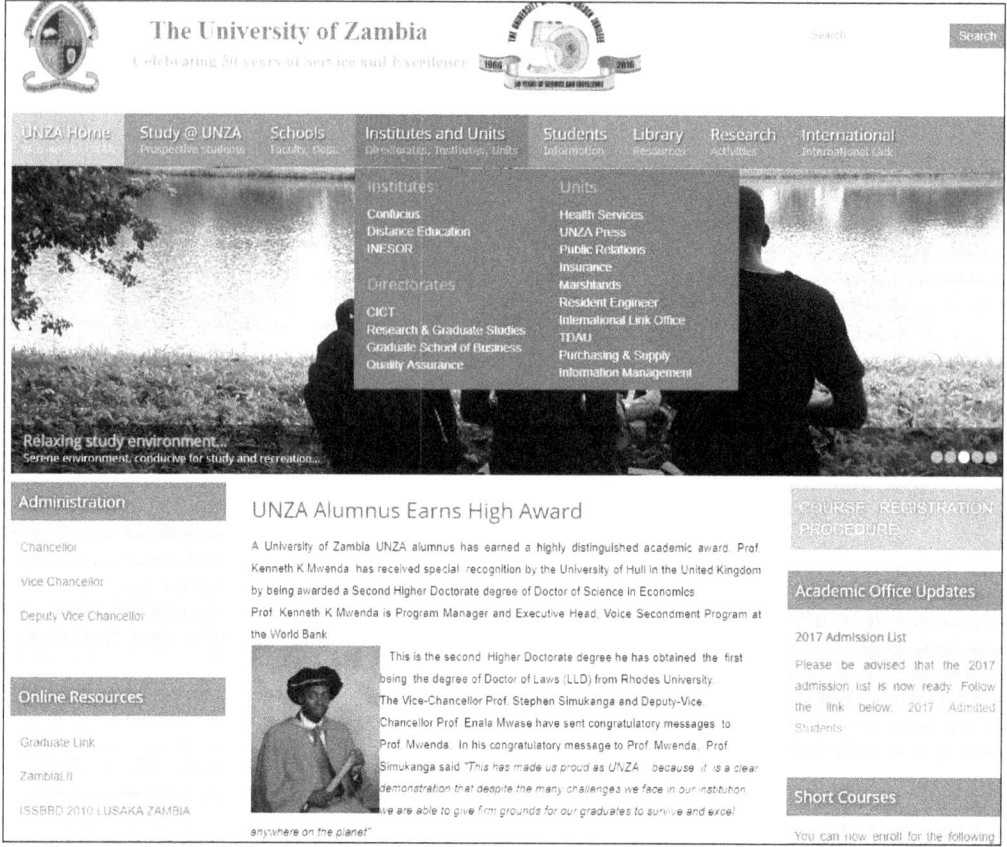

On February 21, 2014, the *Times of Zambia*, a leading State-owned Zambian print and online media publication, carried a lead features article written by Prof Mwizenge Tembo, a Professor of Sociology at Bridgewater College in Bridgewater, Virginia. The article, titled, "What Drives People to Great Achievements?", reads in part as follows:

"The email from Professor Kenneth Mwenda was first surprising as it was later stunning. The email said: 'I am pleased to inform you that I have been awarded a Second Higher Doctorate degree by a leading British university, the University of Hull. This coveted and esteemed academic award came through after the successful examination of another substantial and significant body of my published scholarly contributions by an eminent panel of distinguished professors in the United Kingdom. The decision of the entire board of examiners and assessors was unanimous and without any reservations or referrals.' What was baffling was that Prof Mwenda as he described in his e-mail had already been awarded a first Higher Doctorate (LLD) from Rhodes University in South Africa. Both of these degrees are most superior and different from ordinary PhDs and Honorary Doctoral degrees."

Prof Tembo observes further:

"He describes how he attended Oxford University as a Rhodes Scholar, was to go to the prestigious Yale University Law School in the United States, but was detoured to the World Bank. He mentions that he has taught law to dozens of individuals who later became prominent figures in the legal profession. He thanks God, his family, and friends for all his achievements."

Turning to the question of what drives people to great achievements, Prof Tembo avers:

"What intrigued me about the good news is that I have always been fascinated and have had deep curiosity about people who make great achievements. What drives them to do it? While the rest of us wallow in struggling with every day average no doubt useful achievements, what drives people who do great things reflected in Prof Mwenda's latest achievement? Do people who do great things walk on clouds or the stratosphere way above all of us ordinary people? Prof Mwenda asks similar questions in the email. Does he need so many degrees? He asks: 'Do we all need all those many pairs of shoes or suits in our wardrobes when we can actually do with only one or two pairs of each?' Isn't one degree enough?"

Prof Tembo, drawing on his broad and rich experience as a distinguished scholar, submits:

"In my short human life in which I have done some studying, have read about great people in history, and have been fortunate enough to meet a few of them, I have come to this conclusion: people who make great achievements are driven by a deep force which is inside them. This force drives, compels, and so overwhelms them to pursue with tremendous zeal whatever they set their mind on that they want to achieve and be best at. They breathe, wake up at night, during the day, and that's what they focus on most of the time. They are thinking of many and different ways of achieving whatever it is that dominates and occupies their minds. The people who have great minds perform achievements in any circumstances even when opportunities to do so do not seem to be there. Sometimes the society they are born in or the era, may work very hard to suppress that drive, but it still shows up somehow. People with great minds achieve even in the face of brutal oppression."

No truer words have ever been spoken. Prof Tembo taught at the University of Zambia in the 1980s before joining Bridgewater College in the USA where he served for many years as a Full

Professor of Sociology until he retired a few years ago. He now holds the esteemed position of Emeritus Professor at Bridgewater College. Closely related to Prof Tembo's submission above, Prof Mercy N Mumba, a notable Professor at the University of Alabama in the US and the founding Director of the Centre for Substance Use Research and Related Conditions at the said university, in her October 2023 post on LinkedIn for a fireside chat titled, 'The A to Zs of Becoming a Published Book Author,' referred to me as, "The incomparable Professor Kenneth K Mwenda…" It is humbling to receive such unsolicited accolades and kind words from distinguished and eminently qualified scholars. How your colleagues, peers and fellow published scholars in the academic community view your work matters a lot. Academia is consistently driven by a peer-review philosophy. What are the views of your peers? You cannot fake it. Rather, it is your standing in the eyes of those who are well initiated in the profession that counts most, not the noise or claims that you are making which you would want people to believe. It is indeed wise to let others speak for you. In 2022, *Rhodes Scholar*, a notable publication of Rhodes House at Oxford in England, whose Volume 9 theme was 'Collaboration for Impact', highlighted the following (p.72) among the key contributions of distinguished Rhodes Scholars worldwide during the year 2021/22.

> Kenneth Mwenda (Zambia & Exeter 1992) Professor Kenneth K. Mwenda's latest three books, *Doctoral Degree Programs in Law: An International and Comparative Study of the English-speaking World*, *Contemporary Issues in Public International Law* and *Intellectualism Beyond the University: What They Forgot to Teach You in School* Vols 1-3, were published in 2021. Prof Mwenda attended Exeter College (1992-94) and read for the two-year BCL degree, now the BCL and MPhil in Law degrees. A recipient of the prestigious Presidential Insignia of Meritorious Achievement (PIMA) conferred on him in 2019 by H.E. President Dr Edgar C Lungu, the sixth President of the Republic of Zambia, Prof Mwenda holds a PhD in Law from the University of Warwick as well as two Higher Doctorate degrees in Law and Economics, respectively, from Rhodes University and the University of Hull. He has taught at leading universities in Europe, North America and Africa and continues to serve as the Executive Head of the World's Bank Voice Secondment Program (VSP) in Washington DC.

A quick snapshot of notable scholars from Africa that hold a Higher Doctorate in Law follows below.

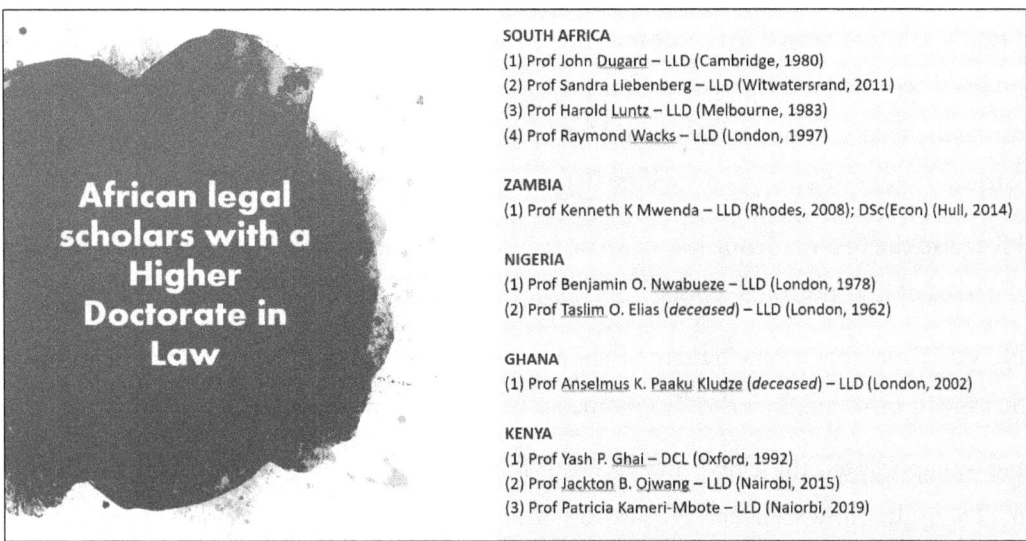

SOUTH AFRICA
(1) Prof John Dugard – LLD (Cambridge, 1980)
(2) Prof Sandra Liebenberg – LLD (Witwatersrand, 2011)
(3) Prof Harold Luntz – LLD (Melbourne, 1983)
(4) Prof Raymond Wacks – LLD (London, 1997)

ZAMBIA
(1) Prof Kenneth K Mwenda – LLD (Rhodes, 2008); DSc(Econ) (Hull, 2014)

NIGERIA
(1) Prof Benjamin O. Nwabueze – LLD (London, 1978)
(2) Prof Taslim O. Elias (*deceased*) – LLD (London, 1962)

GHANA
(1) Prof Anselmus K. Paaku Kludze (*deceased*) – LLD (London, 2002)

KENYA
(1) Prof Yash P. Ghai – DCL (Oxford, 1992)
(2) Prof Jackton B. Ojwang – LLD (Nairobi, 2015)
(3) Prof Patricia Kameri-Mbote – LLD (Naiorbi, 2019)

I was halfway through the writing of this book when news broke that Africa had just lost one of its distinguished intellectual legal luminaries, Higher Doctorate degree holder Prof Benjamin O Nwabueze. On October 30, 2023, the *Punch* newspaper published an online article titled, "Remembering Prof. Ben Nwabueze: 15 things you should know," reporting:

"One of Nigeria's foremost constitutional lawyers and one-time Secretary General of Ohanaeze Ndigbo Worldwide, Professor Ben Nwabueze, is dead. Here are 15 things to know about the legal icon:

1. The Senior Advocate of Nigeria was born in 1931.

2. His academic pursuit started at the CMS Central School Atani, from 1938 – 1945; C.M.S Central School, Onitsha (formerly, African College), 1947 – 1950.

3. He later went to London School of Economics and Political Science, University of London, 1956 – 1961 and School of Oriental and African Studies, University of London, 1961 – 1962.

4. From 1962–1965, he was Senior Lecturer at Holborn College of Law, London, and Senior Lecturer, University of Nigeria Nsukka, between 1967 – 1970. In 1971, he was Dean, Faculty of Law, University of Zambia and Director, Law practice Institute, Zambia, 1973 – 1975

5. Prof. Nwabueze earned his Doctor of Laws (LL.D) at the University of London in 1978, based on his three outstanding books–Constitutionalism, Presidentialism, and Judicialism, thus entering the record books as the second (since the death of Dr. T.O. Elias), the only Nigerian and African holder of a higher doctorate degree in Law by published works.

6. He is also the first academic lawyer to be made a Senior Advocate of Nigeria in 1978 strictly on the basis of his published works.

7. He was a member of the Senate of the Universities of Lagos, Dar es Salaam, Nairobi, Haile Selassie in Ethiopia, Lesotho, Botswana and Swaziland between 1971 – 1978.

8. He was appointed the University Assessor for Academic Appointments, Universities of Ghana, Lagos, Ife (now Obafemi Awolowo University), and Jos between 1978 – 1979.

9. Prof. Nwabueze is the proud author of over thirty books and treatises with an average extent of 400 pages.

10. He has written over 200 articles in academic journals and given more than 100 keynotes at local and international conferences.

11. He was appointed to Professorial Chairs in the following Universities; Zambia, 1970 – 75; Ahmadu Bello university, Zaria, 1974; University of Nigeria, Nsukka, 1975 – 76; Anambra State University of Technology; Nnamdi Azikiwe university, Awka 1989 – 1983 (visiting)

12. Prof. Ben Nwabueze is also a strong advocate for the Igbo cause. He, alongside other prominent Igbo sons like Akanu Ibiam, M.I. Okpara, K.O. Mbadiwe, Chief Ugochukwu, P.N. Okigbo and Udoji, co-founded Ohaneze Ndigbo in 1976.

13. He served as Secretary – General of the Ohaneze Ndigbo between 1978 to 2004, in which capacity he transformed the body into a formidable, highly regarded non-partisan Pan Igbo pressure group.

14. He is a recipient of several chieftaincy titles, and the Nigerian Order of Merit.

15. In 2019, he played a crucial role as a member of the election petitions filed by Atiku Abubakar of the Peoples Democratic Party. These petitions were filed against President Muhammadu Buhari's re-election, adding to the already intense political climate in Nigeria. The team faced defeat in the case."

The passing of Nigeria's Prof Ben Nwabueze in 2023 came a decade after Africa lost another distinguished intellectual legal luminary, Higher Doctorate degree holder Prof Justice Anselmus Kodzo Paaku Kludze of Ghana. As *GhanaWeb* reports, in an online article titled, "Ghana famous people,"

"Anselmus Kodzo Paaku Kludze (1934 – 5 October 2013) was a Ghanaian lawyer, author, and academic who served as a judge for the Supreme Court of Ghana and was also a professor. He was an Emeritus Professor of Law at Rutgers University, Camden, New Jersey, United States, a chairman of the Law Reform Commission of Ghana, a Fellow of the Ghana Academy of Arts and Sciences, and a fellow of the Royal Society of Arts, London…He proceeded to the United Kingdom for further studies in law and was awarded his doctorate degree in 1969. In 2002, he earned a Higher Doctorate degree of LL.D. for his scholarship from the University of London."

On July 21, 2021, one of Zambia's most distinguished and eminent Rhodes Scholar, Mr Chisanga Puta-Chekwe, based in Canada, posted the following commendatory note on his Twitter page:

I am ever grateful to my learned and esteemed elder brother and fellow Oxonian, Mr Chisanga Puta-Chekwe, who is also a Rhodes Scholar and alumnus of Exeter College at Oxford. Much gratitude and respect. Mr Puta-Chekwe is simply an awesome and wonderful human being. The Lawrence National Centre for Policy and Management at the Ivey Business School of Western University in London, Ontario, Canada, provides the following abridged biographical note (Online: 2023) on Mr Puta-Chekwe:

"In 2009 Chisanga Puta-Chekwe became Deputy Minister for Citizenship and Immigration as well as Women's Issues in Ontario. In July 2013 he was also named Deputy Minister for Seniors' Affairs, taking on additional responsibilities as Deputy Minister for international trade as well in 2014. In 1994, he served as adjudication officer and United Nations observer support officer monitoring the South African election, and in 1996 served as election supervisor in Bosnia and Herzegovina. He spent six years with the Ontario Criminal Injuries Compensation Board and was the founding Chair and CEO of the Ontario Rental Housing Tribunal."

In the picture below, I appear with Mr Chisanga Puta-Chekwe and the then Ambassador of Zambia to the USA, Hon. Ambassador Mr Palan Mulonda, at the Zambian Embassy in Washington DC. Ambassador Mulonda, standing in the middle, later went on to serve as a Constitutional Court judge in Zambia.

When I taught at the University of Zambia (UNZA) in 1991 and 1992, Ambassador Mr Justice Palan Mulonda was one of my law students, so it was great to see him appointed as Zambia's Ambassador to the US. Every good teacher takes pride in the success of his or her students. In the picture below, I am with Ambassador Justice Mulonda when he was still serving as Zambia's Ambassador to the US. We were joined by a fellow Rhodes Scholar and Oxonian, Dr. Monde Muyangwa, who later served as the Assistant Administrator in the Bureau for Africa at USAID. Dr Muyangwa and I were together at UNZA and Oxford.

A representative list of some of my former law students who have gone on to occupy prominent positions or offices include: (i) Hon. Chief Justice of the Supreme Court of the Republic of Namibia, Mr. Chief Justice Peter Shivute; (ii) Deputy Vice-Chancellor of the University of Malawi and former Dean of the School of Law at the University of Malawi, Dr Sundu Madise; (iii) Hon. Supreme Court Judge of the Supreme Court of Zambia, the late Mr. Justice Sandson S. Silomba; (iv) Former Minister of Communications for the Republic of South Africa, Hon. Ms. Faith Muthambi; (v) Former Minister of Defense of the Republic of Ghana, Dr. Ben Kunbuor (who also served at some point as Minister of Health and Minister of Interior as well as Attorney-General of that country); (vi) Former Minister of Justice and Attorney-General of the Republic of Gambia, Ms Amie Joof; (vii) Former Minister of Ethics and Integrity for the Republic of Uganda, Dr. Miria Rukoza Koburunga Matembe; (viii) Former Director of the Legal Department of the Common Market for Eastern and Southern Africa (COMESA), Mr. Brian Chigawa; (ix) Former Zambia's Ambassador to the United States of America, Hon. Mr. Justice Palan Mulonda, a judge on the Constitutional Court of Zambia (i.e. the said Constitutional Court ranks at par with the Supreme Court of Zambia); (x) Hon. Mr. Justice Martin Musaluke, a judge on the Constitutional Court of Zambia; (xi) Hon. Ms Justice Maria Mapani-Kawimbe, a judge on the Constitutional Court of Zambia; (xii) Hon. Ms. Justice Mugeni Siwale-Mulenga, a judge on the Constitutional Court of Zambia; (xiii) Hon. Ms Justice Judith Zulu-Mulongoti, a judge on the Constitutional Court of Zambia; (xiv) Several other judges on Zambia's Court of Appeal and High Court benches; (xv) Former First Lady of the Republic of Zambia, Dr. Maureen K. Mwanawasa; (xvi) Former Chief Counsel, Private Sector Operations, African Development Bank Group (AfDB), Ms Sarah M. Ntabazi; (xvii) Director of the Legal Department at the Common Market for Eastern and Southern Africa (COMESA), Mr Gabriel Masuku; (xviii) Former World Bank Country Manager for Zimbabwe, Ms Marjorie Mpundu, now serving as a Chief Counsel in the Legal Vice-Presidency of the World Bank; (ixx) many other prominent lawyers that have served in the Legal Departments of the World Bank, the International Finance Corporation (IFC), the African Development Bank (AfDB), and the Africa Export-Import Bank (Africa EXIM Bank); (xx) Hon. Ms Aisha Ally Sinda, a judge on the High Court of Tanzania; (xxi) Former Chief Executive Officer of Christian Aid (London, UK), and now serving as a United Nations Resident Coordinator in Lesotho, Ms Amanda Khozi Mukwashi; and, (xxii) the Hearing Examiner in the Office of Zoning and Administrative Hearings (OZAH) for the Montgomery County Council in Maryland, US, Ms Khandikile Mvunga-Sokoni; and (xxiii) notable academicians and some deans of leading law schools in Europe and Africa, including Deans of the University of Zambia (UNZA) School of Law and the University of Lusaka (UNILUS) School of Law. Also, I would be amiss if I did not mention Mr Tundu Lissu, a notable opposition leader and former presidential candidate in Tanzania, as well as Mr George Luchiri Wajackoyah, an opposition leader and former presidential candidate in Kenya. Both were my graduate law students at the University of Warwick in England.

In August 2014, when I flew from Washington DC, US, to Manchester, UK, to receive my DSc(Econ) from the University of Hull. I was accompanied by both my wife and son. We connected from Manchester Airport by train to Hull via Leeds. When we got to Hull, we booked in at Royal Hotel Hull. The following day, I went to pick up my graduation gown from the university. Later that day, I got a courtesy visit from my good brother and friend, Mr Robinson K Zulu, who drove in from his UK base in Leeds. A highly successful businessman, Mr Zulu is the Executive Chairman at Meanwood Holdings Limited in Zambia. In the picture below, Mr Zulu appears wearing glasses on the far right. This picture was taken at Pamodzi Hotel in Lusaka, Zambia, when I was launching one of my books on banking regulation. That book launch event was sponsored by Meanwood Holdings Limited and the Bankers Association of Zambia, working in collaboration with the Bank of Zambia (BOZ) and the University of Lusaka (UNILUS). On the far left is Professor Pinalo Chifwanakeni, the Vice-Chancellor of UNILUS. And next to Mr Zulu is Dr Caleb M Fundanga, the then Governor of the Bank of Zambia and the Chancellor of UNILUS. The vote of thanks was given by Hon Mr Justice Michael Musonda, a fellow Oxonian and Rhodes Scholar who currently serves as the Deputy Chief Justice of the Supreme Court for the Republic of Zambia.

Mr Zulu and I were together at undergraduate at the University of Zambia (UNZA) in the 1980s as well as in the UK when we were both pursuing our graduate business degrees. I was extremely humbled and grateful to catch up with him in Hull again when I was there to receive my Higher Doctorate degree. It was particularly humbling that he drove over from Leeds to give me moral support. I know that the long-distance drive from Leeds was probably made lighter by the luxury of the latest Range Rover he was driving. It was indeed good to catch up and exchange some wonderful notes. I am ever grateful to such friends.

The next day was the graduation day. The Hull graduation ceremony was a truly memorable event. I had graduated previously from Hull for my MBA almost twenty years before the Higher Doctorate graduation ceremony, so coming back to Hull after that time invoked some nostalgic sentiments. While based in England in the 1990s, I had moved to Hull after completing my joint Masters degree programs in law as a Rhodes Scholar at Oxford in the summer of 1994. My plan was to augment my corporate law specialization at Oxford with an MBA degree. At the time, there was no business school or MBA program at the University of Oxford. The closest business or management degree at Oxford was a two-year MPhil degree in Management Studies offered by Templeton College. I was however left with only one year funding on the Rhodes Scholarship, so I used the third year of my Rhodes Scholarship to study for an MBA at the University of Hull. I attended from 1994 to 1995. It was good to be back in Hull after such a long time. I had missed Yorkshire.

My wife asked me why my Higher Doctorate graduation gown and hood were different from those worn by the graduands waiting to receive their PhDs. Indeed, my gown had a striking bright red color whereas the gowns of those waiting to receive their PhDs had a maroon color. I simply smiled and jokingly said, "They are receiving Junior Doctorates. I am receiving a Senior Doctorate. That's the difference!"

Indeed, in the olden days in England, the nomenclature associated with the titles of junior doctorates and senior doctorates made a distinction between the two. A PhD was a junior doctorate, whereas a Higher Doctorate was a senior doctorate. And so, when I was receiving my Higher Doctorate from Hull, the 'junior doctors' sat in one corner of the graduation hall while I, as a 'senior doctor', sat in another area. I could tell that many eyes were on me. I was the only one among those receiving earned doctoral degrees who was wearing that gown and receiving a Higher

Doctorate. Many people in the graduation hall kept staring at me and wondered why my graduation attire looked conspicuously different from everyone else's.

After the PhD graduands were presented with their degrees it was time for the only senior doctoral candidate to be presented with his degree. I walked up the stage to receive my Higher Doctorate. All eyes were on me, with many people, including some 'junior doctors', wondering what in the world I was receiving. Given the rarity of Higher Doctoral awards worldwide, not many people had an idea until the citation was read. Even at Rhodes University, when I was receiving my first Higher Doctorate, the gown was different from the PhD gowns. Whereas both types of gowns at Rhodes were red in color, the Higher Doctorate one had long sleeves while the PhD ones had short sleeves.

A few years later, in an online article dated on October 26, 2020, and titled, "Alumnus Prof Kenneth Mwenda awarded Zambia's highest civilian honour," the University of Oxford Faculty of Law had the following statement on its official faculty website, in recognition of my scholarly excellence as an alumnus of Oxford Faculty of Law:

"In 2008 and 2014, respectively, after a rigorous and thorough examination of Prof Mwenda's selected scholarly books and peer-refereed journal articles by two leading universities in South Africa and the United Kingdom, namely, Rhodes University and the University of Hull, Prof Mwenda was admitted to the rarely awarded Higher Doctorate degrees of Doctor of Laws (Rhodes, LLD, 2008) and Doctor of Science in Economics (Hull, DSc(Econ), 2014). He also holds a PhD in Law from another leading British university, the University of Warwick."

As established in Chapter 1, until 2019, there was no other known legal scholar in the entire English-speaking world with Higher Doctorates in two different disciplines. As someone once said: you are either cut out for it or you are not. The picture appearing on the left side of the frame below (i.e. dressed in a red and light blue graduation gown) was taken shortly after I received my DSc(Econ) from the University of Hull in the UK. Then, the picture in the middle was taken shortly after I received my PhD in Law from the University of Warwick in the UK. On the right side of the frame (i.e. dressed in an all-red graduation gown) is a picture taken shortly after I received my LLD from Rhodes University in South Africa.

Kenneth K Mwenda, PhD, LLD, DSc(Econ)
Rhodes Scholar

Having spent almost a decade in England, I did most of my university education there. My Warwick PhD was, essentially, my fourth degree from the UK. I remain ever grateful to my good learned brother Zakary, who is still in academia at the University of Warwick, and my good sister Auntie Sue (Ms Susan Sitemba), who also continues to be based in the United Kingdom, for their hospitality and warm brotherly and sisterly support when I arrived for my PhD graduation at Warwick. The two were my only guests at that graduation ceremony. At the time, I was not married and had no family of my own.

After walking onto the graduation stage to receive my PhD, I remember thinking to myself, 'Is this it? What next now?' Throughout my life, I have never been one to compete with or against anyone. I have always had my own scholarly dreams and ambitions. From adolescence, I knew exactly what I wanted to be. At no point in my life have I ever felt as if I had arrived. Neither do I panic or feel as if others have left me behind. Rather, I work according to my plan and schedule, and my goals are on my own terms.

For me, consistency is key. I have always had the urge to do better and keep improving myself consistently and continuously in whatever I set my mind on. Excellence is about building a culture of continuous improvement. Even when faced with challenges, I look with humility to my strengths and what God has blessed me with, knowing that there are many folks out there wishing that they could have just half of what I have. And my strengths are there to generate opportunities for me. That thought has always kept me afloat. In life, you must have your own game-plan, and not react like a chicken whose head has just been chopped off whenever you see what others are doing. If you keep following the crowd blindly, you will end up lost in the woods. It is important to have your own compass for directions.

Personally, I have followed closely the professional careers of many influencers on the global stage, such as world-class soccer players, internationally acclaimed musicians, worldclass boxing champions, notable basketball players, world record holders in athletics, respectable statesmen and women, global thought leaders and pundits, as well as eminent religious leaders. They all have one thing in common: they never stop working to improve or perfect their art or craft. And they are always trying to do better. So, if I have to outdo myself, so be it. At times, you just have to break your own record if it has to come to that. In 2025, I was honored to make the list of the few distinguished Rhodes Scholars selected mainly on the basis of their global impact and interviewed by the prestigious Oxford-based Rhodes Trust. The recorded biographical interviews for this Oral History project are freely accessible online.

But where does the story of Kenneth Kaoma Mwenda begin? How and when did it all start? In the next chapter, I trace my family roots as far back as I can. Then, in Chapter 4, I will take you back to my early childhood days in Livingstone, Zambia. Chapter 5 provides a transition from Livingstone to the Copperbelt Province of Zambia. I spent much of my middle childhood and adolescence on the Copperbelt before moving to Lusaka for my university studies at the University of Zambia (UNZA). I will take you through that journey and beyond in these and other chapters ahead.

CHAPTER 4

Family roots

Both my father and mother were educationalists. They had both been to school and were well educated. They attained higher education at a time when some of their peers held only a modest primary or secondary school education. Others were simply illiterate, semi-literate or uneducated. Further, both my parents had travelled the world. They had been to the Western world or Global North at a time when most of their peers back home in Africa could only imagine what it felt like to get on a plane. Also, my father and my mother each had their own cars. Yes, both my father and mother would drive at a time when most of their peers were simply pedestrians. So, why am I giving you all this contextual background information? Because the environment in which a child is raised often speaks to how his or her parents can help to shape or influence the child's values and instill discipline and confidence in the child.

In a nutshell, I come from a family of parents who were not only exposed and enlightened but were also committed educators. Hard work, discipline, good character, decency, determination, perseverance, focus, integrity, honesty, and meritocracy were values they imbedded in me from early childhood. And so, I know of no other better or more worthy route for one to succeed in life than through the edifying norms espoused above.

In my father's house, there were bookshelves filled with rich books, not crates and bottles of beer lying around everywhere in the house. My father's house also had a study room dedicated exclusively to reading. That study room housed, inter alia, a rich collection of other scholarly books.

My father, Joseph T Mwenda, or "JT" as he was fondly called, also had smaller bookshelves in other rooms in the house. They hosted, inter alia, rich collections of encyclopedias and other reference books in psychology, literature, education, politics, economics, sociology, public administration, philosophy and so forth. This was at a time prior to the invention or development of the internet. In those days, there was no Google or Yahoo, so encyclopedias, including the other works referred to above, were the main sources of data. These sources often depicted an aura of civility, modernity and intellectual sophistication in a home and were found mainly among the learned and intellectually grounded folks. JT was ahead of his time.

JT, my father and greatest hero, was not only a decent man but an enlightened one. He was a stern disciplinarian, too. Perhaps that is why I was somewhat scared when growing up of marrying early or having a child out of wedlock. I did not want to disappoint him. My father's view, influenced arguably by his strong intellectual and Catholic backgrounds, had always been that you only marry once in life unless you become widowed and then decide to remarry. His other view was that, as a young and single person, before you even entertain the thought of marrying or getting married, you needed to get yourself a good education to provide you with a solid foundation on which to run a home.

JT never drank alcohol or smoked. Also, to discourage me from ever indulging in alcohol and cigarettes, he would often ask me about the benefits of drinking or smoking, if any, even though he knew that I was too young and free of alcohol at the time. Also, I have never smoked in my entire life. The idea was to get me to think ahead of time on the health choices that one makes. In response, I couldn't provide him with any satisfactory answer of benefits in drinking or smoking. Even as I write, I still have not found any benefits in drinking or smoking, though I drink mildly. Maybe the benefit is in the euphoria of calming down the nerves, I don't know. The truth is that I cannot point to any scientifically convincing benefit of alcohol or cigarettes.

During the week, my father would often go to work at 07:30 am. He would be in the office by 08:00 am, and back home around 5:30 . At home, we all knew his schedule. Dad always came home on time from work. I thank God that I did not come from a chaotic home where a father would often go out gallivanting in search of all manner of mischief or morally debased indulgences. In life, some of the seemingly wealthy folks that you see around come from troubled and chaotic homes. You might think they are happy with all that wealth they keep flaunting around. Wait until you get to know them better. You will be shocked by what goes on inside their homes. In the midst of champagne, cigars and caviar, there is misery and pain in some of those homes. Many seemingly rich folks suffer quietly inside while putting up a face and holding out to the rest of the world as if all is well. You might even find, for example, that the father or husband in the home has sired some child or children outside marriage. Also, you could find that the man was found cheating and entangled with someone's wife or was beaten by some young man after being found in a compromising situation with the young man's girlfriend. These things do happen. Yet the adulterous man's wife, wearing dark shades to conceal the tears triggered by the pain of her husband's infidelity, will smile superficially as she drives by majestically in her latest Range Rover or Mercedes Benz. It is what it is. These things happen.

Some afflicted spouses say that it is better to suffer behind the steering wheel of a Mercedes Benz than riding on a bus or taxi with little or no money. Other seemingly rich people owe creditors money. Every other day, you will see them avoiding and dodging creditors, yet they drive fancy luxury cars and talk big, even telling lies about having been or preparing to go on some exotic vacation abroad, just to keep up appearances and give a false impression that everything is under control.

As a child, and later as an adult, I do not recall anyone ever showing up at my parents' home looking for my father because my father owed them money. Even after my father passed on, nobody showed up claiming to be his 'secret' or 'hidden' child born from some other woman. Neither did anyone show up at my father's funeral claiming that my father owed him money. There were no such things. In my humble opinion, that is how one should live one's life and that is how it ought to be.

After my father passed on in 2003, my mother would often tell me how strict JT was and that he was such a disciplinarian. Mum was right. My father was a very focused man who had no time for pettiness. Also, he was very frank. JT would speak truth to power. He was such a decent man, with great virtues of honor, honesty, integrity and prophetic truth. He never minced his words. If he caught you telling a lie, he would sometimes reprimand you in the presence of everyone around so that you felt embarrassed and ashamed of your bad behavior. After working hours, he would always come home straight from work. For him, there was nothing like passing through the tennis or golf club for one or two beers. We all knew his routine. After getting home, he would pick up his books and head to the study room to read. Then he would listen to the news on television at 7:00 before we would all, as a family, have dinner together. And before a meal, we would all pray as a family. Grace before a meal was non-negotiable. There was nothing like, 'I don't believe in God, so I am not praying.' We all had to pray, unless you wanted to leave the house to go and eat elsewhere. It was not a dictatorship or authoritarian system, as today's young people might think or suspect. Rather, we all understood that there is a limit to democracy if you have to maintain discipline in a functional home. There is a thin line between anarchy and democracy. And so, there was nothing like eating like a heathen without praying. We all had to pray and thank God before breakfast, lunch and dinner.

In my father's house, you were not allowed to take your food with you from the dinner table to the living room sofa so that you could watch a movie on TV while eating. We all understood that there was a reason why there was a dining room and a dining table in the house. Our human rights or freedoms to choose where to sit during dinner if a good movie on TV was showing were anchored in the raison d'être of having a dining room and a dinner table in a decent home. Indeed, what is the purpose of having a dining room and dinner table in a home if the children or parents will migrate from the dinner table to the living room to sit on a sofa to watch a movie on TV? And so, we all could not depart from that dinner table tradition, unless you wanted to forgo your dinner. It was all about table manners.

Looking back, I can comfortably say that I had a privileged background. I was raised in a decent home and come from a well-cultivated family. Manners are not something that you can buy with money. And I don't mean to be snobbish or to put down anyone. To illustrate, in my childhood, I had some friends whose parents probably earned more money than my parents. That said, their homes were either a broken home or full of chaos. Money did not make a difference for them. In those days, I remember that when I would go to play with some friends at their home, I would sometimes find them eating on cheap plastic or metal plates bought from some Indian bazaar. If it was breakfast time, they would be drinking tea from large plastic or metal mugs. The tea would be prepared in an old rusty metal teapot from which they would all pour their take. I would watch curiously as they indulged also in crudely cut slices of bread. For me, I never experienced such things. There was none of that at my parents' home. My mother had an assortment of fine kitchenware and chinaware. She hated the idea of plastic and metal cups and plates. Those ancient artifacts, as I call them, were often associated with colonial times when Africans experienced a lot of hardships due to limited economic opportunities. Also, in many circles, plastic and metal cups and plates were associated with backwardness.

Below are two pictures of some of my mother's tea sets. This chinaware is still present today in my parents' home in Luanshya, Zambia.

As you can see from the picture above, there is a healthy assortment of a teacup, teapot saucer, milk jar, teabag holder, sugar bowl, and cupcake holders.

In the second picture, there is a teacup and saucer, teapot, sugar bowl, milk jar, a small jar for custard or cream to pour over a cake, side plate, napkin holder, butter dish and a butter knife.

Looking back, I remember that my mother never allowed us to use a table knife for spreading butter on the bread. Much later, when I went to Oxford, it made a whole lot of sense. It was only then that it sank in that exposure matters. For example, you have to know when to serve your guests a sherry and what kind of drink or wine to order if you are having a meat or fish entrée. Te kunwa fye! (English translation: "Don't just drink anything and everything without knowing what food you are going to eat along with that drink."). Equally, do not sit at the dinner table struggling with a fish knife to cut your steak. Why not ask the waiter or waitress to bring you a steak knife, that is, if you know what that means. There is a difference between a fish knife and a steak knife as well as between a fish knife and a butter knife. When it comes to, say, ordering steak, you must know whether you want it rare, medium rare, medium, medium well or well done. It not just a question of telling the waiter, 'T-bone!' Rather, tell him also how you would like your T-bone prepared.

I remember growing up as a young boy in Zambia when my mother would often make me a cup of tea at 4 pm whilst most of my friends took to 'zigolo' in their parents' homes. Zigolo, also known as 'ichi-koloki', is a local substitute for tea. It is made by pouring several teaspoons of sugar into a cup or mug of cold water and then stirring the mixture briskly to form a sweet drink or concoction. Other people would place a few teaspoons of sugar on a frying pan and then heat it up to melt the sugar. The melted sugar would turn into some brown syrup. Folks would then pour that syrup into a cup of hot water to mimic the color of tea. It was crazy!

From my early childhood, I recall that my parents always insisted on good manners from everyone in the family before, during and after meals. So, there was no room for zigolo in our family. We were all raised with good table manners. For example, though my father never used to drink alcohol, he would always keep a bottle of fine wine or two at home for his guests instead of telling them, 'I don't drink'. Similarly, my mother taught me never to serve her a cup of tea not made in her presence. Otherwise, she would insist that I simply bring her all the ingredients and accessories, including the hot water in a teapot, the teabags on a teabag holder, the sugar in a bowl and the milk in a milk jar, with everything placed nicely on a tray, for her to make her own tea. Also, my mother would insist that one should not drink tea from a coffee mug, but from a teacup that came with a saucer. By contrast, in some homes where I would visit some friends, there were no such traditions or manners. Anything would go. Folks would even insult or blow their nose while drinking tea.

I should add here that the disparity was not about income levels across homes, but simply an issue of cultural exposure. Many parents could afford to buy decent kitchenware or chinaware for their homes, but, for one reason or another, they chose to hold onto the culture of plastic or metal cups and plates. In homes where you found such cultural strongholds, there was nothing like asking you, as a guest, how many teaspoons of sugar you would take before making you a cup of tea. Everything, including tea bags, sugar and milk, would be poured into a metal kettle placed at the center of the family gathering for all to partake. And folks seated on the floor, or sharing some empty tin for a seat, would compete to pour some tea into their respective plastic or metal mugs. It is such encounters that made you appreciate your parents even more. My parents were preparing me for the future before I even went to Oxford.

One evening in Luanshya when I was in Grade 6 or 7, as my father was retreating from his study room with a stack of books in his hands, my mother, who was with me in the dining room, jokingly said to him: "My husband, you are always reading. Why don't you join the golf club and spend a bit of time there with other men after work hours instead of just reading books every day?"

I stood there quietly, wondering what my father would say. JT looked at my mother with a smile, and responded calmly: "Ba mayo, bushe kwena ba lya aba sangwa ku golf club na ine na tu lingana nabo amano? ("My dearest wife, do you think those fellas at the golf club and I are at the same level of thinking or cut from the same cloth?")

My mother was speechless. She just stood there, not knowing what to say. As I said earlier, my father was very frank. He never minced his words. And he was right. There was no comparison between my father and a number of those men at the golf club. JT had character. Those who knew him can attest to what I am saying. I was so proud of him.

With that reply, JT headed to the book rack to place his books back on the shelf before joining us for dinner. Indeed, a number of the men at the golf club had a checkered history of infidelity as well as questionable financial integrity. There was very little, if anything, about them to admire. Even we young folks knew about some of their shenanigans. So my father had a point. You don't mix crudeness with finesse or oil with water. Let darkness remain with the dark, and brightness with the light.

The college where my father worked as principal and executive head was not far from our house in Luanshya. So he would often leave his car at home and walk for five to ten minutes to the office. If it was drizzling, you would see him wearing one of the waterproof trench coats he came with from

Canada, with an umbrella in one hand and a full grain American belted leather briefcase in his other hand. He would also don a lovely woolen hat, matching his suit or tweed jacket. My father had a fine taste in fashion, I must admit, though, like most old folks back then, he would never talk about it openly. You just had to look at his Oxford brogues, suit, trench coat, silk tie, white shirt and cufflinks. After my father passed on, one of the ties I found in his wardrobe was an Yves Saint Laurent (YSL) tie. There was also a good collection of fine dark-colored V-neck cardigan sweaters that had wooden buttons on them, allowing for the elegant look of a fine necktie on a white shirt. Boy, the man had such fine taste in clothing. That was JT, as my father was fondly known. He had such high standards even back then. If it rained, he would wear *rubber overshoes to protect his Oxford leather brogues. It takes some exposure to appreciate such finer things in life. Even with money, if you don't have that exposure, you might not get it. And so*, if you see me dressed in fine garb, just know that it runs in the family. The only difference is that my volume might be slightly louder, as I work mainly with the prevalent levels of volume in the country where I now reside, as opposed to the levels where I hail from. We only aspire to inspire.

I remember that when my father returned from his university studies in Canada, he brought my eldest brother, Kelvin, a new Omega wristwatch. Like a Rolex, Omega wristwatches were only known back then in Zambia as a standard pension-gift for retiring miners. At the time, I was quite young and did not know much about such wristwatches and brands. It was only much later, after I moved abroad, that I realized the real value of an Omega wristwatch. I doubt that even my elder brother, Kelvin, or any of my other siblings, knew the value of that wristwatch gift that Dad got for Kelvin. At the time, only Dad had been overseas in the family. The rest of us lacked exposure and experience of the world back then.

Over the years, I have come to learn that exposure matters. There are certain things that you and I will not understand fully if we lack exposure. Travelling is by itself learning. My father also came with three powerful hunting guns from Canada which he always had licensed at the local police station in Luanshya, in addition to an airgun. He would get a government permit to go hunting. He enjoyed it, as he had back in Canada. The game meat from those hunting sprees was always so tasty. I was, however, too young to accompany my father on those hunting trips when he would drive out into the Zambian countryside with some of my elderly cousins.

My father started his long journey in the education sector way back before Zambia gained political independence from Britain and before any university was established in Zambia. He first attended the then famous Munali Secondary School and Hodgson Technical College (now known as David Kaunda National Technical Secondary School) in Lusaka before proceeding to university studies abroad. Back in the days before any university was set up in Zambia, Munali and Hodgson were the most prestigious institutions of higher education. African men who attended Munali and Hodgson were considered to be among the most learned in Northern Rhodesia, now known as Zambia. For the ladies, Chipembi Girls Secondary School was arguably the most prestigious high school. An elderly Zambian man whose wife is an alumnus of Chipembi Girls Secondary School once told me that it was quite prestigious back in the day to marry someone from Chipembi Girls' Secondary School. As we conversed, I asked him why it was also not uncommon for some Zambian men from his generation to marry women, say, from Zimbabwe or South Africa. He looked at me intently and smiled. He then replied, "Nephew, you are right. You are well informed. The gals from Chipembi Girls Secondary School were often our first choice locally. But if one got the chance to go and study or work in Salisbury, Southern Rhodesia [now known as Harare, Zimbabwe] it was fashionable to marry a woman from there. Then, for those who managed to go as far as South Africa, especially for school at, say, the University of Fort Hare, they would often marry some light complexioned Xhosa lady. It was like that. Marrying from outside often depicted a level of sophistication."

That information helped me to understand why some of my Zambian friends' mothers were from Zimbabwe or South Africa. It started making sense. I probed the man further by asking, "Uncle, what about the Zambian men who went to the UK or the US?" And he replied: "They were not many. The few who managed to go overseas would come back with either an African-American lady, even where one had only been out of Zambia for a year or two, or a white woman. Interestingly, the Zambian men who went to study at the University of East Africa in Tanzania or, later, at the University of Makerere in Uganda, rarely came back with a Tanzanian or Ugandan lady."

I sat back and wondered why this was so. Perhaps it was because Tanzania and Uganda were at the time already independent and being run by Africans, as opposed to countries such as Southern Rhodesia and South Africa, which were still under white minority rule. Some people of color, unfortunately, tend to associate whiteness with civility or civilization. They would rather go where there is some whiteness.

My father once told me an interesting story from his Munali days of how they were all expecting Prof Lamech Goma and one or two other Zambians who had gone to university abroad to return to Zambia as the first Zambians to earn a university degree. Little did people realize that Mr John Mwanakatwe, who also studied at Munali, had already enrolled in a distance learning degree program in South Africa. By the time Prof Goma was returning to Zambia, Mr Mwanakatwe had already obtained his degree from South Africa. Thus, Mr Mwanakatwe became the first Zambian to obtain a university degree. He was also the first African in Zambia to head a secondary school before independence. And when Zambia got independence in 1964, he became Zambia's first Minister of Education.

Education was something that was very dear to my father. As noted earlier, in my father's house, there was always a well-stocked bookcase, with shelves filled with stacks of books. I cannot begin to talk about my parents without referring to the rich bookshelves in their home. As I mentioned earlier, my parents were both educationalists. Thus, they understood and appreciated the value of having a bookshelf or library in a home. Truly, the apple does not fall far from the tree. The well-stocked bookshelves in my own home speak to the way I was raised. I grew up in a home of books. I grew up around books, and was raised by loving and caring parents who understood the value of education. Below is a picture of bookracks in my home library, with several books having no place to sit on the shelves.

When my father was a high school student at Munali in Zambia, that school was highly revered and coveted by many talented native Zambians. A few years after we gained independence, my father left Zambia for university studies in Canada. Many years later, and after my father had even retired from Zambia's civil service, I won the prestigious Rhodes Scholarship to go to the University of Oxford in England. As I was preparing to go to Oxford, my father sat me down and told me jokingly how his parents, especially his mother, would worry, as he was preparing to leave Zambia for Canada for his university studies, saying that he would find them long gone. His parents kept telling him that he would find them dead upon his return. My father just laughed it off. He set off for Canada, and pursued and successfully completed his university studies there, before returning to Zambia. Upon his return from Canada, my father found his parents still alive. He then said to them: "You're not yet dead? I am back." Against this background, my father would encourage me not to worry much about him and my mother, as I was preparing to leave for Oxford.

In Canada, my father attended the University of Toronto and the University of Saskatchewan, respectively. In the picture below, taken in Toronto, Canada, in the early to mid-1970s, my father's Canadian friends from a Catholic Church parish near the University of Toronto hosted a birthday party for him. My father was always a regular and committed Catholic even when he was abroad in Canada.

I was very young when my father left Zambia for Canada, but one thing always stuck with me. If my father could work so hard, starting from his humble beginnings in Mansa, Zambia, and making it to a prestigious university abroad, that is, the University of Toronto which is, arguably, Canada's best university and beats even top-ranked Canadian universities such as McGill University and the University of British Columbia, I had no reason to let myself and my parents down. I had no other option but to excel, because my parents had given me a better platform to spring from than they themselves had.

In the picture below, taken before I was born, my parents can be seen in their early years of marriage with my older siblings and one or two other family relations.

Because of the educational standards set by my parents, I had been dreaming of going to prestigious schools such as Oxford or Harvard, and the dream came true eventually. It is often the dream of many a serious-minded student to end up in such intellectually lofty places. Who wouldn't want to go to Oxford or Harvard? Let's be honest. We all want the best, although some people will tell you dishonestly that school is not everything just because they themselves could not go far with their education or could not make it to a top-ranked school. Some people are not honest. We all want the best in life. And every generation, I submit, has a responsibility to move the notch higher than where their parents left off. And so, I not only ended up studying at both the University of Oxford and Harvard University but also graduated from Oxford with the most highly regarded postgraduate taught law degree in the entire English-speaking world, the prestigious Oxford graduate degree of Bachelor of Civil Law (BCL), in addition to studying advanced management and leadership at Harvard. Further, I got admitted to the best law school in the US, Yale Law School, with a full scholarship, which, as established earlier, I had to turn down for the World Bank. There is no doubt that while I applied myself seriously in order to succeed, my parents also gave me a strong foundation from where to excel. Again, as the old English adage says, the apple does not fall far from the tree. Following below are some pictures of my father, taken in the 1970s and 80s, respectively, after he returned from Canada.

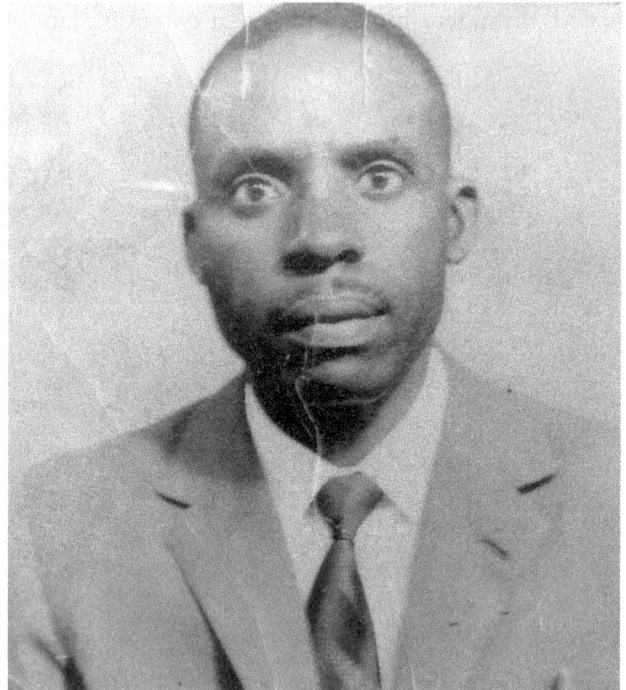

My father often shared with me stories about his Munali student days as well as his university student days in Canada. He had friends and colleagues, as well as a few distant relatives who were with him at Munali in Zambia. I recall some of the names he would mention. A number of them became famous politicians in Zambia's Kaunda Government. But my father was not one who would run back to ingratiate himself with famous people or to beg them to remember him as having been with them at Munali at some point. My father's own credentials were enough. And his rich bookshelves at home gave him more comfort. My father was an avid reader, and, as already established, had a rich collection of books which, by any standards, was very rare in many Zambian homes those days, including in the homes of the so-called famous people.

On my mother's side, I also got to learn that she too, like my father, had some distant and close relatives in prominent Lusaka circles. But both my parents encouraged us, their children, to be self-confident and not to suck up to any allegedly prominent people or to go searching for famous relatives. Integrity and self-respect were important attributes that our parents instilled in us. One had to be self-assured so as to avoid going around seeking validation from other people who had no time for you or who hardly knew you. The last thing you would wish for is for someone to deny knowing you as their relative until they realize that you have made it in life. So, for my siblings and I, the relatives that knew us, we also knew them. Those who did not know us, we also did not know them. There was no time or room for pretense or name-dropping. We did not need any validation from anyone to make it in life.

As the head of a higher education institution in Zambia at a time when there were many expatriates working in Zambia, my father headed an academic institution whose academic staff comprised many white and Asian expatriate lecturers as well as some Zambian lecturers and nationals of other African countries. It was a multi-cultural and inclusive community. I grew up in that environment. There was hardly any racism, xenophobia or tribalism. Following below are some two pictures of my father and some of the academic staff at the higher education institution he was heading.

The picture below was taken in Livingstone, Zambia, when my father served as the Vice-Principal of Livingstone Trades Training Institute and before he was promoted in 1976 to serve as the Principal of Luanshya Trades Training Institute in Luanshya, Zambia.

But let us take a more reasoned look at the issue of inclusivity or the lack of the same in some African settings. Of tribalism, Nonyelum Ossai, writing in an undated Online article titled, "Causes of tribalism in Nigeria and how to tackle them," posits:

"Tribalism is one of the biggest problems of national integration in Nigeria. There are often cases of violent tribal or ethnic conflicts where lives and properties are lost. As the nation gets ready for the 2023 general elections, we have to consider the impact of tribalism in selecting the next leaders to lead the people in the next four years. We already see signs of people's views of their preferred candidates based on their tribal affiliations."

Ossai contends further that 'a tribalist can move heaven and earth for someone from his tribe but will not lift a finger to help someone from another.' However, given the multi-cultural environment in which I was raised, I have never looked at people through the prism or lens of race, tribe, religion, creed, or ethnicity. To me, everyone matters. Indeed, the socialization you undergo often influences how you view the world. And so, I was very proud of my father, especially when I saw how inclusive he was and how much respect all the lecturers and the people around him accorded him. To him, your race, tribe, religion, or ethnic background did not matter. Not even your political connections mattered. That was JT. He was a man of great character. As his son, I learned a lot from that experience. It gave me confidence to excel in multi-racial, multi-ethnic and multi-cultural environments.

Growing up in Zambia, I was never a timid or impressionable boy. Rather, I was quiet but somewhat intellectually inquisitive. I had a very reflective mind. I recall that my father owned different cars at different times even before I was born. He rarely drove any of the college vehicles at the college he was heading, even though he had the authority to do so. Neither would my father ask his driver to run personal errands for him or to pick us up from school, a thing that was common with a lot of men who were in leadership positions back in the day. My father separated work from personal and family responsibilities.

I remember him telling me a story about public procurement before I even knew what the word 'procurement' meant. Before my father was appointed as the College Principal at Luanshya Trades Training Institute (LTTI) in 1976, his predecessor, an Indian man, would award most of the public procurement contracts at the college to his fellow local Asians who were businessmen in the small town of Luanshya. Nobody ever questioned that practice. Many Zambians just looked at it as a normal practice. In 1976, when my father took over as College Principal, things changed immediately. And those corrupt local Asian businessmen knew it that their days were numbered. My father instructed the college's Purchasing and Accounting Departments to cease giving non-competitive procurement offers to the Indian friends of his predecessor. This was a time when there was state capitalism in Zambia. My father reasoned that LTTI was a Zambian Government-owned higher education institution and should therefore be supporting other government-owned institutions through the procurement of goods for the college from Government-owned parastatal companies, and not by supporting non-competitive shady deals with the local Asian businessmen. My father was of the view that there was no way that he would ignore Zambian parastatal companies to go and get instead college supplies and other purchases from private individuals who had not gone through a competitive bid. This was not racism or discrimination, but merely putting an end to favoritism and cronyism. That was my father. He was a man of principle.

My father instructed his staff to procure all goods for the college from Government-owned institutions (parastatals) located in Ndola, the nearest industrial hub to Luanshya. Of course, the shady local Asian businessmen were not happy. They had lost 'good' business. And they knew that they were now dealing with a different kind of African from the ones they had been accustomed to. In the end, they were left with no choice but to respect my father. He was one man who could not be bought or corrupted, a man of strong moral and ethical values. We don't have many men like that nowadays.

People say that behind every successful man there is a woman. My mother was not a housewife. She was a professional woman. Here, I must clarify that there is nothing wrong with being a housewife if that is the choice one makes. Some housewives even have a university education, but choose to stay home to take care of the kids or family. We now also have a lot of men who are househusbands. But during our mothers' times, many mothers who stayed at home as housewives did not simply opt for that. It was because they did not have much of an education. My father gave my mother some good opportunities to get an education and become a professional, and she did utilize those opportunities. My mother trained and worked as a nurse before changing careers later to train and work as a teacher. At a time when most of her friends and workmates did not own a car and could not drive, she had her own car and would drive. She started driving even before I was born, unlike most of her friends, who could only rely on their husbands for transport or take public transport.

My father bought his first car in 1957 when many Zambians were just pedestrians and did not own a car. That was JT. He was a pioneer. He got a loan and bought a lorry, which he gave to two of his siblings, Uncle Robert and Uncle Justin, to start a small transport business of transporting fishermen and other members of the public in and around Mansa area. His brothers then hired a local driver, a Mr Kashimbaya. The business took off, but unfortunately my father's two siblings would squander most of the money earned from the business without servicing the loan. So, my father ended up paying off the loan using his modest earnings as a civil servant.

Decades later, my father met a man by the name of Kashimbaya on the Copperbelt who recognized him. Although my father did not recognize the man, he could have heard from some people of a wealthy businessman in Mufulira by that name. The man asked my father if he was the same Mr Mwenda who had bought a lorry for his siblings in Mansa in the late 1950s. The man also mentioned the names of my father's two brothers, as his former bosses. My father was shocked. My father admitted that he was indeed the same Mr Mwenda. The man explained that he was the driver of that lorry that my father bought for his two brothers in Mansa in the late 1950s. The man had indeed worked for my father's brothers as their lorry driver but was now a successful businessman on the Copperbelt while they were languishing in poverty in the village in Mansa. My father could not believe it. The man then went on to explain that my uncles would have made it big, but for lack of discipline. Each time they made money from that transportation business, they would squander it instead of servicing the loan for the lorry and reinvesting the money in the business.

A few years later, the same two uncles showed up in Luanshya from the village in Mansa, asking my father to render them help again. They wanted my father to give them each one of the three licensed rifles that my father had brought with him from Canada so that they could use the guns for hunting in the village. My father was very upset. He reminded them of how they had let him down when he bought them a lorry for transportation business. In short, he did not give them the guns and asked my brother, Dennis, to escort them to the bus station the next day so that they could go back to the village. My father gave them transport money and some cash for subsistence as they left. Afterwards, he explained to Dennis and my other older siblings how his two brothers had let him down. My father was the youngest or last-born in his family. He was a very fair and reasonable man in his decisions, but also a stern disciplinarian.

Back in Livingstone, when I started school in 1974, my mother would drop me off at school. My father was at the time in Canada for his university studies. At the time, it was uncommon to find African women of my mother's generation driving or owning a car.

At home, we had a houseboy. He lived in the servants' quarters behind the main house, or what some people in Lusaka now call a 'cottage.' We treated him as family and with much respect. And I remember the names of all our houseboys. In Livingstone, we had one whose name was Songolo. He would entertain us as kids by lifting a heavy metal rail bar with his teeth. He would put a white handkerchief on the edge of the rail bar and then with one bite lift it up in the air. He was a dark, shortish and stout fella. When we moved to Luanshya, we had Rabson, then Chibale, and finally

Chama. Rabson later went on to complete his high school education and got himself a good job in Luanshya. Dad would always encourage him to pursue his education further.

Because of the privileged background that I grew up in, my siblings and I made no effort whatsoever to reach out to seemingly 'prominent' relatives who did not know us, or, rather, who pretended not to know us, though it was fashionable back then, and still is somewhat fashionable, for some desperate people who like name-dropping to clamor for attention by claiming to know big names, even asserting that they are related. My father and mother never raised us that way. Rather, they instilled in us a sense of self-assuredness in order to nurture our self-esteem. The idea is that a man is likely to respect you if you meet him on neutral ground, say, in a professional setting, than if you were to go around sucking up to him and trying to explain yourself as his relative. Besides, as we say in Bemba, 'Ing'anda ushi kalamo ba ikumbwa umu tenge.' This Bemba adage reads as follows: 'A house you have never lived in often looks attractive from the outside. But the moment you enter that house, you will be shocked with the type of chaos that goes on in there or the type of problems that the people living there are facing.' Put simply, the grass is greener on the other side.

Here is a picture of my father leaving Zambia for Canada.

The picture below is of my father in Canada, with a Zambian friend of his (wearing a hat), a Mr Nyirenda, who was attending the same university as my father in Canada. The white couple standing next to my father were his Canadian friends.

I have already established above that my mother, Mrs Esther M Mwenda, first trained and worked as a nurse in Zambia before switching careers to become a teacher. After a short career in medical nursing, she quit nursing and went on to train as a teacher. Thereafter, my mother worked as a teacher. Then, my father, who retired in 1983 before my mother's retirement, headed, as highlighted above, a tertiary educational institution in Zambia called Luanshya Trades Training Institute (LTTI). In Luanshya, there were two major colleges located next to each other. Both colleges were Government-owned. One of the colleges was LTTI and the other was the Technical and Vocational Teachers' College (TVTC). The two institutions, LTTI and TVTC, shared a relatively large and modern campus in a gated community. The college principal or head of the other college, TVTC, was a Mr Bwalanda.

Against this background, let me now share some pictures and insights into my good relationship with my parents. I have provided below a picture of my father and mother when they visited me in

England in 1996. We spent the summer of 1996 together. I was at the time an Assistant Professor of Law at the University of Warwick. I was not making much money as an academic with my modest salary, but I was able to save a bit and buy my father and mother air tickets to visit me in the UK. I was at the time living in Canley, a suburb southwest of Coventry near the University of Warwick. I was renting a two-bedroomed apartment. I had only worked for a year at Warwick, and thus did not have much savings. In fact, I could have easily focused on myself with the indiscretion of youth, choosing to party and have a lot of fun as a young and single guy who had become a law professor at one of the top ten British universities. But, I chose otherwise.

I was only twenty-six years old when I started teaching at Warwick. Instead of selfishly focusing on myself, I kept thinking about my father and mother, who had by then retired. They had worked so hard and given us, their children, the best of everything that they could offer. So how was I going to pay them back, or at least make them feel appreciated? This thought kept bothering me. My parents were old now and retired. What was I to do to put a smile back on their faces? I decided to gift them a holiday in the UK. I am talking about a time when very few parents from my hometown of Luanshya in Zambia had been abroad by then. This was in the mid-1990s.

My parents, especially my father, were not surprised. He knew what kind of son he had. At the time, I had not even bought my first car or house yet. And I was not even married, so no one could say that my wife had suggested to me to honor my parents with a holiday in the UK.

On the day my parents were arriving in England from Zambia, I took an early morning coach from Coventry to London's Heathrow Airport. At around 7 am, I saw my father and mother walk through the arrivals section at Terminal 4. It was a dream come true. We greeted each other and boarded the return coach to Coventry. When we got to Coventry, my mother told me how most of her friends back home in Zambia were so envious and kept asking her who had advised me to invite them over to the UK because most young men of my age lacked that kind of wisdom. I just smiled.

We visited many places in England and, more importantly, I took my parents to see the famous University of Oxford and showed them where I studied. I also showed them where I used to live as a graduate student at Oxford. It was a memorable experience. I remembered the old days when I was a student at Oxford and how most of my European, Asian and American friends would have their parents visit them during university breaks while most of us African students could not afford to get our parents over. That era was over. My parents were now here with me in England and experiencing

Oxford. In the picture that follows, my parents and I were coming from my office at the University of Warwick during their visit to England.

In the picture below, taken on a Sunday morning in the late 1980s, my parents can be seen relaxing in the yard of their home before going to church. The photo was taken a few years after my father retired from the civil service. At the time, my mother was still working as a teacher.

That expensive tweed jacket always caught my eye when my father wore it.

The picture below was taken in 1998 in Lusaka when my parents travelled from Luanshya to support me for a family event. I spent some time talking to my father. I could tell that signs of aging were now visibly showing, even though his mind was still very sharp.

The 2005 picture below is of my mother in front of the White House when she was visiting my family in the US. We had just lost my father in 2003 and I had to travel to Zambia to mourn my father. This was a good way to help my mother to find some comfort after losing her husband.

Let me end this section with the photo below, taken at my parents' home in Luanshya. I bought them that house in the late 1990s when I had just moved from England to Washington DC to join the World Bank. The house had once belonged to the Mayor of Luanshya and was a befitting gift from a son to his loving parents. My father was still alive at the time. The picture below was, however, taken many years later after my father had left us and a couple of years or so before my mother passed on unexpectedly in 2019 after a short illness. I had been talking to my mother on the Wednesday of the week she died. She was having lunch, and all seemed okay. She sounded very jovial. Two days later, on a Friday morning, I received a call that she had passed on. The event where this photo was captured was a traditional Zambian ceremony known as 'Ama tebeto'. I was being honored by my in-laws for having been a worthy son-in-law. Not every married man gets to be given such honor by his in-laws. You must prove your worth as a worthy son-in-law for several years before you can be 'tebetad'. Your works must speak for themselves and must show, especially regarding how you have treated your wife throughout your marriage. Nowadays, some families in Zambia host such an important traditional event just to put up a show, even if they know that their son-in-law is just a jerk or an irresponsible fella who does not deserve any formal honor.

My parents, Joseph and Esther, had eight children altogether. There were no stepchildren or half-siblings in the family. My father was married to one woman only in his entire life, and he had no children or known concubines outside marriage. Likewise, my mother was married to the same man all her life. As my father would say, 'Mwana wandi, ukupa upa ta kwa wama.' ('My son, it is not wise for a man to be changing wives now and again or, put simply, to divorce and remarry'). Both my father and mother had travelled widely within and outside Zambia and Africa, and they were both well-educated. They had seen the world beyond Africa. Also, all my siblings have travelled widely outside Zambia and Africa, and they too are all well-educated. Ignorance was not, and has never been, an option in the Mwenda family. One just had to get that international exposure both in terms of education and international travel. It surely does improve your outlook to life.

While no man is perfect, each person has their own reason why they make the type of choices in life that they make, whether or not those choices are good or bad. You can't blame anyone. You are the master of your own destiny. Even in matters of faith, religion and marriage, you are the master of your own destiny. Others can simply inspire you, but you must find your own fit. My father was a staunch Catholic. So, am I. He believed strongly in the inviolability of the sanctity and sacrament of marriage, as espoused by the Christian Catholic faith. So, do I. Those are some of our common choices.

I have shared below some family photos. A number of them were taken in Livingstone in the early 1970s when my father was away in Canada for university studies. I can be seen standing on the far left. Next to mum is my immediate elder sister, Matilda. The baby in the photo is my immediate younger brother, Eugene.

In the photo below, Eugene is being held by my mother. On mum's immediate right is my eldest brother, Kelvin. On mum's immediate left is my first cousin, Michael, the son of my father's only sister. I am the little guy standing on the far left. Standing between me and brother Kelvin is my brother Dennis. On Dennis' left is another cousin of ours, Kaunda. Standing next to Kaunda is my eldest sister, Catherine, followed by my sister Matilda.

In the picture below, I am the shortest guy standing in a suit. Next to me is my eldest sister, Catherine, followed by my sister Matilda and then my brother Dennis. At the time, brother Kelvin was away from home in boarding school at Canisius Secondary School in Monze, Zambia. Cousin Michael was also away in boarding school at St Edmunds Secondary School in Mazabuka, Zambia.

When it comes to family matters, others might choose to see life differently. Many are okay with the idea of divorce and remarriage. They embrace the idea of blended families with different parents. The proponents of this school of thought often challenge the inviolability of the sanctity of marriage, asking why someone should continue to live in an unhappy marriage if things are not working. We all have opinions of one kind or another over different things. Even a cockwomble is welcome to share spiritedly his misguided opinions. So it is understandable that some folks might take a different stance on the matter of the sanctity and sacrament of marriage. We live in a free world where everyone is entitled to his or her opinion. But for me personally, I agree with my father not just because he was my father but for the following logically sound reasons, aside from any Christian edicts: (a) the character of a married person is often seen in the consistency of his or her edifying behavior within the institution of marriage; (b) the stability of a married person's character often informs the predictability of his or her behavior, and it could earn him or her either trust or mistrust from others; (c) the spontaneous or random behavior of a married person often leads to his or her unpredictable conduct, accompanied by short-term immediate gratification and long-term consequences; (d) a man or woman who changes friends frequently, like a married person who changes spouses, cannot be trusted because he or she can become your enemy tomorrow; (e) if a parent divorces, the children are often affected badly by that decision and what follows thereafter; and, (f) in some conservative societies, you can be judged harshly by the public court of opinions (i.e. society) if you divorce since many people tend to be skeptical of the moral and ethical standing of a person whose life is fraught with failed relationships.

But of course, we are awake to the view that to every general rule there are exceptions. Even the Bible allows for divorce in some exceptional cases. An analogy can be drawn here between politicians who change political parties or switch allegiance when the political tide is changing and those that remain steadfast. It is hard to trust politicians who switch sides to follow the wind or sail with the tide. These are opportunistic individuals. They are not loyal and cannot be trusted. Such individuals can switch political allegiance any time when it suits them. By parity of reasoning, you cannot be a Catholic today, then tomorrow a Pentecostal or Evangelical, and the following week a Seventh Day Adventist or Jehovah's Witness. Just what do you want in life? You cannot tell us that now you have found God in the new church that you have just joined, unlike where you were before. Have you seen God there for you to tell us that you have now found Him? God is omnipotent and present everywhere, including in the church that you have just left. Be honest about your own confusion and stop pretending to be holier than thou by giving all manner of lame excuses and scapegoats. We believe, as Christians, by faith, not by sight. By moving around aimlessly from one church to another, you are confirming that you are either confused or simply don't know what you want. Even the police or immigration officers at the airport cannot trust a person who shows up with seven different passports, some of which are expired. Why do you have to have several nationalities? What are you running away from? Or, rather, what are you hiding? Any reasonable man or woman would become suspicious of you.

My parents' eldest child, Kelvin Ng'andwe Mwenda, was born in 1959. He was their first-born child. Like his parents, Kelvin was well educated and never left his spouse to marry someone else. He too remained a Catholic Christian throughout his life. Brother Kelvin passed on in 2012 after a sudden and short illness.

Kelvin was a brilliant economist, with a sharp and critical mind. He studied economics at the University of Zambia (UNZA), the country's premier university, from 1978 to 1982. I recall that in 1977, when Kelvin was preparing to write his high school final exams (known then as Form 5 exams and now as Grade 12 exams) at St Canisius Secondary School in Monze, Southern Province, he, together with some of his friends who had sneaked out of boarding school to go and drink beer outside the school premises, was expelled from Canisius, a prestigious Catholic boarding school for boys. Canisius has produced some of Zambia's top intellectuals.

It was in January 1977 when my parents got a phone call from the headmaster of Canisius to say that Kelvin had been kicked out of school. That same evening my parents were hosting an evening wedding party for one of my aunties, who was getting married to a British educated Zambian engineer. The Guest of Honor at the evening wedding party, the then Minister of Information and Broadcasting, Hon Mr Unia Mwila, was an uncle of the groom. The groom was an engineer in the copper mines in Luanshya.

Later that same night, a second phone call rang. It was from the village in Mansa. My father had just lost his mother in Mansa. The wedding celebrations could however not be cancelled or stopped. Everything continued. Early the next morning, my brother Dennis, my sister Matilda and I were all woken up by my father to get ready to travel with him to Mansa to attend his mother's funeral. In the meantime, my mother tried to draw my father's attention to the plight of his eldest son, Kelvin, at Canisius, hoping that my father would change his travel plans so that he could first save his son from school expulsion before he could mourn his mother in the village. It was a tight call. My father, being a stern disciplinarian he was, would have none of that and simply told my mother, "I told my son several times to stop the bad behavior of drinking alcohol, but he would not listen. I am sorry, I am going to mourn my mother." That kind of tough love was not unusual from my father. He was a man of few words and was very stern. When he spoke, he never minced his words.

We started off for Mansa that very morning around 5 am. My father packed all our bags in his Peugeot 404 van and took to the wheel for Mansa. The rear of the van was covered by a canvas canopy. Then he put a soft mattress at the back for us to relax on as he cruised the van via Congo's Pedicle Road to re-enter Zambia after crossing the Luapula River on a pontoon. We drove all the way through DRC, and crossed the Luapula River using a pontoon, until we reached the village in Mansa. It was a long journey. I was only eight years old at the time and it was the first time I visited the village. We arrived around 1800 hours. Everyone in the village was waiting for my father. They knew they could not proceed with the burial of his mother without him present. My father was highly respected by all his relatives. He was a man of great wisdom and character.

Back in Luanshya, my mother was left shell-shocked by my father's decision to travel to Mansa for his mother's funeral when their son was in serious trouble at school. As a mother, she probably saw it differently. She was hoping that my father would be moved to travel immediately to Canisius to save his son. Ultimately, it was my mother instead who ended up travelling to Monze to plead with the school authorities at Canisius to allow Brother Kelvin to at least write his exams. The expulsion was commuted to a suspension, but all the affected boys would not attend any classes and would only be allowed to take their final exams. My mother saved her son but missed her mother-in-law's funeral. It was a tough decision she had to make.

In high school, Brother Kelvin had dropped a number of subjects that many of his friends were sitting for. He was only left with six subjects that he would sit for in the final exams, meaning that, if he were to fail just one subject, he would not get a full high school certificate. The minimum number of subjects that one has to pass to get a full high school certificate is six. It was a risky thing that Brother Kelvin did. Many students sit for eight to nine subjects, but he took the risk of sitting for only six. It was a big gamble. But when Brother Kelvin went into that exam room, he surprised the school authorities with what he was able to produce. He passed all the six subjects with flying colors and made it to UNZA. That was the brilliance of the man. He was gifted intellectually, with a very sharp mind.

After graduating from UNZA, Brother Kelvin joined Zambia National Building Society (ZNBS), a major parastatal organization, where he rose to a senior managerial role. Later, he left ZNBS to venture intopmentrepreneurship and consultancy. He also lectured briefly at a government educational institution in Zambia.

The second born in the family is Catherine Mofya Mwenda, who holds an MBA degree from Nottingham Trent University in the UK and taught at some point in the UK's higher education sector before returning to Zambia to take up a managerial post in the private sector. Catherine has also done extensive consultancy in the field of human resource management. Prior to embarking on further studies abroad, she earned professional qualifications in human resource management and worked for a major parastatal organization, the Development Bank of Zambia (DBZ). She can be seen in the photo shown here.

The third born is Dennis Chilando Mwenda. Dennis is a UK Chartered Institute of Logistics and Transport specialist, with additional qualifications in the field of automotive engineering. He has not only taught in higher education but also held a number of executive leadership roles as well as worked for the Zambia Consolidated Copper Mines Ltd (ZCCM), the Ministry of Health of Zambia and Zambia's Ministry of Youth and Sport. He can be seen in the photo below with our sister Catherine, at one of my book launch events held in Lusaka, Zambia.

The fourth born is Matilda Ng'andwe Mwenda, who holds a Masters degree in journalism from Cardiff University in Wales. She also holds a Bachelors degree in Mass Communication from UNZA, in addition to a higher education teaching diploma and a three-year college diploma in journalism. Her picture is hown here.

Matilda worked for many years for a notable international organization, the South Africa Development Community (SADC), based in Botswana. She also taught at the University of Zambia (UNZA) as a Staff Development Fellow (SDF) prior to working in a leadership role at the Zambia Revenue Authority (ZRA). Additionally, she served as a journalism lecturer at Zambia's Evelyn Hone College before joining UNZA. Matilda has also worked for the Zambia Chamber of Commerce and Industry as well as the Times of Zambia, a leading print media house in Zambia.

I am the fifth born in the family. Like my brother Dennis was an altar boy in his childhood days when the family was based in Livingstone, I became a Catholic altar boy when my family moved to Luanshya. At one point, I entertained the thought of becoming a Catholic priest or joining the army as a commissioned officer. Additionally, I was not only a talented soccer player in high school and university but also a high school cadet. More importantly, my academic excellence had already started showing as early as my elementary or primary school days. For example, I won some prestigious debating awards while in primary school. In the end, the pursuit of academic excellence took precedence over all other career or vocational considerations.

I have shared a picture below, taken when I was an undergraduate student at the University of Zambia (UNZA) in the mid to late 1980s. I am the guy in glasses wearing cream pants. Standing

on my left is a good brother and friend who was in my law class at UNZA, Noyoo Noyoo. On my immediate right is another good brother and friend, Fortune Michelo Chibamba, who studied social work at UNZA and was in my cohort as well. On my far right is Eugene Haazele, who was my roommate when I was in first year at UNZA. Eugene was then a finalist civil engineering student at UNZA.

As you can see, I have always been very multi-cultural in my outlook on life. While some students at UNZA, especially those from certain rural settings, often stuck with friends from their home villages and tribes, I was far above such insular and parochial ways of thinking. For example, my friend Noyoo was Lozi. Another friend, Fortune, is Tonga. Eugene, my former roommate, is also Tonga. I am Ushi. To me, tribe does not matter. Rather, intellect, social consciousness and humanity are my main drivers.

The picture here was taken at Goma Lakes, UNZA, when I was in my second year of undergraduate studies. In my time at UNZA, student radicalism, inspired by the leftist ideology of Marxism-Leninism, often warmed us up to conscious reggae music. This was a time when Zimbabwe had just gotten independence while South Africa was still under apartheid white minority rule. Namibia was also fighting for independence at the time. And Angola and Mozambique, though independent, still had some internal and external reactionary threats to deal with.

Among my siblings, my brother, Eugene Kalobwe Mwenda, comes after me. I have shared his photo below.

In the picture below, taken in Cardiff, Wales, on Sunday, June 30, 2024, Eugene can be seen with his son, Denzel, coming from Catholic Church Sunday Mass. Yes, we are all Catholics in the family.

Based in the United Kingdom, Eugene holds an MBA degree from Cardiff University, in addition to prior professional qualifications in the field of marketing from both the UK and Zambia. Eugene also taught briefly in higher education and continues to be based in the UK. He now works as a senior manager in the private sector in Cardiff, Wales.

After Eugene comes Francis Mwansa Mwenda, who completed his tertiary education studies at LTTI before embarking on a college teaching diploma to become a college lecturer. Below is a picture of Francis taken in October 2023.

Francis, who worked for a Catholic Church educational institution in Luanshya, Zambia, passed on in March 2024 while I was writing this book. In fact, I had to come back to this chapter to edit his entry, as I had already finished writing the chapter when he left us. Like a Christian martyr, Francis left us while serving God by giving his best with the Franciscan Catholic Nuns at Dagama School to assist children with different physical challenges. He loved his service to God and before his last breath spoke with a kind heart of wanting to return to work to assist the children at Dagama School. His is a very touching story of selfless service to God.

The last born in the family, Joseph Mambwe Mwenda, recently completed graduate studies for the Master of Philosophy (MPhil) degree in International Trade and Investment at the University of Western Cape (UWC) in Cape Town, South Africa. He also holds a post-bachelors Honors degree from MANCOSA in South Africa, in addition to a Bachelors degree from Zambia's Copperbelt University, one of the two leading universities in Zambia, as well as a three-year college diploma in marketing and some professional British qualifications in marketing. Above is a picture of Joseph taken in October of 2023.

When I travelled to Cape Town, South Africa, in 2024 to give lectures at UWC, Joseph and I took the picture below after the conclusion of my graduate lectures. Joseph was one of the graduate students in my UWC class.

Joseph has served in a number of managerial roles as an executive in the banking sector as well as carried out major consultancy work. He, too, has a passion for academia and is considering pursuing a PhD before switching to full-time academia.

My parents have also been blessed with several grandchildren. Many of them are either in university or are university graduates, and some are now parents themselves. Others have already travelled widely across the world. We are 'Mwendas', meaning 'Travelers'.

In my parents' home, selfishness, greed and pride were strongly discouraged. I remember growing up there with some extended family members as well as a few close family friends at various points in time. My parents did not discriminate. If, for example, one of their close friends from a distant city needed their son or daughter to go to school, say, in Luanshya, the town where we were living, my parents would gladly take in that child to allow him or her continue with school in Luanshya while staying with us. No excuses were ever given by my parents to avoid helping. Neither would there be complaints from my parents of one kind or another. We were all a one big happy family. In fact, we children considered the children of our parents' close friends as our cousins, including those that did not stay with us. The parents were our uncles and aunties. It was like that. You don't find that type of humanity with most people nowadays. Today, it is each one for himself and to his own. We have lost that communal sense of a purposeful life. My parents gave a fair chance to everyone around them. They helped to educate many. We lived with cousins, uncles, aunties, and close family friends. You could not even tell the difference between how my parent treated their own biological children and how they treated any extended family member or the children of their close friends. We were all just one big happy family. As my nephew, Bernard M Fungamwango, recalls fondly about his grandfather, that is, my father, after Dad took him in when Bernard lost his father, Mr Gabriel Fungamwango (i.e. one of my father's twin nephews who were both raised and educated by my father):

"Grandpa was in a league of his own. There are very few men like him. I learned so much from grandpa… things that not even my own father taught me. Grandpa would always sit Uncle Joe (i.e. Joseph Mambwe Mwenda) and me down, imploring us to be disciplined, focused and hardworking like you, uncle. He always gave you as an example of exceptional brilliance and excellence in the family. And grandpa would always check our homework and schoolwork to ensure that we were on the right track with school. Even when I got my first job, grandpa called to congratulate me. That is the kind of man he was. Very loving and caring. There are very few men like him."

My nephew, Bernard, continues: "The only one within the extended family who comes close to grandpa is probably you, uncle, but you still are not at the level of grandpa. You have done well, without doubt, and you are so focused, but grandpa was at another level. Uncle, the truth is that, without grandpa, I don't know where we would all have ended up. Grandpa singlehandedly transformed the lives of so many relatives, including me, and gave everyone a chance to get an education." It is always humbling to hear such kind and honest words spoken about one's loving and caring parent. And it is true that my father had a kind heart and great personality. You always felt as if you were in the shadow of a mountain when you looked at the dignity with which he carried himself throughout his entire life. My father was an absolute gentleman, with a certain sense of quiet around him. A man of great learning and inspiring virtue. My father was a God-fearing and prayerful man, full of wisdom and clairvoyance. Many relatives and friends of his would often seek advice from him on various life issues. I, too, often sought counsel from him even when I was planning to get married. My father was a magnanimous man and lived a truly edifying life, with great decency. He never drank, never smoked, never uttered profanities, never cursed, and never engaged in abusive violence towards anyone, including my mother. I never saw my parents fight or quarrel, not even once. Yes, he was human, just like you and I, but he probably knew how to manage his emotions in a more mature and conscientious manner. A lot of people lack that emotional intelligence. Even when my father was quiet, you knew where he stood on a particular matter. You did not have to ask him for an opinion to know his views. You just had to look at his life and the dignified way in which he lived it to know that he would not entertain any nonsense. Indeed, you had to check yourself before exposing your intellectual bankruptcy or moral and ethical impropriety.

My parents got married in Mansa, Luapula Province, Zambia. They were both from Mansa. My parents also lived and worked in Kasama and Isoka before moving to Livingstone and then settling in Luanshya. I was born in Livingstone, the tourist capital of Zambia, although Lusaka is the main capital city of Zambia. Located in Southern Africa, Zambia is home to one of the great wonders of the world, the Mosi-oa-Tunya waterfalls, known also as the Victoria Falls. The Mosi-oa-Tunya lies on the border of Zambia and Zimbabwe. The waterfall is a chasm between the two nations, with waters pouring into the Mosi-oa-Tunya from the mighty Zambezi River shared by the riparian states of Angola, Zambia, Namibia, Botswana, Zimbabwe, and Mozambique.

I was born on a Sunday, January 5, 1969. My father's name was Joseph Toli Mwenda. My paternal grandfather's name was Peter Mwenda. And his wife, my paternal grandmother, was Mrs. Belita Mofya Mwenda. Mofya was her maiden name, and my elder sister, Catherine, was named after her. In the picture below, my father can be seen standing next to his mother, my paternal grandmother, Ba Mama Ba Belita (Grandma Mrs. Belita Mofya Mwenda). She was a rather quiet old lady and never spoke much. I remember her from my childhood days in Livingstone, Zambia, when she visited our home. I was pretty young then, but I remember her like it was yesterday. Standing on my father's right is his nephew, my first cousin, Gabriel Fungamwango. He was a great guy. He took after my father with his kindness and support to extended family members. My mother can be seen holding a baby and standing next to my grandmother. The oldest of the little boys seated is my first cousin, Alex Mukobe Mwenda, who was the young brother of cousin Gabriel, though he maintained the Mwenda name, as opposed to using the Fungamwango name.

My paternal grandmother, Ba Mama Ba Belita, as she was fondly known, had three siblings, a brother and two sisters. One of the sisters was Ba Chileya, after whom Catherine's daughter is named. Ba Chileya had the following children: Ba Sondashi, who lived in the Democratic Republic of Congo (DRC); Bana Chansa, who lived in DRC and whose son was a close uncle that we called, Ba José, and whose full names were Joseph Chunga (Ba José also lived in DRC for some years before he returned to Zambia); Bana Samala (the mother of a close aunt in Mwenda village in Mansa known as Ba mayo Bana Chama Kaloba), Bana Ponde (the mother of my uncles, Ba Mutento, Ba Kaluwe, Ba Chenda, and Ba Makesa); and Ba Kapini (the mother of my uncle, Ba Mwange). So I do have close relatives in DRC. Many of them live in or around Kasenga district and Lubumbashi, though I have never met them. That said, my paternal grandmother's brother was Ba Sumaili, who also lived in DRC for most of his life until he was quite advanced in age, when his sister, my maternal grandmother, Ba Mama Ba Belita, sent relatives to go and fetch him from DRC and bring him back to Mansa. Ba Sumaili lived in a town in DRC called Kasenga, on the border of DRC and Zambia, so he is likely to have left some children or family in DRC, meaning that I have close family members in DRC who I have not met.

I recall seeing my paternal grandmother, Ba Mama Ba Belita, during my early childhood, when she would visit our family in Livingstone city, from her home in Mwenda village in Mansa District. My paternal grandfather, Peter Mwenda, however, died when I was very little or even before I was born, so I never got to meet him, although my mother would tell me stories about him. He worked as a postmaster for the colonialists back in the colonial era. It was a prestigious job back then. He clearly stood out among many of his fellow African peers who were confined to village life with little education. Grandpa Peter, and Grandma Belita, were both Catholics. My grandparents had seven children altogether. All the children shared the same father and same mother. My paternal grandfather only married one woman all his life. And my paternal grandmother was married to the same man all her life.

When my father was born in Mansa in April 1928, and baptized in the Catholic Church, I would like to believe that he was named Joseph after St. Joseph, our Lord Jesus Christ's earthly parent. One thing I know from my reading of the scriptures and looking back at my father's demeanor and personality is that my father did somehow bear the moral and ethical character of the St. Joseph described in the Bible. Additionally, my father was a gamechanger like the other Joseph who was sold by his siblings to a pharaoh in Egypt. My father, like the Joseph in Egypt, was destined for greater things. He would later pave the way for a better life for a whole generation of us, that is, his children and much of the extended family.

My father's middle name was Toli, a corrupted pronunciation of Titus. There was a man in grandpa and grandma's home village in Mansa who was known as Tito, a close relative of my grandparents, so my father was given that man's name as his middle name, but the name had been corrupted from 'Titus' to 'Tito' and then 'Toli'.

My father was the youngest of seven; he had five brothers and one sister. The firstborn was Uncle Jim, who was a pioneer among his peers those days. And he was greatly respected. Uncle Jim left the village in Mansa early to work as an electrician for the copper mines in Mufulira District on the Copperbelt Province of Zambia. This was at a time in the colonial days when few Africans would hold such jobs. My father would tell me stories of how, as a young boy, he would struggle to finance his childhood education in Mansa. He would tell my grandparents that if he had to walk 166 kilometers (103 miles) from the village in Mansa to Mufulira District on the Copperbelt Province just to get money for his school from his elder brother, Uncle Jim, then he was going to do just that. He was truly determined to get his education. My grandparents panicked and told my father, their youngest child, that it was too risky to walk such a long distance alone. They were right. But my father would not compromise his zeal of acquiring a good education with the prospect of remaining semi-literate or illiterate. For him, education was not an option, but a mandatory obligation. It was a must-have.

The journey between Mansa and Mufulira would start with hours and hours of walking from Mansa District to the banks of the Luapula River. After crossing the mighty Luapula, one would then cross the neighboring country, DRC, walking for days before getting to the other side of Zambia. Even when you got there, you still had to continue for hours and hours before arriving in downtown Mufulira District. But my father was determined. He eventually convinced my grandparents that he would travel with some elderly villagers who habitually traversed that route in search of economic opportunities in the copper mining town of Mufulira. I remember when I was a teenager that my father would tell me how he made that long trip from Mansa to Mufulira, walking days and nights just to get money for his school fees from his elder brother, Uncle Jim.

His other siblings in the village almost gave up on the prospects for going further in school, given the risk that it entailed of walking so far just to go and get money for school fees from Uncle Jim. My father's siblings feared their eldest brother for his stern discipline. Uncle Jim did not tolerate any nonsense or indiscipline from any family member. But my father, despite being the youngest in the family, had the courage to face up to him and ask him to pay for his education. The journey from Mansa to Mufulira was not an easy one. It would take several days, and anything could happen along the way. You could be attacked and eaten by wild animals. But the courage and determination to get an education kept my father securely anchored in his beliefs. In those days, telegrams or traditional forms of money transfer were the preserve of the whites. It was tough, but that was the man my father was – a man of courage and faith! He would later return to Mansa with the same villagers, using that same route once again. As a child, I was nicknamed 'Jim' after Uncle Jim. Most of my childhood friends knew me as Jim, not Kenneth. The latter name only became more socialized in my high school days and when I got to university.

The second born in my father's family was Uncle Robert. I recall meeting Uncle Robert on many occasions when he would visit from the village. He was a tall man with the dark complexion that is quite common among some ethnic groups of Uganda and Kenya, and he had a deep baritone voice when he spoke. After Uncle Robert came my father's only sister, Auntie Pauline or Bana Mpundu (the mother of twins). She was married to a Mr Fungamwango and her first children were twins, Gabriel and Cosmas. The twins are likely to have been named after St Gabriel, the Archangel, and St Cosmas. I never really got to meet her, as she probably died before I was born. When she died, my father, as a young and single man back then, took in Gabriel and Cosmas and raised them like his own children. My father would narrate how he, in the small bachelor's residence back then, would share a bed with the two boys, one on his left and the other on his right, just to ensure that they did not fall into hardship after losing their mother. The boys' father, a Mr Fungamwango, was reportedly a Tanzanian businessman who had either moved back to Tanzanian or the Democratic Republic of Congo (DRC). Although my father educated and raised his nephews, the twins, until they became adults and independent, he did not stop them from using their biological father's name, Fungamwango.

After bearing twins, my father's sister and her husband, Mr Fungamwango, then had a daughter, cousin Chola, who unfortunately died in her teenage years. They had two sons after cousin Chola, cousin Alex and cousin Michael. Both Alex and Michael adopted their mother's surname, which was also my father's surname, Mwenda, since their biological mother had left them in my father's care. Thus, the two were Michael Kosamu Mwenda and Alex Mukobe Mwenda. They did not take the name Fungamwango, because it was my father who, essentially, raised them.

Cousin Michael came to stay with us in Livingstone. Cousin Alex remained in the village. My father gave almost everyone around him an opportunity to get a good education. Many years later, one of his nephews, cousin Gabriel, who was a twin, died in a tragic road accident in Chipata District, where he had gone for work from Lusaka. My father took in some of his children to educate them. In many African settings, when a parent dies very few relatives will show interest in looking after or taking care of the deceased's child or children. All they are interested in is looting the estate of the deceased through property-grabbing. But my father was not like that. He was above board. Educated at the University of Toronto and the University of Saskatchewan in Canada, JT was a civilized and enlightened man. All he wanted was to ensure that his nephew's children also received an education, just as he had educated their father.

My father asked one of my sisters, Catherine, to take in and look after one of cousin Gabriel's daughters who was about to complete high school. My father was a visionary. As administrator of his deceased nephew's estate, he made sure that the estate was well managed before he handed it over to the deceased's children when they became adults. There was no primitive property-grabbing. JT was a different kind of guy altogether. He always had a big heart for others.

At the time, my father was retired and advanced in age, but that did not stop him from helping his nephew's children. He did what he had to do. He had also previously taken in one of cousin Cosmas' sons to give him an opportunity for high school education. That was the man my father was. In addition, he had taken in a number of my mother's relatives at various points in time, including two of my first cousins whose father was my mother's brother, Bashi Chibwe, just to help them to get a good education. My father was a man who loved education all his life. If I were to describe him in a few words, I would say that the two things defined his life are: (a) the love of God and the upholding of Christian ethical and moral values and principles and, (b) the unceasing love of education, as well as his own inspiring effort to get an education at a time when many of our people did not appreciate such edifying things.

After Auntie Pauline came Uncle Justin. I saw Uncle Justin several times when he would visit from the village. He was a jovial man and loved his drink. He was also a smoker. But every time he came to visit from the village, I noticed that he would be scared to smoke in the presence of Dad. He would also avoid touching any alcohol when Dad was around. He would wait until Dad had gone for work. Uncle Justin would then smile, light up, and ask me to pass him his cigarettes and beer. With a sigh of relief, he would go on to say, smiling: "Wiso alya fya!" ("Your father is a very strict man.")

After Uncle Justin came Uncle Stephen. Unfortunately, I never got to meet Uncle Stephen, though my mother told me about him. My father never really spoke much about his own family. He was a rather reserved man. Then after Uncle Stephen came Uncle Albert, my father's immediate elder brother. He died very young, before he even reached the age of ten, from what could have been measles. I recall that my father once shared brief anecdotes about Uncle Albert, but it was my mother who would often give fuller details. As I mentioned above, my father was the youngest in the family and became the greatest gamechanger.

On my mother's side, I had met my maternal grandmother on several occasions. It is said that her family came originally from Luwingu district and settled in Ushi land. Some of her family members, however, did not migrate and remained in Luwingi. My siblings and I only knew our maternal grandmother as 'Ba Mama Bana Chibwe' (Grandma, the mother of Mr Chibwe) since her eldest son, my mother's brother, was 'Ba Chibwe'. We also knew one of grandma's sisters as Ba Mama Ba Maggie (Margaret). Katopwa was her first name. My grandmother's surname was Nsamba. Little is, however, known about her father, my maternal great grandfather, Mr Nsamba. Later, I got to learn that my grandmother's first name was Christina. Her middle name was Ng'andwe and her other name was Safie, so she was Christina Safie Ng'andwe Nsamba, and her other siblings included her brother, Ba Speshya, and her sisters Bana Mwansa Nkulu (Chipelo was her first name), Bana Mwelwa Chibalo (Lise was her first name), Bana Bwanga (Mwansa was her first name) and Bana Chamba Malicawa (Mwila was her first name). My maternal grandmother's oldest sibling was Bana Bwanga.

My immediate young brother's daughter is named Christina after my maternal grandmother. My mother had a brother, Ba Chibwe (or Bashi Chibwe, since he named one of his sons after himself), who I have mentioned above. Bashi Chibwe was a miner in Kitwe. The father of my mother and Bashi Chibwe was a man by the name of Mr Kalobwe Mwalimu. He is said to have been a businessman whose ancestry was allegedly Tanzanian. When Grandpa, Mr Mwalimu, died, his brother, Mr Kalasa, together with their mother (i.e. the mother of both Ba Mwalimu and Ba Kalasa), that is, my maternal great grandmother, Ba muka Nsamba, took up the responsibility of educating my mother and her sibling, Bashi Chibwe. My maternal great grandmother's first name was Ng'andwe, and after her my immediate elder sister, Matilda, is named. Then, my immediate young brother, Eugene, is named as 'Kalobwe' after my maternal grandfather. My mother also had three half-siblings later on her father's side. I only met one of them, a lady based in Ndola city. Otherwise I never knew much about my mother's other siblings or my maternal grandfather except that grandpa, known famously as 'Mwalimu' (teacher), died when my mother had just started second grade in Chipili District. I do know, however, that my mother's maternal grandfather was Shikulu (grandpa) Nsamba. My mother's maiden names were Esther Mpande. Her last name was my maternal grandma's surname.

When my mother died, a family member giving a eulogy at my mother's funeral added the name 'Kalasa' as one of my mother's family names. I was taken aback. Then it dawned on me that my mother had a female first cousin, Auntie Rose Kalasa, who once stayed with us in Luanshya. I would thus think that the name 'Kalasa' became an extended family name in my mother's family. I have shared a photo below taken in the colonial days when my mother had just gotten married to my father and way before my father even bought his first car in 1957. My mother must have been in her early twenties at the time. In those days, owning a bicycle was a rare thing and was considered very prestigious among both whites and blacks.

Below is another picture of my mother taken shortly after Zambia attained political independence from the British.

Although I was born in Livingstone city in Southern Province of Zambia, my parents, Mr Joseph T. Mwenda and Mrs Esther M Mwenda, hailed from the Ushi tribe of Mansa District in Luapula Province, Zambia. Mansa remains the provincial capital of Luapula. Before moving to Livingstone, my parents had lived and worked in Isoka and Kasama Districts in the modern day Muchinga and Northern Provinces of Zambia. Then, I noted earlier that from Livingstone my family moved to Luanshya District on the Copperbelt Province of Zambia. That relocation happened sometime towards the end of 1976.

As a young boy, I got to learn from some family elders that my paternal grandfather, Mr Peter Mwenda, founded Mwenda village in Mansa District. This village falls under the umbrella jurisdiction of Chief Chimese, one of the chiefs of the Ushi people of Mansa. My father was born in Mwenda village. However, apart from Chief Chimese, the other chiefs of the Ushi people in Mansa are Chief Chisunka, Chief Mibenge, Chief Mabumba, Chief Kalaba, Chief Matanda and Chief Kalasa Lukangaba. Also, in the nearby Milenge district, the two Ushi chiefs there are Chief Sokontwe and Senior Chief Milambo. Coincidentally, in Chipili district, where my mother spent her early childhood, there is Chief Mwenda of the Chishinga people. But my family is Ushi, not Chishinga. So, where did grandpa Peter come from, since we are told that he was the one who founded Mwenda village in Chief Chimese's chiefdom? Where was he before that? Who was his father? Could it be that grandpa Peter moved with his people from the neighboring areas around Mansa to settle in Mansa and established Mwenda village? Or could he have come from across the Luapula River in DRC, as was the case for many people during the Luba-Lunda diaspora movement when they migrated from the Kola region of DRC into Zambia?

I am, however, mindful of the scholarly work that has been written or published on the origins of the Bemba-speaking people, including the Ushi and other Luba-Lunda diasporans. I do not intend to depart from that literature, but to build on it. I want to narrow down the discussion to the roots of my family tree so as to get a concise picture of where my family possibly hails from. I will touch on this issue before I conclude this chapter. Here, suffice it to say that the Ushi people of Luapula province are said to have come from Katanga region, one of the four large provinces set up in the Belgian Congo in 1914, and which region became one of the eleven provinces of DRC between 1966 and 2015. The Ushi people are also said to be a sub-group of the Bemba people, though they were the first to migrate from DRC's Katanga region to modern Zambia, paving the way for the larger Bemba-speaking group of people to follow along. In 2015, Katanga province, previously known as Shaba Province under President Mobutu Sese Seko when DRC was known as Zaire, was split into the Lualaba, Haut-Lomami, Tanganyika, and Haut-Katanga provinces.

As founder of Mwenda village, known famously as 'pa Mwenda' or 'pa mushi pa Mwenda' in Zambia's Mansa District, my grandfather, Mr Peter Mwenda, was the headman of that village. He was therefore often referred to fondly as 'Mwine mushi', translated directly as the 'owner of the village'. Indeed, the village was named after him. The instruction of family elders has it that my grandfather hailed from Yasakwa village near Mansa district, with some of his relatives from Yasakwa proceeding to settle in or establish Million (pa mushi pa Million) and Chakulya (pa mushi pa Chakulya) villages in or around Mansa area. Yasakwa village is said to be located about 3 kilometers from downtown Mansa on the way to Samfya after Mabumba village. These developments must have taken place in the mid-to-late 1800s because my father, as the youngest child in his family, was born in Mansa in 1928, meaning, I would estimate that my paternal grandfather was between his mid-thirties and mid-forties when he moved to Mansa from Yasakwa village before my father was born. My father's close relatives included Hon Mr Wilson Chakulya, who was a senior diplomat and cabinet minister in the Zambian Government of President Kenneth Kaunda. Hon. Mr Chakulya was my father's nephew, and he hailed from Chakulya village. It is believed that Yasakwa village was the first place of settlement when my father's people came to Zambia from the Democratic Republic of Congo (DRC) during the Luba-Lunda diaspora migration. According to the oral tradition of some family elders and sources in DRC, my father's people are likely to have migrated to Yasakwa village in Zambia from Chief Mpala's chiefdom in DRC. Chief Mpala's chiefdom was under the paramount chieftaincy of Paramount Chief Msiri Ngelengwa Mwenda in DRC, to whom the lineage of my father's royal ties is alleged to flow. The *Oxford Reference: Dictionary of African Biography,* published online in 2012 by Oxford University Press, has the following on the earlier Msiri (c. 1830-1891):

"...political leader in eastern and central Africa, was born Mwenda Msiri Ngelengwa Shitambi in Tabora (in present-day Tanzania) to an ambitious Sumbwa Nyamwezi trader. Msiri rose to become one of the most powerful of a new class of nineteenth-century African rulers who used firearms and long-distance trade to build up spheres of influence independent of clan linkages or hereditary inheritance. Msiri's father, Kalasa, held a chieftainship under the great Nyamwezi ruler Mirambo and was also a very successful copper merchant. Known as the Yeke, Msiri and other Nyamwezi brought the peoples of the Katanga plateau coastal trade goods while providing a market for the heavy copper crosses molded in Katanga refineries."

Interestingly, the names Kalasa and Mirambo (the latter name is written and pronounced as

'Milambo' in Zambia's Luapula Province) are names of some royal chiefs of the Ushi people in Zambia's Luapula Province today. These names are also found amongst many other Luapula people.

The *Oxford Reference: Dictionary of African Biography*, however, continues as follows:

"Msiri's first political strategy was to ally himself with the Wasanga in their war against a Lunda regent. Msiri was able to defeat the Lunda king, earning the gratitude and subordination of the Wasanga. He followed this victory with a series of challenges to local rulers, including the Katanga chief of the Lamba peoples. To the north he halted Luba expansion and broke their control over trade westward. By 1867 he was challenging the Kazembe of Eastern Lunda for regional supremacy. An alliance with the Swahili Arab merchant-potentate Tippu-Tip in 1870 helped Msiri to decisively defeat the Kazembe and further expand his rule onto the Katanga plateau."

So, my paternal grandfather, Mr Peter Mwenda, alleged to have royal ties to the Paramount Chief Msiri Ngelengwa Mwenda in DRC, left DRC to look for employment in Zambia. Paramount Chief Msiri Ngelengwa Mwenda in DRC is said to have had around 500 children born from around 300 wives that he would marry from every tribe that he conquered. According to Mwami Antoine Munongo Luhinda Shalo of the Yeke people, in an online article published in 2021 by [Mwami Msiri, King of Garanganze](), and titled, the "Bayeke Culture: Mwami Msiri Ngelengwa Shitambi," Paramount Chief Msiri Ngelengwa Mwenda is said to have been "...fearless in battle and magnanimous in time of peace. His generosity and loyalty to the Yeke people made him a beloved monarch, whose legend was passed down in the oral tradition of story-telling, later kept alive through written accounts and yeke traditional songs. He was the first Mwami of the Bayeke in Katanga, until the 20th of December 1891, when he was killed by Bodson – a so-called captain of the Belgian expedition, whose sole purpose was to achieve, by any means necessary, total subjugation in the name of the Belgian king Leopold II. After his death, the Belgians continued their pattern of brutality and forced labor in Katanga and the Congo at large. His option to die instead of being enslaved symbolizes the Yeke spirit of refusing to bow to oppressing forces and colonial tyranny. That moral stand lives on strong in the form of a motto, which was uttered by Msiri a few days before he was assassinated: 'Sumbwa Kufwa'. It means: 'I would rather die than be enslaved'."

Mwami Antoine Munongo Luhinda Shalo writes further that three of Paramount Chief Msiri Ngelengwa Mwenda's sons succeeded their father as Kings of the Bayeke, namely: (i) Mwenda Mukanda-Bantu, (ii) Mwenda Kitanika Mabumba, and (iii) Mwenda Munongo Musamfya Ntanga.

Looking back, before I entered Law School at the University of Zambia (UNZA) in the mid-1980s, I studied political science under one of my favorite professors, Dr Angel Mukanda-Bantu Mwenda, who held a PhD in political economy from the University of Leeds in the UK. It is very unlikely that the likeness of my professor's name, 'Mukanda-Bantu Mwenda', and that of Paramount Chief Msiri Ngelengwa Mwenda's son, 'Mwenda Mukanda-Bantu', was a mere coincidence. A combination of such African names is not that common. One would surmise that my professor must have descended from the same royal lineage of Paramount Chief Msiri Ngelengwa Mwenda. I came to learn later that Dr Angel Mukanda-Bantu Mwenda, though Zambian, had, like me, some DRC ancestral heritage. Even more interesting is the fact that he carried both names of one of the sons of Paramount Chief Msiri Ngelengwa Mwenda – that is, Mwenda Mukanda-Bantu.

After Paramount Chief Msiri Ngelengwa Mwenda's death, internal royal wrangles ensued and are said to have led to the dispersion of the paramount chief's family members, with some crossing into Zambia. Others stayed behind in DRC. With these dispersions came the weakening of the Yeke empire and the assimilation of the dispersed people into other tribal groupings where they resettled. Oral tradition has it that grandpa, Mr Peter Mwenda, who was Ushi-speaking, travelled from Lubumbashi in the Katanga Region of DRC to Luapula Province of Zambia, looking for employment opportunities. He finally landed a job in Mansa district, Zambia, as a postmaster at a local post office. He then married my paternal grandmother, Ba Mama Ba Belita, who was also Ushi-speaking and a Zambian national, and, through that union, my paternal grandfather naturalized as a Zambian citizen. And because of his royal blood from DRC, my grandfather, Mr Peter Mwenda, after arriving in Yasakwa village, is said to have moved on to set up his own village, known as Mwenda village, in the Mansa district of Luapula Province near where he had found a job. Some unconfirmed reports, however, indicate that later, around the early 1980s, there were rumors of some xenophobic talk by some native people around the surrounding areas of Mwenda village to have our relatives from Mwenda village evicted from there, alleging that they did not belong to that area and should go back to where they came from in DRC. My father is reported to have been informed of those rumors, and he allegedly wrote a letter to the chief, Chief Chimese, explaining the Ushi roots of his family and how his mother was a Zambian and how his father's family, also Ushi, had Zambian roots, notwithstanding that some of them had settled in DRC. Indeed, there are Ushi-speaking people both in Zambia and DRC. My father's letter is said to have salvaged the situation and ended the xenophobic rumors.

When the time came for my father, as the youngest and only surviving child of my paternal grandfather, Mr Peter Mwenda, to succeed as village headman of Mwenda village, he was reluctant to take up the role. I could understand this. My father had left the village a long time ago, though he was still in touch with his family relations in the village. He decided instead to nominate one of his nephews, a Mr Chungu, to serve on his behalf as the headman. Mr Chungu had to travel from the village in Mansa to Luanshya to get blessing from my father, as was expected under our African traditional norms, so that he (Mr Chungu) could become the headman.

In the course of writing this autobiography, I got to learn that the village headman, Mr Chungu, passed on around mid-May 2024. The question then became whether any one of us in the family, as the Mwendas, would ascend to headmanship of Mwenda village or we would leave it, as Dad did, to other family relations. The answer seemed obvious. My siblings and I had no interest in succeeding as headman. Suffice it to say that I can claim, and justifiably so, that I carry royal blood in me and that I am proper royalty.

I once asked my father about his family lineage. My father explained to me that his paternal grandfather was a Mr Shombo. But it is not clear where my great grandpa, Mr Shombo, came from or lived before his son, Mr Peter Mwenda, founded Mwenda village. Given what has been explained above, it is likely that my great grandpa, Mr Shombo, lived in or around Lubumbashi area in DRC. What is, however, clear is that my great grandpa, Mr Shombo, was the father of my paternal grandfather, 'Mwine mushi.' And it is from the family of my great grandpa, Mr Shombo (and his siblings), that some of my relatives, like the late Mr Francis Kapansa, who was my uncle and one of the first black Africans to be licensed as a soccer referee in Zambia, came. Uncle Francis Kapansa later became a prominent politician in the UNIP Government of President Kenneth Kaunda.

It is also important to bring in the concept of clan or totem here. My paternal grandfather, Mr Peter Mwenda, belonged to the abena Nsengo clan. Then, my paternal grandmother, Mrs Belita Mwenda, belonged to the abena Muti clan. On my mother's side, my maternal grandmother, Mrs Christina Nsmba-Mwalimu belonged to the abena Mwansa clan while her husband, Mr Mwalimu, belonged to the abena Mbushi clan. Now, because many people in Luapula and Bemba-land follow the matrilineal system of succession, a mother's clan tends to be the dominant clan at the family-level. Thus, in sum, on my paternal side, I belong to the 'abena Muti' clan. On my maternal side,

I belong to the 'abena Mwansa' clan. The concept of clan, known locally as 'umukowa', refers to a group of close-knit and interrelated families. It is, however, not something that can be grasped easily by an outsider. Suffice it to say that, in Africa, we not only have tribes but also have totems and clans. My father was from the abena Muti clan. My mother was from the abena Mwansa clan. The two got married in Mansa in the mid to late-1950s. Both my parents were devout Christians and educationists. My mother belonged to the Anglican church before she married my father. My father, as already established, was a staunch Catholic.

After the two got married, my mother converted to Catholicism. She was not forced to do so. Rather, it was a conscious and well thought out decision on her part. In many cultures, it is expected that the female spouse will take up the name of her husband as her last name. The same is true when it comes to matters of faith and religion. And so it came to be. This has nothing to do with issues of patriarchy or misogyny, as some overzealous gender activists might want to assume.

I am mindful that some readers might see things differently on the issues of a female spouse taking up her husband's name and religious denomination. That is perfectly understandable. We all have different historical experiences, and they inform our outlook differently. While some may have no issues with the idea of a married woman taking up her husband's last name or religious denomination, others may have issues with that. Yes, people are free to disagree and maintain their maiden name or religious denomination. Nobody is stopping anyone. Experience alone teaches us some real-life lessons. And every society has different emphasis. From the assertive ubiquitous notions of individual entitlements in the Global North to arguments of individual and communal responsibilities in the Global South, many lawyers and legal scholars have still not come to a consensus on the criticality of context in envisioning and appreciating the scope and scale of the jurisprudence of human rights. Yet the dialectics of nature have shown different emphasis for every society at different epochs.

So, my mother's decision to convert to Catholicism was not because she did not know what she was doing spiritually or that she was confused about her faith. Rather, it was out of an enlightened and well-considered choice. When you get married, you become one before God. It is therefore ill-advised to bring up unnecessary issues of human rights and constitutional freedoms of expressions and conscience here. Marriage, as I know it, at least from the perspective of my culture, is about unity, as opposed to pursuing individualistic or egoistic goals. If anything, marriage places on the married couple responsibilities towards one another and towards their children. Your rights only come in after your responsibilities, though the two co-exist. Your rights and those of your spouse are predicated on your individual and joint responsibilities. Put simply, your rights only become primary if, or where, the responsibilities of the other party are abdicated or neglected.

Although my mother was born in Mansa, she spent her early childhood in Chipili District, a town not too far from Mansa. At the time, Chipili had a strong presence of the Anglican church. My mother began her elementary or primary education at Chipili. Many years later she would recall to me the names of some of her primary school teachers. Some of those teachers included notable Luapulan personalities such as Mr Jason Mfula and Mr Simon James Musonda Mwamba. The latter was the father of my good learned brother, the distinguished Oxford educated Anglican Church cleric, the Right Reverend Dr Musonda Trevor Selwyn Mwamba. Bishop Trevor Mwamba once served as the Anglican Bishop of Botswana and is now the elected President of the United National Independence Party (UNIP) in Zambia. The picture below, taken in April 2024, shows me with Bishop Mwamba when I hosted him to dinner in Lusaka, Zambia.

As I mentioned earlier, my mother lost her father when she was only in the second grade of primary school at Chipili mission (District). My mother moved back to the neighboring district of Mansa, together with her mother, settling pa mushi pa Mwenda. As noted earlier, Mansa was the capital of Luapula, and a Chipili District is not too far from Mansa. Chipili District is said to have been separated from another famous district in Luapula Province, Mwense District, in 2012. Most of my mother's relatives are from Chipili area. My mother always spoke fondly of 'pa Chipili' (Chipili District) where she came from. She once told me humorously how my youngest brother, Joe, once drove to Luapula Province for work and called her from pa Chipili, saying: "Imwe Bana Mwenda, epa Chipili apa mu landapo lyonse ati, pa Chipili?" ("Mum, is this the so-called Chipili that you always talk about as if it is some great place?")

Chipili District shares its western border with the Democratic Republic of Congo (DRC) and its eastern border with the Northern Province of Zambia. Some relatives of my mother who I have never met migrated many years ago to DRC. At the time, DRC, especially the region across the Luapula River, was reported to have better hospitals and business opportunities. So, it is understandable what could have motivated some migration to DRC at the time. My father too had some relatives who moved to DRC, but some of them returned to Zambia later.

I remember meeting one such uncle by the name of José. His English name must have been Joseph, but the francophones refer to 'Joseph' as 'José'. We all knew him as Uncle José. He dressed elegantly like a typical guy from across the Luapula River in modern day DRC. Uncle José returned to Zambia in the 1970s and settled in Chingola District on the Copperbelt Province of Zambia. It was easy for some of our Luapula people to move across into DRC because only the Luapula River separated Zambia's Luapula Province from DRC. On either side of the border, you could find the Ushi people and an abundant usage of the Bemba language. Even today, both DRC and Zambia have the Ushi people, just as you would find the Tumbuka people in the eastern part of Zambia and the neighboring part of Malawi. The current borders of many African nations were drawn out in Europe by the colonialists during the Berlin conference of 1884-85, splitting across many African chiefdoms, kingdoms, clans and families through externally imposed geographical demarcations.

In 2005, I visited Uganda. I was pleasantly surprised to find that names such as Mwenda, Kasolo, Chintu, Katongo, and Mulenga, which I thought were Zambian names, are also found in Uganda. In Zambia, these names are common among the Bemba and the Luapula Lunda-speaking people and many closely allied tribal groupings associated with the Luba-Lunda diaspora. They are all said to have migrated from DRC, although inter-marriages also took place with the people they met or conquered when they arrived in Zambia. Now the question is: how come Uganda has the Zambian names listed above? Could it be that the migrations from the Luba-Lunda Kingdom of Mwata Yamvu in the modern DRC could have included some people moving up north from DRC into Uganda while others headed eastwards towards Zambia? Historical writings, unfortunately, are not of much help. A plausible explanation here could be that, if humanity, as some historical studies suggest, started around the Great Lakes region of Africa, and if we were to take into account the fact that most historical migrations would follow the rivers and lakes to enable the migrants to access fish for food and remain safe from land-based dangerous animals as well as access water to drink and bath, it could be argued that the interlacustrine ('between lakes') migration or trekking of some of these migrants can be traced back to the Great Lakes region. DRC, I submit, could have been a stop-over for a few years or decades before some factions of the migrants that originated initially from the Great Lakes trekked further into modern day Zambia.

This thesis seems more plausible, especially as Paramount Chief Mwenda Msiri Ngelengwa Shitambi, who lived between 1830 and December 20, 1891, was himself a Nyamwezi from Tabora in modern-day Tanzania. Like his father, Kalasa, he was a trader and was involved in the trade of ivory, copper and slaves through the trade route of Ujiji on Lake Tanganyika and then to Lake Mweru and Katanga. Viewed from this angle, the ancestry of my people stretches further than DRC.

My ancestral heritage could also have some Tanzanian roots. I will explain below some anthropological-linguistic similarities between my native language, Ushi (including Bemba) and the Luganda language spoken in modern-day Uganda as well as some languages spoken in countries such as Burundi and Rwanda neighboring Uganda in the Great Lakes region. Here, suffice it to say that the four riparian states that are often considered as comprising the Great Lakes region are DRC, Uganda, Burundi, and Rwanda. The Great Lakes region is the area that lies between western Lake Victoria, northern Lake Tanganyika and lakes Kivu, Edward, and Albert. There are a few other closely adjacent bodies of water such as Lake Rukwa and Lake Mweru that are however often not included in the definition of the Great Lakes of Africa. That said, additional riparian states in the neighboring region, such as Kenya and Tanzania, are often considered as part of the Great Lakes region, though riparian states that lie southwards such as Zambia, Malawi, and Mozambique are often excluded from the definition. Neither is Ethiopia, which lies a bit to the north, considered part of the region. Yet all the four states that are excluded do border at least one of the Great Lakes.

Turning back to similarities between some Zambian and Ugandan names and words, one could argue that it is highly improbable that the people that the Luba-Lunda Diaspora migrants found and conquered in Zambia originated from the Great Lakes region and popularized or socialized their names and language to their conquerors. Rather, it is the conquerors who are likely to have brought those names and words with them when they arrived in Zambia because quite often the dominant culture or ideology of a given society is that of the dominant governing or ruling class. Just how can we explain the fact that some of my Ugandan friends in Kampala, especially those who speak Luganda, could understand most of my telephone conversations each time I called Zambia to speak with some of my extended family members, using the Zambian language, Bemba? Even my young brother, Joe, while studying for his Masters degree at the University of Western Cape in Cape Town, South Africa, was pleasantly shocked to find that he could understand the conversations of a classmate of his from Burundi whenever that classmate was talking to a fellow Burundi national in their native language.

This evidence is not a combination of mere coincidences or anecdotal conjectures. There is a consistent and systematic pattern of similarities such that we can safely surmise that my people must have trekked down to Zambia from the Great Lakes region via DRC, moving alongside the waters of Lake Tanganyika. On the western shore of Lake Tanganyika is DRC. On the eastern shore lies Tanzania. Then Zambia lies further down on the southern tip of Lake Tanganyika. Long journeys of this kind would require some resting along the way for days, months or years. And so, DRC, which also borders Lake Albert and Lake Edward, the lakes right above Lake Tanganyika on the geographical map of central and east Africa, could have been a more convenient route than Tanzania, which has Lake Victoria far up north next to Uganda with a vast area of land in-between. This huge area could have discouraged the migrants from transiting through Tanzania's hinterland. Indeed, in the absence of any scientific DNA testing to test for the origins of a people, it is hard to think otherwise.

Below is a map of the Great Lakes region.

Source: US Library of Congress Blogs, "Detail of Africa showing the many international borders of the African Great Lakes region. Lakes Turkana, Edward, and Kivu do not appear on the map. *Africa*. U.S. Central Intelligence Agency, 2011. Library of Congress Geography and Map Division," accessed online <<https://blogs.loc.gov/maps/2021/12/among-the-greats/>>, March 10, 2024.

Given what I have explained above, it now makes sense why some sources within my extended family allege that some of my paternal grandfather's ancestors came from Tanzania, while other sources claim that our people came from Katanga region of DRC, in particular, in Chief Mpala's chiefdom near Lubumbashi, the capital city of DRC's Haut-Katanga Province. These assertions are not far from my deductions and findings. Put simply, both Tanzania and DRC could have been transit-points for some of my ancestors before they arrived in Zambia, although some of them could have remained in Tanzania and DRC, respectively, and settled there.

CHAPTER 5

My early childhood

In the preceding chapter, I sought to give the reader a glimpse into my family background and roots, going back as far as my paternal great-great-grandfather, Ba Shombo, and my great-great maternal grandfather, Ba Nsamba. In this chapter, I shift gears to take you through my early childhood. As noted in Chapter 3, I was born on January 5, 1969, in Zambia's tourist capital, Livingstone city. I was baptized at St Theresa's Catholic Cathedral in downtown Livingstone. Back then, almost everyone referred to St. Theresa's Catholic Cathedral as "217". The number "217" was the postal box address of the church. But many people do not know the meaning behind that "217" number to this day. The cathedral was right next to a Catholic primary school, Holly Cross Convent School, where I started elementary school. The resident priest at St. Theresa's Catholic Cathedral was Fr. Jude McKenna, an Irish priest who is known famously as the father of judo in Zambia. Fr Jude was a tall, nice and friendly man with a white beard. He could have baptized me when I was born because I do not remember any other priest at that parish when I was growing up. I have followed Fr Jude's work as a priest and a blackbelt judo martial artist. He is now retired as a priest and is back in Ireland after spending about fifty years in Zambia.

My godfather was a Mr Mutale. He and his wife were close friends of my parents in Livingstone. We got to know them as uncle and auntie respectively. Many years later, when I was in the UK, I asked my parents for his contact details. I got his phone number and called him up from my base in England. I was at the time based in the UK as an Assistant Professor of Law at the University of Warwick. It was good to reconnect and speak with my godfather. Mr Mutale had by then long retired from his job in Livingstone and relocated with his wife back to Kasama District in Northern Province where the couple was originally from. I recall that Uncle Mutale asked me to get him a blood pressure machine from the UK. I did the needful and delivered it in Zambia during one of my visits back home. I last saw his wife, Auntie Mutale, at my father's funeral in Luanshya. Uncle Mutale was by then too old to travel for my father's funeral. A few years later, I learned that both Uncle Mutale and Auntie Mutale had passed on.

Let me preface this chapter with a disclaimer that the views that I share below are based on my experiences as a participant-observer, and proceed from the general to the specific. As we lawyers say, to every general rule there is an exception. Indeed, it is not my intention to generalize anything or use stereotypes. So if you have a different view from the one I will share below, it does not mean that you are right. Neither does it mean that I am generalizing or stereotyping. For you have never walked in my shoes. Even in slavery, the views of the enslaver were usually different from those of the enslaved. Against this background, let us take a more reasoned look.

In Livingstone, when my father left for his university studies abroad, I was a toddler. I remained behind with my mother and siblings. I started school in 1974 at Holy Cross Convent School in Livingstone. I was only five years old at the time. When my father left for Canada, a Mr ABC (real name withheld), the man who was my father's immediate senior and the College Principal of Livingstone Trades Training Institute, the college where my father was serving as Vice-Principal, asked our family to vacate the affluent college staff housing that we were occupying as a family, even though my father was simply on study leave and had not resigned from the college. He was, for all intents and purposes, still employed as the Vice-Principal of the college, although he was away on study-leave. My father had only gone abroad for further studies while on study-leave. But, in his own wisdom, Mr ABC saw it differently. He was not only ruthless but heartless. His decision was not only unreasonable but also lacked merit. Where were we going to go? I mean, how can you kick the family of your own staff member out into the cold simply because he is away? On what basis? We had nowhere to go.

Luckily, my mother was educated and had a professional career of her own as a teacher. So, she was able to find alternative housing accommodation quickly in the newly built local council houses in Dambwa North. But even that process of securing alternative housing was not as smooth as it may seem. Had it not been for the intervention and support of my father's close friend, Mr (Uncle) Pembanyali, even that Dambwa North housing would not have been secured easily. To us, as my father and mother's children, Mr Pembanyali was more like an uncle, and his wife, very close friends with my mother, was more like an auntie. As minorities in a place that was somewhat hostile to outsiders, our families formed a social network of minorities for survival. It is natural wherever you go in the world for minority people to unite when faced with discrimination and prejudice from the dominant majority. Mr ABC's decision to evict us when my father was abroad was not free of illogical difficulties and tribal undertones. But thankfully my mother had a professional job of her own as a teacher and, through our minority networks, we found a new home in Livingstone.

My mother owned her own car, a white Datsun 1600, and would thus drive my siblings and I to school. She was already driving when I was born. That really helped when we moved houses. The move was somewhat a social downgrade.. But we had to take what was available even though my father, as I have stated above, had not resigned from the college. He was still a college member of staff and was on study-leave abroad when his family was evicted by his boss and almost thrown out in the cold. Clearly, to Mr ABC, we did not 'belong'. He wanted to make that point very clear.

You might be wondering what was driving all these shenanigans. Tribalism, like racism, can be found anywhere and at any time. It is not limited to certain people or places. And tribalism can be fueled by, inter alia, a resentful attitude towards social groups that you believe, rightly or wrongly, are responsible for your real or self-imagined fears. Some people can hate outsiders, fearing that they are taking their jobs and economic opportunities. Other folks exhibit traits of bigotry for one reason or another, including fearing that outsiders can win over the hearts of their women. Bigotry can extend to the marginalization of minorities, the practice of religious and cultural intolerance as well as that of shared or personal views of tribal pride, the urge by a group of people to access and control national resources, the emergence of ethnic group coalitions built around tribal cousinship, and the presence of a national identity crisis fueled by a poor vision of a nation's leadership. Put in context, you can have clusters of two whites, two Asians, two Hispanics and two black people, with one member of each cluster being racist while the other is not. By parity of reasoning, you can have, in a country such as Zambia, two Bemba men, two Tonga men, two Lozi men, or two Ngoni men, with one of the two in each cluster being a tribalist whilst the other is not. Indeed, not everyone you meet is a tribalist or racist simply because his brother, sister, father, mother, uncle or cousin harbors tribal or racist tendencies.

I am, however, mindful that some people are just too sensitive to have any meaningful and objective discussion on anything to do with tribalism or racism. They would rather pretend that such issues don't exist. Others, out of guilt, would rather attack and counter-accuse the person highlighting issues of racism or tribalism as the actual racist or tribalist. In psychology, we call that 'cognitive dissonance.' The fact remains that tribalism, like racism, is real. We cannot escape from that truth. And being in denial does not help.

My father's boss, Mr ABC (real name withheld), was a man from a certain tribe in Zambia. By contrast, my father was from one of the tribes up north of the country. That, in and of itself, seemed to have been the main source of the problem. Mr ABC showed so much hostility towards my father and his family when my father was away in Canada. But how you treat people along the way matters. For the reader, you can choose to see the experience I have shared above as you wish. But it was not about government housing policy or a mere coincidence. Mr ABC kicked us out into the cold because he probably considered us as 'aliens' and far removed from his tribal or ethnic background. I was never raised to look at people through a tribal lens. We were shocked as a family.

Many years later when I was a student at the University of Zambia (UNZA), I saw some of this tribal-affinity nonsense in some university students. You could tell that even though some colleagues had left their home villages for the university, the village had not left their heads. I was disappointed by some colleagues who I had mistakenly thought were above the village mindset, especially one or two who had presented themselves to me as close friends initially until their true colors started showing as we progressed through the later years of our student life at university. Disloyalty in friendship was mushrooming. Such things destroy a good friendship, even though you might try to pretend later in life that you are still good friends. Someone once whispered to me that some people have a tendency to stick to their own kind as they grow older. To them, if you do not 'belong', then they do not consider you as one of them. And it is not uncommon for such people to switch allegiance and friendship to their 'own kind' and leave you out or abandon you. I saw it and was old enough to put things into perspective. The whole experience eroded the trust and confidence I had in some parochial and tribally inclined colleagues. With time, you get to know people for who they really are.

Be that as it may, in life, I have come to learn that two wrongs don't make a right. You cannot fight prejudice with prejudice. I was not going to start looking for new friends from what one would consider my 'own people'. I was not raised like that. As I stated earlier, I grew up in a cosmopolitan urban setting, not in a rural village setting where exposure to other cultures is limited. I grew up with ethos of diversity, inclusion and equity. Maybe it would have been different if, like some of those fellas I met at university, I had not had that rich background of diversity and inclusion. But, as it is, I have a global perspective of life and am above parochial and insular dispositions.

Many people in Zambia who grew up on the Copperbelt in the 1970s and 1980 can relate to the cosmopolitan nature of the Copperbelt. We had many people living with us from different parts of Africa and other continents, including Malawians, Senegalese, Malians, Zimbabweans, Namibians, South Africans, Egyptians, Indians, Pakistanis, Chinese, Japanese, Lebanese, Filipinos, Americans, Danes, Greeks, Germans, Swedes, Israelis, Congolese, Somalians, Ethiopians, Ugandans, Tanzanians, Angolans, Jamaicans, Ghanaians, Nigerians, Mozambicans and many other nationalities. We all mingled freely. There was no xenophobia or tribalism. It was open for all, regardless of one's tribe, ethnic background, race, or nationality. If you could survive the open competition on the Copperbelt back then, you could make it anywhere on this planet, including in New York, London, Paris, Frankfurt, Los Angeles, Chicago, Miami, Philadelphia, Washington DC, Toronto, Melbourne, Rome, Moscow, Kiev, Podgorica, Warsaw, Bucharest, Bishkek, Dushanbe, Tashkent, Belfast, Belgrade, Tirana, Budapest, Siberia, Damascus, Kabul, Grozny, Delhi, Lahore, Jakarta, Kuala Lumpur, Baghdad, Ramallah, Tel Aviv, Jerusalem, Tokyo, Beijing, Wellington, Rio de Janeiro, Bogotá, Kingston, Georgetown, Bridgetown, Cancún, Fortaleza, Nassau, Legazpi, Port Moresby, Lagos, Kinshasa, Nairobi, Accra, Algiers, Timbuktu, Nuku'alofa, Cairo and Johannesburg.

The lesson that one can draw from this is that you cannot fight tribal or racial prejudices with reverse prejudices. And tribalism or racism cannot go away simply by denying its existence. Certain things are not mere coincidences but socially ingratiated biases. And some of it manifests itself as unconscious bias. Yet, some superficial cynic might be too quick to counter-argue here. You cannot refute or dismiss what you have not witnessed or experienced. Until you experience or witness something, you might just end up misleading yourself with self-pacifying anecdotal conjectures. That you are a black man, for example, does not mean that you cannot be racist. That you are educated or financially wealthy does not mean you cannot be a tribalist. We have to be open-minded about these issues. That you are a white man married to a black woman does not mean you cannot be racist. Even some so-called Christians have racist and tribalist tendencies. Those gangsta proclivities follow them in the church. So, we must remain open-minded to all possibilities. Education or religion alone cannot rid you of racist or tribalist tendencies. Rather, education or religion can help you to mask your tendencies of bigotry or minimize them to a point where, like a virus, they cannot be detected. But what good is education or religion to an incorrigible heart that is filled with nothing but prejudice and arrogance? When we try to contest issues here, let us not argue from without. Emotive outbursts devoid of logical thought are meaningless. Looking back, I'd guess that my father, being a decent man, trusted Mr ABC. In his innocence, my father probably forgot one thing – he did not belong (i.e. the place was not very inclusive).

When my father returned from his studies in Canada, we moved out of Dambwa North to a posher urban residence. I still remember the address of that new home where we moved to, near downtown in Livingstone. It was 66 Nehru Way and was not far from the city center. It was a big house with a big yard and a servant's quarter. The house had five bedrooms and a nice patio. I recall that our neighbor on one side was a Mr Ng'ona. He drove a maroon fuel-injection Peugeot 504. On the other side was a Mr Mweetwa. He had two toddler daughters and a young wife. We would occasionally see him drive in and out. The man seemed somewhat aloof. I suspect he used to indulge in a fair share of alcohol.

Across the street from our house lived a white man who was a medical doctor. His name was Dr Stein. He drove a posh Citroen. Then, down the road at the junction of Airport Road and Nehru Way, was the home of the Permanent Secretary for Southern Province in the UNIP Government, a Mr Sokoni. He would often take an evening stroll to our house to catch up with Dad.

We remained at 66 Nehru Way until late 1976, when my father was promoted to head Luanshya Trades Training Institute on the Copperbelt. In fact, before he took up that appointment, he was being considered for another promotion to head Kabwe Trades Training Institute in Central Province, but in the end, he took up the Luanshya post. So the family moved to Luanshya in late 1976. Many years later, in 2016, as I was visiting Livingstone, I found time to drive to the address where we used live. I arrived at 66 Nehru Way only to find that the place is now a commercial lodge.

The original house that we lived in was allegedly sold by the Zambian Government when many government houses were being sold to sitting tenants. So, now a commercial lodge, Chapa Classic Lodge, sits at that address.

As a teenager in Luanshya, I remember that my father once offered college staff housing to one of my high school teachers, Mr XYZ (real name withheld), who was stranded upon arrival in Luanshya to take up his new teaching job. The man was desperately looking for housing accommodation and would have slept on the streets if my father had not stepped in to assist him and his family. Interestingly, Mr XYZ was of the same tribal and ethnic background as Mr ABC who had kicked us out of college staff housing when my father was in Canada. So, was it time for my father to take revenge? No, he was above that. My father, unlike Mr ABC, was very inclusive. The fact that my teacher, Mr XYZ, was from the same tribal and ethnic background as Mr ABC in Livingstone did not stop my father from helping Mr XYZ. As I said, you can have, for example, two Bembas, one, say, from Chinsali who is very proud and stubborn, and the other, say from Kasama, who is quite moderate. The two, despite both being Bembas, could have different cultural outlooks to life and issues. Even their appreciation of the value of diversity and inclusion could be different. My father studied educational psychology and public administration at university in Canada, and he understood these nuances very well. Besides, he was a Christian. My father would often tell me, 'Son, sometimes, a person who will help you in life may not be from those you consider your 'people'. The parable of the Good Samaritan in the Bible is very instructive, yet some people are just too incorrigible to learn.'

Unlike Mr ABC, Mr XYZ was a nice man and quite friendly. Therefore, you cannot judge someone simply because his brother or cousin was not inclusive and behaved in a weird way. Generalizations and stereotypes are not helpful. They can actually be retrogressive. Mr XYZ was a wonderful man. My father, as an inclusive man, offered him housing accommodation even though he (Mr XYZ) was not a lecturer at the college headed by my father. Indeed, my father rescued Mr XYZ and his family from becoming homeless. Mr XYZ had nowhere to stay in Luanshya when he arrived there for his new job as a high school teacher. Mr XYZ was a high school teacher at Luanshya Boys' Secondary School where I completed my high school education. He taught me in senior high school. My father reasoned, why should an innocent man who is a civil servant suffer when there were vacant houses for college lecturers at the nearby college that my father was heading? While Mr XYZ was waiting for his employer, the then Ministry of General Education, to get him housing accommodation it would not hurt to assist him with temporary housing for some months or a year, my father reasoned. The housing accommodation my father offered Mr XYZ was meant for college lecturers. Zambian public colleges were at the time under the Ministry of Higher Education, not the Ministry of General Education. Now, if you were to reverse the roles here, how do you think Mr ABC would have reacted if he was the one who had come across a stranded and recently arrived high school teacher from up north of the country who was in desperate need of housing accommodation? And imagine if Mr ABC had been disappointed or hurt previously by someone who was of the same tribal or ethnic affiliation as that high school teacher.

Mr ABC in Livingstone was unlike my father. The two were totally different men. Mr ABC should have reasoned, as my father did, that he should enable my family to stay on in the Livingstone college staff house until my father was back from his studies abroad. To put things in perspective, in the Luanshya case, if my father had not stepped in to assist Mr XYZ, the man and his family would have been out on the streets, at least for some weeks, months or even a year, before his employers, the Ministry of General Education, got him decent housing accommodation. My father salvaged the situation, acting with compassion. There was no bitterness in my father. He was a much bigger person in character. My father was not angry at all. He could have easily resorted to malicious tactics of reverse tribalism, but he did not. There was simply no time for retaliation or vendettas. Others would not have done what my father did. Mr XYZ was ever grateful to my father. He simply could not believe that this world could have such kind and humane people. Each time I met Mr XYZ, he would always tell me how my father was such a good man and how he rescued him for a near homeless situation. Mr XYZ would narrate to me time and again:

"Kenny, your father is a good man. He gave me housing accommodation in one of houses meant for college lecturers when I was not even a college lecturer but a high school teacher. Your father could have said it was not his problem that I had no housing accommodation. He did not even know me, yet he gave me a chance. He chose to shelter me and my family, as opposed to sticking rigidly to college staff housing rules, after he realized that I was a teacher and had nowhere to go. Young man, I will forever be indebted to your father."

While writing this book, I had a vivid dream which somehow appeared to connect with the experiences of diversity, equity and inclusion described above. I dreamt that two strangers of South African origin reached out to me for help when they were stranded in Washington DC. Both men were of mixed race and in their mid-thirties to early forties. In South Africa and my native country, Zambia, a person of mixed-race is often referred to as a 'colored' person whereas in the Western world a person of 'color' is anyone who is not white. The two men said that they were from Cape Town, South Africa. They looked haggard and exhausted. Without doubt, they had fallen on hard times. I could tell that they had not eaten for days. Their clothes also looked like they had not been washed for days. The men looked like they had been sleeping on the streets. For the life me, I could not understand why those two men chose to reach out to me. They came looking for me in a high-rise building that looked like it housed offices of major companies. My offices were in that building too. It took a while before I could connect the dots about the dream. The two men must have come across my academic bio somewhere which highlighted my affiliations with a number of South African academic institutions. They probably thought that I was South African.

After getting a call from the reception desk at the main entrance of the building that someone was looking for me, I walked into the elevator from my office on the sixteenth floor to go and meet the two men. They were waiting for me downstairs in the lobby. In the dream, my workplace seemed like some corporate setting somewhere in Manhattan, New York, or yet again the setting could have been in Washington DC. I went downstairs and greeted the men. They greeted me back and explained their desperate situation. I listened patiently. When they were done speaking, I did not ask them to go to the South African Embassy to look for help. Something within me told me to be more humane and to listen to their plight. They had become homeless in the US shortly after their arrival from Cape Town, and now they did not know where to turn to.

As I was talking to them, one of my colleagues, a black South African, who was a director, walked out of the elevator and was just about to exit the building when I saw him. I quickly signaled him over to meet the two guys from Cape Town. I told him they were also from South Africa. I thought he would be happy to meet his fellow countrymen, but he seemed indifferent. The two men opened up to him about their problems but before they could finish he excused himself, saying that he was rushing to a meeting somewhere. The men looked disappointed. I was not surprised, as I was just trying my luck with him that day. I knew the kind of guy that he was. So I was left with the two stranded men. I said to them, "Look, I don't have much to offer you but allow me to do just one thing, if it's okay with you. Can you come with me to that coffee shop at the corner of the street?"

We walked to the coffee shop. Inside was an ATM machine. I withdrew US$100, split in five US$20 bills, and handed them it to them. They were so thankful. As I we walked out of the coffee shop, I said to them: "Sometimes, the person who is going to help you may not be one of your own but a stranger. Remember the story in the Bible, as told in Luke 10:29–37. A man was going from Jerusalem to Jericho when he was attacked by robbers. They stripped him of his clothes and beat him up. A priest and a Levite passed by without helping him. But a Samaritan stopped and took care of him. The Samaritan took him to an inn where he paid for the man's care. So, here we are today. It looks like your own brother has left you in the hands of a Samaritan. Well history has a tendency of repeating itself, doesn't it?"

There was silence from the men. Then I continued: "Look, I saw President Nelson Mandela when he came out of prison. He had just flown into Lusaka to meet the Zambian President, Dr Kenneth Kaunda. I was in my final year of law school then at the University of Zambia. We were told that President Mandela had flown to Zambia to thank President Kaunda for the significant role that Zambia had played in the liberation of South Africa. ANC, the ruling party of South Africa, was fighting apartheid mainly from Zambia. It had relocated its headquarters from Tanzania to Zambia and remained in Zambia until the end of apartheid."

As I spoke, I could tell that the men took great interest in what I was saying. So, I pushed on. "Gentlemen, when Madiba arrived in Zambia, there was a sea of people to meet him. During that state visit, Madiba and his wife, Winnie, and their two daughters, also visited UNZA. President Mandela was being honored with an Honorary Doctorate from UNZA. And the chancellor of UNZA at the time was his counterpart, President Kaunda. It was a memorable event. There he was, Nelson Rolihlahla Mandela himself. Gentlemen, it was history being made and written. I witnessed it with my own eyes."

The two men looked at each other and remained silent as I spoke. They knew that I was speaking from the heart about the importance of love and unity among people of different walks of life and from different parts of the world. I continued further,

"In Lusaka, we often saw the head of ANC, Hon Mr Oliver Tambo. We lived together with some of our brothers and sisters from countries such as South Africa, Namibia, Zimbabwe, Palestine, Mozambique, Angola, Uganda, Nigeria, Ghana and Malawi. We lived with them at a time when the political climate in their respective home countries was not conducive for them. It's called *Ubuntu*. We did not discriminate against anyone. Rather, we welcomed them. If anything, we looked after our brothers and sister very well. Even some Rwandese, Somalians, Chinese, Indians, Europeans, Lebanese and Ethiopians have now made home in Zambia. Perhaps, this is why your own brother, as you can see, chose to ignore you, leaving you in my hands."

I woke up from that dream and wondered what kind of message was being conveyed. Could it have been an extension of my thoughts for this chapter? Or could it just be one of those dreams? Yes, it was true that I saw President Mandela when he came to Zambia. But then, what was the meaning of the dream? Sometimes, dreams can just be dreams. At other times, they can mean something. I was convinced that this dream is a story that belongs to this the chapter. For, it speaks to the issues of bigotry that I discussed above.

In Livingstone, when I was around three to four years old, I remember playing in the neighborhood with a child from a few houses down the road. He would catch grasshoppers and then fry them as a delicacy to eat. I could not believe it. I would just stand there and stare while he laughed and ate. Although many people in Zambia would feast on seasonal flying insects known as 'inswa' which are often caught during the rainy season by putting a dish of cold water beneath a streetlight so that those insects get trapped in that water as they fly down from the bright light, I never thought people would eat grasshoppers. I'd guess I was wrong and naïve. People everywhere eat strange things. In some parts of Zambia's Eastern Province, for example, fried grasshoppers are a delicacy and are often eaten like seafood. Unfortunately, I don't eat seafood, except for salmon, that is, if you consider it as seafood. Otherwise, no prawns, oysters, crabs, lobsters, shrimps, mussels, periwinkles, whelks, snails, abalones, scallops, limpets, octopuses, cuttlefish, sea turtles or frogs for me. And I don't care how well they are described or pronounced by the waiter or waitress using a fancy French or Italian accent. Seafood is seafood. For me, they belong to the sea, just as grasshoppers belong to the grass. Period.

Other folks from Zambia's Eastern Province eat rats, though they claim that they don't eat rats, but mice. But what's the difference between a mouse and a rat? If a rat escapes from the house and runs into a nearby maizefield, how can you tell the difference between a rat and a mouse? Is it not just a question of discrimination between one town-mouse and one village-mouse? In the northern parts of Zambia, some folks there eat monkeys. Very strange. Then, in some parts of Western province, a monitor lizard, known as 'opani' in the local language, Lozi, is a delicacy. Again, I eat neither opani, mice, monkeys, nor grasshoppers. I tried a few times to eat 'inswa', insects which I mentioned earlier on, but gave it up. For me, the aesthetics of how the food looks is important. The food must look presentable, not nauseating. Otherwise, it can disturb and distract the sophistication of my palate for finer drinks.

When my parents noticed that I was struggling with the idea of folks eating grasshoppers and seeing elders catching 'inswa' under the streetlights, they knew it was time for me to go to kindergarten. I had to go there before proceeding to primary school at Holy Cross Convent School. There was a kindergarten located behind St. Theresa's Cathedral, and one of our teachers there was Auntie Polly. Much gratitude and respect to all our former teachers. Kindergarten is where we learned most of the basic manners of human decency, such as potty training, not peeing or defecating on the streets or lawn, washing your hands after making a noble submission in the toilet, flushing the toilet after the said submission, using toilet paper in the aftermath of such submission, not making sounds when offloading your burdens in the toilet, not spitting saliva anywhere in public, not insulting or using profanity or uncouth language, sleeping in pajamas as opposed to jumping in bed naked, not farting in public places, covering your mouth when you are yawning or coughing, not blowing your nose when people around you are eating, making sure that your shoes are polished, tacking in your shirt nicely, how to sit and behave at the dinner table, learning how to use fork and knife, making sure that your hair is combed and your teeth are nicely brushed, not adding cold water to a cup of hot tea (known in Bemba as 'Uku fusha'), not dipping bread in a cup of tea (known in Bemba as 'Uku tobela'), not making strange hissing sounds when drinking or sipping hot tea, avoiding too much sugar in your tea (known in Bemba as 'Chi pumu wa sugar'), not putting too much jam or butter on your piece of bread, and many more. You could actually tell if someone had been through kindergarten or not just by the way the person behaved or carried himself or herself later in life. Even on social media today, you can get a rough idea of who might have been through kindergarten just by looking at people's comments and how they behave. By the time I was going to Holy Cross Convent School, my classmates and I had picked up some fine manners from kindergarten.

Holy Cross Convent School and St Theresa's Cathedral were both built around 1936. Zambia got independence from Great Britain in 1964. So, by the time I was going to Holy Cross Convent School in 1974, Zambia had only been independent for ten years. So, we still had a lot of expatriates working in Zambia at the time, and they would bring their children to this prestigious fee-paying private Catholic school as opposed to taking them to government public schools. Although Holy Cross Convent School was seen somewhat as a school for the white kids mainly, and a few Asian, mixed-race (colored) and privileged black African kids, it was quite multi-racial.

Our parents were paying seventy kwacha (K70) per term for each child to study at Holy Cross Convent School. Back then, the Zambian currency, the Kwacha, was very strong. K70 was a lot of money by any Zambian standards. Most of our Zambian friends could not afford to study at Holy Cross Convent School and ended up at government public schools that offered free education. As a result, Holy Cross Convent School was seen as a prestigious fee-paying school for the 'apa mwambas' (the white kids and some privileged kids from other races).

By design or default, some schools in Livingstone had a stronger presence of kids from a certain ethnic or racial background. For example, Bluegam Primary School was known mainly to be for kids from a mixed-race background (coloreds) whereas Zambezi Primary School was associated mainly with Asian kids, especially those from Indian families. At the time, there was a decent population of colored and Asian families in Livingstone. Some of them came from neighboring Zimbabwe (Southern Rhodesia) and South Africa since the two countries were under the oppressive minority rule of the whites. Livingstone was the first point of entry into Zambia if one was driving from Zimbabwe or South Africa. So, it was easier for migrants to cross over into Zambia, which had by then already attained political independence, and settle in Livingstone. Zambezi Primary School, where many Asian students in Livingstone went, was located right next to Hindu Hall, an arts performance theatre that served mainly the Asian community.

By contrast, Livingstone Primary School was said to host kids from all races, especially black African children whose parents could not afford to send them to fee-paying schools. Similarly, in the health sector, Batoka Hospital was seen as a hospital mainly for Africans whilst white folks and Asians went to Livingstone General Hospital. A few African families, however, who considered themselves affluent enough also went to Livingstone General Hospital. One needs to understand that the racial undertones that were prevalent at the time were a carryover from colonial times since

Zambia had only been independent for a decade or so. Livingstone used to be the capital city of Zambia before the capital was moved to Lusaka. And so, even the shopping areas in Livingstone carried some divisive colonial structure of first-class and second-class shopping areas. The latter was meant mainly for the African natives during the colonial times. A posh hotel such as the North-Western Hotel back then was mainly patronized by white folks. The North-Western Hotel had some nice wooden Victorian-looking architecture in the foyer or reception area, as you entered. The hotel was located near the rail-line and station, perhaps, to ensure the convenience of transportation for the white folks during colonial times. So, I was exposed to a multi-cultural and multiracial environment at an early age, starting from my early childhood. Thus, nothing surprises me when it comes to issues of race relations, as I have studied and lived in various multiracial societies for more than half of my life.

At Holy Cross Convent School, my Grade 1 teacher was Mrs Jacobs. Then my Grade 2 teacher was Ms Boghardt. In Grade 3, my teacher was Sister Anthony, who later changed her name to Sister Rita.. I transferred from Holy Cross Convent School in Livingstone to another Catholic school on the Copperbelt just when I was about to go into my fourth grade. The Catholic nun who took over the class at Holy Cross Covent School in Grade 4 and 5 was Sister Irene. Our headmistress was Sister Margaret Mary. She was a pleasant but stern disciplinarian. My classmates at Holy Cross Convent School from Grade 1 to Grade 3 included my good learned sister and fellow Oxonian Ms Mulima Kufekisa-Akapelwa, and her twin sister, Ms Mutumwa Kufekisa. Mulima has served as Deputy Director for Governance at the USAID offices in Zambia and has previously also served as Executive Director at Civil Society for Poverty Reduction. There was also my learned brother, Mr Maurice Chaiwila, a prominent Lusaka lawyer, as well as Mr Titus Mapani, an engineer in Zambia. In addition, I remember Mr Christopher Chimpuku and Mr Ian Mbewe from that class. Ian had a slight disability and a limp in one of his legs. He was a wonderful and cheerful brother. I often would hang out more with Christopher because we lived in the same neighborhood. Christopher and Ian nicknamed me "Ka J". I would guess it was an abbreviation of the name Jim given to me by my parents after my father's eldest brother, Uncle Jim. Many years later when I went to University of Zambia (UNZA), I reconnected with Mulima, Titus and Maurice at UNZA. My family moved from Livingstone to the Copperbelt when I was just about top of my fourth grade. In Lusaka, I also reconnected with Ian and Christopher on a few occasions. I was then a law student at UNZA. Interestingly, at UNZA,

Maurice and I became classmates again. We both got admitted to and graduated from UNZA Law School. Looking back, I still remember our childhood days in Livingstone. Maurice was one of the smartest kids academically in our class from Grade 1 to 3. He was really good. While we were classmates in Livingstone, Maurice unfortunately lost both his parents. He lost his father first and then his mother within a short period of time. The news was devastating to everyone.

There are other names from my class at Holy Cross Convent School that I can only remember vaguely now. One guy by the name of Gilson Mudzingwa, I think, whose parents were originally from Zimbabwe, was also in my class. Gilson was a bit of a rough guy. He liked bullying his friends. Another naughty boy was Kenneth Huni, who was also from Zimbabwe. Then we had in class a close family friend, Agnes Tembo, who I later met again in Lusaka when she was at Evelyn Hone College of Arts. I was at the time studying law at UNZA. A few years later, Agnes, her siblings and her parents moved to England. I was in touch with Agnes briefly when I moved from the UK to the US but have since lost contact.

I also remember Robert Symington (male), Glenn Wright (male), Ngula Yuyi (female), Derek Pillai (male), Mike Nyangwete (male), Ajayi Tiku (male), Natalie Clock (female), Phillip Ngonga (male), Patrick Malenga (male), Adelaide Smith (male), Keyur Mistry (male), Robert Arogyswammy (male), Auxilia Nawa (female), Ivy Lungu (female), Theresa Kabuku (female), Vaishali Patel (female), Patricia Simeons (female), Grace Nkunika (female), Binah Patel (female), Sisu Simango (male), Manoj Nayee (male), Caroline Mutowa (female), Carol Rodrick (female), Akufuna Mubitana (female), Sangita Devalia (female), Danisile Sibanda (female), Millie Mangalashi (female), and Carmeline Williams (female). There was also a girl by the name of Ida whose surname I can't just remember now. It's been a while. Many of us are now scattered all over the world, including the UK, the US, Australia, Canada, New Zealand, India, South Africa, Botswana, Zimbabwe and many other countries. Others are back home in Zambia, though many have moved out to various other cities. I would like to express my many thanks to all my former classmates and childhood friends for the camaraderie that we shared and the memories that we created which continue to live on. We cannot take that for granted.

During weekends, when I was not at school, I would sometimes hang out with friends like Monday Mwenda and his brother Sunday, who lived nearby. For some reason, the guys' names in their family seemed to have been picked from the days of the week. We shared the same last name but were not related. Monday's elder brother was a guy called Friday. Monday also had an elder sister called Judy. Monday's family moved to Livingstone much later after we had gotten there. We interacted only for a few years before my family moved to the Copperbelt.

In Livingstone, at Holy Cross Convent School, our school uniforms were a delightful blue shirt, grey shorts, grey socks and black shoes for boys. The girls wore light blue gym dresses that had dark blue pinstripes. They would also wear a grey cardigan in the winter.

As pupils, we would perform nativity plays every December at the then famous Hindu Hall. We would also sing such Christmas carols as Silent Night and the Little Drummer Boy. Next to the school was a convenience store where we would buy 'black cat' bubble gum and light snacks. We called that store 'the little shop'.

In winter or the cold season, we would have sports day at school. It was a big event that nobody wanted to miss. We would be grouped into the 'red house' and the 'yellow house', and the two groups would compete against each other. The three-legged race was my favorite sport. You had to coordinate well with your partner to win. We would also have the sack race, the one hundred meters dash race, the egg and spoon race and the 1x 4 relay, among many other athletic sports. Annual prizes would be given out to outstanding students at a formal awards ceremony held at the end of the academic year. At these awards ceremonies, certificates and cups would go not only to the best performing student academically in class, but also to the student with the best handwriting as well as the student who demonstrated consistent academic progress and one who was neatness in class.

As part of the curriculum, we would also go for swimming and art lessons. The school had a swimming pool as well as a room dedicated to art lessons. During art classes, we were introduced to the use of Plasticine and water-based paint brushes. The experience was simply awesome. The school had a rich curriculum.

In the classroom, the teacher would place a star chart in front of the class where the names of each and every pupil in class would appear. Each pupil would be awarded either a blue, yellow, green, or red star, depending on his or her academic performance. Your grade would determine what color of star you would get after taking a class test. Also, we would have music classes in the music room. Then, of course, we would go to the chapel at St Theresa's Cathedral for prayers. As noted earlier, Fr Jude Mc Kenna was the resident priest. He introduced judo as a sport in much of Zambia and is thus famously known as the father of judo in Zambia. There was a Dojo for martial arts near St Theresa's

Cathedral. Also, located next to the Cathedral, Holy Cross Convent School had two tennis courts. One tennis court was clay court while the other was a hard court. The latter sometimes doubled as a basketball court. Also, I remember that the Catholic nuns kept some vicious looking German Shepherd dogs.

One Christmas holiday season when we were in Grade 3, the Catholic nuns at our primary school in Livingstone were preparing us to perform and sing some Christmas carols. Our class teacher, as noted earlier, was Sister Rita. I seem to remember that she wore spectacles and was a young and cheerful Irish nun. I also remember Sister Oliver Plunket, who later took over from Sister Margret Mary as head of the school. Most of the teachers we had at the time were white Catholic nuns from Ireland.

We were rehearsing to sing and perform the famous Christmas carol Little Drummer Boy. Two guys from our class, Robert Symington and Maurice Chaiwila, were selected to play the drums. The rehearsals were going on well but then, just a week or so before Christmas, we learned that Robert Symington had died in a swimming pool accident at the Intercontinental Hotel.

Robert was of mixed race. His mother was a black Zambian lady and his father was white. Robert was so cool. He always had a neatly trimmed table-cut hairstyle with rich, dark curly hair. Robert was on the slim slide, with a slender frame. We often played soccer together at school. Many of us at school only got to learn of Robert's passing the following Monday after the occurrence of the accident. It was devastating news. That was probably the first time that most of us in class had come across the issue of losing a friend. Robert loved soccer so much. His life was taken too early.

After the funeral, Maurice and another Robert, Robert Arogyswammy, were asked to continue with the drum rehearsals, but it was not the same. One drummer was missing. The rhythm was different. Robert Symington was a cool guy.

Back in those days, as primary school pupils, we would get free bottles of milk at breaktime every day. A dairy truck would deliver a free one-pint bottle of whole milk for each pupil. Zambia Daily Produce Board, a parastatal company, made sure that its dairy truck was always on time and that the milk was fresh. This was at the height of a buoyant Zambian economy. Life was so good.

I remember that when my father completed his university studies in Canada, he returned to Zambia immediately. He did not start looking for a job in Canada. As soon as he was done with his university studies, he was on the next plane back to Zambia, even though he could have easily found a job in Canada if he had wanted to stay on. This was a time when the Zambian economy was at its peak. Livingstone was a small thriving city. The major industrial firms in Livingstone included Livingstone Motor General Assemblies, whose CEO was a Mr Lemba. The firm used to assemble Fiat and Peugeot cars. I got to learn later that Mr Lemba was a sibling of one of Zambia's most celebrated scholars in the field of demography, Ivy League-educated Dr Musonda Lemba. Dr Lemba has been a senior academic at UNZA for many years.

Many families in Livingstone knew each other. I remember that when my parents' friends, Mr and Mrs Nsomi, were leaving Livingstone, their son, Chibale Nsomi, remained behind with us to take his Grade 7 exams. Chibale stayed at our house at 66 Nehru Way for a couple of weeks in order to take his primary school final exams. His father was working for ITT, a leading manufacturer and distributor of electronics. I remember that Mr Nsomi used to driver a white Mercedes Benz car back in the days. The UNIP Government under President Kenneth Kaunda was really pushing for industrialization. There was a concerted effort to diversify from a monocultural economy that was almost wholly dependent on copper mining to one that could also promote the growth of such non-traditional sectors as agriculture, telecommunications, fisheries, and tourism. Policies of rural development, together with the introduction of poles of growth to spur further development in the non-traditional sectors, were being prioritized.

The UNIP Government was also pushing for the implementation of policies of import substitution so that the country could be self-sufficient and cut down on the cost of imports while pushing for export promotion. You could actually see what the UNIP Government was trying to achieve. Almost every province in Zambia benefitted in one way or another from the policies of rural development and industrialization.

I will give here just a few examples to illustrate this point. Eastern Province had a state-owned or parastatal enterprise known as Chipata Bicycle Plant. Southern Province, as I have stated above, had Livingstone Motor General Assemblies. Lusaka Province, hosting the capital city, had major industries which included Kafue Textiles of Zambia, Kafue Nitrogen Chemicals, Chilanga Cement, and so forth. At the time, Zambia even had a vibrant national airline, Zambia Airways. Central Province boasted of the state-owned enterprise, Kapiri Glass Factory. Copperbelt Province had two state-owned enterprises, KCM and NCCM, running the copper mines in almost every city on the Copperbelt. The two parastatal companies were later merged into one and became known as ZCCM.

Copperbelt also boasted Indeni Petroleum Refinery in Ndola as well as Seroes Clothing Industry and ZAMEFA, both located in Luanshya. Northwestern Province had a state-owned enterprise, Mwinilunga Cannery, which was the sole pineapple factory in the country. Luapula Province had the state-owned enterprises, Kawambwa Tea Estates and Mansa Batteries Factory. That was Kaunda. He was a visionary leader. Other parastatals such as Zambia Breweries and Daily Produce Board of Zambia had a presence in almost all provinces through various distribution channels. Even in the financial sector, Kaunda was pushing for the empowerment of Zambian people by setting up state-owned enterprises such as Lima Bank, ZANACO, Zambia National Building Society, and many others. Co-operatives were also being promoted to empower Zambians. The leadership of the nation had a vision, notwithstanding developments in the international political economy which were beginning to have a bearing on Zambia. Corruption was unheard of in the Kaunda Government.

When my family was in Livingstone, my mother would drop me off every morning at Holy Cross Convent School before proceeding to her workplace. She was a teacher at a government school, Nalituwe Primary School. I always enjoyed the class exercises and outdoor curricula that the Catholic nuns provided us with at Holy Cross Convent School. Generally, Catholic schools offered the best education in Zambia at the time. There is no doubt about that. Even some parents who were not Catholics or were anti-Catholic took their children to Catholic schools. In fact, a lot of critics of the Catholic Church today benefitted from Catholic education, notwithstanding their uninspiring pontifications against the Catholic church later in life.

After school, I would walk home with one or two of my classmates who lived near our house. Sometimes I would be alone. Up to this day, I still do not understand how I was able to manage. I was very little. I was only about five or six years old. I had to cross the main road in Livingstone, Mosi-oa-Tunya Road, which runs through the heart of the city. We would often have traffic wardens to help us cross the street when leaving the school premises, but that alone was not enough. We were just too young. I remember some crazy driver who drove a Dunlop Company van and was famous for cruising down Mosi-oa-Tunya Road at high speed. People used to call him, 'Kamiji'. His driving was just so reckless and irresponsible.

I am mindful that many small kids in Africa and other parts of the developing world still walk to and from school by themselves. It can be heartbreaking to see the type of risks that these kids are exposed to as they travel to and from school. But it all looks normal if you are in those parts of the world where such things are common. There are simply no school buses to transport pupils to and from most public schools. I grew up in Africa and can attest to this fact. But when I moved to England more than thirty years ago, and then subsequently to America, my perception of life somewhat changed. Maybe I became too soft and began to look at life differently. In the UK and the US, kids at that young age cannot go to school by themselves. Their parents, guardians or an elderly family member has to drop them off and pick them up from school (in the UK) or the school bus has to drop them off and pick them up after school (in the US). There is always someone to play a supervisory role for the safety of the children until they are old enough. By contrast, back home in Africa, you will only get that protective supervision during the first few days or weeks of school. Thereafter, you are on your own. You are left to swim with the sharks on your own. It looked normal and okay, but it is not.

Anyhow, I got used to my lonely walk from school in Livingstone. With the aid of traffic wardens, of course, my friends and I would cross the road from Holy Cross Convent School. I would then walk along the sidewalks past Livingstone Museum towards Livingstone Park. The park was right next to where Fairmount hotel was located back in the day. I would take a shortcut through the park and then walk up Mwela Street, which led to Nehru Way where our house was located. It was an uphill walk, bypassing Moth Club, until you got to Nehru Way. All in all, it was a 30 to 40-minute walk from school.

Sometimes, I would be lucky and would get a ride back home from my mother if she was somewhere near my school. My mother was always very enterprising. Even though she knew I was good at school, she arranged for me to have private classes on weekends under the tutorship of an elderly and semi-retired white Catholic nun who lived not too far from our house. It was as if my mother knew that one day her son would have to study, work, and live in a multi-racial society where he had to prove himself beyond many others around him. I am grateful to both my mother and the Catholic nun who served as my private tutor.

The Catholic nun's name was Sister Gwen. Every Saturday morning, I would wake up early to get ready for my private tutorial classes at Sister Gwen's house, which was across Moth Club and only about a five-minute walk from our house. I would be there early. I would knock on the door and wait for Sister Gwen to open the door. She was a nice, kind old lady. I still remember her as if it was just yesterday. Both my mother and father would encourage me to excel in school to greater heights. They were ever so supportive.

As early as Grade 1, I would really push myself to go over and beyond. This drive of going over and beyond has always been with me. It explains the title of this book. I have had to go over and beyond the PhD. As a black man in a multi-racial society, to improve chances of getting a seat at the table, you have to be two or three times more qualified than most of your colleagues from other races. A black man generally has to deal not only with issues of racial bigotry from some white and yellow folks who look down on blacks and blackness, but also with issues of hate, envy and jealousy from some of his own fellow blacks. Thus, both hands of a black man who is trying to make it in life are often constantly stretched out to ward off both white bigotry and black hate. He has to keep pushing away those distractive forces in order for him to move forward. It can be quite exhausting. But you have to stay the course and persevere. You have no other choice. Trying to ignore something won't make it go away. Neither is giving in an option. For many people, it is easier for them to become envious than to get inspired by other people's success. Indeed, there is a very thin line between love and hate. Those who choose hate over love are often slow to clap. And if they clap, it is only because they want to be seen to be a part of the cheering crowd though they don't mean it and thus end up putting on a face.

Sunday mornings in Livingstone were devoted to church. The whole family would go to church. There was nothing like 'I have the right to choose whether I want to go to church or not'. When it came to matters of faith, our freedom of choice was limited. We all had to go to church, that is, the Catholic Church. In those days, there were hardly any Pentecostal or Evangelical churches, as we know them today. We only had the old traditional churches like the Catholic Church, the Jehovah's Witnesses, the Seventh Day Adventists, the Baptist Church, and the United Church of Zambia. Our Lady of Angels Catholic Church, whose parish priest was Fr Patrick, a wonderful Irish priest who often enjoyed a cigarette, was located near our home. It had just been built a few years before we moved to 66 Nehru Way. I think the Catholics bought that church building from another Christian denomination that seemed to have had difficulties to maintain it.

Since Our Lady of Angels Catholic Church was closer to our home than St. Theresa's Catholic Cathedral, the main Catholic parish in Livingstone, it made sense for my family to attend Mass at Our Lady of Angels. My elder brother Dennis who was somewhere around his seventh grade at Holy Cross Convent School, would, however, often attend Mass, as an altar boy, at St. Theresa's Cathedral.

There were times when Dennis would be asked at short notice to serve Mass, as an altar boy, at St. Theresa's Cathedral, especially on major occasions such as in cases of an impromptu funeral service. My mother always wondered why Dennis never appeared scared each time he was serving Mass during a funeral as he accompanied the priest, together with other altar boys, in prayers around the casket. Fear, it might seem, is only a function of the mind. As human beings, we like to imagine things and thus create our own figment of the mind.

On some weekends, my father would drive the whole family to Maramba Cultural Village to go and see African traditional dancers. I remember that the lead 'nyau' dancer there was a Mr Mkandawire. He had sideburns and danced with grace. He had such finesse and great poise, as he danced the nyau dance. Those drives would often extend to Victoria Falls (known locally as 'Mosi-oa-Tunya') or the Livingstone national wildlife park (known locally as the 'Mosi-oa-Tunya National Park').

At times, we would go for a drive along the Zambezi River. Those riverside drives were simply awesome. Even to this day, I remember them like it was just yesterday. As a result, I still go for riverside drives on some weekends with my family. That is how I raised. I grew up on those edifying norms.

Sometimes, we would go out as a family to tour Livingstone's national museum. Of course, the older siblings would be hanging out with their friends elsewhere. I remember some of my elder brothers' friends like Mr Victor Pembanyali, Mr Andrew Mijere, Mr Gilbert Malulu, Mr Chilufya Masese, Mr Dennis Wina, Mr Charis Muyangana, Mr Andrew Kabalata, Mr Saul Kabalata, Mr Peter Yuyi, Mr Felix Katowa and Mr Geoffrey Katowa. They used to hang out with my eldest brother, Kelvin, and our first cousin, Kosamu (Michael). And, as I said earlier, many families knew each other. Felix seemed to be a Jimi Hendrix fan and would try to dress like Hendrix. He would also often carry a musical record or album in his hands.

Brother Kelvin was then a high school student at Canisius Secondary School near Monze District in Southern Province. So, he would only come home during breaks at the end of each semester. Cousin Kosamu was a student at St Raphael's Secondary School in Livingstone. At St Raphael's, Cousin Kosamu was a very good football (soccer) player. His school team often played against Linda Secondary School, the school where Zambia's highly regarded football player, Fanny Hangunyu, was studying. Fanny and Cousin Kosamu knew each other at that level. Fanny later went on to play professional competitive football for Red Arrows Football Club in Lusaka, Zambia. He also had a stint as a player for the Zambian National Football Team. Cousin Kosamu transferred from St. Raphael's Secondary School in Livingstone to St Mark's Secondary School in Choma when our family moved to the Copperbelt. Brother Kelvin remained at St Canisius, where some of his close friends included: Mr Lameck Maonde, aka, 'Joe Maos'; Mr Tom Chona, now based in Canada and son of a prominent Zambian politician in the UNIP Government, Hon Mr Mainza Chona; Mr Patrick Nabulyato, aka 'Pat Nat', son of former Speaker of the National Assembly, Hon Mr Robinson Nabulyato; and Mr Mwami Maunga, whose father owned Choma Hotel in Southern Province. After St Canisius, both Brother Kelvin and Mr Joe Maos completed one-year compulsory military training for all high school leavers in Zambia before proceeding to study economics at the University of Zambia (UNZA) in 1978 and graduating in 1982.

Then, Brother Dennis had a younger cohort of friends and schoolmates like Mr Nyambe Mundopu, Mr Charles Mapani, and the renowned Zambian DJ of the 80s, Mr Peter Mbewe, aka, 'P Funk', now the Honorable Headman of Kachingwe Village, who also once served as a Director at Bank of Zambia. Mr Peter Mbewe was also a close relative of my childhood friend, Christopher Chimpuku. I think Christopher's father was Peter's grandfather. Dennis' other friends were Mr Tom Phiri, Mr Patrick Pembanyali, Mr Christopher Konsolo, Mr Joseph Mwalongo, Mr Moses Mawere, Mr Danny Malulu, Mr Francis Bwembya Mutale (son of my godfather), Mr Wamunyima Munalula, Mr Francis Matanda, and Mr Gregory Matanda. They were all in upper primary school when I was lower primary school.

I remember also that there were two flamboyant brothers whose family lived down the road near where we lived on Nehru Way, as you drove towards Our Lady of Angels Catholic Church. Their names were Shepherd and Shipstar Kanyika. They were around Dennis' age. Further, there was the Sikanyika family whose two teenage daughters were Nellie and Jessie. They lived a few houses from the Kanyikas. Mr Sikanyika was head of an educational institution. Another family that I remember in that area was the Nkunika family. Mr Japheter Nkunika was the Controller of Customs and Excise at some point, a rank, if I am not mistaken, which is now equivalent to Commissioner-General of the Zambia Revenue Authority.

I also remember the Kondolo family in Livingstone. Mrs Kondolo, the mother of one of the judges of the Court of Appeal in Zambia, Hon Mr Justice Mubanga Kondolo, was a friend of my mother. They were both teachers. Judge Kondolo was a young man then and was around my older brother Dennis' age. My mother's other friend was Mrs Malilwe. She too was a teacher by profession. Mrs Malilwe had a daughter, Prudence, and a son, Ian. There was also Mrs Mbewe, my friend Ian Mbewe's mother, then Mrs Tembo, my classmate Agnes Tembo's mother, and Mrs Filamba, my colleague Jackie Filamba's mother. As noted earlier, both Ian Mbewe and Agnes Tembo were my classmates at Holy Cross Convent School. Then, Ian Mbewe's older brothers, Stephen and Michael, were also good friends, although Michael was a bit older. Then, I got to know Jackie Filamba much later in Lusaka through a mutual friend.

My family left Livingstone in December 1976. It was when we moved to the Copperbelt that I learned to speak both Ichi-Copperbelt and proper Bemba. You might be wondering what the difference is between Ichi-Copperbelt and proper Bemba. Let me start with a quote attributed to some of the writings of a University of Cambridge-educated Bemba intellectual and elite, one Mr Valentine Shula Musakanya, in a book titled *The Musakanya Papers: the Autobiographical Writings of Valentine Musakanya*. Mr Musakanya, who served as Zambia's Secretary to the Cabinet and Head of the Civil Service in Zambia's first post-independence government, is reported to have said: "The Bemba aristocracy always believes not only in their inherent aristocracy but also in the vocal aggression to make others believe so. Their aristocracy has no foundation in wealth or known education but essentially in being a Bemba. Bemba, I must admit, spoken by an arrogant expert, has a mind-boggling and enslaving effect upon those to whom it is directed."

This quote sums it up aptly. And so, Ichi-Copperbelt, as an offshoot of the Bemba language, also draws its inspiration from the psychology of being Bemba. In proper Bemba, for example, one would say things like "Abantu ba lya fya" (people are hard to understand.) The same sentence if delivered in Ichi-Copperbelt would read something like this: "Ba fya ti'ile fyabo! Ba ba intwanikane! Amano uku tumpa!" (Them and their things. That's why they have loose hanging ones. Very silly chaps!)

Ichi-Copperbelt is a corrupted version of Bemba found mainly on the streets of the Copperbelt. In Ichi-Copperbelt, one would say something like: "Iwe ma'ambala, aba nobe ba le lya ibuuku, iwe ule panga ichongo pa social media! Elo mailo ukese mu ku bepa ubufi ati ba la yumfwa. Amano ubu nono!" (Your friends are busy studying [i.e. known in Ichi-Copperbelt as, 'chewing books'] while you are just wasting time and making noise on social media. Then, tomorrow, if your friends make it to Oxford or Harvard, you will be busy accusing them of boasting. Grow up and snap out of it.")

A story was told of how a commercial bus driver, upon getting converted to Christianity, abandoned the street thug life that is often associated with bus drivers and bus station call-boys. Notwithstanding that he was now baptized as a Christian, the bus driver reportedly said in Ichi-Copperbelt: "I would like to thank the pastor for delivering me pantu the life I was leading na ba fikala bamu station ta yali bwino." ("I would like to thank the pastor for delivering me from thuggery and introducing me to Christianity because the life that I was leading with my fellow rascals (i.e. his fellow bus drivers and call-boys at the bus station), as unscrupulous heathens and pagans, was not good.")

Similarly, another Kopala fella from the Copperbelt, speaking ichi-Copperbelt, narrated his predicament of growing up as a toddler without ever using a bath towel to dry himself up after bathing: "Ifi ifyama bathing towel ni nomba tu fishibe. Ifwe ba le tu posa fye mu mulu imiku itatu ninshi twa uma!" ("This thing of drying yourself with a bath towel after bathing is a new experience for some of us. When I was growing up as a toddler my mother would just lift me out of the bathing water and throw me in the air three times. I would land safely back in her arms again and again until I was dry. That was it. There was no need for a towel.")

And if you, as a child, were crying or making noise to protest bathing, you would just hear your Kopala father say "Mu leteni kuno!" ("Bring him here for a beating!")

It meant your fate was now in your Kopala father's hands. And you knew what was awaiting you. You would immediately stop misbehaving and jump in the water to bath so as to avoid the whip.

In Livingstone, I spoke mainly English and Nyanja. I had no concept of Ichi-Copperbelt. My Bemba was average and not good enough to sound like a native Bemba-speaker. In general, many people in Zambia, irrespective of their tribal affiliation or native language, use Ichi-Copperbelt if they want to insult or convey crude humor. Ichi-Copperbelt has come to be accepted as some form of lingua franca in Zambia. As one Zambian woman on the Copperbelt told her niece who had just been dropped off a posh car by an elderly looking man, "Mu le upwa ko so that mwa chindamikako nobu chende! Noti ba le mi lamfya fye for nothing!" ("Get married, as opposed to just being smeared unmentionable things by that old man! Marriage can legitimize and moralize your immorality.")

A certain Zambia woman, married to a white man, was heard telling a fellow Zambian friend in Lusaka: "Ine, echo na upilwa fye kuli bugga. I can't stand ifya bu puba from some African men." ("That's why I am married to a white man. I can't stand the cheating of some African men.")

The friend, married to a Zambian engineer, responded in Ichi-Copperbelt: "Iwe, umu sungu te degree! Wa li mona po umusungu listed pa CV ati, 'married to a white husband', just because of akwata inkanda ya buta, kwati nayo ni qualification? Amano ubu nono. Ukupwa ku musungu te achievement. Na ma fontini ya lopa aba sungu, atemwa ya lopwa ku ba sungu. Just go back to school and get a proper education." ("Listen, my friend, just go back to school and get a proper education. Stop dreaming about elevating your social status by marrying a white man or woman. You can't list your white spouse's 'whiteness' as a qualification on your CV. Merely getting married to a white man or woman is not a qualification or an achievement for you to be making noise. You can't list his or her race on your CV, can you?")

Ichi-Copperbelt often comes with sarcasm and little or no diplomacy. And delivery can be crude and blunt. In my early days in England, I recall going out with some Zambian friends to a nightclub in London. The doorman at the club was a muscular and hefty-looking white guy. He was clad in a muscle T-shirt, and his physique and toned muscles were visibly loud. As we approached the entrance of the nightclub, the white guy asked to frisk us. Then a Zambian brother in our group, speaking ichi-Copperbelt and thinking that the white guy would not understand it, made the following joke:

"Those days pa CB, aba ifi na le wisha. Fi mi nofu fye ifi. Bruce Lee ta pompele." ("In my youthful days in Zambia's Copperbelt region, I would knockout such hefty guys. This chap's muscular physique is nothing. He can't scare us. In fact, powerful guys like Bruce Lee hardly have chunky muscles.')

Unbeknown to us, the white guy had spent his childhood in Zambia's Kitwe city and could thus speak Bemba fluently. So, the white guy turned around to face the Zambian fella who was yapping nonsense. We all wondered what the white guy would say or do and if at all he even understood what had been said, until he went: "Iwe, ka chikala… Ati shani wa landa?" ("You little dickhead, what did you say?")

Before we knew it, the Zambian fella who was yapping had taken to his heels. He fled the scene, leaving the rest of us in harm's way. We all pretended we were not with him, just to buy peace. It was clear that the white guy understood Ichi-Copperbelt and was indeed a proper 'Kopala' (i.e. a native of the Copperbelt region) like all of us.

In Zambia, even a shrewd politician who is not a native Bemba-speaker knows that during, say, electoral campaigns, if he uses Ichi-Copperbelt and says things like, "Iwe, ka chikala", in reference to some little twit, that can help to make him more popular with the rowdy masses that often comprise a large faction of the electorate. As crude as some profanity in Ichi-Copperbelt may sound, they can be appealing to some rowdy audiences that are able to relate to such street lingo, making them feel that the politician is relatable to them because he speaks a language they understand. Relatability can earn a politician more votes. That is how powerful Ichi-Copperbelt can be. A number of Zambian presidents are reported to have used Ichi-Copperbelt at some point to galvanize the masses for political support. One of the presidents, a native Bemba-speaker from the Copperbelt, was reported to have said the following, in reference to some of his political adversaries that were trying to undermine his presidency:

"Ba fya ti'ile fyabo! Kuti ba ba. Ta tu tina aba maka, Tu tina aba mano !" ("Them and their things! We are not scared of brawn. We respect brains, not brawn! They can go to hell with their brawn behavior.") The president's adversary got the message and caught feelings. They tried to rally the masses against the president, insinuating that the man had used unpresidential language and should be condemned in the strongest terms. But the president sprang back to his feet and responded: "Bushe nga na landa ati ba fya ti'ile fyabo, ninshi na tukana?" ("If I say that them and their things, have I insulted? It is a generic expression, with no names of people or body parts mentioned. So, it is not an insult.")

More recently, another Zambian president, who is not a native Bemba-speaker, switched to pontificate in Ichi-Copperbelt as he tried to galvanize the support of the masses. In a baritone voice, referring to the time when he was in opposition and how his political supporters were often beaten up by youths from the then ruling party, he said the following: "Whenever the former ruling party would hear that, I, as the main opposition leader was around, mwa le ponokwa! Kwa le ba uku ponona!" ("Whenever the former ruling party would hear that, I, as the main opposition leader was around, you, my supporters, would be beaten! There would be heavy beating and assaults!")

The use of Ichi-Copperbelt, however, backfired on that president. Some native Bemba-speakers claimed that he was hurling insults and that it was unpresidential of him to use such street language.

The critics insisted that in authentic Bemba, the words 'mwa le ponokwa! Kwa le ba uku ponona' mean, 'Your penis foreskins were being stretched back ruthlessly by the thugs in the then ruling party!' Whether this is the correct Bemba interpretation or not doesn't matter. It is, however, a truism that language or words can have a different meaning depending on the context. The president could have been trying simply to excite the masses with a contrived effort at speaking some Bemba but did not intend to insult anyone, so he can be excused and forgiven because it is doubtful that he intended to insult. In any event, people forget quickly and move on.

A few years ago, another notable Zambian opposition leader, who later became a president and who was known for his crude delivery of Bemba humor, got on the wrong side of the then sitting president of Zambia. The president, a distinguished lawyer, was a former Chiwala Boys' Secondary School student on the Copperbelt. And Chiwala had a reputation of producing some of the roughest fellas on Copperbelt. The incumbent president at the time, who was also a distinguished lawyer, could speak Ichi-Copperbelt and was well-acquainted with the Kopala way of life. But because he was a senior and well-respected lawyer, he never let that side of him show. The opposition leader took it for granted and continued taunting the president, using all manner of unpleasant jokes to disrespect him. This time around, the president could not take it anymore. He lost his cool and turned around to face the opposition leader, and issued him a 'street' verbal warning: "Kuti ca ku bipila apa pene nombali'ine so." ("Things could get really ugly for you right now!")

The president was not talking about unleashing his presidential security detail on the opposition leader, but he himself beating the hell out of that opposition leader. The words, 'Kuti ca ku bipila apa pene nombali'ine so' often mean 'Your attitude can be adjusted right now with a quick headbutt and a few good body punches to your ribs and chin.' The following day, the Zambian media published an article on this 'presidential' incident. In short, never judge a book by its cover. And never underestimate the depth of calm waters. Otherwise, 'kuti ca ku bipila' (things could get really ugly for you).

CHAPTER 6

Moving to the Copperbelt

Life on the Copperbelt was like playing in a live jazz band. Improvisation was often the order of the day. It was normal to improvise. The soulfulness of that improvisation made life interesting and exciting on the Copperbelt. Creativity was in abundance. People were generally happy. Hardly anyone felt excluded. Humor and assertiveness were embedded in the social fabric of society. If your parents could not afford to buy you a modern football – what we called, 'Iya mpapa' (a leather ball) – you would, like the humble beginnings of many world-class Brazilian or Argentinian football players, resort to improvising with a makeshift home-made football known as 'Ichimpombwa', woven from the remains of empty plastic bags, old newspapers, and discarded rubber band. Others whose parents could not afford to buy them 'Iya mpapa' but could only afford something lesser in value would get an inflated rubber or plastic ball known as 'Ka chikanda' or 'Ka Wembley'. So, depending on your station in life, many kids would rise from the low-tier of playing Ichimpombwa to the middle tier of playing Ka Chikanda or Ka Wembley before ascending to the higher tier of playing Iya mpapa. And for the most part, everyone would play football with their bare feet, controlling the Ichimpombwa or Ka Chikanda with great mastery. It was all about improvisation. Football boots would only be worn during formal primary or high school games, not for weekend neighborhood matches.

When it came to swimming, kids who could not afford to go to the affluent swimming pools in the posh neighborhoods would improvise with some alternative venue. They would go to swim 'ku ka dayi' ("Swimming in a dirty local stream, river or dam"). And the swimming styles seen 'ku ka dayi' were somewhat unclassified, ranging from doggy paddle (iya kabwa) to 'underwater walking' as long as you resurfaced on the other side of the stream. That was improvisation at its best. No swimming techniques were ever taught 'ku ka dayi'. It was all about instincts for survival. There was nothing like freestyle, front crawl, backstroke, breaststroke, butterfly stroke, or sidestroke. Such things were for the finer folks at the elite swimming pools in the posh neighborhoods. To swim 'ku ka dayi', you needed no swimming lessons or attire. You could just jump into the water butt-naked with a hippopotamus-styled splash, as opposed to a fine-looking meticulously rehearsed dive. At the famous 'ku ka dayi', your 'birthday suit' (nakedness) and your initiative to swim were all you needed to make it. Whether you succeeded at not drowning or not was your own issue to worry about. There were simply no swimming lessons or rules 'ku ka dayi'. You were on your own. Folks would just jump into the water like a hyena, landing with a heavy thud and splashing water on everyone around them. A common response from those you would splash water on was a heap of unpalatable insults such as: "Iwe ka chi kamba! Wa nsansa amenshi!" ("You little dickhead! Can't you see that you have splashed water on me?"). Or, "Wa aba ibolo! Ta wishibe ati kuti na ku ponona? Ka puli kobe!" ("Your damn balls! I can sort you out!").

Notwithstanding these threats, life would go on happily. After 'ku ka dayi', some guys would go to perform rituals of 'onion daura' in the nearby bushes. To perform this ritual, chaps would pick some wild plants in the nearby bushes known as 'onion daura.' These plants had an onion-like look, with a bulb head. From there, the fellas would start to peel off the respective outer layers of the bulb-head one by one until they got to the moist inner layer. Once the inner layer was exposed, the fellas would then spiritedly rub the bulb against their bald pubic area, believing superstitiously that such a ritual would stimulate the rapid or early growth of their pubic hair. This was boys trying to be men. Other guys would go 'ku ma labo' ("municipal solid waste site"). Many kids with no proper toys at home would improvise by exploring the 'ma labo' option, just in case they could salvage something from there. Copperbelt was all about improvisation if you needed to have or get something you lacked.

If, for example, you wanted to watch a football game featuring stylish Roan United at the local stadium, Kafubu stadium, but could not afford the entrance fee, all you needed to do was wait outside the stadium, pretending to be waiting for a friend or someone. The idea was to wait until the National Anthem started playing prior to the commencement of the football match. When it Anthem started playing, everyone around, including all security personnel, had to stand still. That moment presented an opportunity to sneak into the stadium by climbing the stadium's wall fence and jumping inside before racing into the crowd to hide among those who had paid. You had to move at lightning speed to avoid being caught afterwards. Chaps would run past the cops, waving at them, as the National Anthem played. The cops could not do anything, for they were required to stand still while the National Anthem was playing. Once you succeeded in sneaking into the stadium, you would then enjoy the game, just like those who had paid. It was all about improvisation and initiative. Copperbelt gave you the skills and instincts for survival. But I was just too scared to sneak into Kafubu stadium without paying. Because I was not raised like that. I would always ask myself: what if before I could hide in the crowd that had paid to watch the football match the national anthem stopped playing, wouldn't I get in trouble? Or, what if those who had paid to watch the game were to snitch on me or surrender me to the cops after the National Anthem?

I noted earlier that my family moved to the Copperbelt from Livingstone in December 1976. A few weeks before the relocation, my father went ahead to the Copperbelt to prepare for our arrival in Luanshya. He then returned from the Copperbelt to collect us from Livingstone. Two of my siblings, Dennis and Matilda, and I took the train from Livingstone to Ndola while Dad, Mum and Eugene drove all the way from Livingstone to Luanshya. Francis and Joseph were not born by then. Dad dropped off Mum and Eugene in Luanshya and then came to meet us in Ndola at the train station. When got to Ndola, we found him already waiting for us at the train station. My older brother, Kelvin, and my older sister, Catherine, were in Catholic boarding schools at the time. Kelvin was St. Canisius Secondary School and Catherine was at St Joseph's Secondary School. Both schools are located in Southern Province.

I discovered that Copperbelt was a melting pot of different cultures. While Livingstone had more pronounced ethnic and tribal divisions, the Copperbelt generally was more inclusive, except for the social class distinctions of the haves and have-nots. Let us take a more reasoned look.

On the Copperbelt, the large population of blue-collar African laborers in the mines, in contrast to the few white elite and privileged people of color, could explain some of the social dynamics of class structure. For the most part, the Copperbelt had more social class issues than tribal or race issues. Also, the culture on the Copperbelt comprised bits and pieces of almost every aspect of the socio-cultural fabric of Zambia. There was no such thing as the indigenous people or the rightful owners of the land. Everyone had a stake, except that the economy drew distinctions between or among the social classes. Otherwise, in terms of tribal or ethnic issues, Copperbelt was spared from such vices. It was, indeed, more inclusive. Although the indigenous people of the Copperbelt are mainly the Lamba-speaking people, Copperbelt has never been a region that advancing or promotes the superiority of Lamba culture over the cultures of other people or 'outsiders.' Rather, Copperbelt is a cosmopolitan region that accommodates everyone, including foreigners and people of all races and tribes. Various people would thus migrate to Copperbelt Province from all parts of Zambia and from outside the country to work in the copper mines or do business there. The job opportunities in the copper mines attracted a lot of people to the Copperbelt, making the place probably more cosmopolitan than any part of Zambia. As such, it had a unique character.

Much of the Zambian economy also relied on the Copperbelt region. Copper has always been the country's main export, so you would find there some silos of affluent folks, on the one hand, and some silos of the working class and peasants, on the other hand. That said, these social class divisions did not separate the two silos entirely. For example, if you visited the primary schools known as the 'Trust Schools' on the Copperbelt, that is, schools that were meant mainly for the middle to high-income employees of the copper mines, you would find some children of the working class seated in the same classroom as children of the petit bourgeoisie. The common thread was that their parents all worked for the same State-owned mining company. Interestingly, however, the kind of bourgeois affluence that you would find at most schools run by the mines on the Copperbelt was not always present at most schools in Lusaka, the capital city. Also, within the Copperbelt itself, if you were to visit, say, some of the high-density mining townships where the low-income blue-collar miners lived, you would find primary schools that were no different from those that were run by the Zambian Government in local townships outside the miners' townships. This was so because the State-owned mining companies in Zambia back then, unlike today's privately owned copper mining companies, invested heavily in corporate social responsibility. zx

The ambivalence of the economy on the Copperbelt was striking. The mines provided a duality of economies, namely, one that was designed originally for the white colonial settlers during colonialism and one that was meant originally for the African natives. In Luanshya, for example, many African families whose parents were miners started off life in the low-income blue-collar townships of Roan or Mpatamato before gradually being upgraded to the more affluent housing areas near downtown. Even the new housing areas that these folks would move to near downtown had a pecking order. The new arrivals from the blue-collar miners' townships of Roan and Mpatamato would often be housed on a street called Zaone Avenue. That street was mainly for folks that had just been upgraded from the high-density Roan and Mpatamato townships. A further job promotion would see the family move to other streets that had more senior people. In those days, there were very few university degree holders in the mines. Many Africans would simply migrate from the village to join the copper mines on the Copperbelt. Once they found a job in the mines, they would then rise through the ranks based on experience gained while on the job until they reached some lofty position. And so, even talk of superstition and occult practices to gain promotions at work or to secure one's job were not uncommon amongst many blue-collar miners. It was often believed that one had to be 'fortified' through some superstitious occult practices to survive long enough in certain risky and sometimes life-threatening jobs.

For some time, the mines did not have a high concentration of university and college graduates. A good number of African miners would simply attend some short training courses at the mining company (ZCCM)-owned crafts training schools before launching their lifelong careers in the mines. It was only later in the first republic that the mines started hiring more Zambian engineers with university degrees from UNZA or the UK. In fact, ZCCM later embarked on an ambitious program to send some Zambians to various UK and US universities to train as engineers so as to address this skills shortage in the mines.

By contrast, the residential area located near downtown in Luanshya, for example, that housed many middle to senior-level civil servants in that town had a higher concentration of much more educated Zambians than any other part of the town. This was the residential area where you would find a number of high school teachers and college lecturers. My family lived in that area. Many high school teachers and college lecturers had a decent college or university education. At Luanshya Boys' Secondary School, for example, the high school that I attended, we had many teachers with decent university degrees from the University of Zambia (UNZA). Others had two to three-year college diplomas from leading tertiary education colleges in Zambia. That said, a common link between the haves and the have-nots on the Copperbelt was that nobody escaped the pollution from cloudy fumes emitted by the mines! It did not matter whether you belonged to the haves or have-nots. We were all subjected to that air pollution from what appeared to have been sulfur dioxide emissions from the copper smelting processes. Whatever those smelly fumes were, they surely must have been toxic. For, both plants and people would be affected. Even if you lived in an affluent neighborhood, those fumes would not spare you. And the emissions would occur almost on a daily basis. Olli Suominen and Matti Vilkko (2016), in a conference paper presented to the "26th European Symposium on Computer Aided Process Engineering," submitted: "Copper smelting plants separate elemental copper from copper concentrates through multiple sulphide oxidizing stages. The considered smelting process includes a continuously functioning flash smelting furnace (FSF) and several Pierce-Smith converters operated in batches."

Then, Ravi K. Jain *et al*, in a 2016 scholarly journal article titled, "Environmental Impact of Mining," published in the journal, *Environmental Impact of Mining and Mineral Processing*, made the following impactful observation and finding: "Emissions of lead particulates from mining and *mineral processing* remain a problem throughout the world. Lead particulates can be transported long distances through the air and deposited via rain onto soils. Lead has no known biological function and has a broad range of toxic effects on most organisms."

Although Ravi K. Jain et al's study focuses mainly on lead pollution and was not carried out in Zambia, that study deals primarily with copper mining, like the case of Zambia's Copperbelt Province. Therefore, it would be naïve to discount Ravi K. Jain *et al's* study. The results of that study can help to inform dialog in Zambia's case, regarding the pollution from the Zambian copper mines. For the most part in Zambia's Copperbelt region, many people would probably be high on the sulfur dioxide fumes from the Zambian copper mines. Ravi K. Jain et al contend that:

"Lead exposure is particularly dangerous for children, due to their increased exposure per unit body weight, higher physiological uptake rates, and rapid growth and development... Furthermore, recent evidence indicates that many of the health effects associated with children are irreversible, even with the cessation of lead exposure. Many of the effects of exposure to children, such as lowered IQ, and learning, behavioral, and hearing problems, can have lifelong impacts."

In their study, Ravi K. Jain *et al* provide the following table to summarize the harmful effects on the human body of the smoke that is regularly emitted from the copper smelting plants:

Health effects of lead exposure in selected populations (Agency for Toxic Substances and Disease Registry, 2010; Canadian Council of Ministers of the Environment, 1999; National Toxicity Program, 2012; Pourrut et al., 2011)

Population	Effects of lead exposure
Children	Decreased IQ, increased behavioral and attention-related problems, delayed puberty, decreased hearing, reduced postnatal growth, anemia, coma, convulsions, stupor, death
Adults	Decreased kidney function, reduced fetal growth in mothers, increased blood pressure, decreased fertility, nerve disorders, muscle and joint pain, cataracts, tremors, memory problems
Plants	Inhibition of germination, root elongation, development and growth, transpiration, chlorophyll production, impaired nutrient uptake, phytotoxicity
Aquatic organisms	Increased mortality, decreased abundance and diversity, abnormal development, reduced mobility."

Source: Ravi K. Jain, P.E., Zengdi 'Cindy' Cui, Jeremy K. Domen, "Environmental Impacts of Mining," *Environmental Impact of Mining and Mineral Processing: Management, Monitoring, and Auditing Strategies,* (2016), pp. 53-157, available Online at:

https://www.sciencedirect.com/topics/engineering/copper-smelting, accessed on September 27, 2023.

The intensity of the fumes from the copper smelters was felt more in the African native townships since many of these neighborhoods were located near the mines and on lower ground facing the winds from the copper smelters. During colonialism, the native African townships were developed deliberately by the white colonialist on lower ground to make it easier for the fumes to be directed at the African natives, and not the white colonial settlers' homes. The white colonial settlers often lived far away from the mines and on elevated ground. In a 2019 study, Chibamba Jennifer Chansa, a then final-year PhD candidate in the International Studies Group (ISG) at the University of the

Free State in South Africa, while carrying out fieldwork for her PhD studies on environmental pollution and regulation on the 'old' and 'new' Zambian Copperbelts from 1964 to 2019, noted: "Mufulira is as famous for copper production as it is for air pollution. Most of the town's residents are routinely exposed to sulfur dioxide fumes, locally known as *'senta'*, but it is the communities closest to the mine that are most affected."

Chansa submits further: "…African settlements were strategically positioned in proximity to the hazardous fumes during the initial construction of housing facilities for mineworkers in the colonial period. …white mineworkers were themselves housed further away from the mine, and the potential pollution."

After Independence, Chansa (Online, 2019) submits, Zambia's state-owned ZCCM mines employed several strategies to curb environmental degradation, but those efforts only ended in a general failure to abide by many international standards for emissions and effluent. Chansa contends further that air pollution continues to be a major challenge even after the privatization of the mines. Put simply, we all got a good share of our dosage of the sulfur dioxide fumes emitted by the copper mining plants when it came to inhaling those emissions. The white colonial settlers too could not shield themselves away completely from the pollution. The fumes would still reach them, albeit with lesser intensity given the strategic location of their residences. Air flows freely and knows no haves and have-nots, not even white or black people. It just flows wherever it wishes to flow. You can't stop it as long as there is no filter or scientific inhibitor against pollution. It's like a fart. There is simply no filter in the underpants or nostrils to block the smell of a fart. It will still reach everyone nearby, including the 'owner of the fart' who we often refer to politely as 'the person responsible for fouling the air.'

The polluting fumes from the copper smelting plants were referred to by many African natives as 'senta'. Those fumes would cause your eyes to turn red and itch. Other people would have watery eyes. It was as if you were high on some illicit drugs of some sort. Maybe we were all constantly high on 'senta', but whatever it was, that 'senta' must have had an effect on the Copperbelt character, although many folks would casually brush that view aside, saying: 'Bwa mwana shi mine niba problem…ta bomfwa!', translated in English as, 'Children of miners are a problem…they lack discipline.' There could have been a causal link between the polluting fumes from the copper smelter in the mines and the often militant and mischievous character of many fellas on the Copperbelt Province. But, as usual, we never take most things seriously in our part of the world and simply overlook such issues.

This brings me to my first encounter with the complexity of social life on the Copperbelt. My submission here should be viewed in the light of the scientific evidence provided above from the study conducted by Ravi K. Jain *et al*. I pointed out earlier that, although my family was staying in the urban residential areas that housed civil servants mainly, and not miners, and that our residential area was far from the mines, we too were not spared by the fumes from the mines. Everyone had to inhale those fumes. Surprisingly, it would appear that nobody ever sued the mines for the pollution until 2016 when the British newspaper *The Guardian,* in an online article dated September 18, 2016, and titled, "Glencore court ruling in Zambia may trigger new pollution claims," reported:

"Toxic fumes from one of Glencore's copper plants in Zambia caused the death of a politician, the African country's high court said, in a ruling that could trigger fresh claims against the company. The London-listed mining and commodities trader was ordered to pay 400,000 Zambian kwacha (£30,000) in damages to the widower of Beatrice Mithi, a politician who died after inhaling sulphur dioxide released by Glencore subsidiary Mopani Copper Mines."

So it had to take a politician to die for the mines to be made accountable? This is the reality of life in the developing world. The pollution would occur almost daily in most of the mining towns on the Copperbelt. *The Guardian* article cited above notes further:

"The ruling…means Glencore could face new claims from residents of the Mufulira district, where local people have long complained of health problems allegedly caused by emissions from Mopani's copper smelter."

On November 19, 2019, the *Lusaka Times*, in an online article titled, "Mines Minister calls for action after 200 pupils were rushed to hospital after inhaling emissions from KCM," noted that the then Minister of Mines in Zambia, Mr Richard Musukwa, directed the Mine Safety Department and the Zambia Environmental Management Agency to use all provisions of the law to deal with Konkola Copper Mines (KCM) following a major incident of air pollution where "…over 200 pupils and 40 KCM employees in Chingola were rushed to hospitals after inhaling sulphuric acid which KCM released from its acid plant."

I remember that I was about eight years old when my family moved from Livingstone to the Copperbelt. The Copperbelt was not a place for weaklings. I found Luanshya, in particular, and the Copperbelt in general, to be more of a culture of survival of the fittest. You had to stay alert all the time. If you blinked, it was over. There was a 'senta' culture on the Copperbelt. By contrast, in Livingstone, I would leave my toys outside the house overnight and find them safe the next morning. But when we moved to Luanshya, it was a totally different experience. Right from the very first day when we got there, some boys came from the neighborhood (whose names I will not mention because they are now respectable men in society), pretending to befriend and welcome me. They pitched up at the gate of our house uninvited. I thought they were cool guys just trying to be nice and to welcome me to the neighborhood. I let them in. It was a big mistake. Little did I realize that they were just little rascals trying to rob me of my toys. I doubt those chaps even had any sensible toys in their parents' homes. Now, I am not looking down on anyone here. Neither I am saying that the boys' parents could not afford to get them proper toys. Rather, it was a just an issue of different levels of exposure between those boys and I. For the most part, the Copperbelt culture under which the said boys were brought up was all about improvisation, toughness and using your initiative to survive.

For example, whereas I came with some decent and modern toys from Livingstone, most of the local fellas I found on the Copperbelt had only seen such toys with white children. For the most part, the fellas would be playing with what they called 'impolo' which is a small makeshift toy-gun carved out of a bamboo stick and uses small bush fruits as bullets. Others would get used car tires and pour some water inside the tire before inserting two bamboo sticks. That was a toy for them. You were to hold the bamboo sticks inserted in the tire with your hands and then cruise away like a speeding vehicle. I also discovered that these boys had grown up playing with toy cars made out of wire cables or mud. Improvisation was part of their livelihood. By contrast, in Livingstone, we never had such 'toys', at least not among the boys I used to play with. Rather, we would play with toys bought from the stores, not something made out of mud or wires. We hardly improvised. We also played marbles using proper marbles bought from a kids' toy store. In Luanshya, it was different. Only a few boys were exposed to a culture of playing proper marbles. Most of the kids would simply use expired batteries as a substitute for marbles. I was shocked when I saw that. It explains why, instead of welcoming me as a new arrival, those Luanshya guys robbed me of 'proper' toys. They stole them with impunity. I only noticed that my toys were missing after the fellas had left. I could not believe it. I was in shock. I had never experienced anything like that. In Livingstone, such behavior was very rare. No one among my friends ever stole any of my toys.

On the Copperbelt, I had to adapt quickly both at the family and social levels. It is not every day that people open up about the family dynamics they experienced when growing up. But I am opening up here. Many people try to put it all behind them or put on a fake face as if everything was perfect and rosy. But life cannot be perfect all the time. There will always be good moments and low moments. We must learn from our mistakes instead of trying to sweep the dirt under the carpet. Learning from our mistakes is not necessarily washing dirty linen in public. Rather, it is about honesty and sharing lessons of how you can pick yourself up in the midst of adversity.

At home, I was often teased, bullied and called names by some of my older siblings. Many of you have experienced such things. So, I would often retreat to be alone, either in the bedroom or elsewhere. In Africa, there is usually no such thing as suffering trauma when you are mistreated. You grow up with a thick skin, learning how to cope and survive. So sometimes, I would take long walks all by myself in an area now called Kamirenda where some new houses were being built at the time. Along the way, I would pick some lovely looking colorful stones. I'd guess my eclectic taste for finer things of great aesthetic value started at a young age. One family friend, Mr Gabriel Chingwe, reminded me much later and just a few years before he passed on that I grew up a very quiet boy and was usually alone. He was right. I was often alone not only because of the family mistreatment I have referred to above but also because I found many boys my age in my neighborhood a bit childish. In fact, most of them were a year or two behind me in school. Although I would hang out with them occasionally, I had to pretend for the most part that I was fine with their childish games or pranks. But the truth is that I often struggled understand why they would be excited with what seemed to me to be childish behavior. The kind of things that they would laugh about or get excited over were things that I often associated with much younger boys. Intellectually, I would say that I had matured faster than most of my friends. So, I would keep to myself for the most part unless I was bored or wanted to play some football.

Also, I would collect postal stamps from different countries as a hobby. Young people nowadays spend more time on social media. I am not sure I would call that a hobby. Stamp-collecting was a popular hobby for many kids back then. In addition, I had a pen-pal in Australia whom I would write to occasionally.

Naively, I was under the impression that the family mistreatment that I went through at the hands of some of my siblings went unnoticed, but many years later, when I had travelled from Washington DC to Zambia to attend my father's funeral, my eldest brother, Kelvin, who was a student at the University of Zambia (UNZA) when I was a kid in Luanshya, revisited the issue, offering me kind words of encouragement and moral support. I never knew that he had paid attention to how others were treating me when I was young. He surprised me. I listened to him quietly as he spoke. He went on to narrate how he would notice that I was often mistreated, bullied and called names by some of my older siblings. Brother Kelvin was the eldest in the family and was, thankfully, not part of that bullying and mistreatment. He opened up to me that he would see and notice everything, as we took a walk along one of the roads in Northmead residential area of Lusaka.

I was silent as he spoke, trying to process how far he could remember. Brother Kelvin had his facts correct. I did not say a word. I was touched by the fact that he could remember everything after so many years. I grew up as a quiet child. Although I never opened up to my parents about the bullying and mistreatment, I found strength and courage in exceling in life. I have always been that person, who, when you push me to the edge, I will not break. Rather, I will be motivated to excel even to greater heights. I always turn adversity into hope. And so I would pray quietly, even as a child, choosing to see things differently. Even though I knew that my father would have put a stop to the mistreatment had I reported it to him, I did not muster enough courage to tell him. I knew, however, that dad was a disciplinarian and would not have tolerated such behavior.

I remember one time, during an altercation I had with some neighbor's children, I uttered some unkind words. My mother was informed about the incident by the neighbors. She decided to report me to my father. That day, I sat alone in my bedroom eavesdropping my parents' conversation in the next room, as they discussed my fate. I could hear my mother telling my father to give me a good hiding. I was terrified but helpless. I knew what was awaiting me. My father seemed reluctant to whip me, but my mother kept insisting that I should be disciplined. And so, I received a good hiding for uttering some unkind words to the concerned neighbors, though my words had some grain of truth in them. My father knew deep down his heart that there was no major reason why I had to be punished or given a good hiding, especially that what I had said was not far from the truth, albeit the words not being politically correct.

Growing up on the Copperbelt, I also had to deal with, arguably, some senta-influenced behaviors of some folks on a daily basis. Moving from Livingstone to the Copperbelt was like coming from playing a game of chess or squash with some well-mannered school kids and then getting thrown into a boxing ring with some rough neighborhood boys. You can't afford to be too intellectual when confronted with a thuggery culture. You have to adapt and allow yourself to pick up some game from that thuggery in order to survive. Otherwise, you will be eaten alive. I had to adapt from being book-smart to being both book-smart and street-smart. In Livingstone, as children at convent school, we would compete in intellectually stimulating games and sports at the end of the semester. We would celebrate academic success and achievements, as we looked forward to receiving prizes, awards and medals for those accomplishments. By contrast, on the Copperbelt, it was different. Sports day was not that widely socialized at our primary school. Rather, the main sport that many pupils looked forward to were just football matches against other schools during the semester. On 'Closing Day', as folks would call the last day of the semester, it was a time for physical violence and brutal fights. But some fellas who attended the elite Trust Schools running by the mines will spiritedly tell you that such things never used to happen at their schools. Well, 'senta' was all over the mining towns on the Copperbelt, including at Trust Schools. Senta spared no one. It is just the degrees of intensity that differed. Even white folks got affected by it. And many white folks got initiated in Kopala profanity, and like some native Kopalas, would be heard pontificating a myriad of unprintables, saying, "Ulya ca ti'ile chakwe..." ("That one and his things...")

So, the culture of senta spared nobody even if you went to an elite school on the Copperbelt. We all inhaled the 'senta'. And it affected us. You could even see sparks of 'senta' in many people's personality, no matter how much one tried to suppress it. Today, the psychosocial effects of that senta culture are known simply as the 'Kopala' factor.

At many primary schools on the Copperbelt, Closing Day was the only day when you saw those suspiciously dull-looking big boys who often sat quietly at the back of the class appear excited. Otherwise, during the rest of the academic year they would utter no word in class. But on Closing Day, they would be smiling and looking forward to the fights. Theirs was a world of brawn, not brains. It was a time to settle scores. Those bullies thrived on exchanging punches, not ideas. They would compete with fists, not brains. Fists and blows were their academic awards. In fact, if you were very good academically, you would be bullied by the rough boys who were usually quiet in class. They loathed academic excellence. To them, if you were smart academically it meant you were boastful. They would often falsely accuse the brightest kid in class of boasting, just as a way to find an excuse to bully him or beat him up. The bullies would often warn the brightest kid that, "Ka chi kamba aka ka mona kwati eka kwatisha sana amano mu class. Tu ka ka mona pa Closing Day." ("This guy thinks he is the smartest guy in class. We are going to deal with him [assault him] on the last day of the semester.")

When Closing Day came, you would feel their eyes on you, as they murmured a warning to you that:

"Lelo ule ponokwa nga ta wa ponokwa po!" ("Today, you will be beaten like you have never been beaten before.")

Sometimes, these rough chaps would lay an ambush, waiting to beat you on your way home, forcing you to take a detour to avoid getting a beating. That was the Copperbelt. There was none of that in Livingstone. At other times, a school bully would threaten everyone at school that if they could not go out with a certain chic (*i.e.* a female pupil), then nobody else should date her. And whoever would be seen talking to, or hanging out with, that gal risked being beaten by the bully himself. A number of these bullies are now haters on social media and hiding behind the keyboard while hurling insults at whoever outshines them. They often attack people that have a huge following on social media since they themselves have little or no following. Just check their social media pages and you will see that many haters hardly have any followers. And they have very few likes on their posts. Also, haters like to use fake and pseudo names on social media to conceal their identity because they are cowards.

Some common characteristics of haters on social media include not being as successful in life as the person they hate as well as secretly admiring and envying the person they hate. A hater will often find something negative to say even in the abundance of someone's good or success. If you are dressed in fine designer clothes that the hater can only dream of, he or she will, without any provocation or invitation for a comment, say things like, 'Why are you advertising for that designer clothing company?' instead of just appreciating your fine taste for garb. Also, do not expect a compliment from a hater, unless the alleged compliment is sarcasm veiled as a compliment. If you pass your exams in school, for example, scoring, say, 98 out of 100, a hater will simply insist that you are missing 2 points and that your score is thus not good enough. While others are busy clapping for you, the hater will remain fixated on that 2 that is missing just to make you feel bad. But in life, you do not need anyone's permission to succeed. Otherwise, if you had to get permission from haters, that permission would never be forthcoming.

Like rabid dogs, haters, known also as 'enemies of progress', hate anyone, including people that they hardly know and have never met, as long as the person is doing far much better than them or is more successful than them. Haters often want to blame others for their own failures and shortcomings in life. They try to take it out on innocent people. For example, if you have what a hater wants but cannot afford, or you have achieved what the hater can only dream of, that hater will hate you relentlessly. Because your ability to excel reminds him or her of his or her dismal failure. Haters can even hate an innocent beautiful female celebrity, especially if they themselves are ugly or cannot afford to date her but can only dream of her, as they pitifully squeeze the neck of their rooster in frustration under the bedcovers. As pointed out earlier, for many people, it is easier for them to become envious than to get inspired and to hate than to love. But, as the former Prime Minister of the United Kingdom, Sir Winston Churchill, once put it: "You will never reach your destination if you stop and throw stones at every dog that barks."

Some dogs do bark, and all just to distract you. They are true enemies of progress. They just hate progress. So, if you pay attention to them, you do so at your own peril. Some people cannot stomach the idea of seeing you prosper and do better than them. They will do anything and everything to frustrate you. You do not need such people in your life. Leave them and move on. Other folks have no agenda of their own but just want to see you fail. That is all they are interested in, as if it will improve their lives. But much to their chagrin, you keep resurfacing, like a premium wooden cork from a bottle of fine wine that keeps floating back to the surface when it is submerged. Just when they think you are drowning, they see you swimming safely to the shore. Even in biblical times, Jesus Christ had haters. If you are going to gossip about someone, at least mention the good things that he did for you or how he helped you. Do not try to be clever by muting out the sound on the man's good deeds to you while amplifying your own prejudiced views about him. Many biblical haters were envious of Jesus Christ's ability to draw large crowds and perform miracles which they themselves could not perform but could only dream of. Besides, they hated Him for the fact that He was so frank and would call them out publicly, as He did when they wanted to stone a lady that they accused of committing adultery. Sometimes, as someone once said: 'Most of the enemies that you will have in life are people that you once helped.' I am sure that among the people that wanted Jesus Christ crucified, as well as among those who claimed that He had committed blasphemy by saying that He was the Son of God, were some folks that Jesus Christ had healed, cured or helped, including other folks whose relatives had been healed, cured or helped by Jesus Christ. Many people are like that generally, that is, so ungrateful.

Often times, haters expect you to apologize for your honesty, hard work, success and excellence. But what was Jesus Christ going to apologize to anyone for? Apologize to hypocrites, betrayers and pretenders, filled with evil hearts of malice and envy? Instead of getting inspired, haters choose out of envy to hate. In Bemba, we say: "Ba fya ti'ile ta ba temwa." ("Haters will always be bitter. They are bitter people.")

Some haters will even pretend to mean well, as if they just want to give you some good advice. But if you look carefully, their advice is often unsolicited and tainted with malice. Secondly, their advice often focusses on the negatives, not the positives. This is all because envy, jealousy and insecurity are the main drivers of their frustration. Such people don't like it when someone appears to outshine them. Foolishly, they think that by dimming your light, theirs will glow, when they do not even have a flicker. Their hearts are full of unfathomable resentment, unrestrained anger and debilitating acrimony. They are bitter. So, to avoid dealing with such animosity, it was often safer for the academically gifted kids not to show up at school on Closing Day. Otherwise, you would pay heavily for your intelligence if you showed up at school on Closing Day. For some people, it is a crime for someone else to be intelligent. And if one was intelligent, he or she was not expected to show it. Rather, he or she was expected to hide their intelligence and pretend to be dull. Only then would the bullies consider you a good boy or good gal. Otherwise, anyone who had a bone to chew with you would wait until Closing Day to fight you. If a fight was not happening, someone somewhere was busy with some other kind of mischief, including promoting dog fights.

There was a guy who loved to promote or encourage fights between any adversaries he found. Wherever there was a fight, you would hear that he was there cheering the feuding adversaries to fight on. He went by the name of George. We all feared George. He often walked around with his dog, ready to get it to fight your dog. If he was not promoting a dog fight, he would be promoting a fight between two guys. George was a rough guy. He earned his respect through fights and intimidating others with threats of violence. George was a bit older than most of us. But his reputation often preceded him. You were not to cross his path lest you face his wrath.

When I arrived at the Catholic Convent School in Luanshya, its name had just been changed by the Zambia Government to Buteko Primary School. That was at a time when the Zambian Government was taking over Catholic schools in Zambia. But the grotto remained there at Buteko Primary School until I was somewhere in my sixth or seventh grade. I joined Buteko Primary School in fourth grade. My classmates from Grade 4 to Grade 7 at Buteko Primary School included Linda Singogo (female), Vera Shawa (female), Bertha Mwaba (female), Maureen Khuzwayo (female), Masanguza Thole (male), Malama Ngulube (male), Mwalwa Mwamba (male), Kelly Mwansa (male), Grace Chishimba (female), Anne Chishimba (female), Angelina Chibuye (female), Joyce Shezongo (female), Bianca Mukuka (female), Timothy Mano (male), Gladys Machiya (female), Faith Tembo (female), Irene Munthali (female), Dennis Mukelabai (male), Edwin Mushabati (male), Stephanie Sekanji Nakanyika (female), Vumango Musumali (male), Janet Ngungu (female), Musole Musole (male), Dorothy Ngungu (female), Hector Kalulu (male), Osman Teladia (male), Hugh Chindongo (male), Rickie Thiel (male), Patricia Nkoloma (female), and Pelina Chama (female). There was also Faith Tembo's elder sister and another gal in class (the latter gal's last name was Yuyo), but I can't remember their full names. It's been a while. Many thanks to all my former classmates for the camaraderie that we shared and which I do not take for granted.

Our teachers at Buteko Primary School from Grade 4 to Grade 7 included Ms Bwalya, Ms Mondoloka, Ms Siyatwinda, and Mr Phiri. Ms Mondoloka was my class teacher in Grade 4. She was nice but tough. Ms Mondoloka would sometimes headbutt you if you were misbehaving. She was something else, but very jovial too. When I proceeded to Grade 5, Ms Bwalya took over briefly before handing over to Ms Siyatwinda who had just joined the school. Ms Bwalya was cheerful, though she only taught us for a short period. I found Ms Siyatwinda very motherly. She was also very patient with the pupils. I remember her teaching us some Tonga songs. It felt weird at first because a number of us only spoke English and Bemba. Eventually we got used to singing Tonga songs.

In Grade 6, Mr Phiri took over. He was a tough man and a sports enthusiast. He was also a good teacher, though he liked dictating his way. He was not a good listener. Mr Phiri introduced a few Nyanja songs when he became our Grade 6 teacher. It was another weird experience for the class. Mr Phiri took us through to the end of Grade 7. Throughout my stay at Buteko Primary School, the headmaster was Mr Mpundu, and his deputy was Mr Sichalwe. Both men were stern disciplinarians. Mr Mpundu was well-known for being very strict. Otherwise, Buteko was a great school. And much gratitude and respect to all our former teachers.

In class, I was always in the top three when it came to academics. Only two classmates would pose a threat academically. The two were girls, namely, Linda Singogo and Vera Shawa. These two gals were really smart and would always feature in that top three. I was a playful but naturally talented boy academically. I was never one who would spend hours and hours reading. Thirty to forty minutes of reading was enough for me before running off to play football with friends.

I remember one game where I played for the First Side of Buteko Primary School's Football Team. Our goalkeeper was a guy called Ezron Silomba who was a year behind me in school. On that team, the other guys who I remember are Eddie 'Kims' Mutale, a defender who was in the same class as Ezron, and my good friend Timothy Mano, another defender. Timothy and I were in the same class and were close buddies. That day, we played River Cross Primary School and beat them 1-0 at the nearby football grounds of Mpelembe Primary School. I scored that game's only goal. I was the youngest player on the football field. And, yes, I looked visibly tiny but was nonetheless swift on the ball. I received a low cross pass from the left wing. I did not stop the ball but simply connected with a one-touch to strike it into the back of the net, beating the opposition goalkeeper, my friend, Patrick Sampa. That one-touch finish was classical. I still remember the goal like yesterday. There was jubilation everywhere, as people swarmed the field to hug me and lift me high. It felt like one of those Messi or Ronaldinho free-kick moments when the ball gets to the back of the net miraculously.

The next day, one of the gals in class called me to the side and gave me some cash for the brilliant goal I had scored. I was so touched. I felt really appreciated. Sports can unite people. Off the soccer pitch, I would also do wonders when it came to academics. Although I was always one of the top three pupils in my class, my mother arranged for me again, like she did in Livingstone, private tutorial classes. I would go for the classes on certain days of the week. I did not protest. I knew that my mother had my best interests at heart. There were mainly six primary schools in Luanshya's middle to high-income residential areas, namely, Luanshya Trust School, Buteko Primary School, River Cross Primary School, Gandhi Primary School, Mpelembe Primary School, and Central Primary School. As I pointed out earlier, Luanshya Trust School was mainly for children of middle to high-income earning miners. A number of these kids were whites and Filipinos as well as some Africans whose parents were working for the mines. My school, Buteko Primary School, was a former Catholic convent school and arguably the best primary school in Luanshya run by the Zambian Government. Then, River Cross Primary School, like Luanshya Trust School, and also located in the middle to high-income miners' residential area, seemed to be more tailored for kids whose parents could not afford to send them to the prestigious Luanshya Trust School. There was also Gandhi Primary School that was located in a neighborhood dominated mainly by the Indian community. A number of pupils there were Indians and other Asians, plus some indigenous Zambians from the nearby homes. Finally, there was Mpelembe and Central Primary Schools which were seen by many as the two public schools that accommodated almost anyone and everyone.

After classes at Buteko Primary School, I would walk to Ghandi Primary School for private tutorials. My private tutor was a wonderful Zambian teacher, Mr Kalonga. He was an experienced teacher who had built himself a good reputation of preparing students well for their Grade 7 final exams. A few other kids, especially from the Indian community in Luanshya, would also attend Mr Kalonga's private tutorial classes. Most of the kids came from privileged families whose parents could afford to pay for their private tutorial classes.

When I wrote my Grade 7 final exams in 1980 to qualify for admission to secondary school I came top of the class at my school. I was the youngest pupil in that class, but managed to beat everyone. I was the best graduating student at Buteko Primary School in 1980. I remember that during the exam period I would go quietly behind the school's art room to pray before taking an exam. I would pretend to sneak out to go to the toilet and then make a detour to go and pray alone behind the art room. I prayed quietly and alone. I am disclosing this for the first time so that others can learn about the power of prayer. I have seen and been a witness to what prayer can do. I have experienced the power of prayer. The reason why I would pretend to head to the toilet and then go behind the art room to pray is that I did not want anyone to see me praying or know that I was going to pray. Prayer can sometimes be very personal. I really did not want to be like the Pharisees in the Bible who made sure that everyone saw them when they were fasting or praying.

God, thankfully, answered my prayers. I was only eleven years old but had so much faith in God. And, as I said above, though the youngest, I beat the whole class and was the best graduating pupil at Buteko Primary School that year. I remember my father telling me how the parent of one of my classmates approached my father to ask me to play with his son so that his son could get some inspiration from my exemplary academic performance. So, my journey in thought leadership started way back when I was very young.

Even though Buteko was a former Catholic Convent School, you could feel the impact of the senta pollution in the air. Like the case of the elite Trust School in Luanshya that was run by the mining company ZCCM, we at the former convent school were not spared by the senta fumes and culture. Senta-inspired behaviors were ubiquitous on the Copperbelt. I remember one guy in my class, MM (real name withheld), who was notorious for promoting and encouraging fights at school. He was a smaller version of the George guy that I mentioned earlier. MM's famous line, each time he wanted to impose his authority, was: "Iwe kapuli, kuti na ku ponona. Kuti ca ku bipila apa pene!" ("You little dickhead, don't fuck with me. I can sort you out right here and right now!")

I personally never had problems with my good friend and brother MM. We got on very well. My strategy was simply to avoid crossing his path. Otherwise, we all thought he was a tough guy until he was beaten by a bigger guy who was a year behind us in school. We used to call the bigger guy, Eddie 'Kims' Mutale. Though Eddie was a grade behind us, he looked a bit older than most of us, probably because of his height and physique. So, MM picked on the wrong guy. The fight started and within a few seconds it was over. All I remember was seeing some blood oozing from MM's mouth. From that day onwards, I realized that MM was just about 'ichi ntinya' (intimidation) and 'uku kakata fye pa kanwa' ('being a loud mouth'). There were a lot of guys those days who would try to intimidate you even if they knew that they were not your match. Guys would muster unfathomable courage from nowhere to intimidate others. It was that false confidence spiced with vulgarity that made them appear tough until they got exposed like MM.

I got to learn quickly that one of the most effective tools that many guys were using to intimidate others was the mastery use of street-Bemba. Sometimes, insults and threats alone would be enough to scare someone. The Bemba language, when used tactfully by an overly confident fella, has the effect of intimidating others. Bemba is what I call a 'language of warriors.' That is why many people in Zambia, irrespective of their tribal background, use Bemba if they want to insult. They rarely insult in their native language. Profanity, when delivered in Bemba, can be quite impactful while remaining somewhat more acceptable to the public ear than profanity delivered in any other Zambian language.

The Bemba language, like Swahili, has come to be accepted as some form of lingua franca that is no longer confined or limited to the Bemba people alone. Like English or French, Bemba has spread to many lands and regions afar. It is no longer parochially confined to the Bemba people themselves. Historically, the Bemba language spread quickly wherever the Bemba people migrated to and among the people that they conquered. When I moved to the Copperbelt, I too had to polish up my Bemba language proficiency to fit in. For, it was rare to be bullied if you spoke good street Bemba. But if you only spoke English or any other language such as Nyanja, the local bullies on the Copperbelt would think you were walkover. If you look at President Nelson Mandela, for example, he learned quickly when he came out of prison that mastering the Afrikaans language and associating himself with the rugby game would win him more trust among the Afrikaners. And so it came to be on the Copperbelt. You had to speak some street Bemba and appreciate their football because football was the game of 'ba mwana shi mine' (sons of miners). To that list, you can add a good appreciation of boxing since you had to be seen to be a tough guy as well. I remember an incident when a guy who was an upcoming boxer was walking to a boxing gym, with his boxing gloves hanging from a lace over his shoulder, when he was confronted by two kaponyas (i.e. kaponyas are rough street boys usually found at a bus station selling all manner of merchandize or working as bus conductors). The guy had just alighted from a commuter bus and had done nothing wrong to upset or offend the two kaponyas. Yet, they walked up to him and said in Bemba: "Mwaice, ifwe tu posa aya bishi." ("Young man, don't try to scare us with those gloves. Unlike you, we throw hard and raw punches, not those diluted punches coming from your gloves. Yours are feeble and soft.")

The guy ignored the two kaponyas, but they continued taunting him. In fact, one of the kaponyas slapped the guy on the cheek. Within a second, we saw both the kaponyas on the ground, crying foul that the guy had hit them with a metal bar, yet, there was no metal bar involved. The guy simply unleashed a powerful body shot on one kaponya, forcing him to drop his guard, and then followed that up with an uppercut to his chin, as he himself ducked a counterpunch from the kaponya. We saw the kaponya stagger to the ground. Then, he turned on the other kaponya, who was trying to dance around fancifully, mimicking Muhammad Ali's footwork. The guy cornered him, pinning him against a nearby wall, then faked him with a left before unleashing a devastating right cross to the cheek. That sent the kaponya sprawling to the ground. Both were down. Everyone watching cheered the guy because the kaponyas would often intimidate the commuters at the bus station. The guy picked up his gloves and continued his journey to the boxing gym. The other kaponyas watching the incident said nothing as their eyes followed the guy in awe.

On weekends, I would go to play football with some friends in the neighborhood. Sometimes I would spend time with friends like Masanguza Thole, Chomba Kabezya, and Zambika Banda. The three loved athletics and were often trying out the athletes' racing track at the nearby high school, Luanshya Boys' Secondary School. I would sit and watch them go for the one hundred meters (100m) dash race and the four hundred meters (400m) race. I was not so much into running. Football was my thing.

Sometimes, I would climb up a mango tree at home to get some mangoes. One time, while up in the tree, I came face to face with an ugly looking lizard with a blueish big head. It was a terrifying experience. That lizard species, known locally as 'blue mutwe', looked like an iguana. Once you saw 'blue mutwe' on the tree, the only option would be to let go of the tree and land on the ground with a thud. The blue mutwe was so ugly that you would easily get scared once you saw him staring at you. Occasionally you would find a chameleon crawling on your shirt or even getting inside your shirt, as you climbed up the tree. You would freak out and without thinking let go of your hold on the tree and land with a thud on the ground. It was rough. But the next day, you would be back trying to make another attempt at climbing the mango tree, hoping that there were no 'monsters' up there.

On some days, my friend, Chomba, would come up with the idea of bicycle racing. We would get on our bikes to race. I remember that I had a fancy Swedish-made foot-brake bicycle. Two other guys in the neighborhood who had fast bicycles included Danny Chigubu and Paul Liswaniso. They both had chopper bikes which allowed them to shift gears to increase speed. At the time, chopper bicycles were the ultimate deal.

Chomba always had something up his sleeve. I never knew how to catch birds from the wild using 'ubu limbo' (*i.e.* glue-like substance made out of a liquid drained from a cut or incision made on the buck of a tree and mixed with pieces of nshima) until I moved to the Copperbelt. On the Copperbelt, many guys my age were into 'ubu limbo' in those days. Smartphones and social media were not in existence. So, 'ubu limbo' ruled. I found 'amano ya bu limbo' (preoccupation with 'ubu limbo') on the Copperbelt when I arrived from Livingstone. In Livingstone, my friends and I never went after innocent birds. It was only when I arrived on the Copperbelt that I learned of 'ubu limbo' and 'ama legeni' (catapults used to hunt down birds). Closely related to this, some guys would set up a trap to ensnare birds. They would get an empty dish, basket or metal lid of a big trash bin and rest it halfway on a thin piece of small wood so that underneath that cover they place a bait. The guys would then tie a thin string to the bottom edge of the wood and lie in waiting. The idea was that you had to pull the string once a bird carelessly strayed under the lid to pick up some pieces of corn or bread left there as a bait. These guys would engage in such mischievous activities without obtaining a hunting license from the State. They would just hunt down birds illegally, contrary to the prevailing wildlife protection laws of Zambia. The fellas were committing a crime by hunting down the birds illegally, though it could be argued that most of these guys were underage and thus could not be held criminally liable. Other guys would set up dog traps to deal with free-range stray dogs that would habitually show up in the neighborhood at night to look for food in trash bins or at nearby dumpsites. The stray dogs would sometimes show up in search of a female dog on heat. Quite often, in cultures or communities where you find stray dogs, it is not uncommon to find people loitering in the streets or at street corners. There are some close similarities between the two. Fellas loitering the streets would often unfairly beat a stray dog once it was caught in a snare. Again, cruelty to animals is a criminal offense although the fellas got away with it. Other boys and gals took pleasure in beating dogs that were found entangled in a knot during mating. As a lawyer who values both human rights and animal rights, I would say candidly that such behavior not only constituted unlawful cruelty to animals but also militated against norms of human decency. The kids in the neighborhood would get a big bamboo stick and strike it harshly in-between the entangled female and male dogs, stretching the male dog's knotted private parts with excruciating pain, as the elders nearby either looked away with the shame of guilt or chased the kids. Adults often felt ashamed and guilty if they saw two dogs mating in public. It probably reminded them of familiar sitings. By contrast, the kids would cheer on the mating dogs enthusiastically. It was entertainment.

Quite often, we saw male dogs fighting over a female dog. This can help you to understand why some men fight over a woman. I have lived for many decades in the Western world but have never seen male dogs fighting over a female dog. It is not that dogs in the West are not horny. Far from it. Rather, they are either constrained by their owners from fighting over a female or not given unregulated space to express themselves freely, unlike in some other societies that have no qualms about free-range behaviors. For the more than three decades that I have lived in the US and England, I have never seen a heavily pregnant female dog roaming around the streets of America or Great Britain, notwithstanding any spirited arguments of spaying or neutering. Neither have I seen dogs mating in public, notwithstanding the fact that spaying or neutering can make dogs less aggressive and can also reduce their instinct to mate. Perhaps some dogs in the Western world have bedrooms of their own where they mate. I don't know. Or maybe the spaying or neutering of dogs completely eliminates their libido. Be that as it may, all I can say is that dogs in the West, as long as they have not been spayed or neutered, do procreate just like dogs in any other parts of the world. But in Africa, as young children, we were often entertained by dogs or cats mating in public. Some male dogs would even travel long distances in search of a female dog on heat. They would go missing from home for weeks only to return with heavy scars from fights with other male dogs over a female. Indeed, Africa taught me certain things that a Westerner would not understand unless and until he or she visits Africa.

During my Copperbelt days, sometimes my friends and I would go to pick wild fruits known as 'insafwa' in the nearby forest behind Luanshya Boys' Secondary School. We were young and never understood the risks of going by ourselves into the thick of a forest. A snake or something else out there could have harmed us. Our parents would not even know where we were. I remember one day when we ended up causing a big fire at a nearby school, as we tried mischievously to torch a swarm of bees using a lit bamboo stick with a ball of fire at one end. The swarm of bees was up on a metal pole near a basketball court. There was a lot of dry grass near the pole. When we placed the glowing fire on the swarm, the bees came for us. We dropped the bamboo stick and ran for our lives. The bees were everywhere, and the grass around the pole caught fire. Scared of the bees, we could not go back to put out the fire. Instead, we ran and hid in a nearby trench, waiting to see if someone would put out the fire. After a while, as the fire increased, we heard the siren of a fire engine track approaching. We knew that we were in trouble. We stayed in the trenches and could not go home until it was late around 7 . I kid you not, there are no such games anywhere else in the world except for the Copperbelt. Who goes around starting a fight with a swarm of bees? Luckily, I was not given a whipping that day by my father but was reprimanded harshly.

Sometimes, my friends and I would set up traps for innocent pedestrians walking through a field on a path surrounded by tall savannah grass. The traps were not deadly, but friendly. We would tie some tough savannah grass from, say, the left side of the path to another patch of tough grass on the right side of the path, forming a tough thread connecting the two sides. Now, if you were walking on that path and did not see the tough thread of grass connecting both sides, your foot could get caught up in the thread, leading you to trip and fall. Therein lay our fun. We would make those traps in places where the grass around the path was so high that the thread remained concealed from the view of pedestrians. After the trap was set, we would hide behind the bushes where we could not be seen but had a good view of the approaching pedestrians. We would lie there in ambush, waiting in anticipation of the unfolding drama. If, for some reason, we saw that the approaching pedestrian was the father or mother of one of our friends, we would rush back to disarm or defuse the trap by untying it before the man or woman got there. Again, there are no such games anywhere else in the world except the Copperbelt. These games did not require money for you to play but were quite costly if you were caught. The fun was as high as the risks, so we had to be extremely cautious and meticulous.

When it came to playing football, each neighborhood had a football team. I remember playing football with guys like Kampeshi Chileshe and his older brother, Mata Chileshe. Mata was slightly older but a very talented football player. Mata would have gone places with football had he turned to professional football, but he somewhat abandoned his football talent as he grew older for a more affluent disco lifestyle. Whenever my team played against Mata's team, Mata would opt modestly to be the goalkeeper, though their best goalkeeper was his young brother, Kampeshi. I also played football against guys like Robert Musumbulwa, Kamima Musumbulwa, Joe Singogo, Glory Singogo and a guy called Muyombo. They were a quite formidable team which played some disciplined football. Occasionally, they would be joined by a guy called Andy Kafunda. Andy was from the neighboring city of Ndola and was well known for his street fighting prowess. He was a short and physically fit looking fella, and was extremely vicious on the assault. You were safer not getting into Andy's way. Personally, I never had problems with Andy. He and I got on very well. I was always nice to him to avoid any problems. You gotta be smart to survive out there.

Some of the guys on my football team included Peter Hara, Tom Muchinzi (whose parents were originally from Malawi), Kelvin Nkoloma, Rodney Kapanga, and Owen Kapanga. Owen would be the goalkeeper. In those days football in many parts of the developing world was full of myths. Some guys would say that if you put a dead lizard near your goalpost, the opposition team would miss all or most of their chances of scoring. Others would say that if you put a sewing needle next to your goalpost it would stop balls from going in. Whether these ritualistic myths worked or not is something that we cannot verify.

Suffice it to say that Owen's elder brother, Rodney, together with Peter Hara and Kelvin Nkoloma, were the key defenders on our football team. The three loved executing hard tackles on the opposition strikers. Back in those days we used to call hard tackles, 'uku posa isembe' (throwing an axe at an opponent to chop him down). Tom would be a midfielder. I would play as the main striker. I was very good at tormenting and destroying the defenses of the opposition. They all knew me. I was quick on the ball and my dribbling skills were impeccable. When my team was playing, I was usually the target of the opposition defenders, but I would still dribble past them and score!

I remember particularly one guy by the name of Godfrey 'Mabange' Shamulenge, who was the leader of an opposition team that often played against us, panicking each time I stepped on the ball. We called him Shams, an abbreviation of his last name. He was an older and rough chap, with intimidating reddish eyes. He would ask his defenders to stop me at all costs or just take me down. On his team, Shams had guys like the elegant Fred Kabwe and Fred's young brother, Kafula Kabwe, as well as Bonventure Yombwe, Lewis Tembo, Cuthbert Tembo, Innocent Mweni, and Victor Mweni. Their defenders would come in numbers, and one after another they would all lose sight of the ball each time they faced me. Shams sometimes would step in to assist them. As their goalkeeper, Shams would do everything to foul me in front of the goal so that I did not score. Back in the days, there was nothing like a red card in street football.

A few other guys from the neighborhood who played occasionally on our team included Roger Kasoma, Hector Mbuzi, Musole Musole, Wamunyima Musole, Emmanuel Chatengwa Siame,

Hector Kalulu, Kelvin Nkoloma's young brother, Ivan, and a guy called Mambo. Wamunyima and Hector Mbuzi had a similar style of play. They would just sit and wait upfront for the ball to be passed to them and then score. That's it. Some goals could even have been offside. But still the goals carried the day for us. We would compete against Godfrey's team that comprised mainly sons of college lecturers at the college headed by my father, Luanshya Trades Training Institute (LTTI), and the adjacent college, Technical Vocational and Teachers' Training College (TVTC). On a few occasions, my team played the guys that were staying in the more affluent side of the miners' residential area near Roan Antelope Recreation Center (RARC). My LBSS (Luanshya Boys' Secondary School) classmate and friend, Aaron Chirwa, was their goalkeeper. He was a good goalkeeper. I remember also that there was one guy on their team called Charles. He was left-footed and so gifted on the ball. We called him, 'Chale ma le', meaning, Charlie the left-footed guy. And I remember that Charlie had a very beautiful young sister by the name of Collette. But since he was our friend, we all kept our thoughts to our heads and never acted on them.

Sometimes my team would play against the hardcore 'ba mwana shi mine' (sons of blue-collar miners) from the other side of town, Roan township. Ba mwana shi mine were very good at football. They lived and breathed football. It was their game. But they were also rough. Their township was about 18 miles from Luanshya Boys' Secondary School where we would have our football matches. The games would be quite intense. Each time we played against ba mwana shi mine, both teams would agree to bet a small amount of money like US$10, and then a trusted person would be asked to hold the money, totaling $20, for the team that would win. Sometimes things would get sour towards the end of the game, especially if ba mwana shi mine noticed that they were losing a game. You would hear their supporters saying, "Lelo mwa la ponokwa ba mwana ma yard!") ("Today, you, kids from the affluent neighborhoods, will be assaulted viciously after the game!")

And they would start to sing rough songs like: "Lelo ku leba uku ponona aya ma kula, lelo ku leba uku ponokwa,…lelo ku leba uku ponokwa!" ("Today, there will be vicious assaulting of these fellas who don't know how to play football even if they end up winning this game. We will teach them a lesson!")

My teammates and I would run for our lives without waiting to collect the prize money. As soon as the game was over, we would scamper in all directions to avoid being beaten. We all knew the consequences of the other team's allegedly senta-inspired behavior. So, there was no waiting to see what will happen next after the football match. We would flee the scene immediately. It was rough.

Then there were times when my team would win a game only to be told that the guy who had been entrusted with holding the prize money had disappeared with the cash while the game was on. It was rough. We could not appeal to anyone, but simply walk away empty-handed, in spite of the win. Sometimes, my team would also pull a fast one. If we realized that we were about to lose a game, the guy on our team who was the owner the football that we were using for the match would pick up his football and walk off the field, contending that he was going home to grab lunch and needed to carry his football. That was it. The game would be abandoned and there would be no loser. But such tricks are simply bad manners which often manifest themselves again as people grow older. A person accustomed to behaving like this is less likely to accept electoral defeat, say, in presidential elections if he realizes that he is about to lose. He would rather disrupt the elections and have them cancelled so that there is no winner. You just have to look into the past of some of these narcissistic politicians to appreciate what I am saying.

Sunday mornings were time for church. I became an altar boy at Immaculate Conception Catholic Church when my family moved to Luanshya. At church, some altar boys would try to behave in a holier than thou way as if they were junior priests. We had quite a number of such overzealous characters. They would warm up to visiting seminarians as if they too were headed for the same priestly calling. Many altar boys had fanciful ideas of becoming a priest even though we all knew that they lacked the moral and ethical character to be called to priesthood vocation. A number of those whose parents were staunch Catholics became altar boys simply to align with their parents' religious inclinations. Some Saturdays were thus devoted to altar boys' rehearsals and preparation for Mass on Sunday.

As altar boys, we competed for certain roles assigned to us during Mass. The most prestigious role was that of preparing and carrying the special brazier of burning incense, the thurible. Carrying the thurible for the priest and swinging it at the right moment during Mass was considered a prestigious role reserved only for the senior altar boys, especially those who behaved as if they were junior priests. And some of them would even steal wine from the Sacrist, a thing that some of us never did. For a number of us, it was unfathomable to do such a thing. I never got the chance to be assigned the role of carrying or swinging the thurible. I was one of those quiet ones who never behaved as if

I was a personal friend of the Heavenly Angels. The most I did was handling the communion plate.

On some Sundays, our altar boys' team would play football against other parishes. I remember one game when we played against the altar boys of St Anthony parish in Mikomfwa. On the St. Anthony team was my good brother and friend, Engineer Dr Dennis Mwansa, with his close friend Mr John Mwansa. The two coordinated well as strikers until Dennis got injured and had to be substituted. I think that game ended in a draw.

When I arrived in Luanshya, the parish priest at Immaculate Conception parish was Fr Angelo, an Italian. Later, Fr Angelo returned to Italy and was succeeded by another Italian priest, Fr Charles Milan. After serving as parish priest at Immaculate Conception parish for many years, Fr Milan was transferred to Kitwe. Then, when my dad passed on in 2003, I travelled to Zambia for the funeral and found that Fr Milan had been reassigned back to Luanshya as the parish priest at Immaculate Conception parish again. Fr Charles presided over the funeral Mass of my Dad. It was a moving ceremony. My Dad and Fr Charles had worked together closely over many years, and he knew my Dad very well. At my father's funeral Mass, Fr Charles spoke not only as a parish priest, but also as someone who knew my Dad very well. Before Dad retired from the civil service, he had been an active member of the parish council at Immaculate Conception parish. So, it was not just one of those random things where you get a priest to say Mass for someone he hardly knew. Rather, Fr Charles knew my Dad very well and described him just as we knew him too. Fr Charles needed no prepared script or written text. He simply spoke off the cuff and got it right.

When I moved to secondary school, I was less active as an altar boy, although I would still attend Mass every Sunday. Perhaps senta was beginning to take a toll on me. I don't know. All I can say is that, as you grow older, new or additional interests probably begin to compete for attention in your life.

After graduating from Buteko Primary School in 1980, I proceeded to high school the following year in 1981 at Luanshya Boys' Secondary School. At the time, Luanshya district only had five secondary schools, namely, Ibenga Girls' Secondary School, Luanshya Boys' Secondary School (LBSS), Luanshya Girls' Secondary School (LGSS), Roan Antelope Secondary School (RASS), and Mpatamato Secondary School. Ibenga Girls' Secondary School, an all-females Catholic school, was arguably the most prestigious high school in Luanshya. It was a Catholic boarding school for girls only run by Dominican Catholic nuns. My dearest wife, Dr J, attended that school before proceeding to Medical School at the University of Zambia. Many elites in Zambia, including some government ministers, would send their daughters to Ibenga Girls' Secondary School as well as to other equally good Catholic schools for girls in Zambia such as Fatima Girls' Secondary School, Holy Cross Girls' Secondary School, St. Monica Girls' Secondary School, Roma Girl's Secondary School, St Mary's Girls' Secondary School and St Joseph Girls' Secondary School. But when the Zambian Government started taking over the ownership and running of most schools in Zambia that were set up by the Catholics, including my alma mater, Buteko Primary School in Luanshya, Ibenga Girls' Secondary School, like Fatima Girls' Secondary School in the neighboring Ndola city, fell under what appeared to be a joint or shared governance arrangement between the Zambian Government and the Catholic Church.

By contrast, LBSS, previously known as Luanshya High School, was an all-boys day school that was wholly owned and run by the Zambian Government. Located in the middle to high-income residential areas of civil servants and other non-miners, LBSS was arguably the most prestigious boys' high school in Luanshya. When I arrived there in 1981, my brother Dennis was in year 5. He was in Form 5S1, the pure sciences class, together with his buddies James Kalengo, Boyd Simposya, Sebastian Chinkoya, Paul Ndalama, and many others. I remember that James was the head boy at LBSS that year. Then, Dennis, Paul, Boyd and Sebastian were among the school prefects.

LBSS has produced many distinguished alumni. The names I mention below are by no means an exhaustive list. Rather, I have only tried to identify those alumni who, in my humble view, have a visibly impactful national and international presence. Among them is the author of this books who needs no introduction. As you read the book, you have before you my whole life.

Other notable alumni of LBSS include:

- Professor Ephraim Munshifwa PhD, an alumnus of the University of Cambridge in England, and the Dean of the School of the Built Environment at CBU;

- Dr Evans Mupela PhD, an alumnus of Maastricht University School of Business and Economics, who served as Director of Research Evaluation and Learning at the Government Technical Advisory Centre (GTAC) in South Africa;

- Mr Douglas Mutesha, the former Chief Executive Officer of ZAMTEL Company in Zambia;

- Mr Bright Ngoma, the former Postmaster General of ZAMPOST in Zambia;

- Mr Ben Kangwa, a former diplomat at the Zambian Embassy in Washington DC and a long-time television personality and former Director of Programs at the Zambia National Broadcasting Corporation (ZNBC);

- Mr Henry Ngolwe, a Commonwealth Games medalist in the one hundred meters (100m) race, as well as a gold medalist at the 1988 Southern Region Africa Championships;

- Mr Justin Chola, an MBA graduate of Cornell University in the US, and a successful businessman and former Chief Executive Officer of Bayport Financial Services Zambia, who has also served in other corporate executive leadership roles in Zambia and South Africa;

- Mr Boyd Simposya, an MBA graduate of a leading Norwegian Business School, BI Norwegian Business School, and the Honorary Consul for Norway in Zambia, who has also serves as the Country Director of Norconsult AS in Zambia and has served previously in various other corporate leadership roles in Zambia;

- Mr James Kalengo, an MBA graduate of Texas A&M University in the US, and a former Chief Executive Officer of Commerce Bank in Zambia, who has also served in various other corporate executive leadership roles in Zambia;

- Zambia Air Force (ZAF) Brigadier-General Sam Simwanda, who also served as a diplomat at the Zambian Embassy in Brussels, Belgium;

- ZAF Brigadier-General Jonathan Chola Makanta, who has also served as the Director of ZAF's Legal Department;

- ZAF Brigadier-General Marcelino Chiluba;

- Dr Dennis Mwansa, who holds a PhD in Computer Science from Nagasaki University in Japan, and serves as the Managing Director and Asia Pacific Head of CIB Solution Architecture at J organ Chase in Singapore, in addition to having held previously many other corporate executive leadership roles in Japan, Europe and South Africa;

- Mr Arthur Ndhlovu, a Zambian based UK chartered accountant, who is also successful businessman;

- Dr Sebastian Chinkoya MD, a prominent physician who has also served as Executive Director of Ndola Central Hospital;

- Dr Charles Masase MD, a prominent physician who also served as Director of Clinical Care at Ndola Central Hospital;

- Mr Steve Chungu, former Zambian Government Chief Whip and former Member of Parliament for Luanshya Central.

- All in all, some top universities where alumni of LBSS have studied, graduated from or taught include the University of Oxford, Harvard University, Yale University, Massachusetts Institute of Technology (MIT), Stanford University, the University of Cambridge, the University of Warwick, London Business School, INSEAD, Cornell University, Georgetown University, the University of Cape Town, and the University of Pretoria.

On the other side of town was Roan township which housed RASS. As a school, RASS was located in the corridor of senta emissions from the mines. RAS, however, produced some of the greatest football players in the history of Zambian football and they include Jack Chanda, Emmanuel Mwape, Kenny Mwape, and Vincent Chileshe. Then, among other notable alumni of RASS are the following: the Hon Minister of Energy for Zambia, Mr Peter Chibwe Kapala, who holds, inter alia, a Masters degree in Structural Engineering from the University of Sheffield in the UK; Dr Kanyanta Sunkutu, a physician who holds an MPH degree from the University of Leeds in the UK, with extensive experience in international health, particularly in sexual and reproductive health, family planning, and supply chain management, and currently serves as a Technical Specialist at the <u>UNFPA</u> East and Southern Africa Regional Office; Mr Christoper Mulenga, the Deputy Managing Director of Grant Thornton in Zambia who is a Fellow of the Association of Chartered Certified Accountants (UK) (FCCA) and the Zambia Institute of Chartered Accountants (FZICA); and Dr Andrew Mwaba, a seasoned economist and retired Country Manager at the African Development Bank, who holds, inter alia, a PhD in Economics from the University of Manchester in the UK and a Masters degree from Columbia University in the US.

After RASS came Mpatamato Secondary School in Mpatamato township. Among the notable alumni of Mpatamato Secondary School was the former Vice-President of the Republic of Zambia and eminent lawyer, Hon. Mr George Kunda, who also served previously as Minister of Justice in the Government of the Republic of Zambia. Mpatamato Secondary School was located further away from downtown Luanshya. The said school was for both girls and boys. Like RASS, Mpatamato Secondary School was also located in low-income residential areas designed mainly for blue-collar miners. Probably because of the presence of some female students at Mpatamato Secondary School, most of the boys there behaved somewhat much better than some RASS students. RASS had a reputation of having some crazy students who may not have benefitted much from kindergarten grooming in their early childhood.

As freshmen at LBSS, we were placed in seven different Form 1 (Grade 8) classes, based on our academic performance during the final Grade 7 exam in primary school. The top class was 1G1. That is the class in which the best students from different primary schools in Luanshya were placed. I was in that class. Again, I was the youngest in class. One of the subjects we took was French. After 1G1 came 1G2, followed by 1T1, 1T2, 1C1, 1C2 and then 1C3. My classmates in 1G1 included Clement Katulwende, Katongo Lukwesa, Anthony Kasonde, Winstone Makukula, Joseph Mofya, Boniface Mushimata, Teddy Nsofu, Aaron Chirwa, Paul Nshale, Victor Kapika, Rex Mungaila, Joseph Kapya, Francis Kasempa, Charles Chileya, Charles Chileshe, Adolph Katebe, Stephen Mwape, Kelvin Chiluba, Elijah Chanda, Hitler Sinyangwe, Lamech Chavula, Hugh Chindongo, Langizya Langson Mbewe, Felison Banda, Bernard Nkhata, Oliver Kafi, Charles Malama Chileshe, Amit Patel, Alison 'Harrison' Nkhuwa, Renton Chisenga, and Joseph Mubanga. This was the crème de la crème of the freshmen at LBSS in 1981.

When we arrived at LBSS as freshmen, talk started going around in class of who had scored the highest points in the entire district of Luanshya during the Grade 7 exams. Apparently, it was a Filipino guy at the elite school owned by the copper mines, Luanshya Trust School. But the Filipino guy never joined us at LBSS and either returned back to the Philippines or went to Europe for his high school. We also learned that after the Filipino guy came some indigenous Zambian guy from some primary school in a local township in Luanshya, Mikomfwa township. We all wondered who it was since we expected that it would be someone from one of the elite primary schools located near downtown (i.e. 'Ama sukulu ya ku ma yard filya'). Indeed, that is what unconscious bias does. You begin to form a priori assumptions. But when I met my good friend, Clement Mwila Katulwende, I knew immediately that that was the guy that everyone was talking about. With a quiet and pensive demeanor, Clement was an all-rounder powerhouse academically. He was exceptionally brilliant in all the class subjects. It did not matter whether it was mathematics or English, Clement would 'wire' them (score highly).

I remember that Clement would sometimes shave his hair and show up with a bald head when it was time to write end-of-semester exams. Some superstitious fellas in class would panic, especially that Clement had a reputation of scoring very high marks. In contrast those fellas, I would just laugh it off. For me, Clement just wanted to look smart and to focus instead of worrying about combing his hair every morning when heading to write exams. But some superstitious guys in class began spreading false rumors that Clement shaved his hair and remained with a bald head so that he could absorb all the knowledge from all his classmates using some 'maximum absorption frequency'. It is the craziest thing that I had ever heard of. Insecure people panic even when they see a fly pass by. Folks would just panic for nothing. Of course, none of those rumors were true. Your friend gets a simple haircut to look smart, and you are busy panicking because of your own insecurities. Clement was always presentable and dressed neatly. That was all. So, those spreading rumors in class were simply hallucinating from their own insecurities, as they struggled to cope with Clement's stellar academic performance and thus had to look for scapegoats. Interestingly, both Clement and I were not so much into excessive hours of studying for us to grasp ideas in class, unlike some students who read like crazy even on weekends. For some of them, it paid off. But Clement, as I remember him, was naturally gifted academically. He was the only one in that class, G1, who I considered seriously as a powerful motivator in terms of academic performance. His academic performance pushed me to work harder. He was consistently good in all the subjects from Form 1 to Form 3. I remember that each time the class sat for a test, one of our mutual friends, whose name I will not mention, would sneak around to find out the grades of the other students. He would often start by asking quietly, with a cheeky smile:

"Nga ka Clement, ka lile shani?" ("What about Clement, what did he get?")

And I would respond:

"You write exams to pass, not to beat Clement."

Another guy would go directly to Clement to challenge him to produce his exam results, insisting that this time around he (the snoopy guy) had beaten Clement even before he had seen Clement's exam results. But it would often turnout otherwise. Competition is healthy, but not when it becomes too personal. In life, you do not have to dim your friend's light for yours to glow. You can have both lights on. Don't you think the room will even glow more brightly if both lights are on, as opposed to one light only? Put simply, you can both benefit from a better lit room if you have two or more glowing lights in the same room. So, why do you want to dim your friend's light so that only yours is glowing? You can easily lose focus if your goal is to derail or beat someone instead of aiming to accomplish your own objectives. Always remember that you cannot put a good man down. There is a tendency for some people to suspect some supernatural force behind a person's brilliance. That is so because they cannot fathom or comprehend why they can't catch up with their friend. I remember asking my good brother and friend, Kalusha Bwalya, one of Africa's most celebrated soccer icons, about his inspiring free-kick conversions in the dying minutes of a number of football matches that he played for Zambia. Some people would say that those free-kicks were not normal free-kicks, implying that there was some superficial force behind them. But Kalusha laughed it off and explained to me that it was all about intensive and focused training when he was playing professional football abroad which included mastering the execution of set-pieces like free-kicks. I agree with Kalusha. If you have watched Messi, Neymar, Ronaldo (CR7) and many other world-class soccer icons, you will realize that they too have often scored from similar set-pieces as Kalusha's free-kicks. All these guys have been top-notch professionals. Like a sniper on top of a building taking out people in the streets, they have perfected their skills to the highest levels. So, just because you are struggling to process or understand someone's brilliance does not mean that you should now turn to arguments of superstition. When I got my second Higher Doctorate, someone whispered to me what some folks were saying. I just laughed it off. Some folks were saying that:

"Aba ama guys ba ku Luapula ba lya fya. Ta kwaba fye, mdala. Ta umona nomu nankwe Kalu ama free-kicks yakwe!" ("These guys from Luapula Province are a problem. No person with normal human capabilities does that. Who gets two Higher Doctorates in two disciplines? That's not normal. You can even see from his friend Kalusha, another one from Luapula, how he scores those inexplicable free-kicks when a game is almost over. Who does that?) Ta kwaba, mdala. Aba aba lumendo ba ku Luapula ba ku leka fye. ("There is something about these Luapula fellas and how they are able to perform inexplicable wonders and 'miracles'. We know them)."

But look, the truth is that if someone is good at what they do, there is no need for you to even entertain thoughts of superstition. It's simply a question of great talent, hard work, focus, vision, determination and discipline. My friend, Clement, who ironically is also from Luapula, explained to me why he used to shave his hair and remain with a bald head before writing exams. He said to me:

"There was a time when I was preparing to write exams in primary school. I shaved my hair and remained with a bald head. When the results came out, I had beaten everyone. They all started suspecting something about my neatly shaved bald head. I could tell that they were so scared and intimidated. So, I figured that I might as well use the same trick in high school to scare them. And it seemed to work."

Though the guy in my class who would often ask about Clement's grades was himself equally good academically, he would not go directly to Clement to ask him for the grades. It would appear that he was scared and chose instead to go to others, asking them what Clement had got. Life is like that. There will be some people who cannot face you directly but will go around asking others about you, as if you have refused to talk to them.

As a class, we proceeded in 1982 from 1G1 (Form 1) to 2G1 (Form 2). A couple or so guys joined us in Form 2. They came on transfer from other schools. One of them was my friend, Fwambo Mambwe, a cousin of a childhood friend and former classmate in primary school, Ricky Theil. Fwambo had just come back from Canada with his parents and siblings when he joined us at LBSS. So, one time, our mathematics teacher, Mr Donald 'Don King' Chanda, who was sitting in for the civics teacher, asked Fwambo the meaning of the acronym, 'MP'. Good ol' Fwambo, having just arrived from Canada, innocently replied with a Canadian accent:

"Mountain Police."

We all burst out laughing. Then, Mr Chanda smiled and tried to help the innocent Fwambo.

"No, Fwambo, its Member of Parliament, not Mountain Police!"

I felt sorry for my friend, Fwambo, because it was not his fault that he thought that the acronym 'MP' stood for mountain police. That is what he had learned in school in Canada. So, you cannot fault him. The question asked by our teacher should have been phrased in a better way, given that 'MP' can indeed stand for mountain police, unless and until the teacher specifies that he or she is asking about 'MP' in the Zambian context. Put simply, the question should have been phrased as follows:

"What do the letters, MP, stand for in Zambia?"

That way, the student would not have been misled to think that the teacher was asking about the mountain police in Canada.

In 1983, we proceeded from 2G1 (Form 2) to 3G1 (Form 3). I remember that we had a few violent chaps in junior and senior secondary school at LBSS. Some of them were older chaps from Mikomfwa township or Roan township who had failed and repeated Grade 7 several times before making it to secondary school. Others would claim that they were karatekas. None of those fellas went far in life. Some of them unfortunately died young. Others are now faced with grinding poverty and severe economic hardship. Indeed, many who are still alive are suffering financially and economically. Violence does not pay. Being preoccupied with 'uku ponona umu nobe' (beating your friend) can never take you far in life. The language of 'kuti naku ponona' (I can beat you) was common among those who were not bright in school. The dull ones often thought that 'uku ponona' (fighting) would take them far. Today, they look so old, frail and haggard by the ailing economy. Many are a shell of what they used to be because they focused on 'uku ponona' (fighting) instead of concentrating on school. It is better 'wa ponona ko ama buku' (you excel academically) than 'ule ponona aba nobe' (unleashing physical violence on your friends). If you are preoccupied with 'uku ponona aba nobe' (beating your friends), instead of focusing on school, in future, people will not even believe you if you say that you were classmates or in the same school as someone who has made it big time out there at the national or international level. You will even be afraid to greet that person if you see him. For, it is often a truism that 'ba lya wa le tinya' (those you used to bully) often end up doing well in life while you can only console yourself in abject poverty, saying that:

"Ba le ntina. Na le ponona." ("They all used to fear me. I used to beat.")

But now the economy has really beaten you. Such is life. Brawn can never excel over brains. Form 3, now known as Grade 10, was the final year of junior high school before we wrote our exams to qualify to senior high school. Some of our teachers from Form 1 to Form 3 included Mr James Malama (English), Mr Donald 'Don King' Chanda (Maths), Mr Frank Chipunka (Art), Mr Libingi (History), Mr Simukoko (History), Mr Juvenal Malembe Kaoma (French), Mrs Abrahams (General Science), Mr Kangwa (Geography), Mr Percent (Civics), and Mr Kawonga (Civics). Indeed, much gratitude and respect to all my former teachers and former classmates. Mr Malama was always a fine gentleman. He was often well-dressed and quite methodical in his teaching. All in all, Mr Malama was a very good English teacher. Then, our art teacher, Mr Chipunka, was such a humble and quiet man. He was also an extremely talented artist. Mr Chipunka appeared to be a strong Christian with very strong Christian family values. He was often so meticulous in his art classes. Then, we also enjoyed the stories about Zaire or Democratic Republic of Congo narrated to us by Mr Kaoma, our French teacher. Mr Kaoma had lived in Zaire for twenty (20) years before returning to Zambia. In the civics class, Mr Percent was our teacher. He was a mixed race (colored) man, possibly from Cape Town, South Africa. Mr Percent was a comedian, but also a very good teacher. He would pull your nose as punishment if you were caught misbehaving. Then, of course, we had the legendary Don King (Mr Chanda) who was very charismatic. For each Form 1 class he took, he would start the math lessons with the topic of sets and subsets, and then pose the following question deliberately to the students:

"What is the set of people in this class who have been to the States?"

Everyone in class would say, 'zero'. Then, Mr Chanda would drop his chalk in a somewhat rehearsed act of disapproval, saying:

"No, you are wrong. Baice (young men), let me tell you about when I was in the US. In fact, that is where I learned how to drive a car. As you know, my car is the only car with a surname. I drive a Toyota Mark II. When I was in the States, I drove a Cadillac. I went to the States for the scout jamboree."

That story about the set of one person who had been to the US would go on and on until the bell rang for the next class and teacher. That was Don King. Otherwise, he was a very nice man and a great mathematician. For general science, we had Mrs Abrahams as our teacher. She was an elderly

Indian lady who often dictated good class notes to us. You did not have to read many textbooks in biology once you took down her class notes. I remember that two of my classmates, Stephen Mwape and Katongo Lukwesa, were the ones she often handed class notes if she was running late. In the picture below, Katongo, who is an IT specialist and professor in the Middle East, can be seen greeting my mother when he was visiting Zambia. Katongo's parents and my parents were very close. Luanshya, like Livingstone, is a small place and many families knew each other.

Following below are two pictures taken in May 2023 when I was visiting Zambia. In the first picture, I can be seen with one of my close friends and a former classmate from Form 1 (Grade 8) to Form 3 (Grade 10), Clement Katulwende, who I mentioned above and who is an accountant by profession and a graduate of Copperbelt University (CBU). The other gentleman in the picture is another good friend and LBSS alumnus, Professor Ephraim Munshifwa (standing in the middle). Professor Munshifwa is a graduate of the University of Cambridge in England. He and I are arguably the only two Oxbridge graduates from LBSS. I was honored to receive a courtesy call from Clement and Ephraim when I was visiting the Copperbelt in May of 2023. I was staying at the Garden Court Hotel in Kitwe, and they came over to see me. We had a good time over some fine drink and good food.

In the picture below, I appear alongside my good friend and brother, Professor Ephraim Munshifwa, in his office at Copperbelt University (CBU). I was paying a courtesy call on him at CBU. Professor Munshifwa was at the time serving as the Dean of the School of the Built Environment at CBU. He now heads the Lusaka campus of CBU. From our LBSS cohort of 1981-85, Ephraim and I, went on to study at the Universities of Cambridge and Oxford, respectively, and became accomplished scholars. So, yes, LBSS has produced notable Oxbridge graduates as well as a distinguished Rhodes Scholar. Today, LBSS continues to be a great high school. Not many schools can boast of producing such a cadre of distinguished alumni who have gone on to make a big impact on the global stage.

Generally, LBSS had good infrastructure, including well-stocked laboratories, nicely furnished classes, and excellent teachers. We even had a dedicated lab assistant, Mr Raphael. As students, we only knew Mr Raphael by his first name, 'Ba Raphael'. He was a wonderful and extremely helpful old man. Another name among the LBSS non-teaching staff that comes to mind is that of Mr Chikumbi. Mr Chikumbi was a fine gentleman. He was always neatly dressed, with a jacket and tie, and a good disposition of exceptionally fine manners. A well-spoken man, Mr Chikumbi was an administrator in the front office that supported the work of the headmaster and deputy-headmaster. Whenever Mr Chikumbi found us playing table-tennis in the foyer, he would ask for a quick game. He was really good at table-tennis, beating even some of our best table-tennis players. The only guy who would give Mr Chikumbi a tough time at table-tennis was my friend, Masanguza (Sangu) Thole, a UK-chartered accountant based in the UK. Sangu was a brilliant table-tennis player. And we would see Mr Chikumbi take off his jacket when playing against Sangu. But even that would rarely help. Sangu was too good. I remember also Arthur Ndhlovu, another a UK-chartered accountant but now based in Zambia, who was two cohorts ahead of me at LBSS, as another talented table-tennis player. Also, Jonathan Mulenga, who later trained as a medical doctor in Cuba, was a damn good table tennis player. Jonathan was known at LBSS for his meanness as a school prefect. He seemed to enjoy inflicting pain on noisemakers and latecomers.

During breaktime as well on some lunch breaks, some of us would play football rondos and position games on the basketball court using a tennis ball instead of a proper football. As you might know, a tennis ball is so much smaller than a football. So, we needed to be very skillful to juggle and control a tennis ball played on the surface of a basketball court using our feet. Also, one had to make sure that an opponent did not dribble you or get you megged. Megging is a skillful and masterful way of kicking or sliding the ball so that it goes through in-between the legs of an opposition player, as you dribble past him or her. We would play rondos and position games with a tennis ball on a basketball court, while wearing school shoes. We called those rondos 'pomo'. Closely related to this, we also played position games. As you might know, position games are a version of rondos. Position games often involved more players occupying spaces like in a regular football match e.g., outside back, center back, center midfield and so forth. When playing 'pomo', if an opponent megged you by getting the tennis ball go through in-between your legs, everyone on the field would descend on you to beat you up until you were able to run for your life and touch a designated object such as a gate or tree. Only then would you be redeemed and readmitted back to the game. In short, the rondos of 'pomo' helped to perfect our cognitive structures and motor actions for playing football. Koto was another form of rondos. Koto involved two guys and two goalposts, with each player guarding his or her goalpost, as they took shots at each other's goalpost to see who would concede a goal. Great goalkeepers were born out of the 'koto' rondos. There were also certain days when I would walk off the pitch in the middle of a game to go and grab a cup of coffee at home. Our house was right next to the school. And that would irritate some folks. But, hey, why not take a stroll for a coffee at home if you live right next to the school!

Some friends with whom I played the rondos included Dr Dennis Musonda, now a highly respected medical doctor in Zambia, Engineer Mr Simon Kunda, now a distinguished Zambian engineer, Mr Preston Luchelo (who was a fellow cadet like me), Mr Chris 'Kayaman' Musonda (who later worked for the mines in Mufulira), Mr Derrick 'Dugan' Tembo (who also played for ZAMEFA Football club), Mr Moses Mutale (who also had served as a Catholic altar boy at the same parish as I did), Mr Moses Sinyangwe (who I shared a desk with in Form 4 and Form 5, and now an entrepreneur currently based in Monze), and Mr Remmy Sinyangwe (Moses Sinyangwe's cousin). In general, LBSS had excellent sporting facilities. The school had more athletic tracks and football fields than many high schools on the Copperbelt. As a result, LBSS would usually host the annual seven (7) aside men's football tournament for all secondary schools on the Copperbelt. We saw guys like the legendary Great Kalu (Kalusha Bwalya, former African Footballer of the Year), Jack Chanda (the Zambian Pele), Vincent Chileshe, Baron Mung'omba, Ashios Melu, Edgar Mulenga, Ken Mwanza, Jericho Shinde, Harrison Bwalya, and many others (who at one point or another played for the Zambian national football team) featuring in games at the LBSS annual 7-aside football tournament. As high school students, some of those players were already playing for the Zambian National Football Team. The national team was known famously as the "KK 11", named after the then Zambian President, Dr Kenneth Kaunda, who was a great fan of the Zambia National Football Team.

The high school or secondary school students who played for the Zambian National Football Team were known as 'Schoolboy International'. That's how high the standard of high school football was back then. And it was not easy to make the cut into the national team. Many high schools on the Copperbelt produced excellent football players who benefitted greatly from the excellent sporting facilities of the mining company, ZCCM Ltd. I have shared a picture below where I appear with my good brother and friend, Kalusha Bwalya, known famously as Great Kalu. Kalusha, one of Africa's most illustrious and celebrated soccer icons, was a Schoolboy International and went on to play professional football in Belgium, the Netherlands and Mexico, respectively. In 1988, he was named the Africa Footballer of the Year. Then, in 1996, he was nominated for the 1996 FIFA World Player of the Year award where he was voted the 12th-best player in the world. Great Kalu gave us good football. Much gratitude and respect to the man. He played competitive football for a number of decades in three different continents, namely, Europe, South America and Africa. Great Kalu is also a qualified football coach and has served as President of the Football Association of Zambia (FAZ), in addition to carrying out international responsibilities in the administration of football globally.

When I arrived at LBSS in 1981, the headmaster was Mr Musumali, whose young brother, Vumango, was my classmate in primary school at Buteko Primary School. The Deputy headmaster was Mr Chaikatisha. Later, Mr Chaikatisha left and was succeeded by Mr Sakeni. After Mr Sakeni came Mr Kalobwe. For the headmaster post, Mr Musumali was succeeded by Mr Mumba, a close friend of my father.

While a student at LBSS, I joined the Zambia Combined Cadet Force in my fresher year. I was promoted to the rank of Lance Corporal within a few months of joining by the head of the cadet force at our school, Second Lieutenant, Charles Mibenge. Charles was a fair guy. He also had good character and a strong presence. I had no idea that I was going to be promoted when it happened during parade. Indeed, I had no idea that Charles had spotted leadership talent in me. While on parade, I just heard my name mentioned for promotion. I was pleasantly shocked. Charles was one of those guys that we all, as cadets, looked up to. He took over cadet leadership from his predecessor, Wisdom Konta. They both had very imposing but admirable personalities. Cadet was fun. We would sometimes have joint cadet parades with guys from Roan Antelope Secondary School (RASS). My contemporaries from RASS included Dr Kanyanta Sunkutu, a medical doctor who I mentioned earlier. He was then known as Braceford Sunkutu. My other cadet friend from RASS was Mr Donny Mpande, an engineer based in South Africa. Then, the gal's school, LGSS, had a very pretty cadet leader, Ms Juliet Nankolongo. She was our senior and ahead of us in school. We were small boys and cadet beginners at the time. I remember a good friend at LGSS from Zimbabwe. Her name was Sarah Muzumara. She too, and a young Zambian lady called Fayidess, was a cadet. Cadet was so much fun. I remember guys like Mulenga Chokwe and Sam Lindo. We had so many humorous fellas. We also had some weird guys who, like the altar boys that behaved like junior priests at the Catholic church where I served as an altar boy, were somewhat overzealous cadets and behaved as if they were already junior soldiers or military officers. Most of them never went far in school because the cadet business got to their heads. They would iron their cadet uniform meticulously with starch, looking so neat and presentable. In class, they would sit like a robot to avoid making any wrinkles on their well-starched and meticulously ironed cadet uniform. And many would not even focus during class. All they would wait for was the end-of-class bell so that they could go for cadet business. Very few of those overzealous fellas, if any, ended up as Zambia army or Zambia air-force commissioned officers. Many just ended up drinking the local opaque 'Chibuku' beer in the townships. The same was true for a number of overzealous prefects at school. I remember one guy, in particular, MJ (real name withheld), who punished me severely for playing a prank on him by giving him a false list of noisemakers that were actually non-existent. The guy was older and in his final year of high school. He showed up as a prefect during prep-time, spiritedly looking for noisemakers to punish. Here, I do not mean to embarrass anyone, but many school prefects behaved as if they were junior teachers. They enjoyed inflicting physical pain on other students. They spent more time running around school as prefects instead of studying. When MJ showed up in our class to collect names of noisemakers, I pretended to be the class captain. I gave him a list of fake names. MJ was happy. But when he called out the names, the whole class burst out laughing. The guy asked why they were laughing. Upon discovering that he had been played, MJ was mad. He took things personally. MJ inflicted severe punishment on me. The guy was so furious. Much later in life, I found MJ at the University of Zambia (UNZA). He was also a student there, but a few years ahead of me. At UNZA, MJ did not last long. He flunked. Then, he turned to an alternative degree or diploma program at another university and had to study some law courses. Life can be humbling. MJ later reached out to me for assistance with some study materials. Such is life. I had already forgiven MJ and thus gave him the advice that he sought. There is no point in keeping grudges. UNZA had already punished MJ. Besides, we were young at LBSS. MJ was seemingly excited with the whole idea of being a school prefect while I was a class prank-star. I enjoyed cracking jokes and playing pranks. It was fun. It was part of the 'senta' culture on the Copperbelt.

More recently, I ran into some of my former teachers at LBSS. I have provided below some pictures taken with two of my former LBSS teachers, Mr James Malama and Mr Charles Suwali, when I had travelled to Zambia in 2019 for my mother's funeral. The first picture appearing below was taken in Lusaka with my former English language teacher at LBSS, Mr James Malama. He was my teacher at LBSS from Form 1 (Grade 8) to Form 3 (Grade 10).

Then, the picture below was taken at my parents' home in Luanshya soon after we had just come from putting my mother to rest. In the picture below, my chemistry teacher in Form 5 (Grade 12), Mr Charles Suwali, who was also a close friend of my eldest brother, Kelvin, can be seen standing next to me. Mr Suwali attended my mother's funeral and was also there for us when we lost brother Kelvin and brother Francis. Also in attendance at my mother's funeral was my former geography teacher in Form 4 (Grade 11) and Form 5 (Grade 12), Mr Benson Chalwe. Mr Chalwe was also my uncle on the paternal side of our family.

After we had put my mother to rest, and before leaving Luanshya for Lusaka enroute to the US, I went to thank the then Mayor of Luanshya, His Worship Mr Nathan Chanda, who was in attendance at the funeral. His Worship played a key role, as a leading government official and senior civic leader in Luanshya district, in leading the procession for the burial at my mother's funeral. He was also instrumental in providing some logistical support during the funeral. In the picture below, I can be seen with His Worship, Mayor Nathan Chanda, in the mayor's office. When I went to see the mayor, there were a lot of people waiting outside his office to see him. But I was exceedingly humbled and honored to be given priority and ushered into the mayor's office, especially that I had a tight schedule trying to get into Lusaka enroute to the US. Much thanks and respect to His Worship, Mayor Nathan Chanda.

Back in the days, when I was in high school, junior secondary school in Zambia ran Form 1 (Grade 8) to Form 3 (Grade 10). Things have since changed. Junior secondary school now runs from Grade 8 to Grade 9. As noted above, I entered Luanshya Boys' Secondary School (LBSS) as a freshman in 1981. In 1983, just before I sat for my senior secondary school qualifying exams at the end of Form 3, my father unexpectedly got his retirement letter. He was up for retirement from the civil service. My father had not expected the retirement letter to come so soon. He had been of the view that he was left with couple of years or so before retirement. My father was born in 1928 but had signed up in the civil service as having born two years earlier, that is, in 1926, with a view of taking early retirement and going into farming. But as years went by, he forgot that the government records had him registered as having born in 1926. In his mind's eye, he was working with his real age, as having been born in 1928, and thinking that he still had some two years to go. So, the notice of retirement took him by surprise. He had to make alternative plans immediately.

In 1983, soon after my Dad retired, I wrote my Form 3 exams and my immediate elder sister, Matilda, also wrote her Form 5 school leavers' exams. We both passed, despite the disruption that the family went through with my father's unexpected retirement. Dad had just bought a four-bedroom house in a new settlement for retirees in Mboya, Section C area. It was a bit of an adjustment. That is where I linked up with some good reggae music enthusiasts like Amos Tembo and his friends, Eddie and Noah, who would play renditions of Bob Marley's music on an acoustic guitar. Eddie was a really good guitarist. My family had just moved from our residential home near LBSS, whose address was 1 Shala Road. During school days, my friend, Masanguza Thole, who used to live near LBSS, would often invite me to their place for lunch. We used to live in the same neighborhood before my father retired. So, we were close family friends. Sometimes, I would hang out with my classmates, and we would head into downtown Luanshya to grab lunch at some famous lunch hotspots where the female students from Luanshya Girls' Secondary School (LGSS) were often found. The gals were the magnet. A couple of years later, I left Luanshya for university studies at the University of Zambia (UNZA) in Lusaka. Later, I moved my parents out of Mboya and bought them a lovely spacious home that once belonged to the City Mayor of Luanshya and is located in the same residential area near downtown and LBSS where we used to stay before the family moved to Mboya.

In 1982, my eldest brother, Kelvin, graduated from the University of Zambia (UNZA). That was a year before Dad retired. Kelvin worked as a manager for Zambia National Building Society in Lusaka. My eldest sister, Catherine, had also graduated by then from a secretarial college in Southern Province of Zambia and was working in Lusaka. My older brother, Dennis, was at college in Ndola. So, there was only Dad and Mum as well as my immediate elder sister, Matilda, together with Eugene, Francis, Joseph and me at home. I was always confident in my intellectual abilities. In 1983, soon after Dad retired, when the Form 3 exam results came out at LBSS, all the guys from my school, together with some parents and many folks from the neighborhood rushed to see who had made it and who had failed. Those days, school exam results would be posted on the wall for the public to see. As expected, I was on the first list of the top thirty (30) students at LBSS in 1983/4 who had made it to Form 4. The total number of students at the school who made it to Form 4 that year was one hundred and forty-four (144). The first list, ranked from number one (1) to number thirty-tine (39), based on academic performance, contained thirty-nine (39) names. That was the A-list. I was on that list. The second list, the B-list, ranked from number forty (40) to number seventy-six (76), based on academic performance, contained thirty-six (36) names. The B-list was followed by the C-list, ranked from number seventy-seven (77) to one hundred and fourteen (114), based again on academic performance. The C-list contained thirty-seven (37) names. Finally, there was the D-list, ranked in terms of academic performance, starting with number one hundred and fifteen (115) to one hundred and forty-four (144). The D-list comprised twenty-nine (29) names.

A few years before I wrote this book, one of my former high school teachers, Mr James Malama, shared with me copies of the lists that I have summarized above. I was shocked to find that he had kept a good record of the same. Tactfully, Mr Malama did not disclose to me fully what was contained in an envelope that he gave me when we met in Lusaka, Zambia. He simply said it contained a draft of a paper that he wanted me to look at and give him some feedback. But when I got back to Washington DC, I realized that the envelope did not only contain the draft paper, but also a treasure trove of the lists described above. Indeed, the elders have a way of sharing valuable information clairvoyantly. I am ever grateful to Mr Malama. I would not have had my hands on the said value document had it not been for him.

Now, I have mentioned above that only 144 students from my 1983 Form 3 cohort at LBSS made it to senior high school. I will, however, not disclose the names of those who failed or those who passed but were on the C-list or D-list, especially that some of them might be prominent people in society today. Suffice it to say, when the academic year started in 1984, those of us who had made it to Form 4 were ushered into the school sports hall to be assigned to our respective Form 4 classes. Out of seven (7) classes in Form 3, we were reduced to only four (4) classes in Form 4. The rest of the guys did not make it. As I pointed out earlier, the junior secondary school classes at LBSS, ranked in terms of academic performance, and, starting with the top class, ran as G1, G2, T1, T2, C1, C2, and finally C3. I was in the G1 class throughout my junior secondary school. G1 was the top class and the only one that took French while G2 folks took Bemba. Apart from this difference, we all took general subjects such as civics, mathematics, general science, history, geography, and English. Both G1 and G2 classes also took art. Then, T1 and T2 folks took subjects such as technical drawing and metal work, in addition to the general subjects mentioned above, whereas C1, C2, and C3 folks took subjects such as book-keeping and office practice, in addition to the aforesaid general subjects.

In Form 4, the arrangement was different. There was 4S1, 4S2, 4A1 and 4A2. The letter 'S' stood for 'sciences' whereas the letter 'A' stood for 'arts.' So, as we reported for Form 4, we were being assigned to any one of those four classes. The guys in the S1 and S2 classes would end up taking subjects such as Additional Mathematics and what was then known as Pure Sciences whereas the guys in A1 and A2 classes would end up taking ordinary mathematics and physical science (chemistry and physics) subjects. The A1 class would also take biology, as a standalone subject, whereas the A2 class would focus more on zoology in their biology class. And so, the A2 class became known famously as the 'zoo'. That nickname was compounded by the fact that those who barely scrapped through to get to Form 4 were placed in A2. So, there we were, as Form 4 students, waiting to be assigned to classes.

My name was the first one to be called out. I was caught unawares. I was hoping that since I was on the A-list my natural home was S1, like my elder brother, Dennis, who had previously made it to S1. To my surprise, I was singled out from the A-list and thrown into A1. I was disappointed and devastated. How could it be, I said to myself? I was on the A-list. I could not understand what had happened. To me, it did not make sense. Most of the other guys on the A-list proceeded to S1. Interestingly, the A-list comprised a combination of students from my former G1 class in junior secondary school and folks from the less academically gifted classes of T1, T2, C1, C2, and C3 classes. Some guys from the T and C classes had finally redeemed themselves academically after a weak start in junior secondary school. I was thrown into A1, a class that had folks mainly from the B-list and C-list. I realized later that actually my teachers had done me a favor by putting me where I would excel the most. They saw my strengths in the arts subjects. I was very good at the social sciences. I did my own introspection and realized that although I was one of the best performing students at Grade 7 in the entire Luanshya district, my maths was not that excellent. By contrast, I scored exceptionally high marks in all the other subjects to beat everyone at my primary school. This pattern somewhat repeated itself at Form 3. My grades in the art subjects or the social sciences were simply impeccable and untouchable. However, my mathematics was not that excellent. I accepted, adapted and adjusted to life in 4A1, maintaining my academic excellence at the helm of the class. I was undoubtedly ahead of everyone academically in that class.

Some of my teachers in senior secondary at LBSS included Mr James 'Buffalo Solider' Mukosha (Literature in English), Mr Mpandashulu (Form 4 Geography), Mr Hachaamba (Form 5 Mathematics), Mr Paedar MacGowan (Form 5 English – Irish-Zambian national and a former national squash champion of Zambia under whose tutelage LBSS' squash player, Chambo Phiri, excelled), Mr Armitage (Biology – British national), Mr Leeuw (first part of Form 4 Chemistry – South African national who was rumored to be a black belt martial artist), Mr Nyirenda (latter part of Form 4 Chemistry), Mr Charles Suwali (Form 5 Chemistry), Mr Donald Chanda (Form 4 Mathematics), Mr Jayarej (Form 4 English – Asian national (possibly from India)), Mr Alexander (Physics – Egyptian national), Mrs Abrahams (Biology – Indian national) and my uncle, Mr Benson Chalwe (Form 5 Geography). Each one of them brought a different touch to the subject that they taught. Mr Chalwe, for example, was never short of jokes, though he was also a very good teacher. He would sometimes throw shade at us with his wicked sense of humor. The students nicknamed him 'spitting cobra' because spits of saliva would escape from his mouth as he kept making jokes nonstop. Then, Mr Leeuw, rumored to have been a blackbelt martial artist, never smiled much. His chemistry class was very intense. He knew his stuff. And all the students avoided getting in trouble with Mr Leeuw because of the blackbelt rumors they had heard. Then, our biology teacher, a British man, was once introduced to some Zambian English. In one of the biology classes, when we were learning about diffusion and osmosis, one of my classmates asked our biology teacher, Mr Armitage, a question about how osmosis can possibly take place if you sliced an avocado pear in half and put some sugar on one half. Now, in Bemba, the name 'avocado pear' is 'kota pela'. If one does not know the real name of an avocado pear in English, you would be tempted to think that 'kota pela' is an English name. No, it's not. Unknowingly, my classmate went:

"Sir, what about if you cut a 'quarter pellar' and put some sugar on it, would osmosis take place?"

Mr Armitage could not get what the guy was trying to say. He looked baffled. So, we all burst out laughing until one of my other classmates came to the rescue of the guy that had just 'butchered the word', explaining to Mr Armitage that:

"Sir, he meant to say, 'avocado pear.'"

The erring classmate that had said 'quarter pellar' felt so embarrassed though tried to muster some courage, as if nothing wrong had happened.

Also, I remember one other funny incident when we entered Form 4. I was selected by our teachers to be on a provisional list of new school prefects. But when the list was forwarded to one of my Zambian colleagues, who was a fellow student in Form 4 and charged with the responsibility of finalizing that list, he dropped my name and replaced it with the name of an Asian friend of his. When you are young, you think that that is disappointing news. So, I decided to make it known to my Zambian colleague that that is not how friends treat each other or behave towards one another. He had acted inappropriately, of course, but then you realize later that, after all, being a prefect was not an achievement. If anything, it was a distraction and many students who were school prefects did not go far with their education. Like those who would sometimes bully their friends, many school prefects got derailed academically and are now a sorry sight, that is, for those who are still alive.

Generally, this thing of giving preferential treatment to people of a different nationality, color or race is too ingrained in some of our people. In 1981, thieves broke into our family home in Luanshya. My father was alone at home and fast asleep when this happened. The rest of us had travelled to Lusaka for Christmas holiday while my older siblings were in university and college, respectively. Dad could not hear the break in. The house was quite big, and the master bedroom was at the end of a long passage or corridor. The thieves cut a big hole in the security barbed wire fence around the yard through which they hauled out the stolen good. They stole a number of precious items, including a then trendy Akai X1810 cartridge stereo musical system that my father had bought when he was abroad in Canada as well as the home television set in the living room and many other items. When we got back from Lusaka, we found our neighborhood cordoned off by police and college security. We arrived at night. The cops were patrolling the streets. They stopped us and asked us where we were coming from and going. Then one of the cops recognized us and broke the news that residence of the Principal of LTTI had been broken in recently, leading the cops to provide some additional security in the neighborhood.

We later came to learn that the suspected thieves were some house servants from the neighborhood. The rascals allegedly sold the Akai X1810 cartridge stereo system cheaply to some white man who owned a restaurant in downtown Luanshya. Someone saw that musical system playing in the white man's restaurant and alerted my father. A complaint was lodged by my father with the police, but the police did nothing. It would appear that either the white man managed to bribe the cops to silence them, or the police were just afraid of confronting and arresting a 'white man'. It comes back to the point that I was making above that a number of our African folks like to give preferential treatment to people of a different color, race or nationality. It is some kind of inferiority complex and self-hate. To be associated with a white person or someone from another race or nationality is not an achievement. So, even though the police in Luanshya could have done more to investigate the matter of theft at my parents' home, they simply froze maybe because the matter involved a white man knowingly purchasing stolen goods. For some unknown reason, the police could not just do anything. Interestingly, even those who stole from us stole from fellow black people to enrich or empower not themselves, but a white person. Looking back, one could argue that the rascals could have been hired by that same white man to go and rob their fellow black man and disposes him of property. In Africa, when the white slave traders came to get slaves, they were only able to succeed because some Africans were quick to help them. On their own, the white slave traders would not have succeeded. It was only possible for them to succeed because of the help and complicity of some selfish and foolish Africans who received such cheap items as salt, mirrors and empty bottles of whisky in return for the betrayal of their fellow black men and women. Even today, it is quite common in Zambia to see preferential treatment being accorded by the natives or locals to people of a different nationality, color or race. It is something that is too deeply ingrained in the psyche of some of our people. And many non-indigenous folks living in Zambia, especially Caucasians and Asians, know this fact fully well and will often exploit it to their own advantage.

In other countries, if you are a foreigner or non-native, you know your place, notwithstanding that the law is there to guarantee equal rights to all regardless of race, religion, nationality or gender. Growing up in Luanshya, I noticed that most of the major shops and businesses in downtown were run by foreigners. And a number of those foreigners were political refugees or self-exiles from other countries, yet many local Zambians looked up to them as the elites of the town. It was a sad culture of self-hate by many Zambians. Indeed, it was not common to walk into a butchery in Luanshya and find that the butchery was owned by a Malawian who had fled from Dr Hastings Kamuzu Banda's tyrannical rule in Malawi. Where were the Zambians? In the transport sector and retail industry, too, it was the same. You would find a Zimbabwean, for example, who had fled from the then white minority rule in Zimbabwe, or some colored guy who had fled the brutality of apartheid in South Africa, running buses or other businesses. Some Malawian refugees too owned some buses and would dominant the public transportation sector. The indigenous people, the Zambians, were nowhere to be seen. If anything, the few Zambians who had tried out some form of private sector business would operate mainly from the outer fringes in the second-class trading area of Luanshya or in Luanshya's highly populated townships of Mikomfwa, Roan and Mpatamato. Generally, business ownership in downtown was a preserve mainly of Indian businessmen, some white traders, some Jewish traders and a few Caribbean folks as well as some Malawians and Zimbabweans. So, the mindset of many a native Zambian was that foreigners were superior to Zambians generally. Even illegal emerald dealers from Senegal and Mali infiltrated the Copperbelt and took advantage of that mindset of the Zambians. Some Zambians were now working for Senegalese and Malian illegal emerald miners or dealers, risking their lives to mine emeralds illegally for some undocumented and uneducated Senegalese and Malian migrants. It was unbelievable yet so true!

I look back today and tell myself that God has a way to preserve you from losing direction. I was never one who idolized contrived friendships with people of a different race, color or nationality. It was a blessing that God took me away from the prefect responsibility in high school and allowed me to be the Chairperson of the LBSS Debating Society when I got to Form 5. I succeeded a colleague, Lawrence Muleka, as Chairperson of the LBSS Debating Society in 1985. Lawrence is now based in Livingstone where he runs a media business firm. Back in the days, Lawrence was quite popular with the young gals at LGSS for his Michael Jackson dress and hair styles. Other guys whose names were popular among the gals at LGSS included Masauso Tembo (i.e. he became headboy at LBSS as well as a cadet leader and later graduated from UNZA as an economist), Bruno Jere, Mugaba Mwase (later went into the public relations profession and returned to Malawi, his native country), Kennedy Chishimba, Victor Kapika, Danny Mukena, Charles Kang'ombe, Lloyd Makombe, Philip Mwape, Teddy Makungu (later graduated from UNZA as an economist and held corporate leadership positions in South Africa and Zambia), Melvin Makungu (later graduated from UNZA as an agriculturalist and is now an academic in South Africa), Victor Chanda, and many others. We also had folks who liked to patronize Caesar's Palace disco in Luanshya. But unfortunately, many disco heroes and heroines of the late 1970s to late 1990s era died young and never lived long enough to experience the real European or American lifestyle abroad that much of the disco life was trying to mimic. Others who are still alive today could have gone far academically and professionally but for their intellectual martyrdom to disco life that distracted and derailed them. It was often not easy to bounce back academically once you boarded the soul train's disco life. Only a handful disco heroes and heroines came out of that era without scars.

There were two famous nightclubs in Luanshya, namely, Caesar's Palace and Olympia Disco. Caesar's Palace was in the first-class shopping area while Olympia Disco was in the second-class shopping area. I think they were both owned by some Greek businessmen in Luanshya. When Caesar's Palace was being built, it was the talk of town. The debate ran rumor mills of what the nightclub would be called when it was open. Eventually, the place was opened and named Caesar's Palace. My brother, Dennis, and his friends, Sankwe Kabezya, Paul Kasochi, Victor Ndhlovu, Aggrey Kasonkomona, Charles Kasonkomona, Griffin Musonda, and Evaristo Yombwe, as well as some guys like Charles 'Chado' Chishimba whose names would often pop up in the LGSS circles were regular patrons of Caesar's Palace. My good friend, Kelvin Nkonda, and his buddie, Moore, would often pitch up in the company of a lady called Barbara Shawa. The popular deejays at Caesar's Palace included a colored guy (mixed-race guy) by the name of 'Kenny the Roman' and a guy called Martin 'Brutus' Mwape. Brutus was originally from the neighboring city of Ndola. I recall that Brutus was also a very good football player. But it appeared that deejaying had taken over his soccer interests. For me, I only went to Caesar's Palace on not more than five occasions. I was not one who was easily impressed with the flava of the day. From childhood, I knew that I was destined for better and greater things. And it came to pass. So, I decided to stick to my books and football. But my cousin, Mutamba Bwalya, who joined us from Ndola and was about my age, would often tag along with Dennis and his Caesar's Palace crew. I remember Dennis' friend, Paul Kasochi, winning a dancing competition at Caesar's Palace. He became popular with the gals, especially that he often used to travel back to the capital city, Lusaka, for school holidays. Guys from Lusaka often would pull that stunt as if Lusaka was some sophisticated place. I remember Evaristo Yombwe also arriving in Luanshya with some Lusaka umph. Those were the good old days. Later, Sankwe Kabezya also won one of the dancing competitions at Caesar's Palace. Folks would dress in Hawaiian shirts, baggie pants, legwarmers and schooners. A few years later, moccasin shoes came on the scene. That was all part of the disco era. I remember when Dennis' friend, James Kalengo, landed from the UK on his vacation from university. Rumor went around town that the guy had come with the latest music from England. I recall that James had the Jheri curl hairstyle and often wore a black leather jacket. And he would move around with his Walkman and headset on. He became a star overnight. A few weeks later, he returned to England for his university studies.

At the LBSS Debating Society, Daniel Ng'andwe succeeded me as Chairperson when I completed high school at the end of 1985. The oratory skills picked up from the debating society helped me later to hone my advocacy skills as a lawyer. As Chairperson of the LBSS Debating Society, I would lead the school's debating team on trips to Ibenga Girls' Secondary School and Luanshya Girls' Secondary School (LGSS), respectively, for debating tournaments. That leadership role gave me some visibility at both the gals' schools. So, by any measure, I was not doing bad. I remember that the chair of the gals' debating society at LGSS was a pretty young lady by the name of Gwen. Gwen always looked elegant, with very good looks and some fine oratory skills. She became a close and trusted friend, and we worked together very well. Like I said, I was not doing bad at all.

Outside class, I had many other activities going on. As noted above, I was an active cadet at LBSS. I rose to the rank of Warrant Officer Class II. Some of the guys that I remember from the cadet days include Andrew 'Mulans' Mulala, Masauso Tembo, Bruno Jere, Paul Muzumara, Arthur Mukuka, Innocent Kwesha, Paul Mukonko, Michael Banda, Preston Luchelo, Wilson Phiri, Patrick Sampa, Cephas Chafumapunda, Twavula Witola, Ntavizi Witola, Eric Chola, Moses Mutale, Anthony Kasonde, Geoffrey Chokwe, Mulenga Chokwe, Sam Lindo, Lawrence Muleka, Elias Kangwa, Frank Kapika, Johnson Machiya, Raphael Mutesha, Victor Simfukwe, Michael Banda, George Kapasa, Misheck Mhango, Victor Chanda, Masanguza Thole, Amos Tembo, Wilfred Chirwa, Victor Kalesha, Robert Mtonga (Dr), and Boniface Mushimata. Then, Mr Peter Chaikatisha, the Deputy Headmaster of LBSS, and Prof Chola Chisunka, one of our Literature in English and English language teachers, played a leadership role of overseeing the cadet force at LBSS. Both Mr Chaikatisha and Prof Chisunka served as full lieutenants, a rank above the highest rank that a student could ever attain as a cadet. For students, the highest rank you could attain was that of second lieutenant.

Apart from cadet, I was also active in football. Although most of the guys who played for our school football team were much older, I was able to make an impression during trainings. Age was the only limiting factor. I was a bit too small. Some of the older guys were big and had by then started playing competitive football for such established football clubs in Luanshya as Luanshya United, Buseko United, Red Phase Football Club, and Roan United. Thus, they would easily grab spots in the LBSS football team automatically whenever we would play against other schools. I found this same 'big boys' mentality at the University of Zambia (UNZA). Some older UNZA students who were playing for competitive football clubs, such as British Petroleum (BP) football club and Lusaka Dynamos football club, whether these guys were talented or not, would simply pick up a jersey to play in the UNZA students' football team even if they had not been training with us. The rest of the folks would just assume that those guys were good simply because they played competitive league football. Yet, some of them were quite average and just played 'bola ya bu kaka' (physique type of football) that was not even technically and tactically sound. So, those of us who were much younger and smaller in stature would be left out of the football team in spite of our indisputable talent. Anyhow, it really did not bother me much, given that I already had a well-secured position in the UNZA Law School football team. I was well-respected there and was their star player.

At Luanshya Boys' Secondary School (LBSS), we also enjoyed watching football matches between our high school teachers and the teachers from such neighboring high schools as Luanshya Girls' Secondary School and Roan Antelope Secondary School. Our high school, LBSS, would usually host those games since we had the many football grounds. My geography teacher in junior secondary school, Mr Frank Kangwa, was usually the goalkeeper. As students, we nicknamed Mr Kangwa as 'Buffalo'. He would try his best as a goalkeeper but would sometimes let in goals that should not have been a goal had he parried off the ball for a corner. Other teachers on our school staff team included Mr Katongo as a defensive midfielder, Mr James Malama as a striker, Mr Peter Chaikatisha as a defensive midfielder, Professor Chola Chisunka as an attacking midfielder, Mr Donald Chanda as an attacking midfielder, Mr Hachaamba as a striker, Mr Hansakali as a striker, Mr Huge Mulenga as a midfielder, Mr Lawrence 'Zwizwi' Mwamba as a winger, Mr Cyril 'Mad Scientist' Mwansa as a defensive player, Mr Kainde Daka as a midfielder, and Mr Charles Suwali as a winger. Mr Suwali was probably the youngest teacher in the staff team and had exceptional dribbling skills but would often run out of steam quickly and walk-off the pitch for a cigarette, leaving us all disappointed. We all knew that Mr Suwali was capable of doing amazing things with the ball, but he would tire quickly and walk off the football field to smoke. Mr Chaikatisha was always calm on the ball. He was the Deputy Headmater and often played with spectacles on, releasing some good passes on first or second touch. He was a selfless player. Mr Hachaamba and Mr Hansakali brought striking power upfront, combining good physique with skill. Then, Mr James Malama would build from the midfield, strategically holding on to the ball for a short while in order to draw in opposition players before releasing some neat and accurate passes into the stage-spaces left open by the advancing opposition players. Those passes would often find Mr Mwamba or Mr Suwali on the wings. Mr Malama also had good speed and good shots at the goal when on the offense. It was hard to keep up with him if a defender was not fit enough.

On our LBSS teachers' football team, Professor Chisunka was a true professor of the game. Whenever he stepped on the ball, he played like a real gentleman. He reminded me a lot of Michel Platini, playing with great poise and finesse with every touch on the ball. Professor Chisunka was a marvel to watch in the midfield, controlling the ball with such mastery before unleashing a visionary triangular pass to Mr Donald 'Don King' Chanda who would then aim for a finish. Those were the good old days. The school had a nice grandstand next to the main football field. The grandstand would be packed with students and other teachers watching the game. Then, we also had one Mr Kainde Daka in the team. He was a bit overweight with a potbelly but was a master dribbler. You would not believe what you were seeing when Mr Daka stepped on the ball, as he dribbled one player after another, and then unleashed a powerful shot. One other the player that got many students cheering each time he stepped on the ball was Mr 'Zwi-Zwi' Mwamba, probably because of his great sense of Kopala humor. Mr Mwamba was a tall and lanky man. He was a bit clumsy on the ball and would run awkwardly with the ball like an eagle about to take off. But the students just loved him. They would cheer wildly each time he touched the ball. Mr Mwamba was a people's man. The people just loved the man. There is also a trio that deserves special mention here. Mr Donald 'Don King' Chanda would masterfully coordinate with Professor Chola Chisunka and Mr James Malama in the midfield, causing panic in the opposition team. The three, Mr Malama, Mr Chanda and Prof Chisunka had a unique touch to the game, and they coordinated very well. I got to learn later that the three brought that beautiful game with them from their youthful days in Chililabombwe. They were simply reenacting history like when Messi is playing on the same team with his former Barcelona FC team-mates. On the other team, especially the teachers' team from Luanshya Girls' Secondary School, would be a gentleman by the name of Mr Selemani. He was a soccer wizard. Mr Selemani terrorized defenses and would walk through tightly marked spaces as if there were no defenders standing in his way. He was so skillful and talented. The man would do things with the ball that you only see in professional football. But then, he was probably the only major threat to the opposition on his team.

The interschools sports events in Luanshya were always eventful. It was the only time in the year when students from all secondary schools in Luanshya would gather for sporting activities. The much admired gals from the girls' Catholic school, Ibenga Girls' Secondary School, would show up for the sports events in their school bus. They would be led by some Catholic nuns. Each secondary school had a school bus of its own, including Roan Antelope Secondary School (RASS) that had a reputation of being a school for rough boys.

The Interschools sports events would be held at Kafubu Stadium, the home of Roan United Football Club. We had great athletes at LBSS. One of Zambia's greatest athletes in the one hundred metres (100m) sprint race, Henry Ngolwe, was a student at LBSS. Henry was the Zambian 100m champion for many years and even competed in the Olympic games. We also had some good long-distance runners like Moses Phiri and a guy called Miles Chisenga who would often compete fiercely with a guy from Mpatamato Secondary School by the name of Preston Mwanamulai. Their races were always intense and nerve-racking to watch. Preston had consistency of pace whilst Moses and Miles had this impeccable ability to pick up speed towards the end of the race, leaving everyone watching dazzled. A number of these guys would also represent the country in various international athletic tournaments through the Zambia Athletics Association (ZAA). I also remember one Alex Chisenga with a very small voice but well-bult body. He and Lordmayor Nsalange were good athletes too. Lordmayor was a high jump guy. Alex was more of a javelin and shotput guy. There is also a guy who was so multitalented in academics and in almost all manner of sports. His name was Ephraim Phiri. He later went to England for university studies, and we never heard much from or about him after that.

In the 4 × 100 meters relay race, an athletic track event run over one lap, with four runners in each section of the track completing over a 100 meters distance each before passing the baton on to the next four and so on, LBSS had the indomitable quartet of the sprint-master, Henry Ngolwe, accompanied by Ken Banda, Abina Banda, Anthony Kahokola. It was like watching the Olympics.

The brothers had speed, flair and style. Those were the good old days. After those guys graduated from LBSS, we had guys like Masauso Tembo and Guy Kahakola, whose 100-meter dash echoed the high standard set by the then Zambia 100 meters national champion, our own LBSS, Henry Ngolwe. Closely related to that, Masanguza (Sangu) Thole was outstanding in the 400-meter race. The guy would take off as if he was a 100-meter sprint athlete, as the onlookers and other athletes thought he would tire somewhere around halfway the field only to find that the guy has begun to increase his pace with more acceleration halfway through the race, leaving no chance for his competitors. In the game of rugby too, LBSS had a great team. Some of the great rugby players at LBSS included Robby Kabeli, Sam Mwase, Obed Koloko and Patrick Wamulume. I recall that we lost a guy by the name of Pelvic in a rugby fatal accident. Then, in long distance running, a guy like Mc-Gyver Muyeke had the Ethiopian and Kenyan pace of endurance and consistency with the track. Our high school teacher, Mr James Malama, was a dedicated athletics and football coach. He made sure that he prepared the boys to the best of his abilities.

When it came to football, RASS had an advantage. They often produced more footballers than running track-athletes. RASS usually overshadowed LBSS in football. But on the running track, they usually trailed behind us. Mpatamato Secondary School, by contrast, was more balanced and was fairly good at both track-athletics and football. Also, Mpatamato was a co-education school for both guys and gals. For the gals' teams, there was no doubt that the gals from Ibenga Girls' Secondary School were the stars. They often seemed so focused and disciplined. The Catholic nuns would prepare them so well. Most of the guys at the tournament rarely paid attention to gals from Luanshya Girls Secondary School or Mpatamatu Secondary School if the gals from Ibenga Girls Secondary School were around. The gals from Ibenga Girls Secondary School attracted more attention and had a powerful reputation of being some of the brightest students academically that Zambia would produce. Of the female students in Luanshya district who would make it to the University of Zambia (UNZA) and Copperbelt University (CBU) annually, a significant majority came from Ibenga Girls Secondary School. My wife, Dr J, as noted earlier, actually attended Ibenga Girls Secondary School before studying medicine at UNZA's Ridgeway Campus Medical School and proceeding for postgraduate degree studies at two leading universities in the United Kingdom. The Catholic nuns must be commended for their excellent work in the field of higher education in Zambia. In many Zambian districts and provinces, the Catholic nuns had this model of academic excellence at the schools that they were running. Reputable high schools such as Ibenga Girls Secondary School in Luanshya, Fatima Girls' Secondary School in Ndola, Roma Girls' Secondary School in Lusaka, St Mary's Secondary School in Lusaka, St Monica's Girls Secondary School in Chipata, Holy Cross Girls' Secondary School in Mongu, and St Joseph's Girls Secondary School in Monze have produced some of the best of Zambia's intellectuals and professionals. Even some non-Catholics and staunch critics of the Catholic Church would take their children to these schools. Indeed, if they are honest enough, they will admit to what I am saying. This is something you cannot take away from the Catholics. They gave us some of the best schools and education.

While RASS had dominated the football scene for high schools in Luanshya, especially that a good number of their players, such as Jack Chanda, Vincent Chileshe, Abel 'Zaga' Banda, Paul 'Yankey' Banda, and Roy 'Shanana' Kalunga played for Roan United at some point, it took us, at LBBS, years to upset the tables. In 1985, when I was in Form 5, for the first time in the history of the Copperbelt Secondary Schools' Seven (7)-Aside Football Tournament, LBSS qualified to the finals. It was a tough game. I don't know how many times our fans kept squeezing their private parts each time the opposition team came close to scoring against our team. There was a myth that if someone was about to take a penalty or score against your team, all you need to do to stop him from scoring was to squeeze your private parts. So, each time the other team would be close to scoring, a number of our LBSS football team fans would hold and squeeze their private parts firmly. It was an exciting but tense game. The Seven (7)-Aside competition was a prestigious high school tournament that would bring together the best of the best of Zambia's football talent on the Copperbelt. Soccer legends such as Kalusha Bwalya, Jericho Shinde, Jack Chanda, Vincent Chileshe, Edgar Mulenga, Baron Mung'omba, and many others featured at some point at the Seven (7)-Aside tournaments.

The 1985 LBSS football team had guys like Mulenga 'Dynamite' Sasa, Elijah Chanda, Kennedy 'Confuser' Malipilo, Linos Makwaza, Ralph Mutesha, and Derrick 'Dugan' Tembo. Elijah and Derrick were my classmates and close friends. We would train together, though I was a small fella and could thus not make the team of the bigger boys. Elijah was playing for Luanshya United Football Club whilst Derrick was playing for ZAMEFA Football Club. During that 7-aside football tournament, we faced some tough teams before we could make it to the finals. RASS was eliminated by another team. At LBSS, we had one deadly striker, Mulenga Sasa, a short and stocky guy, who was clearly the man of the tournament. He was a version of Diego Maradona, with a good physique, and could dribble like no man's business. Looking back, I remembered Mulenga as a defender in primary school at Mpelembe Primary School. Then, suddenly, when we met at LBSS, he had converted from being a defender to becoming a striker. He became a deadly striker. Mulenga would combine so well with Kennedy Malipilo in our qualifying games. Kennedy joined LBSS in Form 3 or 4 from Chililabombwe. He brought with him a fresh touch to the game at LBSS. Kennedy had the good physique and built of an ideal midfielder, and his technique on the ball was superior. The guy would shield the ball impeccably and run circles around the opposition. And he would never tire, with visionary passes from the midfield. In the defense, Linos Makwaza, who is now a football coach in Zambia, held the back tight, together with Ralph Mutesha. When we reached the finals, I saw Mulenga Sasa put up a stellar performance, destroying the defense of the opposition in the Diego Maradona fashion and comfortably putting the ball at the back of the net as if it was not a final. We overwhelmed the opposition. For the first, I saw our teacher and sports master, Mr James Malama, who was always calm and composed, jump in the air with jubilation. Mulenga Sasa had scored. At first, I did not react. I thought it was only us the students who were supposed to jump in the air with excitement until I saw all the teachers excitedly running on to the field to celebrate the victory. That 1985 LBSS football team made history. Football was no longer a preserve of sons of miners (Ba mwana shi mine, Ba RASS). We proved that we could also do it.

In 1985, as Form 5 students at LBSS preparing to sit for our O'Level exams, we were all invited by the school authorities to apply to go the University of Zambia main campus (UNZA) in Lusaka or the University of Zambia Ndola campus (UNZA-NDO). There was only one university in Zambia at time, UNZA, though it had two campuses. We were asked to fill in application forms for admission to either of the UNZA campuses. There was a lot of hype. Guys were excited and everyone was pitching about who would go where or end up where. You know, as young people, dreaming and fantasizing is okay, but life gives you some hard lessons to show you reality. Some guys who scored highly at Grade 12 struggled with their post-secondary school education. Many never went far. Others married too early and got derailed or distracted. There were also some who could not just adjust well to pedagogical systems beyond high school education. They were accustomed to the memorization and regurgitation of information that is quite common at secondary school-level, as opposed to the critical analysis expected at university-level. Then came those who showed consistency from primary school, high school and through university, maintaining the momentum of excellency all the way up to PhD-level. Indeed, we are all gifted differently. Some will show temporal flashes of brilliance momentarily and then fizzle away quickly. Others will retain a consistent trend or record of brilliance, notwithstanding any temporal setbacks that they may suffer or encounter along the way. It is the consistency and sustenance of outstanding performance that really defines a champion. For example, Muhammad Ali lost to Jimmy Young once, but he later recovered and won back the belt. He also lost to Joe Frazier. Yes, Ali lost some fights, and his belt was once taken away from him by the State, but his endurance to come back and his consistency and longevity at the top is what set him apart from the rest.

As we gathered in the physics lab of LBSS to fill in the forms for admission to UNZA and UNZA-NDO, I recall the excitement of many guys. It was as if they had already arrived at UNZA or UNZA-NDO. The majority applied to go to the School of Natural Sciences at UNZA, hoping to study medicine or engineering like a number of our seniors who had gone to UNZA. Most of the guys in my cohort were simply trying to copy what our seniors had done. There was no originality of thought-process. Few, if any of the guys in my cohort, had a gameplan of their own for developing their careers. It was just a matter of following blindly what our seniors had done. A number of our seniors at LBSS went on to study engineering or medicine at UNZA, but most guys in my cohort had no idea what it took to qualify as an engineer or medical doctor. Folks were just excited with the idea of a university and were busy trying to copy the career paths of their seniors. We had no career master at our school. You were basically on your own in making such life-changing decisions. A few students applied to go to UNZA-NDO, a campus of UNZA which later, around 1987, became an autonomous institution from UNZA. As an autonomous institution, UNZA-NDO got renamed as Copperbelt University (CBU). Those vying to go to CBU were aiming mainly for accountancy and architecture degree programs. Those were the most two prestigious degree programs at CBU.

When we finished filling in the application forms for UNZA or UNZA-NDO admissions, we all gathered outside the physics lab to compare notes. Many guys were all hyped up and started interrogating each other regarding which school or degree program one had applied to. All I could hear was 'UNZA School of Natural Sciences' and a few others say, 'UNZA-NDO'. When I was asked, I pretended that I had also applied to: 'UNZA School of Natural Sciences'. Because that is what the folks wanted to hear. So, you simply tell them what they want to hear to avoid giving lengthy explanations as to why you have chosen to be different from everyone else. Almost everyone who applied to go to UNZA went for the 'UNZA School of Natural Sciences' flava. Deep down, I knew what I wanted and what my choices were. I was probably the only one who had applied to go to UNZA's School of Humanities and Social Sciences. Apart from a couple or so guys who applied to go to UNZA's School of Education, everyone else targeting UNZA applied to go to the School of Natural Sciences. Some of them even started calling themselves 'UNZA Squad'. For me, I did not want to take chances. I had to be honest with myself, given my little skirmish when I was singled out from the A-list at the start of Form 4 to be placed in an arts class instead of the science classes. So, I made sure that my focus was strategically on the social sciences. My first choice was law, with an entry via UNZA's School of Humanities and Social Sciences. My second choice was Mass Communication at UNZA (direct entry). My third and final choice was a degree in the School of Education at UNZA, with a focus on arts subjects. But then, it is wise not to tell people what your game-plan is, especially if they are so hyped up with the flava of the day. I chose to just play along the 'UNZA School of Natural Sciences' vibe, knowing very well that I wanted to be a lawyer and had little interest in the natural sciences.

We sat for our O'Level exams towards the end of 1985. When the results came out in the first quarter of 1986, not everyone who had been so hyped up by the 'UNZA Squad' nomenclature had made it to UNZA. Some guys would have entered UNZA if only they had been more honest with their choices. What do I mean? There were some guys with good grades who did not make it to UNZA, not because they were not smart, but because they were not very honest in the choices they made. Most of these guys knew from the beginning that they were not very good at mathematics or science but chose to pretend instead that everything was okay. That dishonesty got them in trouble when their final grades were not that impressive to get them admitted to the School of Natural Sciences at UNZA, notwithstanding that these guys generally did well in all other subjects. So, they were left out of UNZA and UNZA-NDO, and thus ended up going to two or three-year diploma granting colleges. Others barely scrapped through to make it to UNZA or CBU. And once at UNZA or CBU, they again struggled and took longer to graduate than the usual duration of the relevant degree program. Some even got re-directed to lesser attractive degree programs that were far removed from the initial programs that they had hoped to study. UNZA had a way of humbling people. Guys would come with the best of high school or O'Level grades from some seemingly fanciful high school and get humbled at UNZA. It did not matter whether you got six (6) points (GPA 4.0) at Grade 12. UNZA would humble you if you were not careful. Many guys and gals would fail and get excluded from UNZA. Many failed in first year and had to exit UNZA or switch to a lesser competitive school at UNZA, especially folks who attempted the School of Natural Sciences but had limited abilities to excel in the relevant disciplines. After dropping out of UNZA, some of these fellas went to Chingola School of Accountancy on the Copperbelt to pursue the accounting qualification offered by the British Association of Chartered Certified Accountants (ACCA). Others would transfer to two or three-year diploma programs at various public colleges in Zambia. Then, there were also those who would leave the country on Zambian Government-coordinated foreign scholarships to study in the then socialist countries of Eastern Europe, Central Asia, and Cuba. Most of these fellas would later return to Zambia as medical doctors or engineers after having failed at UNZA initially. Zambia Airforce (ZAF) and the national airlines, Zambia Airways, as well as many banks in Zambia, would also absorb some students who had dropped out of UNZA.

From our LBSS cohort, we had a few brilliant guys who turned down admission offers from UNZA or UNZA-NDO in preference to studying for the professional accounting program offered by the British Association of Chartered Certified Accountants (ACCA). At the time, there was so much hype about ACCA. Some guys even said that ACCA was better than a degree program in accountancy from UNZA-NDO (now CBU). But when I moved to the UK, I realized that the British people themselves rarely study for the ACCA qualification immediately after coming out of high school. Rather, they first get a university degree before embarking on a professional program such as ACCA. Why? Because ACCA is not an academic program. Rather, it is a professional program. And so, I came to understand these nuances and why many people in Zambia were struggling with completing their ACCA studies. In the UK, as I have explained above, ACCA is rarely taken immediately after you complete your high school education, unlike was the case in Zambia. In the UK, ACCA, as a professional qualification, is often taken by those who already have a university degree. The difference between someone with a high school certificate and one with a degree is quite obvious as soon as they both step into the ACCA class. In many cases, those with a high school certificate tend to struggle and rarely get exempted from any courses or subjects because they do not have a strong academic foundation. Lately, many people who turned down UNZA or CBU back in the days, in preference to pursuing ACCA immediately after completing high school, have now knowingly or unknowingly realized that they miscalculated their bets and are now rushing back to university to get MBA degrees to validate retroactively their academic pedigree. Most of the initial ill-informed choices they made were mainly due to the fact that many high schools in Zambia had no proper career masters or advisors. For the most part, we would just hear stories or rumors about the standing or status of a certain course and take that information as gospel truth. Relatives, friends, elders, and neighbors would peddle misleading information about certain courses or programs based on their poor understanding of issues or simply to massage their own egos especially if they themselves had studied for or held that qualification.

CHAPTER 7

The good ol' days of the African university

In Chapter 5, we travelled together on a journey through my primary and secondary school days in Zambia's Copperbelt Province. In Chapter 6, it is time to leave the Copperbelt for the capital city, Lusaka, to pursue university studies at the University of Zambia (UNZA). Opened officially on July 13, 1966, UNZA is Zambia's leading university and was set up by an Act of Parliament, the University of Zambia Act 1965 (Act No. 66 of 1965). UNZA was the only university in Zambia from 1965 until 1987 when the Zambian Government decided to merge UNZA's Kitwe-based campus, UNZA-NDO, with the Zambia Institute of Technology (ZIT), to form, through an Act of Parliament (Act No. 19 of 1987), an autonomous university called Copperbelt University (CBU). So, CBU became Zambia's second public university in 1987.

Like many first-generation African universities, UNZA was well-funded by the State after it was set up, with an ambitious Staff Development Fellowship (SDF) Program to educate indigenous Zambian academicians through lucrative scholarship opportunities for graduate studies abroad. The economies of many post-colonial African States were buoyant and thriving at independence and in the decade or so that followed. Zambianisation, a policy of the Zambian Government to create more jobs in the economy for indigenous Zambians after the country got independence, included pushing for institutional capacity-building programs such as UNZA's SDF Program to educate more Zambians as lecturers at UNZA so that they can take over when foreign academics returned to their home countries. UNZA was a vibrant and dynamic intellectual hub of the country and sub-region. But before I get into the specifics about UNZA, kindly allow me to provide you with a contextual background that will help to explain some political-economic nuances underpinning the plight of the first generation of African universities today. Some of the truths that I share below might cause some discomfort to some readers, but we must not allow cognitive dissonance to be a distraction.

In his famous treatise, "Black Skin, White Masks," Frantz Fanon decried the apologetics that often choose to rationalize the misconception of truth. Fanon posited, "Sometimes people hold a core belief that is very strong. When they are presented with evidence that works against that belief, the new evidence cannot be accepted. It would create a feeling that is extremely uncomfortable, called cognitive dissonance. And because it is so important to protect the core belief, they will rationalize, ignore and even deny anything that doesn't fit in with the core belief." Does this sound familiar? Many an African intellectual has had to deal with this type of thing in the post-colonial African State. A good number, such as university professors, lecturers, medical doctors and engineers, ended up leaving Africa as they felt neglected, frustrated, rejected and let down by the State.

Over the years, as many African economies started losing their buoyancy, the continent witnessed a sustained and increased hemorrhage of its intellectual power to the Western world. It was called "brain-drain". A cadre of learned individuals that were expected to be more rational and objective in their thinking, relying on intellect rather than emotional sentiments or feelings, continued to leave Africa leaving behind a handful of equally outstanding intellectual leaders, but some of whom became overwhelmed and compromised by the prevailing economic hardship and have since been in bed with the local corrupt politicians. A fable is often told of an old maverick professor, or rather a schizophrenic or eccentric, as some people might say, who always wore the same old sweater and carried a heavily battered and ragged leather briefcase. The professor was once seen walking in town in broad daylight with a heavily lit kerosene lamp. It was daytime and many people wondered what was going on. They thought the professor had gone mad or was going berserk. So, someone mustered some courage to ask the professor what was going on. The professor was patient with the inquirer and answered thoughtfully:

"I am looking for an honest man, and I can't seem to find one!"

Does this sound familiar? Indeed, honest men are hard to find nowadays. Because many people are not honest. The professor had a point, although almost everyone misunderstood him. And many were too quick to judge him. Over the years, several African intellectuals have left the continent because many felt neglected, rejected and unappreciated. Their stories, with a few exceptions, are similar. Although not everyone that left Africa found fortune or fame where they went, the frustrations of leaving Africa came with some pain and nostalgic sentiments of the yesteryears. The issues of limited State budgetary allocation to support the higher education sector as well as uncompetitive emoluments has had serious implications on the delivery of quality education in many an African university. Generally, the salaries of academics in many parts of Africa are not that inspiring. Besides, there are hardly any funds to support academic research in many disciplines. As noted above, many of our African intellectuals have often felt neglected and slighted, as well as maligned and disrespected, especially when the post-colonial African State continues to accord audience to ideas of the so-called Western experts, ignoring the views of the indigenous local experts. Yet, some of these Western experts are not even as qualified or prolific as our local experts. Other foreign 'experts' are just plain mediocre, although many African governments still listen to them.

In the time of détente, those African intellectuals that embraced radical leftist ideology often found themselves at cross-roads with the State machinery of the post-colonial African State. Criticizing the State in many nations can get you into harm's way. At that time, the world was quite polarized between NATO and the Warsaw Pact, with each claiming sympathizers from various corners of the world. Within Africa, the debate between African socialism and socialist Africa continued. There was also the movement of non-aligned States which tried to stay out of the diatribe between the West and the East. Some African Heads of State propagated ideas that they viewed as indigenous African ideologies such as Humanism, Negritude, Ujamaa and Pan-Africanism. Most of these ideas were Afro-centric, though some had a modest infusion of tenets of foreign ideologies. This period in time was when the post-colonial African State, especially in those countries that pursued State Capitalism, witnessed the growth and proliferation of several State-owned enterprises. Almost every African nation that had just attained political independence built or developed its own national university, including many other institutions of higher learning. Most of these academic institutions were well-funded by the State until the economies of many post-colonial African States began to crumble. The African university then entered a critical phase of underfunding.

Even as some African intellectuals tried to offer solutions to post-colonial African States on Africa's economic ills, much of that advice fell on deaf ears. And those African intellectuals that persisted, especially with their leftist ideas, became victims of State brutality or were blacklisted by the State intelligence system. Robert Witanek (see: "The CIA on Campus," Online, 1989) observes that, at the time, the US Central Intelligence Agency (CIA) was also infiltrating many African universities by covertly sending to Africa some academics to teach at these universities. A number of these academics were said (see Witanek, above) to have been CIA operatives. During that time, military dictatorships and One-Party States in Africa were beginning to mushroom. Many African intellectuals began to look elsewhere and far beyond the geographical limits of their home nations. They sought some decent space that could allow them to think independently and where they could find the right kind of incentives to carry out their intellectual work respectfully. Some only sought the professional respect and recognition that they thought had been denied of them by their home countries. As Frantz Fanon would say, 'He who is reluctant to recognize me opposes me…'! The post-colonial African State, in particular, was reluctant to recognize and value academic freedom. Overall, the post-colonial African State remained ambivalent, struggling to appease a growing domestic governing class of emerging petit bourgeoisie and a foreign-based or inspired international ruling class.

Given all these contradictions, many African intellectuals either had to leave their native home countries or bury their heads in the sand. Others opted instead to join (or as they would argue later, were "co-opted" into) the State system of the post-colonial African State. Those that crossed the chasm of ideological divide to join the State system had to become mute or make frantic efforts to try to 'intellectualize' some poorly conceived policies and ideas of the State so as to safeguard and protect their newly found fortune. As they would say in Kenya, the guys had to protect their Ugali (i.e. protecting their Nsima). Such has been the plight of many an African intellectual. He or she had to adapt and adjust quickly, changing colors like a chameleon so as to make ends meet, while also dusting off his or her bookshelf by confining to the archives most of the great works of such eminent intellectual luminaries as Amilcar Cabral, Samora Machel, Eduardo Mondlane, Kwame Nkhruma, Joe Slovo, Frantz Fanon, Walter Rodney, Samir Amin, Archie Mafeje, Abdul Rahman Mohamed Babu, Mahmood Mamdani, Yash Gahi, Dan Wadada Nabudere, Issa Shivji, Thandika Mkandawire, and many others. And the language of class struggle had to be abandoned and desecrated. Good governance and human rights became the new vocabulary of these new converts of capitalism. They had now embraced liberal and conservative ideology, seeking out what is supposedly referred to as 'peace', as opposed to 'equal rights', while overlooking the deepening social class divisions around them. Any type of association with Marxist ideas, it was feared, would deny them a chance to take a bite at the cake.

The African intellectual was by now compromised. But what if Marx was right? Prof. Terry Eagleton asks this question in his book, *Why Marx Was Right*, published by Yale University Press in 2011. He argues, "What if all the most familiar objections to Marx's works are mistaken?" As a fable would show, in a certain African country, a staunch critic of the President was appointed as a Cabinet Minister. Suddenly, he stopped being critically outspoken against the President. People began to wonder what had changed. A journalist asked him during a television interview as to why he had stopped 'talking'. The newly appointed Cabinet Minister thought for a moment, trying to find the right words, and offered the following response:

"In Africa, it is bad manners to talk when you are 'eating'..."

At the time of all these socio-economic and political contradictions, Marxist-Leninist leftist ideas were the mantra of the day for many an African intellectual. But like culture, ideological persuasions also change and evolve over time. Today, most of these African intellectuals have now shed off or literally abandoned their Marxist-Leninist ideals for a petit bourgeois lifestyle. But back in the days, the increasing financial neglect of the African universities by the post-colonial African State, as well as the deposition of excessive power in the instruments of the State, left many African intellectuals disillusioned. As noted earlier, some decided to leave and have never gone back. They simply went into self-imposed economic exile. However, a good number stayed behind, continuing to wage the ideological battle from the ivory towers of the academe.

By the dawn of perestroika and the eventual demise of détente, and with the increasing internationalization of capital through what is now called globalization, the African university had become a different place altogether. It was a shadow of its old self. For example, the Ugandan newspaper, *New Vision* (Online version: Wednesday, February 24, 2010), in an online article on Prof. Mahmood Mamdani when he was appointed in 2010 as the head of Makerere University's Institute of Social Research (MISR), reported that:

"In 2007, he published a book, *Scholars in the Market Place*, that caused unease within the university's administration. The book criticized the commercialization of university education in Uganda and the lack of academic research and publications by professors. He accused the university of duplicating courses for the sake of generating revenues from private students."

Critically underfunded, many African universities now have less intellectually rigorous public debates and have been transformed ideologically into less intellectually stimulating habitats. For the most part, academic research and scholarship has declined. Closely related to this, hardly do you find in the developing world any meaningful think-tank or policy institution collaborating with most universities. Also, the venue of many academic conferences and workshops are not at university campuses but at hotels and other luxury resorts. And a number of conference attendees are more interested in getting their per diem, as opposed to making intellectual contributions. Besides, many intellectual luminaries have left Africa, and a new crop of young academics are coming on board to join the vicissitudes of a few old guards. In some instances, even the curricula of some degree programs have been revised to water down some radical ideas and bring on board some moderate right-wing notions of globalization. For example, many Marxist and leftist ideas have been watered down or dropped altogether from the curricula not because such ideas are completely obsolete or debunked but because many people now believe so much in what they read, watch or hear from the West. Not even the chasm between the left and right is considered an alternative. Also, the cry for more monetary incentives by many academics today has gained a lot of prominence and primacy over the need to pursue and conduct sustained scholarship and edifying intellectualism. As a result, Western donor agencies have now become more visible in the lives of some African academics, offering these academics lucrative consultancy contracts that they cannot turn down easily.

Other African intellectuals have tried to form political parties in order to have a chance at redressing the economic ills of their countries. Some of these fellas simply want to share the national cake that is being enjoyed by those in power. Yet, there is also a small fraction that has joined some public international organizations. In the end, scholarship and intellectualism have suffered at many African universities. And due to poor State funding, a number of these universities are not even able to fill some of their vacant academic positions. That said, some parts of the economy have gained over the years from absorbing some African intellectuals that were afraid of committing class suicide – to use the words of Amilcar Cabral – by remaining with their colleagues in academia. Opportunism began to show in some African intellectuals. Some were appointed by the State to senior management positions in State-owned enterprises. The making of these appointments continued in the era of privatization and free-market economy. And when most State-owned enterprises were being privatized or liquidated, many African intellectuals that had sought economic refuge in these institutions had to come out. They quickly reinvented themselves. Some went back to the university. Others became full-time "street" consultants, providing consultancy services in virtually anything and everything, whilst also peddling a bit as academicians on the side or selling some chickens to make ends meet. Some even ran taxi businesses or sold vegetables at their residential homes. A few others went as far as setting up some private universities. Then there was also a crop of those African academics that just left the country altogether for greener pastures elsewhere or took up political appointments of some sort. Such is the plight of many an African intellectual today. Things have really fallen apart. And the African intellectual is no longer at ease. In many cases, the African intellectual has felt alienated from his profession, leaving him or her hopeless and desperate for any means to sustain himself or herself economically.

I arrived at the University of Zambia (UNZA) in January 1987. My UNZA intake was delayed by the untimely closure of the university the previous academic year. So, instead of the academic year starting in August of 1986, we had to wait until UNZA was reopened in early 1987. As freshmen at UNZA, we were all asked to report to our respective schools where the deans would address us. Those of us who were admitted to the School of Humanities and Social Sciences (HSS) gathered in lecture hall, LT1, where the then Dean of HSS, Prof Gatian F. Lungu, a Harvard educated scholar, addressed us. In his welcoming remarks, Prof Lungu averred:

"Welcome to the University of Zambia. The essence of a university, if I may remind you, is to liberate you from the shackles of ignorance. The school to which you have been admitted, HSS, is where much of the critical thinking happens. Otherwise, without HSS, the rest of the university would just be a collection of blocks of colleges."

While some natural scientists might have difficulties with Prof Lungu's submission that HSS is where much of the critical thing takes place, Prof Lungu had made his point to motivate and inspire us. At the time, UNZA was the only university in Zambia. It was very competitive to get into UNZA. And even when you got in, there was no guarantee that you would stay afloat and sail through easily. Many students who arrived at UNZA with the spirited umph of having gotten six (6) points at Form 5 (Grade 12) never lasted. Like the GPA of 4 in the US, that is, summa cum laude

(GPA of 3.8–4.0), 6 points in Zambia is the highest grade that one can score at Grade 12, although now many young people are getting 6 points and it has somewhat lost its original value. Back in the day, 6 points was rare. They would only be a handful of individuals in the entire country of Zambia who would graduate with 6 points from high school.

Some UNZA students who arrived with 6 points from their respective high schools flunked in the first year of UNZA and were either excluded from the university altogether or redirected to apply to other schools within the university. This fate also befell those students who thought that the apparent elite status of their former high school was a guaranteed passport to sail through university. UNZA was quite unkind to such mindsets. Other UNZA students who arrived with 6 points or were engrossed in delusional grandiose and fanciful ideas of the assumed prestige associated with their former high school barely scrapped through UNZA, proceeding mainly with an overwhelming stagger caused by the overload of carryover courses every year (i.e. course arrears and supplementary exams due to a student's poor academic performance). A good number of these individuals ended up with 'carbons' at graduation, meaning that their transcripts were so bad and filled with such poor grades as C and C+. A number of these 'carbon-rated' poor-performing students would graduate with a 'silent' or basic 'Pass' degree. UNZA was a humbling experience. You had to prove your worth all over after getting admitted to UNZA from high school. Put simply, you had to forget your high school academic heroism.

It is important to highlight that some of the UNZA students who showed up with 6 points from their Form 5 exams had benefitted from what we called 'spoon feeding' in high school. Many high schools where these students were coming from were well-resourced elite schools for kids from privileged families. Their teachers would do everything to prepare the students for the Form 5 exams. In the process, not much attention was paid to nurturing the students to study independently. There was a lot of handholding. So, when left alone, these students would struggle to adapt to a university style of learning. Indeed, there was no 'spoon feeding' at UNZA. We were all considered to be adults and expected to grasp university life on our own. Nobody was going to police or monitor your study hours. Also, not even the memorization of past exam questions or model answers would help you. You just had to study and understand the material critically, as opposed to memorizing and reproducing information with little analysis, if any. So, a number of students who came from some privileged high schools that would 'take care of them nicely' found UNZA to be a bit of a challenge. Nobody was going to babysit or handhold you at UNZA. And relying on lecture notes alone was not enough. You had to go to the library to read books and journal articles and then abstract and synthesize the data on your own. Yes, the lecturers and professors were there to give lectures and tutorials, but you were also expected to work hard on your own to supplement whatever you got from the lectures or tutorials. In essence, a university is about the universality of knowledge. So, your knowledge cannot be confined to lectures notes only. You must go beyond that, demonstrating that you have a full grasp of issues, concepts, theories, and contexts. Some students found that to be a bit overwhelming. But many students who came from poorly resourced government secondary schools, especially folks from the rural areas, were able to adjust quickly at UNZA because they were already used to working independently. Indeed, many folks from poorly resourced rural schools grew up improvising where, for example, standard textbooks were missing. That agility was an asset for them at UNZA.

In the first year of UNZA, all students were required to take four courses, irrespective of the faculty of admission. For many first year students in the School of Human and Social Sciences (HSS), the two most sought-after degree programs were law and economics. All first year HSS students were required to take one mandatory course, Fundamentals of the Social Sciences (SS120), in addition to three electives. Those who wanted to pursue law from HSS were required to take English (E110), as an additional mandatory course, plus two electives. That would make up for the four courses in first year. So, I took SS120 and E110, in addition to Introduction to Developments Studies (ADS100) and Introduction to Political Science and Administrative Studies (PA110). You could not go into Law School directly from high school. You had to spend your first year at UNZA in HSS. Admission to UNZA Law School was contingent upon getting excellent grades in first year. Only about fifteen percent (15%) of the best performing HSS students who were aspiring to study law would be admitted to UNZA Law School. The rest would be left to seek alternative degree programs from the electives that they took in first year. Admission to UNZA Law School was extremely competitive. Many could not make it at first attempt and ended up pursuing degrees in other fields before making a second spirited attempt much later in life, as mature-age students, at studying law at UNZA. After graduating with a degree in a cognate field, many would later reapply for admission to UNZA Law School as mature-age or non-school leaver students. They would then join UNZA Law School directly in second year because they had already completed the relevant foundation courses of first year in HSS. As we shall see below, this type of backdoor entry into the legal profession was also common in the medical profession. Here, suffice it to say, for those who wanted to pursue economics they had to take, in addition to SS120, Introduction to Economics (EC110), Mathematics for the social sciences (M160), and one elective course which would often be their minor once they got admitted to majoring in economics. Again, like in the case of those aspiring to study law, there would be some casualties who would not make it into the economics quota. Such individuals often ended up majoring in a degree program in the line of the elective course that they took in first year. A good number majored in demography, sociology, public administration, political science, psychology, and so forth. Some of them would muster spirited courage after graduating from UNZA to scout for an international scholarship so that they could go abroad to get a Masters degree in Economics as a way to launder themselves into mainstream economics arena and thereby legitimize their claim to being an economist. It was like that. This is the uncomfortable truth about many Zambian 'economists.' The only degree programs in HSS at UNZA that had direct entry from high school were Mass Communication and Social Work.

In the School of Natural Sciences (NS) at UNZA, the typical first year courses were M110 (mathematics), P110 (physics), B110 (Biology), and C110 (chemistry). NS had a reputation of having the highest dropout rate of first year students at UNZA. The majority of NS students were aspiring to be medical doctors or engineers. Other degree programs in NS were merely seen as a fallback if one failed to get into the School of Medicine or the School of Engineering. Like in the case of the study of law, you could not go directly into UNZA Medical School or UNZA School of Engineering. You first had to score high marks in first year of NS before you could be admitted to the quotas for UNZA Medical School or UNZA School of Engineering in second year. Many first year NS students would flunk a number of courses, especially M110 and P110. Some would be excluded entirely from UNZA whilst others would be excluded only from NS but given the option to reapply for admission to another school at UNZA. Thus, it was not uncommon, for example, to find one or two UNZA Law School students who had flunked in NS initially, but later got admitted to HSS and then eventually found their way into Law School. That said, many NS students who made it to second year but did not qualify into UNZA School of Medicine or UNZA School of Engineering ended up in the School of Agriculture, the School of Veterinary Medicine, or remained in NS to pursue degree programs in fields such as mathematics, biochemistry, biology, chemistry or physics. Among these students, some who veered into the Biochemistry degree program as well as the veterinary doctors' degree program found the courage to redeem themselves later by reapplying for admission to UNZA Medical School. Like in the case of mature-age and non-school leaver entry into UNZA Law School, there are a number of medical doctors who entered UNZA Medical School through the backdoor. Others who struggled or failed in first year of NS, together with some folks who could not even make it to UNZA, left Zambia on foreign scholarships to study medicine in some socialist and communist countries. Later, these fellas resurfaced in Zambia as medical doctors. So, there were a couple or so backdoor entry routes to both the medical and legal professions in Zambia. Then, among the first year NS students who qualified to be admitted in second year to the School of Engineering some ended up in less attractive engineering fields whilst others made it to the much sought after engineering degree programs of Mechanical Engineering and Civil Engineering. It was like that.

After completing my first year in the School of Humanities and Social Sciences (HSS) at UNZA in the latter part of 1987, I qualified among the top students admitted to study law at UNZA that year. Prior to law school, some of my first year lecturers in HSS including Dr Caleb M Fundanga (SS120, offering fundamentals of economic theory), Dr Angel M Mwenda (PA110), Prof Oliver S Saasa (ADS100), Mr Paul Potts (E110), Dr Mable Milimo (SS120, offering fundaments of gender studies), Dr Fred Mutesa (SS120, offering pertinent aspects of modernization theory in development studies), Mr Donald Chanda (SS120 – main course coordinator and lecturer), Mr Kabwe Tiyaonse (SS120 – tutor), Dr Edgar Bwalya (PA110 – tutor), Mr Mbwayu (E110 – tutor), Mr Roni Khul Bwalya (SS120, offering fundamentals of philosophy), Mr Pieter Boele van Hensbroek (SS120, offering fundamentals of philosophy), Dr Peter Machungwa (SS120, offering fundamentals of psychology), and a few other expatriate and Zambian lecturers whose names I now forget but who offered lectures in the other social sciences. UNZA was a dynamic and vibrant academic community. There was a strong culture of intellectualism and academic scholarship. Guys like Roni Khul lived and walked philosophy, as he puffed away from his smoking pipe before jumping on a motorbike with his Asian female friend to head home after lectures. Roni always wore different t-shirts with different university logos. His love for university apparel sat well with his Dr Walter Rodney-styled black Afro. And Roni often wore colormatic spectacles or dark shades, and a blue pair of jeans and some fancy canvas shoes, as he walked with a cool bounce to deliver his eloquent and enlightening lectures. Roni was not only cool but also somewhat of an enigma, with a great aura of intellectual sophistication around him. UNZA had some of the best scholars that the country has ever produced. Then, there was also the Ghanian scholar, Prof Ferdinand Akuffo, an Oxford alumnus who taught development studies. Old Ferdinand was among the intellectual luminaries at UNZA. Although I was not taught by Prof Akuffo, he and I became good friends when many years later I left Zambia for Oxford. We shared the same alma mater, Oxford. And that helped to cement our ties. He often referred to me as 'my good friend from Oxford.'

Some misguided and misinformed folks will often tell you that people from the university, or rather, academicians and people with PhDs, often struggle to make it in industry outside academia. That is not true. I have lived and experienced both sides of the aisle and can speak authoritatively against such prejudicial insecurities of those that are often intimidated by the 'big papers' of academicians. Let us take a look at a fable that speaks to this issue. A shortlisting panel was constituted to shortlist candidates for an executive position in a quasi-governmental institution. Some panelists averred that one of the candidates who had a PhD was overqualified. That candidate was the only one with a PhD. Other panelists were of the view that the candidate was too academic simply because he had a PhD and publications.

Irrespective of how well a CV is structured, the 'big papers' syndrome is quite common among insecure folks, especially those folks who themselves do not have big papers. Often times, people like to clone or replicate a prototype of themselves when making choices. That bias often comes up unconsciously. At other times, it can also result from deep-seated insecurities. But then, why the 'big papers' syndrome, or what in Ghana is called 'book-long'? The answer is simple. It is the misguided assumption that people with advanced degrees such as PhDs are too academic and not practical enough for practitioner type of professional work. This unfortunate assumption is often steeped in a fallacy that lacks any systematic empirical evidence to support it.

One of my mentees, armed with a freshly minted PhD, reached out to a hiring manager of a notable institution to explore some career prospects. The said mentee was given an appointment for a coffee meeting with the hiring manager. The young man, the mentee, prepared his résumé and made sure that it was well structured and tailored to the objectives of the organization and industry. But upon looking at the résumé and noticing the PhD qualification, the hiring manager said, "Oh, you have one of these (referring to the PhD degree)! Here, we need people who are practical."

My mentee was shocked. The hiring manager did not even listen to him or read his résumé further. She simply went on to say how a PhD is a total waste of time and not useful in industry. My mentee was left dumbfounded. The young man was a victim of the 'big papers' syndrome. Another young PhD graduate told me how she was advised by a senior colleague that she was working with in the private sector to consider a career in academia, as opposed to the corporate world, simply because she had a PhD. This happened in a meeting with her boss after she raised some questions that made the boss uncomfortable. The boss said, "This is not a university, young lady. You understand? You people with PhDs, you just don't get it. We don't' have time for theories here!"

The young lady wondered what she had done wrong. Her boss' highest qualification was a Masters degree. Obviously, he had limited knowledge, or no clue whatsoever, of what is involved in a PhD program, yet he was quick to 'insult' the PhD qualification. What else would motivate such behavior if not insecurities? The man was simply assuming that a PhD is all about theorizing. And even if it were all about theorizing, isn't it a truism that nothing is as practical as a good theory? Put simply, an employee does not become more practical or productive simply because he or she has 'small papers', as opposed to 'big papers.' There is no correlation between the two. Having 'small papers' does not make you more practical. If anything, you could be underqualified for the job you are holding.

At UNZA, I spent all my four years in the students' halls of residence known as the 'Ruins'. My room was Kwacha 6-1. On weekends, I would spend some time at my elder brother's place in downtown Lusaka. My elder brother, Kelvin, had a two-bedroom penthouse on the top floor of Century House, located along Cairo Road and right in downtown Lusaka. Cairo Road is the main business street in downtown Lusaka. It was at Brother Kelvin's place that I got to meet most his friends who were with him at UNZA or St Canisius Secondary School. But the majority were from his UNZA days. Some were now our lecturers at UNZA. So, it was quite inspiring to be amongst some of the brightest Zambian intellectuals as early as when I was just about to enter university. A number of brother Kelvin's friends and colleagues had just returned from abroad after completing their Masters degrees and PhDs. The majority were lecturers at UNZA. It was so inspiring to be in the company of such learned people. Even the atmosphere was different from being in the company of average folks. Brother Kelvin would give me a bit of cash every other week to supplement my UNZA student allowance. I also inherited much of his extensive collection of academic books.

Brother Kelvin had a rich collection of scholarly books. So, the bookshelf in my room at UNZA was well-stocked and filled with popular social science books. I give much thanks to him for all the support and for instilling in me a stronger value for education. Dad and Mum had provided a strong foundation, but Brother Kelvin provided a living example of what education can do to improve someone's life. Some of the guys that I met through Brother Kelvin came from humble backgrounds while others were sons of prominent cabinet ministers and famous politicians. What brought them together was simply education. Indeed, education is an equalizer. Looking back, among his peers from UNZA, I would confidently say that Brother Kelvin had a good head start in the corporate world. He was hired after graduating in economics from UNZA by the then Managing Director of Zambia National Building Society (ZNBS), Mr Simon Mwewa, who was a good friend of one of our uncles, Mr Francis Kapansa. Mr Kapansa was a Governor in the UNIP Government of President Kenneth Kaunda.

In my first year at UNZA, I bonded quickly with fellow freshmen from my hall of residence, Kwacha, especially those who took a number of the same first-year courses I was taking and who were also aspiring to study law. Among them were Mr Noyoo Noyoo, Hon Judge Isaac Kamwendo, and Mr Sydney Phiri. Then, Mr Fortune Chibamba, a close friend who was a direct entrant in the social work degree program, was also with us in Kwacha Hall of Residence. From the group that wanted to study law, we all made it into law school. We entered UNZA Law School through the front door, not the backdoor. When we got to UNZA Law School some of our lecturers and professors in the first year of law school included Dr Joshua Kanganja (L210 – Legal Process), Dr Enoch Simaluwani (L240 – Criminal Law), Dr Anthony Mulimbwa (L230 – Law of Torts), Prof Melvin L Mbao and Prof Robert Kent (L220 – Contract Law), Prof Lawrence Shimba and Prof Robert Kent (L250 – Constitutional Law), Mr Raphael Mungole and Mr Billy Simamba (L250 – tutors), Prof Alfred Chanda (L220 – tutor), Prof Kalombo Mwansa (L240 – tutor), and a Jamaican lady who led us in tutorials for L230, but whose name I now forget. All I remember is that she was very beautiful and intelligent. The adjustment or transition from HSS to law school was not easy for many. There is a way in which legal reasoning is developed and legal arguments are made. It was somewhat different from writing essays or assignments in the (other) social sciences. So, we started learning slowly how to summarize the facts of a case, how to identify or spot the issues, how to apply the general principles of law as well as the exceptions, if any, or how to distinguish the legal reasoning in different dissenting or concurring rulings of judges and how to treat precedents that are binding and those that are merely persuasive. In first year of UNZA Law School, my classmates and I in the four (4) year Bachelor of Laws (LLB) degree program shared classes with colleagues mainly from the Zambia Poice who were pursuing a one-year certificate program in law, and these colleagues included Akende Akende, Peter Lombe Chanda, Sapheli Chikolwa, Lombe William Chongo, Pumulo Kachana, Mike Shula Katongo, Geoffrey Masumba, Moola Milimo, Elias Muzyamba Moole, Peter Mulenga, Joseph Mwape, Lastor Ntobolo, Joseph Phiri, Felix Lyson Phiri, Emanyeo Tubama Phiri, Leonard Punza, Evanson Siame, and Nyambe Sililo.

Then, my classmates in the 4-year LLB degree program, including some colleagues who remained behind at UNZA to complete some courses, as they were either studying on a part-basis or had some courses to repeat, were as follows: Maurice Chaiwila; Muyoya Chibiya; Fraser Chishimba; Zunaid Coovadia; Isaac Kamwendo; Kephas Katongo; Adam Kauzeni; Kawana Kawana; Emmanuel Lukonde; Christopher Mayowe; Maria Mkandawire; Gershom Mubanga; Maureen Mukelabai; Killian Ives Mulenga; Lawrence Munalisa; Hodges Munsanje; Kingsley Musongo; Marcellina Kasweka Musumali; Iris Chiseche Mwanza; Imbuwa Mwiya; Kapya Chibale Ndalameta; Noyoo Noyoo; Anthony Phiri; Maxwell Phiri; Anne Sampa; Christopher Mofu Sampa; Kennedy Shepande; Dennes Simwinga; Liswaniso Siyunyi; Pengani Yangailo; Joseph Sarandos Zaloumis; Fulgency Mwenya; Sidney Phiri; Joyce Namuyobo Shezongo; Fanuel Mumba Kingsley Sumaili; Chimbeka Sakala; and, Philip Stuart Wood. Following below are some pictures taken at our LLB class reunion luncheon held at one of the top hotels in Lusaka. In the pictures below are some of my classmates from the December 1990 UNZA Law School graduating class.

In the picture above, on my left and wearing a tie, is Mr Maurice Chaiwila. To my immediate right is Mr Hodges Munsanje, followed by Mr Fraser Chishimba, Mr Noyoo Noyoo, Mr Chris Sampa and Mr Pengani Yangailo.

In the picture above, with Mr Noyoo Noyoo.

In the picture above is Mr Chris Sampa, dressed in a red sweater, and Mr Fraser Chishimba, dressed in a white shirt and dark color tie.

In the picture above is Mr Fraser Chishimba, dressed in a white shirt and dark color tie.

In the picture above are Mr Maurice Chaiwila, dressed in a white shirt with cufflinks and a dark color tie, and Mr Chris Sampa.

In the picture above is Mr Maurice Chaiwila and Mr Hodges Munsanje, dressed in a dark suit and striped tie.

Aerial view of the whole crew at the lunch table.

In the picture above, with Mr Hodges Munsanje and Mr Maurice Chaiwila.

In the picture above is Mr Pengani Yangailo, dressed in a brown tweed jacket.

Then, the picture above, with Mr Kephas Katongo, was taken in 2023 when I visited Ndola, Zambia.

In first year of law school, I remember having a discussion with some classmates and other fellow second year students who were admitted to UNZA School of Human and Social Sciences (HSS), UNZA School of Natural Sciences and UNZA School of Education about the standard of British 'A' Level courses and how they compared with first year courses at UNZA, given that almost all government high schools in Zambia only offered education up to O'Levels. I got to learn later that UNZA first year courses were allegedly intended to be bridge the gap between 'A' Levels and a three-year degree program akin to the British undergraduate degree program. At the few private schools in Zambia that offered 'A' Level courses, the exams for those 'A' Levels were often set by foreign-based educational institutions, especially British institutions. The Zambian schools would only serve as teaching and exam centers. One of my friends who had taken an 'A' Level course with the British Associated Examining Board (AEB) before coming to UNZA often posited that 'A' Levels were tougher and more intellectually demanding than first year courses at UNZA. The debate went on and on. We even had amongst us someone who had completed 'A' Levels in India before joining us at UNZA. He too posited that 'A' Levels were tougher, so I kept wondering what in the world was the hullaballoo about the so-called 'A' Levels. Of course, I was aware that the ZCCM-run school, Mpelembe Secondary School in Kitwe, and International School in Lusaka, both had students who pursued 'A' Levels. After completing O'Level exams taken in Form 5, the students who proceeded to Form 6 normally spent two (2) years reading for two (2) or three (3) 'A' Level subjects before taking the 'A' Levels exam. The British system of education at the time required that, to be admitted to a good university in the UK, a student must have passed at least two (2) 'A' Level subjects. So, for many ZCCM-sponsored Zambian students who were planning to proceed to university in the UK, they had to complete Form 6 and pass their 'A' Levels in Zambia. Almost all the 'A' Level exams in Zambia were not set by a Zambian examination board, but by a UK-based examination board. Zambia only provided for a few teaching and examination centers for 'A' Levels.

As a second year student at UNZA, I was not convinced that British 'A' Levels were tougher than UNZA first year courses. I wanted to find out more about this whole thing of 'A' Levels and the noise it was beginning to garner in our social circles. Out of curiosity, and to prove my friends wrong, I registered to sit for two 'A' Levels with University of London. I got some money from my UNZA student bursary and used it to pay to write exams in two University of London 'A' Level subjects, namely: (a) Government and Political Studies; and (b) Law. First, I knew that I had studied political science in the first year spent in the School of Humanities and the Social Sciences (HSS) at UNZA. Secondly, I knew that I had covered some fundamental law courses during first year of law school. So I was confident that I could pull it off. I made the payment for the University of London 'A' Levels at Evelyn Hone College in Lusaka where the administration center for most British examination bodies was located. Thereafter, it only took me three months of light studying and private preparation. Within that short period, I was ready to sit for the exams that normally took students two (2) years of full-time Form 6 classes and study. As noted above, I was sitting for these Form 6 exams while I was a full-time student at UNZA, and thus could not commit myself to full-time Form 6 studies. In the evenings and on weekends, I would read a bit on my own and refer to some of my UNZA lecture notes. I was basically on my own, without any teaching aid or guides. When I sat for the University of London 'A' Level exams at Kabulonga Boys' Secondary School in Lusaka, I was the only black African student in the exam hall. All the other students were either Asians or whites, and possibly preparing to go abroad for university studies. They were writing exams in natural science subjects, focusing mainly on mathematics, biology, chemistry and physics. Not only were those 'A' Level subjects the popular subject choices at the private schools that these Asian and white students attended, but they could also have been the prerequisite subjects to foreign degree programs eyed by the students. I was the only guy taking exams in the social sciences. So, I was placed in a corner all by myself. All in all, we were not more than ten (10) of us in that exam room. I aced the University of London 'A' Level exams, essentially completing my Form 6 in 3 months only of self-study, and without ever stepping into a full-time Form 6 class. When the 'A' Level results came out, I shared them with my friends at UNZA. They all could not believe it, and nobody ever spoke about 'A' Levels again. It ended the debate, confirming that UNZA was UNZA!

In third year of UNZA Law School, some of my law lecturers and professors included Dr Enoch Simaluwani (L310 – Law of Evidence), Dr Anthony Mulimbwa (L320 – Property Law and Succession), Mr Luke Muleya (L230 – tutor), Prof Michelo Hansungule (L330 – Commercial Law), Professor Kaye Turner (L340 – Administrative Law and Local Government), and Mr Saidi

Phiri (L350 – Family Law). We also took a course in Legal Methods (L360) which involved, inter alia, the preparation for and participation in a moot court. Then, in the final year of UNZA Law School, that is, the fourth year at UNZA, we had Prof Lawrence Shimba (L410 – Jurisprudence), Dr Nyambe Mukelabai (L410 tutor), Dr Nyambe Mukelabai (L411 – Obligatory Essay Supervisor), Dr John Mulwila (L420 – Business Associations), Dr Frederick Ng'andu (L430 – International Law), and Dr Beatrice Kamwanga (L450 – Trade and Investment Law) as our law lecturers and professors. Also, at the beginning of the final year of UNZA Law School, the school tried to introduce Labor Law as a new course offering, and the lecturer, Hon Dr Justice Winnie Mwenda, even started giving lectures before the course was discontinued.

Student life at UNZA was interesting. A single guy with no chic on campus was known as a 'monk.' Then, some monks who would just hang out with ladies on campus but with no prospects of every dating those ladies were known as walking sticks. Such guys symbolized an old lady's walking stick, and hence the name 'walking stick.' Many walking sticks were like toothless puppies. They could not bite. A walking stick was some guy who would often be in the company of some lady or ladies, yet none of them were his chic. He would simply tag along wherever the gals were going, like a walking stick, or visit their rooms to hang out with them but with no defined agenda. Walking sticks liked to gossip. They would tell the gals everything about whichever guy tried to show interest in the gals. As a result, walking sticks were not popular among the serious brothers. If anything, they were considered a distraction, especially where the walking stick knew that you were about to present your 'manifesto' to the young lady but chose not to leave the side of the gal. Many a walking stick were happy just to be seated next to the gal so as to block any guy from having her for his girlfriend.

A single lady without a boyfriend on campus was known as a 'nun.' Then, a campus guy dating a chic on campus was known as a 'mojo' while a campus chic dating a campus guy was known as a 'momma'. There were also some guys from outside the university who would date some UNZA gals. We called these guys 'absentee landlords' or simply a 'landlord'. Absentee landlords were usually older chaps with a steady job or some banker in one of the commercial banks in Lusaka. Other notorious landlords included some airline stewards working for the national airline, Zambia

Airways. Most UNZA monks had little regard for landlords such as airline stewards, referring to them as 'ba waiter ba pa ndeke' (waiters that serve food on the plane). Little did the UNZA gals dating the airline stewards or other less educated landlords realize that, upon graduating from UNZA and getting jobs in the corporate world, most of those UNZA gals were likely to become bosses to the same absentee landlords that they were dating, especially for those landlords that had no university education. Sometimes, as a student, you can get impressed by a quack masquerading as a somebody simply because you lack exposure. But once you are done with your university studies and start working, you will then realize your true potential and value, making you regret or feel sad about some of the dating choices you made in your student days. If you had known perhaps, you would not have dated or married some of the characters you got involved with.

Turning to UNZA guys, within the category of guys known as monks, there were those who were full of uncouth behavior. Such guys often used vulgar and abusive language, especially after coming from a drinking spree of imbibing cheap local brew known as Chibuku or Kachasu. Occasionally, they would indulge in some beers known as Mosi. These guys were known as 'Lumpens', a name drawn from Marxist-Leninist nomenclature pertaining to the term, 'Lumpen proletariat.' Lumpens often acted sobber during the day and even appeared shy in the presence of gals. If anything, they would avoid getting close to the gals. Because of their poor social skills, lumpens had it difficult to find love on campus. Frustrated, they would resort to alcohol and smoking weed. When high on booze or weed, lumpens would insult on top of their voices during the night, directing their profanity at anyone who they deemed a nuisance, or a pretentious or snobbish person. I came to understand much later that the current nomenclature associated with the pontifications of lumpens is now known as 'shooting' or 'uku shooter'. Indeed, lumpens would shoot. Lumpens often resided in the secluded male-only halls of residence at UNZA known as the 'Ruins', named after the Zimbabwe Ruins. But an interesting feature about the lumpens is that they often brought about sobriety where utopia was beginning to take center stage in some people. Utopia was particularly common in chongololos. The word chongololo means a millipede. Chongololos were folks who wanted to come out like they had grown up with a soft-landing bourgeois lifestyle, spoke their English with a self-styled imitation of American or British accents, and probably played some basketball or rugby, or had lived outside Zambia at some point in their life. A chongololo would fantasize about snow and how life is out there in England or the States where her cousin lives.

Others would place a nicely framed childhood photo by their bedside, just to show whoever would walk into their room how they used to play in the snow when they lived in England or America. It was hard for such folks to let go of the past. Some male chongololos too would pull similar stunts just to woo the chics, especially the impressionable wannabe chics. There was also a guy who had never been to the UK or the States but had memorized the map of London underground trains and would explain to the unsuspecting gals the various London tube stations, as if he had lived there. Many believed him. They actually thought he grew up in England. Yet, the chap was from Lusaka's Chilenje or Kabwata townships.

Other smaller chongololo versions came from some convent schools or other seemingly elite schools. Otherwise, many chongololos had been nowhere outside Zambia. But they walked and behaved in an elitist manner like a millipede moves, majestically and elegantly. So, Lumpens were basically the vanguard of the student community and would neutralize such behaviors. Even the University of Zambia Students' Union (UNZASU) could not ignore the lumpens when it came to the realization of the main student ideology. Over the years, however, the nomenclature associated with UNZA-student social stereotypes has evolved, and certain appellations, such as 'Ba Bungwe' and 'Hijackers', have since lost traction due to shifting priorities and related cultural dynamics of the student populace.

Be that as it may, many lumpens and monks would trek to some nearby townships to drink and look for some township gals since they could not manage to get themselves some campus chics. Once in the townships, the monks and lumpens would throw around their UNZA student ID cards to impress the local township gals. The most frequented townships were Ng'ombe and Kalingalinga. A number of these gals were from underprivileged families and thus thought highly of UNZA students. The lumpens and monks would make an impression and 'import' the gals to their UNZA student rooms for an evening or night of lustful redemption. After UNZA administration allowed students to cook in their rooms, some lumpens and monks even started 'importing' gals that were selling tomatoes or vegetables by the roadside. At some point, some UNZA female students voiced out their disappointment with the monks and lumpens' behavior, arguing that why can't the lumpens and monks find themselves fellow university students to date instead of taking advantage of the vulnerable, poor and often illiterate gals from the nearby townships. After a deafening silence from the monks and lumpens, which many mistook for victory in support of the rebuke from the UNZA ladies that had accosted the monks and lumpens, one lumpen mustered some courage and voiced out his response, whilst looking sheepishly on the ground and avoiding eye contact with the gals.

"Ahhh, you people, why can't you be honest? If you go to buy milk, do you ask if the cow that the milk came from was fat or slim? Milk is milk. You just drink. It tastes the same."

Put simply, the lumpen reasoned, an orgasm is an orgasm, irrespective of the looks or level of education of the person who facilitated the orgasm. That response marked the end of the discussion. It was a great comeback. Everyone around was left stunned with the immutable humor of the lumpen's sarcasm. Interestingly, many monks and lumpens were alleged to be students from the School of Natural Sciences and the School of Engineering where there were fewer female students, leaving room for a strong masculinity culture to fester. Once these monks and lumpens graduated and started working, some of them would marry the very first gal to warm up to them at a pub or in the neighborhood. It was called "engineers' choice".

Some UNZA guys and gals came from humble backgrounds but would want to behave as though they grew up in London or New York. Rapid urbanization, as we called it back then, was not uncommon among UNZA students who were trying so hard to fit into Lusaka lifestyle. Suddenly, you would find that someone wanted to upgrade from drinking the opaque Chibuku beer that he was so accustomed to during his high school days to drinking a fine whisky or some gin and tonic, bypassing the middle stages of ordinary lagers. UNZA student life was something else. With time, many former students sobered up after facing the realities of life upon graduating from UNZA. But, while at UNZA, some of them would even claim that they don't eat nshima, the Zambian staple food. But, today, the same people are the nshima warriors in their homes. If you were to remind them, they will tell you that, 'fya kale naiwe (That was then), I was young' or that 'culture evolves, and we move with time'. All the pretense is now gone, especially if she married a man who was one of those monks or lumpens that she never looked at during the UNZA days. You will find her justifying to her friends that her man has changed and is no longer a lumpen. Others will even add that the man is a good father and a God-fearing man. Then, there are also those who will avoid meeting, or hanging out with, their former UNZA friends, fearing that the friends might ask if their man or husband is still a lumpen or has stopped 'lumpenizing' (i.e. thuggery behavior).

We also had mature-age students at UNZA. They were often referred to as 'chuwi', a pseudo name for 'mature' that was given to them by younger students. Some mature-age students were well-behaved whilst others would behave like young students, spiritedly indulging in the infamous 'gold rush' of chasing after young skirts among the first-year arrivals. I remember an incident of one young pretty Tonga first-year student from Monze district. She was stunningly beautiful. A friend of mine from the Copperbelt really liked her but she kept avoiding him. So, another friend of mine who was Tonga asked the young lady why she kept avoiding the guy. She hesitated a bit and then confided in him, saying:

"Tu ba Bemba, tu la beja!" ("These Bemba-speaking boys are very crafty!")

The young Tonga lady had gotten some counseling from her grandmother before she came to UNZA, warning her to be careful with the fanciful urban city boys. There was also an incident where some male law student was after a pretty young damsel. The young lady was a fresher from Mungwi district near Kasama. She was very good-looking. It was her first time to be in the capital city, Lusaka. So, the Mungwi chic, like the Monze chic, had never interacted with urban city boys before.

While pursuing the Mungwi chic, the male law student discovered that some engineering male student was also after the same chic. The engineering student, who was in his final year at UNZA, would embellish his credentials before the poor Bemba chic from Mungwi, telling her how marketable he was on the job market and that he had received so many job offers from leading companies both in Zambia and abroad that he did not know what to do. It seemed like the guy was really an 'engineer'. For, he could 'engineer' stories. He went on to add that those offers included attractive job offers from several mining companies in Zambia and the Zambian State-owned electricity supplying company, ZESCO, but that he had turned most of them down. The guy went to the extent of even asking the Bemba chic for her advice on which company he should accept to work for without ever producing evidence of those alleged job offers. Unsuspectingly, the Mungwi chic excitedly congratulated the guy, saying 'I am lilly appy for you', instead of the usual, 'I am really happy for you.' Then, one day, the engineering student and the law student collided or met accidentally at the gal's room. It was tense. Each one showed up without a prior appointment since there were no cellphones or email back then to use to make an appointment if you wanted to visit someone. As soon as the engineering student left, the law student went:

"Aba ama guys aba jobber ama course yaku lungisha imi payipi noku fwasulula ifimbusu, too much ichi-kwela!" ("These guys who major in degree programs that focus on fixing broken water and sewer pipes as well as unblocking toilets and sinks are a nuisance!")

On hearing this, the gal got worried. After listening to what the law student was saying, she started questioning her own wisdom, wondering if it was worth it to continue entertaining visits from the engineering student. But, as the law student was just about to conclude his manifesto and leave, an economics student showed up. The latter looked at the law student intently, as their eyes locked. Then, he waited for the law student to disappear before saying to the Mungwi chic:

"What was he looking for here? These chaps who study courses to deal with criminals, you can never trust them. For them, everything is about telling lies. What type of a profession is it where you can't even produce anything except for speaking English with a fake and flamboyant accent? In fact, anyone who befriends criminals is also a criminal. As they say, birds of a feather flock together, not so?"

Confused, the poor Mungwi chic nodded. But before the economics student could conclude his 'poison pills' manifesto, another aspirant showed up. It was a medical student from UNZA Medical School. The guy was just in his second year of medical school but showed up in a doctor's white coat with a stethoscope hanging around his neck, as if he was such an accomplished physician. The gal got more confused further. Feeling outdone, the economics student left. As he was leaving, the economics student asked the gal to walk him out. As the gal walked him out, he said to her:

"I know that guy. He has been failing in medical school and repeating courses for many years. This must be his fifteenth (15th) year now, as he continues to struggle over a simple degree program that has to do with changing bandages, injecting patients and giving painkillers."

Being new to the university, the gal was at a loss. She did not what to do or say. She was so confused from the overload of falsehoods and misleading information that she was left speechless. When she returned to her room, the medical student who had been waiting for her proceeded to present his manifesto, pontificating as follows:

"Most students who come to this university wanting to study economics never make it into the economics quota. They end up studying less prestigious courses like demography where they just count people during census or fi sociology filya. Others are redirected to social work to deal with social misfits in society. Look, you have to be very careful with chaps around here. The Zambian economy is not doing so well right now because of these same chaps we call 'economists'. They just like to be on TV, busy talking nonsense. Anyone, including a mathematician or physicist, can become an economist tomorrow. What kind of profession is that? Your friends are busy saving lives in hospitals, and you are busy arguing over the exchange rate! Who does that? In fact, some of them eventually become our mental patients when life becomes hard on them."

Gold rush had its moments. Fellas would devise all sorts of disingenuous 'manifestos' to stand a chance at de-monking into 'mojo-hood'. Outside the gold rush arena, some mature-age students would import ladies from off-campus or date fellow mature-age female students on campus. I remember one afternoon when my classmate in law school, Kingsley, a mature-age student, and I were walking from lectures to our rooms in the Ruins. It was around 4 pm. Kingsley suggested that we pass through one of his fellow mature-age student's room to check on the man. That mature-age man's room was in President Hall of Residency in the Ruins, near the common room where some students would watch television from. When Kingsley and I got to the man's room, Kingsley did not knock on the door. He simply flung the door open. And there, before our eyes, was his fellow mature-age student, like a Boeing plane positioning itself to land on the runway tarmac, lowering himself in a compromised position on top of a female janitor (cleaner). The man was probably too rushed to even lock the door. The female janitor or cleaner was just giggling like a small gal, as the mature-age man was lowering himself on top of her. It was a traumatic sight. I could not believe what I was seeing. Kingsley and I retreated quickly, as Kingsley pulled back the door. It was so embarrassing. I was really shocked. Prior to this incident, I had heard stories of how some older-looking monks and some mature-age students would miss lectures to wait, like poachers lying in ambush for some game-meat, for some female janitors who they had an 'arrangement' with. Until that day, I did not believe those stories. The mature-age man suddenly emerged from his room after the distraction we had caused him. He invited us back into the room, pretending as if nothing had happened, as the female janitor sheepishly left the room to carry on with her daily work chores. It was so awkward. I kept quiet throughout the saga, as Kingsley chatted with his friend before we left. On our way to our rooms, Kingsley and I laughed so hard. It was hilarious. I had never ever seen anything like that.

We also had UNZA students who were so steeped into religiosity and often behaved as if they were the first cousins of our Lord Jesus Christ, or as if only they knew God best. Some of them never lasted long on campus or they ended up overstaying to repeat some courses they had flunked. Indeed, many either flunked in first year or struggled with their studies, often repeating some courses before they could graduate, all because of misplaced priorities. Others even fell pregnant. There is nothing wrong with being a religious person, but just don't overdo it and start judging others while placing yourself on a holier than thou pedestal as if you operate on a higher moral ground when, in fact, you do crazy things behind closed doors. Thankfully, the lumpens would often put such holier than thou church people in their rightful place through unfiltered and unrestrained pontifications. Then, there were also guys who were fond of 'importing' gals from outside campus. I remember one incident vividly. One monk came back to UNZA late at night with a chic from a nightclub. Now, each student room was shared by two students. There would be one bed in either side of the room, with two big wardrobes in the middle of the room to partition the sides. That way, each occupant had some privacy on his side of the room. However, if your roommate came with a gal, the silent code was that you would have to leave the room and go in 'exile' until the next day. You had to find a place elsewhere, for example, at one of your classmates or friends' places, where you would spend the night. Unfortunately, the monk that had imported a chic that night had a roommate who was a holier than thou Pentecostal fella. After a successful 'tow' of the 'import' from the nightclub, the monk sneaked the chic into his room, hoping that his Pentecostal roommate will leave obviously go into exile. Unfortunately, the roommate chose to stay. In fact, the chap even pretended not to have noticed the importer and importee enter the room. He continued studying, as if nothing had happened, with his sidelamp fully lit up. As soon as the importer and his chic, the importee, jumped into bed and turned off their side lamp, the roommate started boiling some water in a kettle, as if trying to make a cup of tea or coffee for himself. The importer ignored the shenanigans of his roommate and started kissing the importee. Incensed by the sound of two people kissing on the other side of the room, the roommate, itching now to distract the proceedings, blurted out to the importer from his side of the room:

"Ba roomie, na mu kwata ko tu sugar na ama samba?" ("My dear roommate, can you kindly help me with some teabags and sugar? I would like to make a cup of tea but have runout of groceries.")

That obviously distracted the importer who got up and gave the roommate some teabags and sugar. A few minutes later, after the kissing sounds resumed, the Pentecostal roommate called out again.

"Ba roomie, na mu kwata ko change ya K10? Mfwile ukuya ku town mailo ulu chelo. ("My dear roommate, do you have change for a K10 note. I need to catch a bus into town tomorrow morning.")

Again, the importer got up and gave the roommate some money hurriedly, hoping to incentivize him to leave the room promptly. But, as soon as the importer went back to bed and the kissing sounds resumed, his roommate started singing some Christian songs loudly against fornication and adultery. The singing was so intentionally loud that the importer and the importee got distracted instantly. Obviously, the importer was now beginning to lose it. He woke up, looking visibly frustrated and agitated. There was a bitter exchange of words between the two. The importer left the room momentarily, leaving the importee in bed, to go and call one of his lumpen friends from a room nearby. There was pandemonium. We all woke up from the noise. On arrival, the importer's lumpen friend begun 'shooting' (shouting profanity) at the Pentecostal guy in Kopala Bemba (because English was not going to work):

"Iwe kapuli, waya sana. You saw that umu nobe ale fwaya uku doda, but ule chilinganya! Na wishiba, ni pa Camp pano. Ukawa mwaice pa NS nga tauli careful…ne fya bu Pente fi ka shala. Next time I hear that you are behaving like this nkesa ku pomponsha. And don't even think about it. Chi ka ku bupila, mwaice. This is not your father's university, you understand? Nga tau doda mambala, fyobe ifyo. Don't think bonse ba fwile fye uku la wanka kwati ifyo iwe uwanka."

("You dickhead! Stop right there. You friend is trying to grab a cookie and watch Netflix but you are busy distracting him. This is UNZA. If you are not careful, my friend, you might not even make it to second year of studies, especially if you continue with that obsession with religiosity. If you ever behave the way you did, we will come and sort you out. And don't even think about it. This is not your father's university, you understand? So, behave yourself. If you can't afford some cookie, don't think that everyone else, like you, has to squeeze the neck of their chicken.")

We always had free entertainment on campus. One time, a mature-age UNZA student 'imported' a young lady from one of the neighborhoods in Lusaka. The lady looked quite polished and too sophisticated for him. The mature-age man went to take a quick shower and asked the young lady to wait for him in his room. After showering, the man rushed back to his room spiritedly, with only a towel wrapped around his waist. He found the young lady seated quietly and looking at some books on his bookshelf. Lacking finesse, the mature-age man took off his towel unromantically, exposing his nudity, before telling the young lady, 'Ale nomba…ta ba ku funda?' ('Okay now, don't you know the deal? What are you waiting for?') The young lady was shocked. She ran for her life.

There was also a time when some students in the then all-male students' hall of residence, Africa, started complaining that they would lose their clothes each time they did some laundry and left the clothes to dry on the balcony. The guys would leave their clothes on the rail of the balcony while attending lectures only to find the clothes gone. Nobody could track down the thief. It appeared that whoever was stealing the clothes was so meticulous and knew when to strike. So, one engineering student devised a plan. He bought a set of three new underwear. Wearing some hand gloves, the guy laced the three underwear with poison ivy, especially on the inside of each underwear, and left them on the balcony rail to appear as laundry. Now, the Zambian version of poison ivy, known locally as 'sepe', can be quite vicious. The unsuspecting thief showed up while everyone was away in class and fell for the bait. Later that evening, there was a students' party on campus. The party was packed with both female and male students. The thief that had stolen the underwear was also there, dressed in one of the three underwear he stole earlier in the day. At first, everything looked okay and there was no drama. Then, all of a sudden, we heard someone start to scream. The poison ivy was beginning to work. The deejay stopped playing the music. The screaming was so alarming, and the guy dropped to the floor. Within a minute or so, his private parts were swollen. He could not get up or walk. He was in so much pain. The students who had set the trap knew that that was the thief. They pretended to be sympathizers and even helped to 'airlift' him to the hospital. The chap was admitted immediately to the intensive care unit (ICU), as the doctors were not so sure what had caused the unusual swelling of his testicles and penis as well as the excruciating pain he was going through. The guy kept on screaming in Bemba, "Na fwa, mayo. Nsha ka bwekeshepo." ("God help me. I will never steal again.")

At some point, he even lost consciousness and fainted. The intensity of the pain caused by 'sepe' was too much for him to bear. It was then that the students who had set up the bait revealed to the doctors that the chap was wearing stolen underwear laced with 'sepe'. Another incident involved a monk in the Ruins who was expecting his chic from outside campus to pay him a visit on one weekend. The chic was based in Ndola, and she promised that she would travel to Lusaka by bus to visit the guy. Excited, the guy even went and bought some African traditional herbs that are known to produce a prolonged and intense erection when mixed with any beverage and taken as a drink, at least, one hour or so before a sexual encounter. One is supposed to drink only one cup of that concoction. But because the guy had not touched a woman for years, he decided to double the dosage. He wanted to be more effective and to impress with a stellar performance. Unfortunately, his girlfriend did not show up. She was not able to travel because her mother was taken ill. But by then the UNZA monk had already taken his aphrodisiac in significant amounts. It was agony. With bulging red eyes, as if his eyes were about to pop out of the sockets, the chap began pacing up and down like a mad man. He was restless. He started talking to himself, and one could visibly see the burdensome bulge in his crotch area. That led the other students to call university security (UNZA Blue). By the time UNZA Blue was arriving, the chap had collapsed. He was rushed to the hospital quickly, where he was eventually resuscitated.

Sometimes, UNZA drama would come from some mature-age students. One time, a certain mature-age student had 'towed' or 'imported' a sex worker to his room but failed to pay her the next morning. Insults rained on the mature-age student from the sex worker, as other students cheered on. Other times, if your roommate was a mature-age student and was expecting his wife, or some 'import', over the weekend, he would simply tell you that,

"Young man, your auntie is coming to visit this weekend."

Immediately, you would know what to do. You were expected to go in exile. There was nothing like asking the mature-age man to clarify what he meant. You would know that it was time for you to go in exile. UNZA life was something else. One guy broke his leg after jumping from the fourth floor of one of the lady's Halls of Residence at UNZA. The guy had gone to spend a night at his girlfriend's room when he heard university security personnel knock on the door around 1 am. It was past visiting hour, and no guys were allowed to spend nights in the female students' Hall of Residence. So, the guy opted to take flight to escape the dragnet of the university security personnel by jumping out of the widow. Unfortunately, he could not fly. So, he landed with a thud on the ground and broke his leg.

Some UNZA students would squander all their student stipend or bursary within the first month of the semester. Others were simply frugal and would resort to eating nshima with fried eggs or kapenta (*i.e.* anchovies). After downing the heap of nshima, they would then swallow a tablet of vitamins, believing that that was a way of ensuring that they got a 'balanced diet' out of a 'healthy' meal. I refused to be part of that misguided frugal way of life. Throughout my UNZA student days, I ate from the dining hall. I never cooked in my room. I believed in enjoying a quality student life, and not starving myself or preparing food in the student hostels using hazardous cooking utensils and improvised cookers. I found such cost-saving measures unappealing. Many students who lived a frugal life on campus did so not because the government bursary or stipend that they were getting from the Zambian Government was not enough, but because they wanted to solve poverty-related issues in their parents' homes through that same government bursary or stipend by sending much of it to their families back home so that they could support their siblings and aged parents. But that was not the purpose of the government bursary stipend. We were not government employees but rather students at a government-run institution of learning. And so, we were not salaried by the government. By contrast, we were on student stipends. Indeed, the money that we would get was not a salary, but a student stipend. Unfortunately, whenever some students ran out of money, they would start to instigate other students to join them in rioting, as they complained that the student stipends were not enough. For me, although my eldest brother, Kelvin, would supplement my student stipend or allowance every other week, I think that the money we were getting as a stipend was enough if one did not try to live beyond his or her means. Those student stipends were enough if used specifically for the purpose for which they were given. But some students wanted to dress like they were working class people and wanted to compete with people who already work. You can't expect the government to finance your expensive lifestyle through a student stipend. That is not the purpose of the student stipend. Besides, student stipends are not a salary for you to be using that money to pay for your young sibling's school fees now that your parents are retired or not working. At the end of the day, we all must be honest with ourselves. Students often question the intelligence of politicians, but they themselves never question their own. If we all can be a bit more honest with each other, we can avoid more than half of the problems that we encounter in life.

During some weekends, I would sometimes go out with friends to the disco. Lusaka had Moon City nightclub when we just got to UNZA. Then, Studio 22 was just about to be closed down. When Moon City started losing popularity, Valentino's nightclub sprang up. Moon City was eventually closed. I remember asking my brother, Dennis, for some 'back-up' when I wanted to take out a childhood female colleague to Valentinos nightclub. That female colleague was a student at one of the colleges in Lusaka. She decided to invite a friend of hers from some small town on the outskirts of Lusaka to tag along. As a student, I didn't have much cash. So, I turned to Dennis for some support. Dennis was already working by then and so he had the power of the wallet. And so, the four of us set out to Valentinos nightclub that night. After a few drinks, the lady from the outskirts of Lusaka looked so excited and started talking to one of the deejays in the club. By the time we were leaving, that chic had moved to sit with the deejay and his friends. It was so embarrassing. We had to leave her behind, and she made no effort to go with us. Out of shame, her friend, my colleague, could not say a word about the embarrassing behavior of the lady she brought to join us.

In my final year at UNZA, that is, in 1989/1990, UNZA students started agitating for the reintroduction of multiparty politics in Zambia. At the time, not many people could raise a voice against President Kaunda or the UNIP Government. People were scared. The one-party-state system was quiet authoritarian. You could be crushed easily. The general mood and political tide in Africa were however beginning to change and tilt in favor of multipartyism. Some talk was coming up in many African States against the one-party State system. I recall that, as UNZA students, we had the opportunity of sitting in many lectures in the social sciences where a number of our lecturers condemned the one-party State system as a mere dictatorial and totalitarian system of government. We were made to believe that a one-party State system was some kind of evil, especially that it was not based on what was known as scientific socialism. Some African leaders, such as Kaunda, Nyerere, Nkrumah, and Senghor, had crafted their own African ideologies around what was known as African socialism. Kaunda came up with humanism. Nyerere advanced Ujamaa. Senghor pushed for Negritude. Nkrumah advocated for Pan-Africanism. But a number of African intellectuals condemned these ideologies, arguing that they were not even ideologies. Some scholars would shoot down African socialism, arguing that, unlike scientific socialism that draws heavily from Marxist-Leninist ideology, African socialism was not based on class struggle and was therefore not scientific. But is class struggle the only criterion for determining how scientific an ideology is? And what is an ideology, anyway? Suffice it to say that if you are going to criticize the ideas of someone who has made an effort to come up with his own original ideas, kindly give us your ideas instead of just shooting down your friend's ideas. It is easier to criticize than to come up with your own original ideas. Sometimes, one is better off looking at how we can improve an idea, as opposed to how we can kill it. For, you cannot kill an idea. Many of our intellectuals fall short on this approach. They would rather rely heavily on Eurocentric models of ideological persuasion, without considering the merits of the Afrocentric context.

Be that as it may, many African leaders who introduced the one-party-State system reasoned that that system would help with getting rid of, among other things, sectionalism and sectarian tribal politics in the post-colonial African State. Although, admittedly, some of these African leaders, like their counterparts in the former socialist countries of Eastern Europe and some parts of Asia, meant well when introducing the one-party State system, they also used it to hold on to power and get rid of any possible threats or opposition. Ideally, for the Marxists, the one-party State system was meant to promote the dictatorship of the proletariat, not that of individual politicians. For the African socialists, the one-party State system was meant to promote national unity, not tribal politics. As young students, we were indoctrinated with Marxist-Leninist ideas such that if you had never been to any former socialist country in Eastern Europe and Central Asia, you would think that all was rosy in the then Warsaw pact. At UNZA, we were told that the socialists and communists from the East supported Africa to fight off capitalism from the West which came in the form of colonialism. And so, we were made to believe that the East, not the West, were our friends, without realizing that the East came to ward off the West from winning Africa over. Africa has always been an orphan, used and abused for convenience by both the East and the West. Both Warsaw pact and NATO had their own interests. It was not so much about saving the Africans but about pursuing their own interests. We saw, for example, the fate of the constitutionally elected Prime Minister of the Congo soon after that country gained political independence. Patrice Lumumba, frustrated with some reactionary forces in the West turned to seek the support of the East, but got limited support. This left him exposed and at the mercy of his adversaries from the West and locally within the Congo. Yet, many Zambian scholars condemned Kaunda's ideology of humanism and the one-party State system. Not even the idea of the non-aligned movement of States got much traction among many of our leftist African scholars. Time and history, however, have a way of vindicating those who mean well. Many who cried foul against the Kaunda regime where those who tried to cross President Kaunda's path or tried to be funny with him. It is quite likely that you and I would equally not tolerate someone trying to be funny with us. Put simply, those who stayed in their lane, stayed out of harm's way.

I think that President Kaunda and his friend, President Nyerere, were way ahead of their time. The introduction or reintroduction of multi-party politics in Africa has seen a spike in the rebirth of sectionalism and sectarian tribal politics. Even the much touted privatization programs in African have not translated much into the envisaged growth of a number of African economies, as we expected it to happen. These are the things that our founding fathers, the Kaundas and the Nyereres, were fighting against. We cannot therefore focus solely on the shortcomings of the one-party State system without appreciating its positives. For example, in Zambia, the industrialization and diversification of the Zambian economy was probably at its best during the Kaunda Government. That is one example of the successes of the one-party -tate system. Under President Kaunda, the one-party-state system also promoted national unity, as opposed to pushing an agenda of sectionalism and sectarianism tribal politics. President Kaunda was far way ahead of his time. Many people misunderstood him and were misled by the propaganda that was mounted against him by both external and internal forces that wanted him out of power for one reason or another. Some of them said twenty-seven (27) years was too long a period for one and the same person to be running the country without anyone else challenging him in an election. Thus, many UNZA students, excited with western ideas of democracy and the propaganda against President Kaunda both domestically and internationally, started pushing for the reintroduction of multiparty politics. Now, what many people forget is that most western countries themselves did not start with an open free-market democratic society. Their economies were built on the back of slavery. And slavery was a dictatorship. Slavery was never democratic. If you have read Karl Marx on historical materialism, you will appreciate that many societies have had to go through different historical epochs. So, without doubt, there were serious dictators in the Global North too.

It is important to stress that the fight for the reintroduction of multiparty politics in Zambia was started by UNZA students, not the Movement for Multiparty Democracy (MMD). It was the students at UNZA who started the fight for the reintroduction of multiparty politics in Zambia. I was there as a final year student at UNZA. At the time, no notable politician anywhere in Zambia had the guts of facing Kaunda. Many were scared of him. Kaunda was a disciplinarian and no-nonsense type of man. His discipline saw some politicians kicked out of the UNIP Government (the United National Independence Party (UNIP) was sole party in the country), especially those that lacked discipline. So, when the UNZA students started pushing for the reintroduction of multiparty politics in Zambia, some politicians who had been kicked out or forced out of the UNIP Government saw a window of opportunity to gang up secretly with some trade union leaders who had beef with Kaunda in order to form an alliance to unseat Kaunda. They were joined by some young academics from UNZA. A good number of these guys were in their thirties (30's) or early to mid (40's). So, MMD was really formed by the coming together of three main fronts, namely, (a) politicians kicked out of, or frustrated by, the UNIP Government, (b) trade union leaders who had some type of beef with President Kaunda, and (c) some young academics from UNZA. These three fronts brought with them their supporters. But MMD could not come out in the open initially. Even when they did, they kept saying that they were not a political party but just a movement. The fear of the wrath of the one-party state was real. But when the UNZA students put pressure on the Zambian Government to open up to multipartyism, marching to State House to protest before President Kaunda, the Head of State listened. President Kaunda gave us audience at State House. He listened to us, as students. He did not send the police to brutally assault us. He allowed us into State House as a mob of students. And he listened to us and addressed us respectfully. After that, it did not take long before President Kaunda asked for multiparty elections to be held on October 31, 1991. We must give credit to the UNZA students, not politicians, for having fought for the introduction of multiparty politics in Zambia. MMD only rode on the back of the courageous UNZA students who had confronted the Kaunda Government. I know that some views have been aired and books written to paint MMD as a heroic party that fought against the one-party-state system in Zambia and brought about multipartyism. That is not entirely correct. I was there. We, the UNZA students, marched to State House to meet President Kaunda. MMD, as a political party, was not even existence at the time. MMD was only born in July 1990. Earlier that year, UNZA was closed due to some student riots. A number of our fellow UNZA students were picked up and locked up by security forces. Their whereabouts were not known for some time.

On November 2, 1991, a day after the 1991 multiparty elections were held in Zambia, the Washington Post, in its online edition, reported that (see Karl Maier, "Kaunda swept from office in lopsided Zambian vote," (Online, November 2, 1991)):

"LUSAKA, ZAMBIA, NOV. 1 -- One of Africa's most well-known and longest-serving presidents, Kenneth Kaunda, suffered a crushing defeat today in Zambia's first multi-party elections in two decades, marking the first time in English-speaking Africa that an entrenched one-party system has been smashed at the ballot box."

Many Zambians were of the view that democracy had finally arrived in Zambia. They equated multiparty politics with democracy unfortunately. The Washington Post article goes on state that:

"News of the defeat of Kaunda, who has ruled for 27 years, set off wild celebrations in the capital with cars and trucks full of Zambians honking their horns and chanting the opposition slogan, 'The hour has come.'"

Many western commentators expected President Kaunda not to concede defeat or not to honor the results of the ballot. They were wrong! They thought that he would try to cling on to power unconstitutionally. They were mistaken. In fact, the man called for elections earlier than the constitutionally mandared date for Presidential and General elections. We were there. And before the counting of the results of the 1991 elections was over, President Kaunda conceded defeat magnanimously. He called the victor, then president-elect, Mr Chiluba, to congratulate him. There was no need for foreign negotiators to convince Dr Kaunda to step down. Even some of his critics and those who had been throwing verbal missiles at President Kaunda realized that he may not have been the man they thought he was. President Kaunda meant well for Zambia. He may have had his weaknesses as any other human being, but he never amassed unexplained wealth by stealing from or exploiting the Zambian economy. And there was hardly any noticeable corruption in Zambia under the one-party State system. President Kaunda's UNIP Government had a Leadership Code that barred key ruling party and government functionaries from owning major commercial or business interests in the national economy. President Kaunda could foresee the temptation that might have befallen these key ruling party and government functionaries had they been permitted to engage in private commercial businesses and investments. Put simply, President Kaunda prevented a culture of bribes, kickbacks and other corrupt practices from thriving among key public officials. Interestingly, when President Kaunda lost power, he was accused by the then incoming MMD Government of having amassed a lot of wealth from the national coffers. As the *Zambian Chronicle* reports in its online edition (see: *Zambian Chronicle*, "Chiluba witch-hunting, KK busy working," Archived entry, May 22, 2007):

"All this…talk about how President Kaunda stole this and that while he was in office is to say the least bordering on mere childishness. When Dr. Kaunda left office, Dr. Chiluba instigated fraud charges on the founding father and went out of the way to hire the famous Scotland Yard. They investigated Kaunda for almost two years, and he was actually exonerated of all the purported charges. This was the first time we actually had a foreign law enforcement entity investigate a former head of state in Africa."

What is even more interesting is that a number of those who accused President Kaunda of having stolen from the national treasury were themselves implicated in theft cases after they left office; that is, for having looted the national treasury, of course, while they were in office. But our people never learn, or perhaps they forget quickly. Sometimes, the people who cannot themselves explain their wealth will be the ones prosecuting others for having stolen. It's a vicious cycle of tragicomedies. Anyhow, on the 1991 Zambian multiparty elections, the *Washington Post* article concluded:

"By ending the reign of one of the key figures identified with Africa's independence era nearly three decades ago, the elections thrust Zambia to the forefront of the process of democratization transforming the way much of Africa is governed. Over the past two years, popular movements demanding political pluralism and economic change have swept aside more than a dozen single-party governments of often unaccountable and harsh rulers. Kaunda 'promised to cooperate with us,' Chiluba told a news conference after talking to the president tonight. 'He is ready to move out of State House {the presidential palace}, but we are not chasing him.'"

CHAPTER 8

Unza Graduation and Bar admission

After a premature closure in June 1990 prompted by student riots for the reintroduction of multiparty politics in Zambia, the University of Zambia (UNZA) was reopened in August 1990. When UNZA was closed that June, it was not clear when it would be reopened. I was in my final year and looking forward to graduating. The disruption of the academic calendar was unwelcome and left many of us feeling frustrated at the prospects of a delayed graduation. I started considering the idea of just leaving Zambia altogether to go for further studies abroad. I saw an advert in the newspapers of some scholarships to study in Russia. The scholarships were being administered by the Zambian Government Bursaries Committee. I was not too sure if going to Russia was a good idea. But I decided to apply anyhow just to test the water. Russia was not really on my list of places where I wanted to go for further studies. My plan was to proceed to the UK or the US. But the Russian scholarships were the only ones that were showing up on the radar. So, I applied and was called for the interviews. I applied to study international law. I was then in my fourth and final year of Law School at UNZA. My elder brother, Kelvin, was disappointed to learn that I was applying to go to Russia for an undergraduate program when I was just about to get my law degree from UNZA. And, yes, he was right. I had acted out of frustration and just wanted out after the untimely UNZA closure. I remember that the interviews for those Russia scholarships were just a joke. The panel selected a female candidate who was a student at Evelyn Hone College pursuing an associate degree (college diploma) to go and study international law in Russia. She was not even at UNZA and had never been to UNZA. I had performed well at the interviews, yet there I was placed as a reserve candidate, notwithstanding all my legal education background from UNZA. I could not believe it. By then, I had even completed my Form 6 'A' Levels, in addition, of course, to my UNZA legal educational background. I'd guess the only thing that I did not have on my CV was the name of a relative who was well-connected in the 'system' and would push or speak for me. I was naïve to think that everything would be done transparently and on merit. Later, when I asked around, I learned that the father of the young lady that was picked was well-connected in the 'system'. It was, however, a blessing in disguise because UNZA reopened a few weeks later and I went back to UNZA to complete my law degree program, graduating as one of the top two law students in my class.

I graduated from UNZA on December 15, 1990. The graduation ceremony was held at Mulungushi International Conference Center. In my heart of hearts, I knew that that was only the beginning and that one day I would make my parents even more proud than I did with my UNZA education. I just did not know when that would be. All I knew was that one day my old folks will look back with a proud smile of a loving parent on the indelible intellectual milestones of their son. And this, as prophecy would have it, came to be.

After graduating from UNZA, I arrived at the Law Practice Institute (LPI), now known as the Zambia Institute of Advanced Legal Education (ZIALE), in the second half of 1990. LPI, like today's ZIALE, offered a one-year full-time Bar admission graduate program that had the reputation of high student failure rates. I can estimate candidly that more than three-quarters of the practicing lawyers in Zambia today, including many other lawyers who are not in practice but are admitted to the Zambian Bar, failed to pass LPI or ZIALE exams on first attempt. You can ask them if you want. Many only passed after making several attempts. Very few clear or pass all the bar admission exams in Zambia on first attempt. Many lawyers have had to retake those notorious bar admission exams over and over again before finally qualifying to change their legal status from an 'unqualified person' to a 'qualified person' at the Bar. It is a harsh truth that many Zambian lawyers are uncomfortable with and don't want to talk about. If anything, some of them get upset when you remind them about ZIALE because it was a struggle to get admitted to the Bar. So, they would rather make you believe that they are successful in private practice, and constantly pointing you to the material possessions that they have accumulated over the years through law practice. But the truth is that, at ZIALE or LPI, many practicing lawyers came out with scars. They only healed in private practice. A media commentary I made some years back on the low pass rate of Bar admission students at ZIALE made headlines in one of Zambia's leading newspapers, *Sunday Times of Zambia*. The said article was published in the *Sunday Times of Zambia* on December 12, 2021, as can be seen in the picture below.

At LPI, my UNZA graduating class was joined by some repeaters from the previous LPI cohorts. They were preparing to retake the Bar exams. There were many repeaters. But since some of them are now reputable members of society, I will save them from embarrassment and will not mention their names here. Suffice it to say, the Zambian Government was renting a lecture room for us at Evelynne Hone College for our LPI lectures. As LPI students, we were housed at the neighboring National Institute of Public Administration (NIPA). In the mornings, we would go for our apprenticeship work at the respective law firms where we were attached. In the afternoons, we would attend LPI lectures. Then, in the evenings, most guys from the class would unwind over a beer at NIPA club. We were all on government bursaries as Bar admission students, making things easier for us. Life was good. If you had money and the beers were flowing, it was not hard to find happiness. Life was good, especially for colleagues who spiritedly pursued dating at the neighboring higher education institution, Evelynne Hone College. We also played some football matches occasionally against the other students at NIPA who were mainly middle-aged mature-age students from the Zambia Air Force (ZAF) and the civil service pursuing diploma (associate degree) programs.

While a student at LPI, I was attached to Jacques and Partners, which, at the time, was one of the most prestigious law firms in Lusaka. I was hired by the main partner of the firm, Mr Damson Chindeni Katongo, a 1967 law graduate of the University of East Africa. Mr Katongo also qualified as a Barrister and Solicitor in the UK. The two main lawyers working under Mr Katongo were Sunday Nkonde and Ernest Mwansa. Both Sunday and Ernest were my coaches and would give me assignments to work on. The other LPI student who was with me at the firm was Anne Sampa, the elder sister of Miles Sampa, a key political figure in the Patriotic Front (PF) political party and who served as a Member of Parliament, Mayor of Lusaka and Deputy Minister of Finance in Zambia. I remember Mr Katongo taking me through the history of the firm. Notable lawyers in Zambia like President Levy Mwanawansa, a former Head of State of Zambia, Mr George Chilupe, a former Attorney-General of Zambia, and many others had all passed through the hands of Mr Katongo at Jacques and Partners. So I was at the right law firm. Sunday Nkonde later became the Solicitor-General of Zambia after practicing law at Jacques and Partners. After his stint as Solicitor-General, Sunday was appointed as a High Court judge. Ernest later served as a Member of Parliament for Chifunabuli Constituency, Deputy Minister in the Ministry of Energy and Water Development, as well as Deputy Minister in the Ministry of Information and Broadcasting Services. Also, Ernest served at some point as a Deputy Minister in the Ministry of Health and a second Deputy Speaker of the Zambian parliament.

At LPI, we had to take nine (9) courses in preparation for the much dreaded Bar admission exams. The following were the 9 courses that we took.

1. Professional Conduct and Ethics;
2. Book-keeping and Accounts;
3. Conveyancing and Legal Drafting;
4. Probate and Succession;
5. Commercial Transactions;

6. Company Law and Procedure;
7. Civil Procedure;
8. Domestic Relations; and
9. Criminal Law and Procedure.

Professional Conduct and Ethics was taught by a Mr Bwalya who was also the Director of LPI, whereas Book-keeping and accounting was taught by Mr Muyenga. Conveyancing and Legal Drafting was taught by Mr Solly Patel while Mr George Chilupe taught us Probate and Succession. Then, Commercial Transactions was taught by Mr Lwatula while Company Law and Procedure was taught by Mr Ben Ngenda. Civil Procedure was taught by Mr Jitesh Naik and Mr Ndhlovu, while Domestic Relations was taught by Ms Harriet Tentani-Sikasote. And Criminal Law and Procedure was taught by Hon Mr Justice Peter Chitengi.

One Friday afternoon, I had to miss Mr Ben Ngenda's Company Law and Procedure class at LPI. Like in the case of my private studies for the University of London 'A' Levels while I was a young student at UNZA Law School, I went and paid for private studies to sit for the London Chamber of Commerce and Industry (LCCI) Group Diploma in Law exams. It was the second time that I was going beyond and above 'the normal call of duty', so to speak. I got some money from my LPI student allowances and went back to the same place at Evelyn Hone College where I had registered for my 'A' Level exams. I made sure that I paid all the fees required to sit for the LCCI Group Diploma in Law exams. And I had already planned to devote about an hour or two in the evenings daily to prepare for those exams over a period of about two to three months. I would rely mainly on my collection of law books and study materials used at UNZA Law School. I had no other study materials or lecture notes for the LCCI Group Diploma in Law program, though I knew that it was a British qualification based on English law for which many people in England would take two to three years to complete. There I was again, an African student, remotely stationed in the middle of Africa, studying on my own and without the aid of any lecturer, tutor or study texts from the UK. Yet, that did not deter me. I was confident that I would pull it, just as I did for the University of London 'A' Levels. After all, I had already graduated from UNZA Law School and was now at LPI, I reasoned. I proceeded on the basis that I just needed a little brush up on the law and would be good for the LCCI Group Diploma exams. So, that Friday, I missed class to go and sit for the LCCI

Group Diploma in Law exams. My plan was to catch up with my LPI classmates after the exam and get from them lecture notes from the class that I was going to miss that day. I did not tell my friends where I was going. I simply disappeared.

As I entered the exam room, who did I see? My Company Law and Procedure lecturer, Mr Ben Ngenda, whose class I should have been attending at that very moment. He was with me in the same exam room, though we were taking different exams. He was sitting for ICSA professional exams. ICSA is the acronym for the UK-based professional body, the Institute of Chartered Secretaries and Administrators, whose name was changed in September 2019 to the Chartered Governance Institute UK & Ireland. I smiled and realized that Mr Ngenda had also missed his own class, meaning that my LPI classmates were going to wait in vain and the lecturer was not going to show up that day. For, how would he have shown up when he was with me in the same exam room? I sneaked into the exam room quietly to avoid my lecturer seeing me. I went and sat in the corner of the room at the back. He was seated somewhere in front. There were many people sitting for different exams, but we were all using the same venue. My lecturer left the exam room earlier than I did. After the exam, I went back to my room at NIPA. I found my LPI classmates relaxing and chatting before the usual dinner time. I asked them how the class went. They said that the lecturer did not show up. I smiled and said to them:

"I was with him. We were both writing our respective exams in the same building and room. He and I were just a floor above where you guys were waiting for him."

They all looked shocked! I was always an industrious student who would go beyond just my routine daily academic endeavors. Yes, I passed all three of my LCCI exams in one sitting and got the LCCI Group Diploma in Law whilst studying as a full-time LPI (ZIALE) student. Not many people knew about this. I kept it low key. For, it was not the first time that I was getting an additional qualification beyond the usual qualifications that my friends had. I had done this before when I got my University of London A's levels whilst studying full-time at UNZA as a first year Law School student. And it would not end there.

When we wrote our LPI midyear exams, only two people from the entire class cleared or passed all the courses. You might be wondering who those two were. Yes, I was one of them. I had cleared everything. Another student who cleared everything was my classmate, Maria Mkandawire. I can't speak for the others. All I can tell you is that many failed Criminal Law and Procedure at midyear.

That course was being taught by Hon. Judge Peter Chitengi. The judge was so mad at our class. He summoned all of us to class and gave us a stern warning to be serious with LPI studies. When time for the final exams came, again, I cleared everything on first attempt, graduating with distinctions. I graduated for Bar admission as the overall best student in Zambia that year.

On December 15, 1991, those of us who had passed all courses on first attempt, together with the repeaters that eventually cleared their course arrears, were admitted to the Zambian Bar, as Advocates of the High Court for the Republic of Zambia (AHCZ). We were sworn in by the then Chief Justice of the Supreme Court for the Republic of Zambia, Hon. Mr Chief Justice Annel Silungwe. My mother, representing both herself and my father, and accompanied by my older siblings attended my swearing in ceremony at the Supreme Court when I was being admitted to the Bar. And my brother, Dennis, and my sister, Matilda, hosted a barbeque party for me after the swearing-in ceremony. In the picture below, taken in front of the Supreme Court shortly after I was officially sworn in and admitted to the Bar, my mother can be seen on my left. On my immediate right is my childhood friend, Masanguza Thole, to whom I am indebted with sincere gratitude for his kind and brotherly support. On my far right is my young brother, Eugene. I am exceedingly grateful for all the warm support from family members and friends who have stood with and by me in my professional journey and intellectual pursuits.

In the picture below, my mother and I posed for a picture in front of the Supreme Court shortly after my admission to the Bar in Zambia.

The group picture below was taken with my LPI cohort shortly after we were all sworn in as Advocates of the High Court for Zambia (AHCZ). The Chief Justice can be seen standing in the middle towards the right side of the gentleman seated on a wheelchair.

While in Law School at the University of Zambia (UNZA), I was taught by a distinguished American law professor, Prof Robert Kent. Bob Kent, as we often called him, had come back to Zambia as a Visiting Professor of Law at UNZA. He had taught previously at UNZA. Many senior lawyers in Zambia who were among the first graduates of UNZA Law School were his students. Prof Bob Kent began his academic career at Boston University School of Law, his alma mater. He then spent a couple of years in Zambia as Professor of Law and Dean of UNZA Law School. Prof Kent also served as Professor of Law at Cornell University Law School where he retired and became Emeritus Professor before serving as a Distinguished Visiting Professor at Roger Williams University School of Law. So, it was an honor to be taught by Prof Kent. I remember the advice he left us with on the last day of his classes before he went back to the US. He stressed to us the need for anyone contemplating entering academia to ensure that he or she gets admitted to the Bar before going into academia. It was good and sound advice. In Zambia, in particular, it is much easier if you are young and straight from university to study for and pass the Bar exams, although you still have to work hard, than when you show up later in life with a Masters degree or PhD from overseas and attempt to take the Bar exams. Experience has shown that working or studying under someone who is less qualified than you are can sometimes attract unnecessary issues. Many lecturers at the Bar admission school in Zambia (ZIALE) only hold a first degree in law. I will leave the rest to your own imagination.

After Prof Bob Kent encouraged us to get admitted to the Bar before joining academia, I took that advice and went to LPI soon after graduating from UNZA. My heart was in academia. I wanted to be an academic but not one without Bar admission. It is pointless, as an academic, to keep justifying to people why you are not admitted to the Bar, especially if section 2 of Zambia's Legal Practitioners Act 1973, as amended, provides that: "'unqualified person' means a person who is not a practitioner and includes a practitioner who has not in force a practicing certificate.'

Many legal academics worldwide are not active legal practitioners, though a number hold practicing certificates and have been called to the Bar. So, in the wording of section 2 of Zambia's Legal Practitioners Act 1973, does it mean that they are 'unqualified persons'? Certainly not. In Zambia, where a legal academic is not serving as a legal practitioner, but has a practicing certificate, he or she cannot be considered as an 'unqualified person.' Rather, he or she is a 'qualified person' for purposes of section 2 of Zambia's Legal Practitioners Act 1973. So, I wanted to be a 'qualified person' before entering academia, as opposed to being an 'unqualified person' with postgraduate degrees such an LLM or PhD but without Bar admission. Academia should not be seen as excuse for not getting admitted to the Bar. Otherwise, some overzealous young practicing lawyers can challenge your legal opinions or views on any legal issue, contending contemptuously that you are not even called to the Bar and do not have the right of audience before any court of law.

When I was registering for the Bar admission program at LPI, I knew many Zambian legal academics who had been shunned by LPI, given that Bar admission was not a requirement for one to serve or be appointed as an academic. The said legal academics would simply proceed after graduating from UNZA Law School to postgraduate studies abroad or at UNZA. Very few would bother to get admitted to the Bar until the Zambian economy began to weaken and the salaries of academics could no longer provide you with a decent lifestyle. Many folks with Masters and doctoral degrees in the Law Faculty of UNZA then started running back to LPI to study for Bar admission. The idea was that Bar admission could help them get some opportunities for part-time law practice to supplement their earnings in academia. Others figured that Bar admission could also open doors for them to be appointed as judges or to senior executive positions in the corporate sector. So, as years went by, it was no longer uncommon to find yourself in the same class at LPI or ZIALE with your former UNZA Lecturer.

www.ingramcontent.com/pod-product-compliance
Lightning Source LLC
Chambersburg PA
CBHW081153020426
42333CB00020B/2491